Canadian Social Policy

Issues and Perspectives

edited by Anne Westhues

Canadian Social Policy

Issues and Perspectives

THIRD EDITION

Edited by
Anne Westhues

Wilfrid Laurier University Press

We acknowledge the financial support of the Government of Canada through the Book Publishing Industry Development Program for our publishing activities.

National Library of Canada Cataloguing in Publication Data

Canadian social policy / edited by Anne Westhues.—3rd ed.

Includes bibliographical references and indexes.
ISBN 0-88920-405-5

1. Canada—Social policy. I. Westhues, Anne.

HN107.C355 2003   361.6'1'0971   C2002-905584-9

© 2003 Wilfrid Laurier University Press
Waterloo, Ontario, Canada N2L 3C5
www. wlupress.wlu.ca

Cover and text design by P.J. Woodland.

Every reasonable effort has been made to acquire permission for copyright material used in this text, and to acknowledge all such indebtedness accurately. Any errors and omissions called to the publisher's attention will be corrected in future printings.

∞
Printed in Canada

To Ken and Jonathan

Table of Contents

Acknowledgements

Editing a book with twenty contributors is a bit like managing a very large family. Everybody has a shared commitment to a general purpose, but they need to be permitted to make their contributions in a way that is consistent with their interests and their particular competencies. I want to thank each of the authors involved in this project for agreeing to be part of it, but for doing it their own way. The book is richer for the variety of theoretical orientations and writing styles that they have used. I want to thank Brian Henderson and Elin Edwards at Wilfrid Laurier University Press for supporting this approach rather than insisting on a single, prescribed way of exploring policy issues. Special appreciation goes to Brian for inviting me to take on this project.

Thanks are also extended to the people with technical skills and resources who made this project possible: Judith Levene and Carol Stalker, who approved funding from the Faculty of Social Work to hire student assistants; Kristine Allison and Naomi Ives who developed the indexes; Matt Regehr who designed the graphics; Pam Woodland who designed the cover; and Carroll Klein and Valerie Ahwee who copyedited the text.

Finally, warm thanks to Ken Westhues, Brian O'Neill, and Sheila Neysmith, who were generous in taking time to help me think through the options when I came up against especially knotty problems. Your wise advice was appreciated.

Preface

One of our chief complaints when I was a social policy student at Wilfrid Laurier University in the mid-1970s was that few of the class materials spoke to us as Canadians. We used primarily American and British texts and articles, which taught us legislation that would not affect our practice, the history of a welfare state that was not ours, and described policy-making processes that were only generally applicable in Canada. We found ourselves scouring the library, looking mostly in primary sources in the government documents section, for anything to do with Canadian social policy. While this may have given us a competence as researchers that is uncommon in students today, and breadth in our understanding of how other countries had addressed a range of policy issues, it left us feeling disconnected from—and somewhat confused about—Canadian social policy, with no sense of understanding about how, as social workers, we could change the social policies that would shape our practice.

Shankar Yelaja recognized this gap in knowledge, and produced the first edition of *Canadian Social Policy* in 1978 as part of the remedy of this situation. The considerable success of the book, and the subsequent second edition in 1987, is testimony that other students and teachers of social policy were also hungry for Canadian content. The first edition prompted one reviewer to say "With its wealth of theoretical and factual material, assembled in a single volume, *Canadian Social Policy* will prove a valuable resource to teachers charged with the responsibility of introducing students to this subject area. It will also, one would hope, reach a much wider circle of readers, including policy makers themselves, and thereby contribute to a clearer understanding of major social problems facing the country."

In the years since the first edition of this book, social policy scholarship has flourished in Canada among social workers as well as political scientists, historians, and sociologists. Today, we can find journal articles on most policy issues as well as edited or authored books on a number of specific issues. The Internet gives us access to the most immediate information about legislation that has been introduced, and allows us to be well-informed about the reactions of various stakeholders to proposed policy or legislation. There are now a handful of excellent books by Canadian social workers that teach us about the history of the welfare state in Canada, and the policy-making process here.

There are still few books that address the full range of the objectives of the first edition: to help students of Canadian social policy begin to understand social welfare concepts, ideology, the process of social policy formulation, and the substantive issues from a Canadian perspective; and, to stimulate discussion and debate on major social policy issues confronting Canadian society today. While the language we use has changed somewhat, these two primary objectives in introductory social policy courses remain. It therefore seemed that a revised and updated third edition of *Canadian Social Policy* would continue to be a valuable resource for both students and teachers.

The organization of the book remains essentially the same. It opens with a chapter defining social policy. Contributors then introduce readers to issues at the forefront of the policy agenda and the range of theoretical perspectives used to define policy issues The third section focuses on the policy-making process and the book closes with a fourth section identifying the challenges ahead.

A number of things have changed, though. First is the consciousness, reflected in all chapters, that policy is now made in a context that is global, not national. This is most explicit in the addition of the international level to the definition of policy-making levels. Second is the greater emphasis on advocacy or activism—efforts to change policy—which is discussed from both the perspectives of working within the system and from outside of the system. Third is the conceptualization of issues. In the first edition, issues were framed broadly—for instance housing, child welfare, income security, or policy for the elderly. In this edition, housing has transformed to homelessness, child welfare to child poverty, income security to workfare, and "the elderly" to caring and aging. We see new issues on the policy agenda, like heterosexism and ableism. Fourth, new theoretical perspectives inform the substantive analyses. Today, we see a feminist perspective incorporated into the analysis of issues like aging and caring, workfare, immigration and refugee policy, Aboriginal issues, and policy toward single mothers, while in the earliest edition this perspective was restricted to the chapter on social policy concerning women. We also see the use of new perspectives, like constructivism, postmodernism, anti-colonialism, and anti-oppression.

Perhaps most striking is the change in the disciplinary background and gender of the contributors, which I see as evidence of the maturation of the social work education system in Canada. In the 1978 edition only three of the sixteen contributors were female, and five of the sixteen were social workers. In this new edition, ten of the twenty contributors are female, and fifteen of the twenty are social workers. This dramatic change is not just a reflection of different kinds of choices being made by the editor but indicative of the changes in the pool of social policy scholars now teaching and writing in Canada. In 1978, there were still only two schools in Canada that offered prospective social policy students an opportunity to study social work at the doctoral level, and the majority of graduates were male. Now there are eight programs spread across the country. As predicted, this greater accessibility has made it easier for women to engage in doctoral studies and the majority of graduates are now female, almost in proportion to the number of females graduating from master's programs. Policy analysis, once regarded as a male interest within the discipline, has been embraced by this new generation of female scholars.

Several of the contributors to the first book have passed on now, among them my two teachers at Laurier, Shankar Yelaja and Maurice Kelly. Both toiled through the 1970s and 1980s to create policy analysis and evaluation capacity within the profession. One of their dreams was to build the doctoral program at Laurier; five of the scholars who have contributed to this edition of *Canadian Social Policy* have, or soon will, graduate from this program. This book is a tribute to the foundational work they did in paving the way for a new generation. I hope they would be proud of what they have inspired.

I **Introduction**

Introduction to Part I

This section introduces you to the debate about what is meant by the term "social policy," and offers a definition that is inclusive of a broad range of human services and recognizes the inextricable link between economic policy and social policy. A brief review is made of models of policy development, followed by a discussion of the dimensions of policy, or the levels, from the international to the organizational, at which it is made. The argument is set out that social workers have a responsibility to engage in advocacy in an effort to shape social policy to reflect the values that they support—values that are often inconsistent with the neo-liberal thinking of most governments in power in Canada today.

An Overview of Social Policy[1]

Anne Westhues

Social policy has a fundamental influence on our practice as social work-ers. It identifies what a majority of Canadians accept as legitimate pub-lic issues—issues for which we share a collective responsibility. It also gives direction to how that majority, represented by the government of the day, believes these issues should be dealt with. Social workers, along with others like nurses, teachers, and police officers, are hired to implement these policies. We also have a responsibility, as reflected in the Canadian Association of Social Workers Code of Ethics (1994), to advocate for changes to existing policies that we believe will enhance social well-being: eliminate discrimi-nation; increase equality of distribution of resources; increase equality of access to resources, services, and opportunities; create a clean and healthy environment; and promote social justice.

During the post-World War II period, we saw a broadening of areas where Canadians were willing to make collective statements about the kind of soci-ety we wanted to create. Where once we saw violence against women and children as private matters to be dealt with by the family, for instance, we now have taken a stand, reflected in the Criminal Code of Canada and in child welfare legislation in every province, that there are specified limits to what is acceptable behaviour. This process of defining and redefining our vision of what we want to be as a society is continuous. There are supporters and there are critics for every policy decision taken, reflecting the variety of different interests within any society. There are new issues that emerge as demographic, economic, and political realities change, and as individuals and peoples come to understand their realities differently than in the past, and to dream of a healthier future.

Our purpose in this book is to introduce you to the discussion about what is meant by social policy and policy analysis, to provide an overview of the major social policy issues currently being debated in Canada, and to famil-iarize you with the policy-making process at the provincial, federal, and orga-nizational levels. In closing, we offer some ideas about how to evaluate the effectiveness of social policy. Included in these last two sections are sugges-tions about how social workers can engage in advocacy to influence policy outcomes.

Defining Social Policy and Policy Analysis

There has been a long-standing debate within the literature as to what is meant by the term "social policy." The central issue that frames this discussion is how inclusive is the domain of social policy. Does it encompass only those areas that have been described as "personal social services," like income security, child welfare, and counselling (Kahn, 1979)? Does it include related human services like education and health care, or an even broader range of what some consider economic policies like labour legislation, decisions with respect to the reduction of the budget deficit, or free trade agreements with the United States and Mexico? Does it include only decisions made with respect to the allocation of rights and resources by governmental bodies, or does it also include decisions made by transfer payment organizations or by non-governmental collectivities like unions? Is the role of policy analysts that of detached, dispassionate observers, or do they have a responsibility to advocate for a value-based position? While the debate may seem somewhat esoteric, the position that one takes defines how broad is the range of policy issues about which one believes social workers have a responsibility to be informed, and on which the profession has an ethical obligation to try to effect change.

Canadian authors have tended to emphasize a broader definition of social policy, though a few have taken a midpoint on the spectrum. Yelaja (1987, p. 2), for instance, offers this definition: "Social policy is concerned with the public administration of welfare services, that is, the formulation, development and management of specific services of government at all levels, such as health, education, income maintenance and welfare services." In the same vein, Brooks (1993, p. 184) says: "Many of the most expensive activities carried out by the state in advanced capitalist societies are associated with the area of social policy. These functions include public education, health care, publicly subsidized housing, and the provision of various forms of income support to such segments of the population as the unemployed, the aged, and the disabled." At the opposite end of the spectrum, in keeping with Rimlinger, and Wilensky and Lebeaux, McGilly (1990, p. 12) suggests: "The least misleading simplification of social policy is to define it as society's struggle to keep up with the consequences of advancing industrialization." This broader definition, which recognizes the unequivocal linkage between social policy and economic policy, is reflected in the writing of Canadian social workers like Armitage (1988); Collier (1995); Graham, Swift, and Delaney (2000); Lightman (1991, 2003); Moscovitch (1991); Moscovitch and Drover (1981); Riches and Ternowetsky (1990); Tester (1991, 1992); and Wharf and McKenzie (1998). As we have inexorably shifted into a global economy over the past twenty years, it has become clear that social policy can no longer be discussed in a meaningful way without understanding the economic context of policy decisions.

At the same time that there has been a shift to defining policy issues in a more global context, there has been a parallel shift to thinking about policy as it relates to practitioners locally. Pierce (1984), writing from a social work perspective, suggests that there are eight levels at which social policy is made that shape our work as practitioners. These include the three levels of federal, provincial, and local government that political scientists like Pal (1992) and Brooks (1993) include in the domain of public policy. Pierce also suggests that they include what Flynn (1992) calls "small scale policy systems" like social service organizations and professional associations. This reflects his understanding that an integral part of practice is the development of operational policies that define how a service user will experience a policy that is generally set at a larger-system level, for instance, "minimum intervention" into the lives of families with children, "normalization" for people who have disabilities, or a commitment to the equality of women.

Pierce (1984) includes the family and the individual practitioner as relevant system levels to understanding social policy as well. He argues that decisions made by the individual practitioner in relation to the implementation of public policy define how service users experience social services, and the social policies that shape those services. Every worker has some discretion in how he or she interprets policy. For instance, a social assistance worker may choose to accept as part of a recipient's work requirement volunteer time at their child's school, or not. Or a child care worker determining the eligibility of an applicant for subsidized child care may choose to advise the applicant on how to become eligible for subsidy by buying a refrigerator on credit rather than saving for it. How the worker chooses to act in these two instances gives a very different message to service users about the social policies affecting them. Similarly, decisions taken by a family with respect to the care they are willing to provide to an elderly family member or a child with a disability will have an influence on social policy.

Flynn (1992) reinforces the importance of this broader perspective for the social work practitioner. Citing Kahn, he says that policy shapes and delineates what the practitioner does, how he or she relates to the client group, and the manner in which discretion is allowed or exercised. Further, he argues that understanding how policies at the agency, or even individual level, affect what the practitioner may or must do, and how they can be changed, is a way to empower practitioners.

Another important issue discussed in the current literature is the role of the policy analyst. Mirroring the debate in the social sciences about whether positivist, constructivist, or critical theory approaches are most appropriate for social science research today (Cresswell, 1994; Kirby & McKenna, 1989; Lincoln & Guba, 1985; Maguire, 1987; Neuman, 1994; Strauss & Corbin, 1990), the question explored is whether the role of the policy analyst is to provide information to decision makers which will help them make more informed decisions (Friedmann, 1987), or whether the analyst has a responsibility to engage in some form of social action with his or her analyses (Moscovitch, 1991). As we saw above, this latter position is consistent with the Canadian Association of Social Workers Code of Ethics.

Defining social policy and policy analysis

So how do I propose to use the term "social policy"? Following Pal (1992, p. 2), I would define social policy as "a course of action or inaction chosen by public authorities to address a given problem or interrelated set of problems." My definition of "public authorities" would be very broad, however, including individuals who make decisions at the various levels of government, in social service organizations, and in collective agreements, in order to implement policies intended to address social problems. Further, I would add the phrase "which deal with human health, safety or well-being" (Flynn, 1992) to the definition to differentiate social policy from the entirety of public policy issues that governments address.

If social policy is action taken to address a given problem, policy analysis is "the disciplined application of intellect to public problems" (Pal, 1992, p. 38). Pal differentiates between academic policy analysis and applied policy analysis, the domain of social work practitioners. The academic is primarily concerned with theory, explanation, understanding policies and how they came into being, and attempts to retain some objectivity in making the analysis. The practitioner, by contrast, is more interested in specific policies or problems than in theory, in evaluation rather than explanation, in changing policies, and in advocating for the interests of consumers of service (Pal, 1992, p. 24). Moroney (1981) explains this difference in orientation between the traditional academic approach to policy analysis and the practice-based approach as being about making value-based choices. In support of this position, Kelley (1975, cited in Flynn, 1992) suggests that there are three criteria that must be considered in all policy analyses. These include adequacy, the extent to which a specified need or goal is met if program objectives are carried out; effectiveness, the extent to which the outcomes obtained are a result of policy intent and program activity; and efficiency, the measure of goal attainment in terms of the expenditure of the least number of resources. Other values that may be basic to social policy issues include impact on client identity and impact on self-determination. Values that may guide the process of policy development might include informed decision making, public accountability, procedural fairness, and openness and accessibility to the process (Ogilvie, Ogilvie, and Company, 1990).

Models of Policy Development

Another way in which academics and practitioners have tried to understand social policy and policy analysis is through the conceptualization of a model that captures the complexity of the policy-making process (Kahn, 1969; Mayer, 1985; Meyerson & Banfield, 1955; Pancer & Westhues, 1989; Perlman & Gurin, 1972; Pierce, 1984; Westhues, 1980; Wharf & McKenzie, 1998; York, 1982). The earlier models, as one might expect, were less detailed than are more recent ones. Meyerson and Banfield (1955), for instance, defined only three stages in policy development: 1) the decision maker considers all options open to him or her; 2) the consequences of adopting each alternative are identified and evaluated; and 3) the alternative that seems to have the best fit with the valued ends is selected.

As the social sciences moved into a period in which positivism and rationality were highly valued, models became more detailed, and emphasized the technical skills of the policy analyst as researcher (Kahn, 1969; Mayer, 1985; York, 1982). When our competencies in these areas developed more fully, concern arose that insufficient attention was being given to the political, or value-based, aspects of policy development, and models were proposed that attempted to rectify this imbalance (Gil, 1981; Perlman & Gurin, 1972; Wharf & McKenzie, 1998). A model that is useful in thinking about the policy-making process in each of the systems and domains explored in this chapter is: 1) defining the problem; 2) agreeing on goals; 3) identifying alternatives; 4) choosing an alternative; 5) implementing the policy; and 6) evaluation.

Policy Dimensions

One of the difficulties of developing a model that captures the complexity of the policy-making process is precisely because it is such a complex process, as is so ably described by Kenny-Scherber in chapter 14. Social policy can be made at the international, federal, provincial, and local levels of government in Canada, as well as within the agency setting. The policy initiative may fall into one of four subsystems within each of these systems: the strategic framework; the legislative framework; the program framework; or the operational framework (Ogilvie, Ogilvie, and Company, 1990). These dimensions of social policy are explored in more depth below.

Traditionally, we have thought of social policy issues in a national context. The generosity of the safety net that a country put into place has been related to its level of industrialization, its level of affluence, and the extent to which its cultural values have supported the assumption of a collective responsibility for the well-being of all citizens (Moscovitch & Drover, 1981). As we have moved into a period of global capitalism (Collier, 1995; Teeple, 1995), however, international policies have begun to have important influences on our social and economic well-being. Following the introduction of the Free Trade Agreement between Canada and the United States in 1989, and the North American Free Trade Agreement between Canada, the United States, and Mexico in 1992, for instance, it has become evident that there are economic and political pressures to "harmonize" social policy in all three countries. While ideally that may have meant that American and Mexican social policy would come to look like Canadian social policy, in fact the safety net that was so carefully woven over a period of at least fifty years in Canada is gradually being weakened, taking on the appearance of its less sturdy American cousin.

United Nations agreements like the UN Convention on the Rights of the Child (1989) also shape social policy initiatives in Canada. Article 8 of the

Policy
dimensions

convention, for instance, says, "State Parties undertake to respect the right of the child to preserve his or her identity, including nationality, name and family relations as recognized by law without unlawful interference." This entitlement, which Canada had agreed to by becoming a signatory to the convention, has implications for international adoption, for instance. If a child has a right to maintain his or her identity, Canada must now ensure that information is gathered on the child's background, and that there is a mechanism for passing this information to the child at some specified age, in both non-identifying and identifying forms.

Policy at the international level may be made in each of the four subsystems identified above. The strategic framework includes development of a vision and mission statement, goals, and objectives, and is associated with what we have come to call strategic planning. The legislative framework includes legislation and the regulations, directives, and guidelines that are intended to facilitate its implementation. The program framework involves program design, the service delivery structure, and the implementation plan. This area of policy is sometimes called program planning. Lastly, the operational framework includes human resources policies, budgeting, and defining an operating structure, the policy domain that we have traditionally associated with administration (Ogilvie, Ogilvie, and Company, 1990). This policy may be set through bilateral or multilateral agreements like free trade legislation, or through administrative agreements between Canada and individual countries with respect to a policy issue like international adoption. International policy may also be made by international organizations like the United Nations or the newly formed World Trade Organization (WTO). We are coming to understand the enormity of the influence that the establishment of the WTO has had, and will continue to have, on all aspects of public policy through a variety of multilateral agreements. Developed out of the Uruguay Round of the General Agreement on Tariffs and Trade (GATT) talks, this body defines public policy in areas such as the environment, genetically modified food, and labour rights as part of its mandate to regulate international trade (Shrybman, 1999).

Social policy in Canada is shaped by what is called the "divided sovereignty" (Van Loon & Whittington, 1976) of the British North America Act of 1867, and now the Constitution Act, 1982. This means that jurisdiction has been given to the federal government for some areas of policy development and to the provinces for others. Provinces are responsible for "the establishment, maintenance and management of public and reformatory prisons in and for the provinces," and "the establishment, maintenance and management of hospitals, asylums, charities, and eleemosonary institutions" (Splane, 1965). While it is generally agreed that the intention of the legislation was to limit the role of the provinces, and to create a strong federal government, judicial interpretations of the legislation, over time, have limited the role of the federal government in the direct provision of human services.

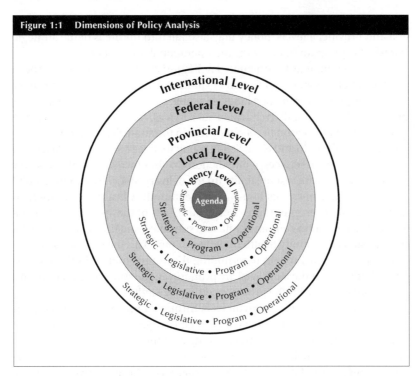

Figure 1:1 Dimensions of Policy Analysis

Depending on the policy area of concern, then, the federal government may play a greater or lesser role. Legislation pertaining to young people in trouble with the law—the Youth Criminal Justice Act, for example—falls within the federal jurisdiction. Each province has enabling legislation to serve as an implementation guide, however. In all cases this is a section of each province's child welfare legislation. By contrast, the federal government has no jurisdiction within the area of child welfare. This means that it cannot pass legislation that will shape the provision of child welfare services. The one way in which the federal government has influenced child welfare is through the provision of federal funding for approved child welfare services. The Canada Assistance Plan was the mechanism for this provision until recently. It allowed for the federal government to match provincial spending on approved child welfare services, a so-called cost-sharing agreement. This federal-provincial agreement was replaced in 1996 with the Canada Health and Social Transfer. This legislation will still allow for the transfer of federal funds to the provinces, but the transfer is now in the form of a block grant, meaning that the provinces will have more control over how the funds are allocated within the areas of health, education, and social services than under the Canada Assistance Plan or the Established Programs Financing Act, which facilitated the flow of money to the provinces in the areas of health and education. In addition to policy being possible within the legislative framework at both the federal and provincial levels, policy may also fall into the areas of the strategic framework, program framework, and operational framework.

Local governments have a limited policy jurisdiction with respect to social services in all provinces in Canada (Tindal & Tindal, 1984). Their primary areas of responsibility include land use, water, roads, and recreation. In most provinces they do not deliver any social services, and so have no legislative jurisdiction or any reason to set policy within the strategic, program, or operational areas. Ontario and Nova Scotia municipalities have some jurisdiction in the area of social services, a jurisdiction that has increased in the past few years in Ontario, with responsibility for the delivery of social assistance, child care, long-term care, social housing, and community health. In addition, in Ontario local government must contribute 50% of the spending on social assistance, long-term care, and childcare subsidies, and the full cost of social housing and community health (Melchers, 1999). This means that local governments play a key role in determining the annual budget in these areas. Policy initiatives at the local level are primarily in the strategic, program, and operational areas, with the province setting legislation.

Service delivery in all provinces is through some mix of government offices and transfer payment agencies; that is, organizations that enter into purchase of service agreements, generally with the provincial and local governments. A few small agencies provide service without government funding. The programs of these agencies are shaped by the legislative framework defined by the province, or sometimes the federal government. The domain of their policy work tends to fall within the strategic, program, and operational frameworks, though they may assume a responsibility to advocate for policy changes within the legislative framework set by the provincial or federal governments. These dimensions of social policy are summarized in Figure 1.1.

Influencing Policy Development

Social work practitioners, as noted above, have a responsibility to advocate for social change that will improve the well-being of the people we work with. A key way in which this can be done is by attempting to influence the policies that shape their experience of the services we deliver. To do this effectively, one must first identify the appropriate system to be addressed for the policy issue of concern. If you are interested in changing some aspect of child welfare legislation, making it easier for an adopted person to obtain identifying information about his or her birth parents, for instance, the appropriate system would be the provincial government, not the local Children's Aid Society. While it may be useful to have child welfare organizations supporting your efforts, they are not the decision makers on this issue.

Once the appropriate system has been identified, it is necessary to understand the policy-making process within that system. Figure 1.2 outlines this

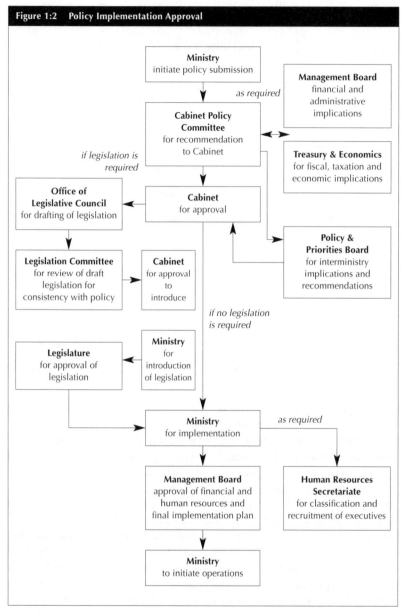

Figure 1:2   Policy Implementation Approval

Source: G.G. Bell and A.D. Pascoe (1988). The Ontario government: Structure and functions. Toronto: Wall and Thompson, p. 28.

Influencing
policy
development

process in detail for the provincial level, as well as the international, federal, local, and agency levels. Figure 1.3 provides further detail on this process, specifying the approvals required for each type of policy change, whether a change to legislation, regulations, or operational policy, procedures, or guide-

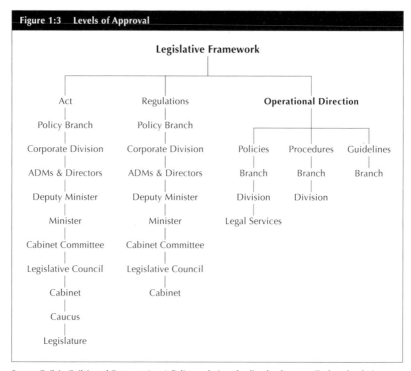

Figure 1:3   Levels of Approval

Source: Ogilvie, Ogilvie and Company (1990). Policy analysis and policy development: Tools and techniques. Course handbook. Toronto, p. 4.

lines. What is striking about these two figures is how many approvals are required before any change can be effected.

At the federal level, the process of effecting change is even more complex, with the additional approval of each of the provinces required. The failed agreement on the Meech Lake and Charlottetown Accords is testimony to this complexity, though the recent agreement on the Social Union demonstrates that it is possible (Mendelson, 1999). At the local level, it is much simpler, generally requiring only the approval of the social service department, the commissioner of social services, the social services committee, and regional or municipal council. At the agency level, the process is similar, with approvals required by the program unit, executive director, and the board of directors. Depending on the model of board governance, approval may be required by a standing committee of the board and the executive committee before the matter is presented to the board of directors itself (Carver, 1990).

What these models fail to convey is the politically charged environment in which many policy decisions are made. While Bell and Pascoe (1988) identify the first step in the policy-making process as the ministry initiating a policy submission, in fact there is often considerable political activity, sometimes

Influencing policy development

over a prolonged period, before a ministry sees an issue as a sufficient priority to address it. Kenny-Scherber describes the variety of institutions, interests groups, and ideologies that interact with one another, vying for influence in shaping a policy outcome in chapter 14. These political efforts are sometimes conceptualized as social advocacy, or community organizing (Ross, 1967; Taylor & Roberts, 1985; Tropman, Erlich, & Rothman, 1995), and planning and policy analysis are described as more rational processes. Further, it is important to understand that both internal and external politics are influential in this process, that is, not only various stakeholders but the bureaucrats making decisions themselves will promote different interests (Tindal & Tindal, 1984).

The effort to educate the general public about wife assault is a good case example of this political process, one that is lucidly described by Gillian Walker (Walker, 1990). Through the women's centres set up to raise consciousness about women's rights in the early 1970s, it soon became evident that a major concern of women experiencing relationship difficulties was being assaulted by their partners. In response to this concern, women's shelters began to spring up across the country as places for women to take refuge when they were under attack. To obtain funding for these shelters, it was necessary to convince the United Way, local, and provincial governments that wife assault was sufficiently widespread that funding was warranted for shelters. Walker makes an insightful analysis of defining the problem of wife assault, and the conflicting politics of feminists and professionals in defining the issue. For feminists, it was an instance of women's oppression, grounded in the patriarchy that influences family relationships and social institutions like the law. The only possible remedy, for them, was fundamental social change, with the objective a system that supports social, political, and economic equality for women. For professionals, by contrast, the problem was defined as that of outdated sex roles, traditional attitudes, and inadequate institutional procedures. Their remedy was to develop programs that educate men and women about gender equality, and that institute therapeutic interventions to deal with the trauma of assault.

Skills Required

Whether policy analysis is a social worker's primary job responsibility or a secondary one, two sets of skills are required: what has been called process (Rothman & Zald, 1985), interpersonal (Tropman, 1995), or interactional (Perlman & Gurin, 1972) skills; and task (Rothman & Zald, 1985), intellectual (Tropman, 1995), or analytic (Perlman & Gurin, 1972) skills. Table 1.1 outlines both the analytic and interactional skills required at each stage in the policy development process. The analytic skills identified draw heavily from an earlier article by Pancer and Westhues (1989).

In addition to the general skill of thinking analytically, at the initial stage of the policy development process, when *the problem is defined*, analytic

Table 1.1 Skills Required at Each Stage of Policy Development

Stage in Policy Development	Analytic Skills	Interactional Skill
Defining the Problem	**Values Analysis** • opinion polls • key informant interviews • group approaches (nominal group technique, Delphi, community forum) • preference scaling **Needs Assessment** • social indicators approaches • surveys • group approaches	**Leadership** • creating a safe environment • ensuring participation • active listening • public speaking • clear, concise writing
Agreeing on Goals	**Goals Analysis** • *Goal formulation:* surveys, community forums, rating of goal characteristics • *Priority Setting:* estimate– discuss–estimate procedure, Q-sort, paired comparisons, multiattribute utility measurement, decision- theoretic analysis	**Engaging People in Process** • clarifying intent • brokering • mediating • persuading
Identifying Alternatives	**Policy Logic Analysis** • review of theories of causation • review of outcome evaluations in policy area • concept development	**Sharing Knowledge** • facilitating
Choosing an Alternative	**Feasibility Study** • investigation of funding sources • cost-benefit analysis • cost-effectiveness analysis • PRINCE analysis • administrative feasibility assessment	**Sharing Knowledge** • facilitating • guiding
Implementing the Policy	**Implementation Assessment** • Gantt charts • milestone charts • PRT-CPM networks	**Information Gathering** • manufacturing commitment
Evaluating the Policy	**Process** • collection of data from information systems • peer review ratings • client satisfaction surveys **Outcomes** • experimental approaches • quasi-experimental approaches • single case design • client satisfaction surveys • social impact assessments	**Sharing of Expertise** • safe environment • ensuring participation in developing design • communication of results

skills are needed in two areas: values analysis and needs assessment. To complete a values analysis, the analyst must know how to conduct opinion polls or to cull useful information from opinion polls conducted by others; carry out key informant interviews; use group techniques like the nominal group technique, the Delphi technique, and community forums; and do preference scaling. To complete a needs assessment, the analyst has to know how to identify and interpret social indicators; carry out surveys; and use the group approaches identified above. Interactional skills required at this critical first stage of the process include leadership in setting up a process that will allow for the exchange of ideas on the issue; creating a safe environment so people feel they can express their feelings about the issue; ensuring that all stakeholders have an opportunity to participate in the process of constructing the problem; active listening skills, to ensure that the nuances of different stakeholder perspectives are not missed; public speaking skills, if one is going to advocate for a particular policy position; and clear, concise writing skills, whether one is playing the role of neutral internal policy analyst at some level of government or community-based advocate.

At the next stage, *agreeing on goals,* analytic skills are again needed in two areas: goal formulation and priority setting. To formulate goals, skills are needed to carry out surveys; conduct community forums; and rate goal characteristics. Procedures like the estimate-discuss-estimate procedure, the Q-sort, paired comparisons, multiattribute utility measurement, and decision theoretic analysis can be used to set priorities. To support the analytic tasks, interactional skills that permit the analyst to engage stakeholders in the process of reaching agreement on goals are needed, as well as skills in clarifying, brokering, and mediating. If the analyst is acting as an advocate, she or he will also need to be skilled in persuasion.

Policy logic analysis, a variant of program logic analysis (Rush & Ogburne, 1991), can be used to facilitate the *identification of policy alternatives* that, in light of a specified theory of causation of the identified problem, could be expected to achieve the policy goals agreed upon. A review of any outcome evaluations of these policy alternatives would identify empirical evidence, which could either support the implementation of a particular alternative or suggest that it would not, in fact, achieve the anticipated outcomes. Theory often precedes practice so another skill required by the analyst is the ability to discern the practice implications of a particular theoretical perspective for policy development. The interactional skills required at this stage include being able to summarize and share knowledge in a way that is both interesting and concise and the ability to facilitate discussion to generate alternative ideas.

Feasibility studies provide information that assists in *choosing among policy alternatives.* Assessing feasibility includes determining whether funds would be available for the various alternatives; completing cost-benefit or cost-effectiveness analyses on each alternative; completing a political feasi-

Influencing
policy
development

bility assessment using a technique like PRINCE (Probe, Interact, Calculate, Execute); and assessing the administrative feasibility of the alternatives. Good skills in presenting information in an interesting and concise way are required at this stage as well. In addition, the analyst must be able to guide the process in selecting an alternative.

An implementation assessment permits the analyst to identify how much time would be required to implement the alternative selected, which jurisdictions would need to be involved, and which approvals required. Pressman and Wildavsky (1973) alerted us to the importance of this stage thirty years ago, when they discovered that many policies never have their intended effects because they fail to make it through the long string of decisions necessary for the policy to be implemented. Analyzing these approval processes beforehand, and identifying potential blocks, will provide greater assurance that the policy will, in fact, be implemented. The primary interactional skills required at this stage are the ability to gather information on complex systems and to manufacture commitment on the part of service providers to the new policy alternative, so that it will, in fact, be implemented as intended.

Finally, any policy must be systematically evaluated to assess what has happened in light of its intended effects. Process evaluation includes a review of who has been served, for what reasons, and what service they have received. Peer reviews are made of cases to determine whether defined standards of care have been met. Client satisfaction surveys assess whether consumers received the service expected, in a timely fashion, and whether they found it helpful. Outcome evaluations may focus on individual goals or program goals, and are intended to assess the extent to which the changes that are intended to occur for the client have, in fact, occurred. The interactional skills required of the policy analyst as evaluator include sharing his or her knowledge about how evaluations may be designed; creating a feeling of safety with respect to the evaluation; ensuring that all those affected by the evaluation participate in its design; engaging service deliverers in the data collection process; and communicating the results of the research to all those involved.

Limitations of Policy Analysis

With all of its promise for improving the well-being of our clients, what are the limitations of policy analysis as an area of practice? First, the process may be exceedingly slow. Even within an agency setting, to make a change in policy may take a year or longer from the point that a concern is identified until a new policy has been implemented. If the local, provincial, or federal governments are the focus of change, it is likely to be even longer. This means that a commitment to effect change must be a long-term one.

Second, efforts to make changes in policy can be very resource intensive. It takes time, energy, and money to raise awareness about an issue. The more complex and controversial the issue, the more resources will be required. It is Conclusions essential to learn to build coalitions, to create organizations where none exist to advocate for an issue, and to identify and link with existing ones that might share your concern. It may also be necessary to raise funding to support your policy change initiatives. This means that a commitment to effect change is an opportunity to develop a set of social work skills that are quite different from those within the clinical domain.

Third, even with the investment of considerable resources, it may not be possible to effect changes that are consistent with social work values at a particular time. In Ontario and Alberta, for instance, governments have recently introduced mandatory workfare. While most social workers support the development of job training opportunities for people on assistance, requiring people to work in return for benefits is in conflict with the value we place on self-determination. Data abundantly show that a great majority of people work when given the opportunity. Job readiness programs offered by the various levels of government in Canada have typically been oversubscribed (Snyder, 2000). In spite of this empirical evidence, the ideology continues to exist that people on assistance are lazy, and we need to coerce them to accept work. As long as a government in power holds this belief, and refuses to alter it in light of evidence to the contrary, efforts to change this particular social policy are unlikely to be fruitful. This means that a commitment to effect change may not always be successful in the short run, and can be the source of considerable discouragement if a longer-term perspective is not maintained.

Finally, for the policy analyst working within an organization or at some level of government, it is essential that there is a clear understanding between the policy analyst and the employer about which kinds of political activity are acceptable. Traditionally, the role of government employee was defined as that of a rational, apolitical analyst. Political activity was not only discouraged but could be the grounds for dismissal. While that has now changed, there may still be limits on what is allowed. An employee at the local government level may be free to engage in efforts to change provincial legislation with respect to regulation of social workers, for instance, but not to lobby his or her member of Parliament to withdraw the mandatory aspect of the workfare program. This means that a commitment to effect change requires a careful assessment of one's work environment, and clear communication about the boundaries on political activity.

Conclusions

Social workers have come to accept social policy development as an essential component of our work as professionals. While the prospect of trying to change legislation, the vision of an organization, or agency policy with respect to service delivery may seem daunting, our successes in these efforts not only

Note

References

provide us with an opportunity to develop a complementary set of skills to those we use as clinicians but also teach us that it can be done. Whether we choose to focus on issues at the international, federal, provincial, local, or agency level, our efforts improve the well-being of individual clients, build a sense of community, and empower us as individuals and as a profession. Ultimately, the values we stand for, infused in social policy, will shape and give definition to the vital, ever-changing culture that we know as Canadian.

Note

1 Reprinted with permission. Adapted from A. Westhues. (2002).

References

Armitage, A. (1988). *Social welfare in Canada: Ideals, realities and future paths.* Toronto: McClelland & Stewart.

Bell, G.G., & Pascoe, A.D. (1988). *The Ontario government: Structure and functions.* Toronto: Wall & Thompson.

Brooks, S. (1993). *Public policy in Canada: An introduction* (2nd ed.). Toronto: McClelland & Stewart.

Canadian Association of Social Workers. (1994). *Code of Ethics.* Ottawa: Author.

Carver, J. (1990). *Boards that make a difference: A new design for leadership in non-profit and public organizations.* San Francisco: Jossey-Bass.

Collier, K. (1995). Social policy versus regional trading blocs in the global system: NAFTA, the EEC and "Asia." *Canadian Review of Social Policy, 35*(1), 50–59.

Cresswell, J.W. (1994). *Research design: Qualitative and quantitative approaches.* Thousand Oaks, CA: Sage.

Flynn, J.P. (1992). *Social agency policy: Analysis and presentation for community practice.* Chicago: Nelson-Hall.

Friedmann, J. (1987). *Planning in the public domain: From action to knowledge.* Princeton, NJ: Princeton University Press.

Gil, D.G. (1981). *Unravelling social policy* (3rd ed.). Cambridge, MA: Schenkman Publishing.

Graham, J., Swift, K., & Delaney, R. (2000). *Canadian social policy: An introduction.* Scarborough: Prentice Hall Allyn and Bacon Canada.

Guest, D. (1985). *The emergence of social security in Canada* (2nd ed.). Vancouver: University of British Columbia Press.

Kahn, A.J. (1969). *Theory and practice of social planning.* New York: Russell Sage.

Kahn, A.J. (1979). *Social policy and social services* (2nd ed.).New York: Random House.

Kirby, S., & McKenna, K. (1989). *Experience, research, social change: Methods from the margins.* Toronto: Garamond.

Lightman, E. (1991). Support for social welfare in Canada and the United States. *Canadian Review of Social Policy, 28*(2), 9-27.

Lightman, E. (2003). Social policy in Canada. Don Mills: Oxford University Press.

Lincoln, Y.S., & Guba, E.G. (1985). *Naturalistic inquiry.* London: Sage.

Maguire, P. (1987). *Doing participatory research: A feminist approach.* Amherst, MA: University of Massachusetts, Centre for International Education.

Mayer, R.R. (1985). *Policy and program planning: A developmental perspective.* Englewood Cliffs, NJ: Prentice-Hall.

Mayer, R.R., & Greenwood, E. (1980). *The design of social policy research.* Englewood Cliffs, NJ: Prentice-Hall.

McGilly, F. (1990). *Canada's public social services: Understanding income and health programs.* Toronto: McClelland & Stewart.

Melchers, R. (1999). Local governance of social welfare: Local reform in Ontario in the nineties. *Canadian Review of Social Policy, 43* (2), 29-57.

Mendelson, M. (1999). The new Social Union. *Canadian Review of Social Policy, 43* (2), 1-11.

Meyerson, M., & Banfield, E.C. (1955). *Politics, planning and the public interest.* New York: Free Press.

Moroney, R.M. (1981). Policy analysis within a value theoretical framework. In R. Haskins & J.J. Gallager, (Eds.), *Models for analysis of social policy: An introduction* (pp. 78-102). Norwood, NJ: Ablex Press.

Moscovitch, A. (1991). Citizenship, social rights and Canadian social welfare. *Canadian Review of Social Policy, 28* (Winter), 28-34.

Moscovitch, A., & Drover, G. (1981). *Inequality: Essays on the political economy of social welfare.* Toronto: University of Toronto Press.

Multiculturalism and Citizenship Canada. (1991). *Convention on the rights of the child.* Ottawa: Minister of Supplies and Services Canada.

Neuman, W.L. (1994). *Social research methods: Qualitative and quantitative approaches* (2nd ed.). Toronto: Allyn & Bacon.

Ogilvie, Ogilvie, and Company. (1990). *Policy analysis and policy development: Tools and techniques. Course handbook.* Toronto: Author.

Pal, L. (1992). *Public policy analysis: An introduction.* Toronto: Nelson Canada.

Pancer, S.M., & Westhues, A. (1989). A developmental stage approach to planning. *Evaluation Review, 13* (1), 56-77.

Perlman, R., & Gurin, A. (1972). *Community organizing and social planning.* New York: John Wiley & Sons.

Pierce, D. (1984). *Policy for the social work practitioner.* New York: Longman.

Pressman, J.L., & Wildavsky, A.B. (1973). *Implementation.* Berkeley: University of California Press.

Riches, G., & Ternowetsky, G. (1990). *Unemployment and welfare: Social policy and the work of social work.* Toronto: Garamond Press.

Ross, M.C. (1967). *Community organization: Theory, principles and practice.* New York: Harper & Row.

Rothman, J., & Zald, M.N. (1985). Planning theory in social work community practice. In S.H. Taylor & R.W. Roberts (Eds.), *Theory and practice of community social work* (pp. 125-153). New York: Columbia University Press.

Rush, B., & Ogborne, A. (1991). Program logic models: Expanding their role and structure for program planning and evaluation. *Canadian Journal of Program Evaluation, 6* (2), 95-106.

Shrybman, S. (1999). *A citizen's guide to the World Trade Organization.* Ottawa: Canadian Centre for Policy Alternatives and James Lorimer.

Snyder, L. (2000). Success of single mothers on social assistance through a voluntary employment program. *Canadian Social Work Review, 17* (1), 49-68.

Splane, R.B. (1965). *Social welfare in Ontario 1791-1893: A study of public welfare administration.* Toronto: University of Toronto Press.

Strauss, A., & Corbin, J. (1990). *Basics of qualitative research: Grounded theory procedures and techniques.* Newbury Park: Sage.

Taylor, S.H., & Roberts, R.W. (1985). *Theory and practice of community social work.* New York: Columbia University Press.

References

Teeple, G. (1995). *Globalization and the decline of social reform.* Toronto: Garamond Press.

Tester, F.J. (1991). The globalized economy: What does it mean for Canadian social and environmental policy? *Canadian Review of Social Policy, 27* (1), 3-12.

Tester, F.J. (1992). The disenchanted democracy: Canada in the global economy of the 1990's. *Canadian Review of Social Policy, 29/30*(2), 132-157.

Tindal, C.R., & Tindal, S.N. (1984). *Local government in Canada* (2nd ed.). Toronto: McGraw-Hill Ryerson.

Tropman, J.E. (1995). Policy management in the social agency. In J.E. Tropman, J.L Erlich, & J. Rothman (Eds.), *Tactics and techniques of community intervention* (3rd ed.) (pp. 288-291). Itasca, IL: F.E. Peacock.

Tropman, J.E., Erlich, J.L. & Rothman, J. (Eds.), *Tactics and techniques of community intervention.* (3rd ed.). Itasca, IL: F.E. Peacock.

Van Loon, R.J. & Whittington, M.S. (1976). *The Canadian political system: Environment, structure and process* (2nd ed.). Toronto: McGraw-Hill Ryerson.

Walker, G.A. (1990). *Family violence and the women's movement.* Toronto: University of Toronto Press.

Westhues, A. (1980). Stages in social planning. *Social Service Review,* (September), 331-343.

Westhues, A. (2002). Social policy practice. In F.J. Turner (Ed.), *Social work practice: A Canadian perspective* (pp. 315-329). Toronto: Prentice Hall.

Wharf, B., & McKenzie, B. (1998). *Connecting policy to practice in the human services.* Toronto: Oxford University Press.

Yelaja, S.A. (1987). *Canadian social policy* (Rev. ed.). Waterloo, ON: Wilfrid Laurier University Press.

York, R.O. (1982). *Human service planning: Concepts, tools and methods.* Chapel Hill: University of North Carolina Press.

Additional Resources

Kaus, M. (1995). *The end of equality.* New York: Basic Books.

Lal Das, B. (1999). *The World Trade Organization: A guide to the framework for International trade.* New York: Zed Books.

Olsen, G. (2002). *The politics of the welfare state.* Toronto: Oxford University Press.

< www.spo.laurentian.ca >

< www.policy.ca >

Current Social Policy Issues Part II

II   Current Social Policy Issues

Introduction to Part II

The major policy issues currently under debate in Canada are introduced and discussed in this section. A range of theoretical perspectives, identified in the chapter descriptions that follow, is used by the authors in making their analyses. The specific questions addressed in each chapter include:

- What is the nature of the problem?
- How are the key concepts used to describe the problem defined, and how have they changed over time?
- Who is experiencing the problem, and what are their characteristics?
- What social values are being threatened by the problem?
- What efforts have been taken to address the problems of, for instance, legislation, funding allocation, or advocacy?
- Who defines the conditions as a problem?
- What are the causes of the problem, including relevant theoretical considerations and political, social, and economic factors historically?
- Are there gender, class, and/or ethno-racial considerations necessary to understand the problem?

The section opens with Garson Hunter addressing the critical issue of child poverty. He shows us that the child poverty rates in Canada remain high in spite of a series of attempts, which go back to 1975, to restructure the way in which we transfer income to families with children. He argues that the explanation for this failure to alleviate child poverty rates, in spite of an all-party resolution to do this in 1989, is that any commitment to reducing child poverty has been tempered by an even greater concern that any transfer of funds to families with children should not impede the incentive to work. He concludes that a different strategy is needed if we are to be successful in reducing child poverty—a strategy that focuses on the inadequacy of current minimum wages.

In chapter 3, Barbara Waterfall challenges the reader to think about the impact of colonization on Native peoples. She argues that the effects of historical and ongoing colonial processes imbue the social work profession and social work education. She uses the case example of child welfare practice

with Native peoples to substantiate this argument, tracing the roots of colonial practice to the Indian Act of 1876. The profession of social work is called
on to disengage from current neo-colonial and constitutional colonial politics
in favour of advocating and supporting anti-colonial initiatives. Schools of
social work are viewed as one site for mapping and developing strategies to
move the profession toward relations of equality and respectful coexistence.

Lea Caragata ably illustrates a constructionist perspective with the issue
of homelessness in chapter 4. She identifies and analyzes the three major
perspectives that have been used to understand homelessness and to shape
policy solutions to address it. These include the liberal perspective, the structural, and the more recent social exclusion perspective. She outlines the
beliefs associated with each of these perspectives, and the social expectations that result from them. She argues that there appears to be agreement
across the spectrum that homelessness exists, and that it is time to address
the issue. Depending upon one's construction of the problem, a sufficient
response may be as minimal as providing temporary services like emergency
shelters or as comprehensive as finding ways to re-engage people in the economy, socially and politically.

In chapter 5, Iara Lessa uses a postmodern perspective to analyze the
changes in what we understand to be role expectations for single mothers
since Mother's Allowance legislation was first introduced in Manitoba in 1916.
Using Foucaultian concepts like governmentality, she shows how motherhood was once seen as a sufficient responsibility to make a woman "deserving" of social assistance. While eligibility was extended to a larger group of
single mothers in the post-World War II period, she demonstrates how single
mothers came to be defined as "unemployable" for family reasons, establishing a connection between single mothers and the labour force. Once children were of an age that they no longer needed a mother's care full-time,
these women were considered employable. She argues that the Canada
Health and Social Transfer has shifted our definition of single mothers to that
of potential labour force participants first, with their mothering role clearly
secondary. These role definitions shape eligibility for social assistance.

Linda Snyder identifies herself as working from a social democratic perspective in chapter 6. This positions her as a critic of the current shift in public policy with respect to social assistance from that of an entitlement for
people who are not able to support themselves to a requirement that welfare recipients participate in work and related activities in order to receive
financial assistance. She demonstrates how these policies, known as "workfare," are inconsistent with social democratic values, and reviews the research
literature, which shows that an exit from social assistance under workfare
programs is not necessarily enduring, and often fails to result in the recipient
finding work that raises his or her standard of living above the poverty line.

Brian O'Neill offers us a useful introduction to the concepts associated
with same-sex sexual orientation in chapter 7. He then provides a historical

perspective on heterosexism in Canada, explaining how this belief system has led to oppressive policies pertaining to gay men and lesbians over the years. The belief that same-sex acts were unacceptable was sufficiently pervasive that they remained in the Criminal Code until 1969, and were classified as a psychiatric disorder until 1973. There has been a shift to greater tolerance of gays and lesbians within the past decade, as reflected in opinion polls and a revision to the Canadian Human Rights Act in 1996 to include gays and lesbians as a protected group. He argues that the next big challenge for social workers is to make the mainstream services we provide sensitive to the needs of people with a same-sex sexual orientation. O'Neill's perspective could be described as anti-heterosexist, or anti-oppressive.

Using an anti-racist, anti-oppression perspective, Usha George provides a sobering historical overview of our racist immigration and refugee policies in chapter 8. She outlines how the major policy shifts in 1967 and 1976 addressed the most blatant of these inequities, but failed to address others. The newest legislation, Bill C-11 was passed in June 2001, and has been criticized by social justice groups like Amnesty International and the Canadian Council for Refugees for its continued lack of transparency, its potential for human rights abuse, and its failure to address gender and class biases. She tells us that this shortcoming can be explained by the valuing of economic objectives in setting policy rather than more humanitarian considerations, even in the case of refugees.

In chapter 9, Mike Burke and Susan Silver identify the normative foundations of Canadian medicare that have shaped the challenges we now face in the provision of medical services. They argue that the legacies of equity of access through national standards and strong federal leadership in the making of health care policy, along with public opinion, which strongly supports the maintenance of these values, help prevent the erosion of our health care system. The neo-conservative policy environment nonetheless presents us with challenges such as renewed interest in user fees, de-listing of services, private clinics, and the privatization of home care. They challenge the argument that the current system is inefficient, an argument frequently heard from critics of publicly funded health care.

In chapter 10, Sheila Neysmith stimulates our thinking about how we can best meet the caring needs of an aging population. Working from a feminist, constructivist perspective, she reminds us that most of the elderly people requiring care are women, and that most of the care they receive is through the informal care system of family and friends. The majority of these carers are also women. She is particularly effective in illustrating the relationship between how we define a problem and the policy alternatives that we are likely to generate.

Finally, in chapter 11 Peter Dunn gives us a comprehensive overview of the policies that affect the lives of people with disabilities. Using a constructivist, anti-oppressive perspective, he describes how the UN declaration of

1981 as International Year of the Disabled Person served as a catalyst in Canada to put in place a range of policies that would promote a shift from an institutionally based, expert-driven model of service delivery for people with disabilities to one that is community based and consumer-driven. While this new model is still more an ideal than a reality in many contexts, the ideas have been identified that would make its realization possible. The challenge is to continue to implement the model in the face of reduced government spending.

The Problem of Child Poverty in Canada   2

Garson Hunter

To address the problem of child poverty in Canada, the federal minister of Finance, Paul Martin, presented the New Canada Child Tax Benefit (CCTB) program on February 18, 1997, as part of the 1997-1998 federal budget. The federal, provincial, and territorial governments negotiated an agreement known as the National Children's Agenda to advance the income and living standards of families with children (National Council of Welfare [NCW], 1999a). Certainly, it was with good reason that a program to address child poverty was introduced in Canada. A comprehensive household survey of twenty-three industrialized nations, based upon data from the Luxemburg Income Study, ranked Canada's relative child poverty level[1] at seventeenth out of twenty-three industrialized nations in 1994 (UNICEF, 2000, p. 3). Canada's child poverty rate is higher than the child poverty rate in countries such as the Czech Republic, Hungary, Greece, and Poland.

A high child poverty rate in rich nations such as Canada is a serious issue; solid research exists that identifies the correlation between a lack of adequate income and its potential impact on families and children. UNICEF's *Innocenti report card no. 1: The league table of child poverty in rich nations* noted this basic fact when they wrote:

> Such statistics represent the unnecessary suffering and deprivation of millions of individual children. They also represent a failure to hold faith with the developed world's ideal of equality of opportunity. For no matter how many individual and anecdotal exceptions there may be, the fact remains that the children of the poor simply do not have the same opportunities as the children of the non-poor. (UNICEF, 2000, p. 3)

Research on child poverty in Canada demonstrates that the disadvantages for children in poor families include being more likely to grow up in substandard housing, living in neighbourhoods with drug dealing and vandalism, suffering health problems such as vision, hearing, mobility, and cognition, and having less participation in organized sports or arts program (Ross, Scott, & Smith, 2000). Obviously addressing child poverty is a serious issue. However, analyzing child poverty is not an easy task, as "The political landscape is already littered with political rhetoric about children, broken promises and token efforts that provide very little real help to families or help only a minuscule number of the families who are in dire straits" (NCW, 1999a, p. 1).

The year 2000 marked the eleventh anniversary of the House of Commons' unanimous resolution to achieve the goal of eliminating child poverty by the year 2000. As the data[2] indicate, by 1998 the federal and provincial governments had failed to achieve that goal. In 1998, one in five children in Canada were still living in poverty according to Campaign 2000 (2000), an organization dedicated to seeing the government of Canada adhere to its resolution of eliminating child poverty. When discussing child poverty however, we need to remember that we cannot discuss children in isolation from the economic situation of their parents. All children, except those who live in an institutional setting, live in some definition of a family.[3] Joan Grant-Cummings incisively apprised the audience at the Eighth Conference on Canadian Social Welfare Policy (Regina, June 25, 1997) that child poverty is being presented to the public as if it fell from an impartial sky to settle among us as a gentle rain. She reminded the audience of what is obvious: poor children live in poor families. Any attempt to try and separate poor children from their poor families is a circuitous diversion from the class and gender issues of child poverty. This chapter will examine the key concepts used to describe the definition and measurement of child poverty; who are the poor; who experiences child poverty and what are their characteristics; social policy measures to address child poverty; causes of child poverty; the political, social, and economic factors involved; and social policy suggestions to address child poverty in Canada.

How Child Poverty Is Defined and Measured

In reporting child poverty numbers, Campaign 2000 relies on Statistics Canada's Low Income Cut-Off (LICO) measure, the most common unofficial poverty line used in Canada. LICO is used to calculate the incidence of poverty represented by the number of economic families that are measured against a definition of low income.[4] The LICO calculation is a relative measure of poverty. It measures relative deprivation based on income compared to a defined community standard. In other words, a relative measure of poverty is informed from the position that "people's experience of hunger and poverty is directly related to the societies in which they live and the standards of living which are customarily enjoyed" (Riches, 1997, p. 10). LICO is based on the average family or individual expenditures for food, shelter, and clothing: "The LICOS represent levels of gross income where people spend disproportionate amounts of money for food, shelter and clothing. Statistics Canada has decided over the years—somewhat arbitrarily—that 20 percentage points is a reasonable measure of additional burden"(NCW, 1999b, p. 3). Most income data from Statistics Canada contain two base years, the 1986 base or the 1992 base. Using the 1986 base, the average Canadian family spent 36.2% of gross income on food, shelter, and clothing in their spending patterns. From this, it was judged—somewhat arbitrarily—that low-income Canadians spent 56.2% or more on these necessary items. If the 1992 base is used, then a low-income Canadian spent 54.7% or more on these necessary items (NCW, 1999b). When using LICO to measure the child poverty rate, the Statistics Canada measure takes into account family size and differing costs of living in larger urban areas. The following table lists the LICOs for 1998:

How child poverty is defined and measured

Table 2.1 Low-Income Cut-offs for 1998 Using LICO 1992 Base					
Size of Family Unit	Urban Areas				Rural Areas
	500,000 and over	100,000 to 499,000	30,000 to 99,999	Less than 30,000*	
1 person	17,571	15,070	14,965	13,924	12,142
2 persons	21,962	18,837	18,706	17,405	15,178
3 persons	27,315	23,429	23,264	21,647	18,877
4 persons	33,063	28,359	28,162	26,205	22,849
5 persons	36,958	31,701	31,481	29,293	25,542
6 persons	40,855	35,043	34,798	32,379	28,235
7 persons	44,751	38,385	38,117	35,467	30,928

* Includes cities with a population between 15,000 and 30,000 and small urban areas (under 15,000).

Source: *Measuring low income and poverty in Canada: An update* by M. Webber, May 1998, Ottawa: Statistics Canada, Income Statistics Division, Catalogue No. 98-13.

LICO is not actually a poverty measure; rather, it is a measure of low income. Statistics Canada does not consider its LICO measure to be a poverty line. If a family unit or individual is below the LICO, Statistics Canada considers that situation to be "straitened circumstances."

Canada actually has no official poverty line and there is no general agreement in Canada on what constitutes poverty (Fellegi, 1997). On the issue of poverty lines, Ternowetsky (2000, p. 1) comments: "We have come to understand, for example, that even the concept of poverty is elusive. It is difficult to define, hard to measure and it is seemingly impossible to obtain a level of agreement on what it means to be poor in Canada." Although LICO is the most commonly used measure of poverty, there are other poverty measures used in Canada. Additional *relative* measures of poverty include the Low Income Measure (LIM) from Statistics Canada, the Toronto Social Planning Council measure, the Canadian Council on Social Development measure, the measure devised by the 1971 Senate known as the Croll, and the Gallup Poll. Others argue that provincial welfare rates are implicit poverty lines, with welfare rates serving as the minimum income a family or person should receive (Ross, Scott, & Smith, 2000). There are also two *absolute* measures of poverty commonly used in Canada, the Montreal Diet Dispensary measure and the Fraser Institute's Sarlo poverty line. Absolute poverty measures differ from relative measures of poverty in that they do not link levels to an average standard of living. Rather, these measures examine the absolute minimum an individual or a family needs to survive.[5]

There is currently an initiative underway by the provincial and territorial ministers of Social Services and the federal Human Resources Development Canada (HRDC) to devise a needs-based measure of poverty based upon the Market Basket Measure approach (MBM), which is similar in concept to the absolute measures of poverty (Statistics Canada, 1999). This initiative should be approached with some skepticism. The federal government acknowledges that using its MBM approach to measure poverty will reduce the extent of child poverty immediately by a third without any improvement in the standard of living for those children (Shillington, 2001). Additionally, the problem with all MBM approaches is the issue of identifying what constitutes life's necessities, as everyone has an opinion about what is necessary (Ross & Roberts, 1999).

Using Income Measures to Define the Condition of Child Poverty

Using the Statistics Canada LICO measure,[6] high levels of child poverty have persisted up to and including 1998 in Canada. In 1989 (year of the declaration to end child poverty in Canada by 2000) the child poverty level in Canada was 14.4%. Disturbingly, the incidence of child poverty in Canada increased to 19% for the year 1998 (Campaign 2000, 2000). The clear and disconcerting outcome from an analysis of the data is the continuous high incidence of child poverty in Canada.

A related concept to the incidence of poverty is the *depth* of poverty as described in Table 2.2 below. Depth of poverty refers to how far below a poverty line an income falls (Ross et al., 2000). The average low-income gap is calculated by determining the sum of all the income amounts that are below the income cut-off level for any given category (see Table 2.1), and dividing that sum by the number of units (individuals, families). The measure is useful as it provides some idea of how much is needed to raise the income of people to a predetermined low-income cut-off level.

The depth of poverty measure is also useful as it can provide us with a means of arriving at an estimate of what proportion of Canada's real (constant dollar) gross domestic product (GDP)[7] would be required to raise all families below LICO to the income cut-off line. Using the depth of poverty figures, it would cost .39% of Canada's real GDP for 1998 to raise all families with children below LICO to their cut-off levels.[8] *The innocenti report card no. 1* estimates that it would take .46% of Canada's gross national product (GNP)[9] to raise all poor families in Canada to their poverty line (UNICEF,

Who experiences the problem of child poverty? Class and gender issues

Table 2.2	Prevalence and Estimated Number of Average Income Gap 1989-1998 Using LICO 1992 Base									
	Average income gap ($)									
	1989	1990	1991	1992	1993	1994	1995	1996	1997	1998
Two-parent families	6,898	7,692	6,968	7,467	6,852	7,405	7,479	7,391	7,307	7,342
No earner	8,172	11,802	8,862	8,552	8,606	9,825	10,266	9,253	9,202	10,508
One earner	6,647	7,162	6,827	7,205	7,114	6,540	6,920	7,325	7,738	7,174
Two earners	4,233	4,930	5,182	5,271	4,429	4,203	4,735	4,123	3,865	5,247
Lone-parent families	5,648	6,322	6,555	6,159	5,946	7,068	6,505	6,023	6,895	9,247
Male lone-parent families	—	5,835	6,340	—	5,814	5,192	4,839	5,730	6,186	6,259
Female lone-parent families	5,685	6,353	6,567	6,024	5,955	6,016	5,916	5,508	6,033	6,189
No earner	6,088	6,738	6,717	6,247	6,047	5,978	6,519	6,099	6,513	7,456
One earner	5,318	6,007	6,327	5,446	5,765	6,210	5,179	4,527	5,307	4,899

Source: Income in Canada 1998. p. 107, by Statistics Canada, November 2000, Ottawa: Statistics Canada, Catalogue No. 75-202-R.E.

2000). As a reminder, however, the *The innocenti report card no. 1* states that achieving a poverty line measure should not be the limit of ambition.

Who Experiences the Problem of Child Poverty? Class and Gender Issues

There are four major sources of income available to people: 1) private material resources such as dividends, savings, insurance, property; 2) employee compensation from a job; 3) personal familial support and community support; and 4) state subsidies in the form of pensions, unemployment insurance, welfare, etc. The poor obviously do not have private material resources for a source of income. The poor either do not have employee compensation, or, if they do, it is barely adequate to meet basic needs. The poor often rely on the support of family and friends, the services of charities such as food banks, and the services of social income programs to survive. Unlike those who have private material resources, the threat to working people and the poor is income insecurity. Those who can work are utterly dependent on

Who
experiences
the problem
of child
poverty?
Class and
gender issues

securing and maintaining waged labour, and therefore are constantly faced with the threat of unemployment. The unemployable who are poor, and the poor who cannot obtain decent employment, must rely upon state subsidy programs. The threat to these programs is similar to waged labour. They are constantly faced with the threat of program elimination, program cutbacks, and being denied services from these programs. The lesson is very clear: if you are not wealthy, you had better have a good job or a responsible government (Hicks, 1999).

There are thousands of Canadian children who are poor and live in families that do not have a decent steady job and are without relatives or neighbours who are wealthy and generous. The highest incidence of child poverty is among female lone-parent families at 42%,[10] or 243,000 families, out of the total of 580,000 female lone-parent families. The highest incidence of poverty using the LICO cut-off for the year 1998 is among female lone-parent families with no earner, a 51.8% incidence of poverty, or 126,000 families of the total of 243,000 female lone-parent families below 1992 LICO. Female lone-parent families with one earner have a poverty incidence level of 45.7%, or 111,000 families of the 243,000 families. The figures indicate two thing: the inadequacy of social income programs (e.g. welfare; CTB and its replacement the CCTB) in bringing female lone-parent families with no earner anywhere near the LICO cut-offs; and a female lone-parent family with one earner reduces the incidence of poverty (actually the 1992 LICO measure) by only 8.9% when compared to female lone-parent families with no earner. Employment for this group does reduce the incidence of poverty, but it does not do so in an effective method that alleviates poverty.

The next highest group experiencing child poverty is that of two-parent families with children. For 1998 there were 3,062,000 two-parent families with children in Canada. Of that total, 225,000 (7.3%) are below the low-income cut-off for 1998. Among two-parent families with children below LICO, families with no earner have an incidence of poverty of 24.8%, or 56,000 of the total of 225,000 two-parent families below the 1992 LICO. Two-parent families with one earner have an incidence rate of 89,000 (39.5%), and two-parent families with two earners have an incidence of poverty rate of 72,000 (32%).

The obvious fact that can be observed from the data, especially for female lone-parent families, is that having a job is not an assurance of escaping poverty. Jackson, Robinson, Baldwin, and Wiggins (2000) write that Canada has experienced a continuous increase in wage inequality with employment becoming more clearly polarized into streams of good jobs and bad jobs. It is not just employment that employable people need, it is decent employment with a decent salary that is required.

Evidence from the research of Jackson et al. (2000) indicates that when examined in aggregate, the collective bargaining process raises employment remuneration for union workers as compared to non-union workers doing similar jobs. In fact, the advantage of unionization is greatest for those who

Who
experiences
the problem
of child
poverty?
Class and
gender issues

would otherwise be low-wage[11] earners. The union advantage for women can clearly be seen in the fact that almost half of women who are non-unionized are in low-wage employment, while less than 10% of women who are unionized are in low-wage employment (Jackson et al., 2000). There are many other factors that affect the quality of life outside of wages; many union contracts also provide for holidays, sick days, dental plans, maternity-leave provisions, and occupational pensions that are not available to women in low-wage, non-unionized employment.

Quite obviously, wages are extremely important when examining characteristics of poverty. Data published by the Canadian Council on Social Development (Jackson, 2001) demonstrates that a household with a single earner working forty hours per week for the *median salary* of $13.86 per hour is unlikely to be defined as low income using the LICO measurement. Of course, the LICO measurement is dependent on the size of the family and the area of geographical residence. However, that is not the situation for a low-income family. The report states: "Indeed, a single parent family with one child cannot climb above the low income line on earnings from a *low wage* job alone" (Jackson, 2001, p. 2). A full-time job at the median wage in Canada is likely to bring a single-parent family with one child above the LICOs; a full-time job at a low wage is not enough to bring a single-parent family with one child above the LICOs.

Also important when studying poverty is the characteristics of length of time one is poor. The *Survey of Labour and Income Dynamics* (SLID) data from Statistics Canada was to provide information on issues such as duration of unemployment and poverty duration, but this data set is currently not available. The SLID data would provide demographic information, as well as longitudinal information about households on labour market (employed part time or full time, for instance) and income characteristics (like total family earnings, and how many earners there are in a family). At this time, the status of when and in what form this data set will be made widely available is unclear. The data that is available indicates that, on average, 41% of the poor escape poverty within one year of becoming poor. Over a ten-year period, the average number of years a family remains poor is five years (Ross, Scott, & Smith, 2000). The likelihood of escaping poverty varies according to different years, which suggests that economic factors play some part in the incidence and depth of poverty. Additionally, the number of employable people on welfare appears to follow seasonal variations as well as economic factors.

In summary, some important factors in answering the question of who is poor are the level of support from social income programs, the type of wages that can be secured in the labour market, the unionization of employment, and economic cycles.

What Are the Causes of Child Poverty?

One method of approaching theories about the causes of poverty is to use the classification system of Townsend (1979), which includes theories of poverty that encompass sociological, economic, and political domains. Townsend's classification system is useful in examining poverty. Dunn states that "Peter Townsend's work follows the Fabian tradition in so far as its object of scrutiny is poverty and its strategy is redistribution, but at the same time it goes beyond the tradition in identifying structural problems whose solution requires structural transformations" (Dunn, 1999, p. 296).

One of the sociological theories of poverty described by Dunn (1999) as particularly salient among the general public in Canada is the subculture of poverty theory. Culture of poverty theory is described as "a way of life passed on from one generation to another. The poor have similar value systems, spending patterns, and time orientations. They buy as their needs arise, are heavy drinkers, and live in crowded quarters. The solution to these problems is to have social workers change the values and patterns of the poor and break their cycle of poverty" (Dunn, 1999, p. 296). Katz (1989) explains that the culture of poverty theory originated among liberals who wanted to advocate for generous and active programs to help the poor. According to Katz (1989), their arguments were developed from the work of Oscar Lewis and his ethnographic descriptions of Mexicans and Puerto Ricans. In Lewis's work, the behaviours of the poor were viewed as common adaptations to common problems of being poor (Katz, 1989). However, during the 1970s culture of poverty theory became a conservative concept (Katz, 1989), according to which the culture of poverty became the cause of continued poverty.

In its substance, culture of poverty theory is the concept of deferred gratification; that is, the poor wish to have immediate gratification of rewards, while the prudent middle-class person can wait and therefore obtain long-term rewards (Ryan, 1976). Summing up the debate about the merits of culture of poverty theory, Ryan (1976) writes:

> A related point—often the most overlooked point in any discussion of the culture of poverty—is that there is not, to my knowledge, any evidence whatever that the poor perceive their way of life as good and preferable to other ways of life. To make such an assertion is to talk pure nonsense. To avoid making such an assertion is to admit, at least implicitly, that the culture of poverty, whatever else it may be (if, indeed it is anything more than a catch phrase approximately as respectable intellectually as the concept of The Pepsi Generation) is, in no conceivable sense, a cultural phenomenon.
>
> Lee Rainwater has developed perhaps the most broadly acceptable formulation of these issues. He notes that there is relatively little difference in descriptions of the *behavior* differences that characterize the poor and suggests that, from a policy point of view, the crucial issue is to view

this behavior as *adaptive,* adaptive to a state of being deprived, excluded, and demeaned. (Ryan, 1976, p. 134, italics in original)

Culture of poverty theory is an individual theory of poverty, that is, the *cause* of poverty is found within the individual.

Another sociological theory of poverty identified by Dunn (1999) develops from the feminist theory formulation of patriarchy. This perspective expands on theories of poverty as it introduces the concept of active discrimination that is beyond general structural accounts as usually presented in the poverty literature. Commenting upon Townsend's (1979) analysis of poverty and women, Williams (1989) observes that Townsend sets his analysis in class terms. Although Townsend (1979), within his class analysis, identifies the underclass as comprising different groups including the low paid, lone parents, and older people (many in those groups are women), he does not identify an interaction between class and gender (Williams, 1989).

Economic and political theories of poverty suggest the economy as the cause of poverty. Classical economists would find the cause of poverty in a deficit of human capital, including education, skills, ability, and experiences that separately or in aggregate lead to poverty (Dunn, 1999). This theory of poverty would suggest that structural unemployment leads to job loss and perhaps poverty if adjustments are not made to combat the changing workplace structures (Ternowetsky & Thorn, 1991). Dealing with structural unemployment necessitates years of retraining workers, and results in ongoing job vacancies and unemployment. A short-term type of unemployment that is derived from the economic system is the pattern of cyclical unemployment. Cyclical unemployment is tied to the cycles of the market economy. This type of unemployment represents the difference in the incidence of unemployment, between the peak and trough years of a business cycle. Periods of economic growth produce lower unemployment levels, whereas recessionary periods result in higher levels of unemployment and the need for social income programs. Unfortunately, during recessionary periods there is less social wage to devote to social programs just when the demands for these programs are at their highest.

The federal and provincial governments and territories have suggested that social income programs create dependency among the recipients and therefore actually harm recipients by keeping them from paid employment. The familiar argument is that people are poor because they do not have a job, and if they are moved off welfare by supports such as the Canada Child Tax Benefit (CCTB) program and into employment, then employment will lead them out of poverty. Even writers who present themselves as progressive state that social income programs like welfare contain disincentives from taking employment and create dependency among social income program recipients:

What are the causes of child poverty?

What are
the causes
of child
poverty?

Paradoxes of intervening in the economic life of some Canadians have long been recognized: financial assistance programs may sometimes decrease the incentive to paid work for some recipients, that is, they contain inherent labour force participation disincentives. Authors of this textbook, like other progressive observers, insist on the need for plentiful jobs offering meaningful employment and decent wages. More than any other factor, decent jobs would alleviate much of the problem of labour force participation disincentives. (Graham, Delaney, & Swift, 2000, p. 57)

As these authors and others suggest the creation of decent jobs and meaningful employment as a way to overcome the disincentives of social income programs, should not then the argument about welfare dependency be rearranged? Rather than creating programs such as the CCTB to help working poor families, the focus should shift to concentrate on the labour market disincentives to employment. Should it not be argued that it is the labour market that creates the disincentives to employment and that the labour market needs to change to create meaningful employment, unionized workplaces, decent wages, and decent jobs? In doing so, attention would be refocused from the individual poor and individual solutions for poverty to an examination of the market system as a cause of unemployment and poverty requiring solutions based upon universal social policies. Although government programs for the poor concentrate on lack of employment skills (e.g., how to look for work, resumes, personal behaviours at work) or work discipline (e.g., poor who have lost the skills of work such as being on time, being rested for work, proper work deportment) or lack of moral responsibility among the poor, the structural and cyclical nature of unemployment and poverty are not easy to ignore. The market cycles of expansion and contraction in the economy require attention if the issue of child poverty is going to be addressed in a serious manner. Jackson et al. (2000, p. 33) comment that: "It can easily be shown that both unemployment insurance program demands and social assistance caseloads ratchet up in times of recession, and fall in times of recovery." Regarding poverty, the recession of 1990-1991 drove up the incidence of poverty to where, in 1995, the incidence of poverty among children in Canada was 1.5 million, or 20.9% (NCW, 1999b).

Recessions are often identified as one of the main causes of the rise in unemployment in Canada (Gonick, 1987; Riches & Ternowetsky, 1990). Part of that increase in unemployment is viewed as eventually filtering down to social assistance and increasing welfare caseloads. The federal government comments that economic slowdown has contributed to increased welfare caseloads: "Many Canadian families lost economic ground during the 1980's and early 1990's. Overall, average disposable family incomes have not grown since the early 1980's. In recent years, increasing numbers of Canadians who cannot find jobs have turned to social assistance" (Government of Canada, 1994a, p. 19). However, recessions are not the same thing as welfare creating a dependency among working people on that program, nor is it the same thing as the lack of the proper type of "employment and training support" that governments are anxious to provide for the poor. We do well to remember that economic policy is also social policy (Durst, 1999).

What are the causes of child poverty?

When examining economic policy as a component of social policy, an understating of the importance of the relationship of recessions and inflation to welfare necessitates an understanding of the relationship between inflation and unemployment. When unemployment falls, wages rise, along with a rise in consumer demand and price levels (inflation), which together push against profits. Conversely, when unemployment rises, wages fall, because people out of work are forced to underbid the wages of those working and the reduction in aggregate consumer demand lowers the inflation rate. Unemployment and inflation can be seen as trade-offs. One of them can be controlled through a deliberate emphasis on the other.

However, unemployment and price inflation can be viewed as alternative strategies with which capital can maintain and enlarge profit shares (Piven & Cloward, 1982). Price inflation can erode wage increases that are gained by workers in tight labour situations. Inflation is not as effective a means for capital to maintain and enlarge profit shares for a number of reasons. Workers in unionized sectors can keep pace with price increases with cost-of-living clauses (Gonick, 1987). Price inflation also complicates corporate dealings with suppliers and customers, and the uncertainty generated by inflation hampers long-term corporate planning and investment (Piven & Cloward, 1982).

The government in Canada has also utilized a monetary policy of high interest rates to control inflation: "the idea of fighting inflation was identified solely with the policy of high interest rates as practised by a succession of federal finance ministers and governors of the Bank of Canada" (Krehm, 1993, p. viii). A number of other writers have also commented on the monetary policy of high interest rate policy adopted by the Bank of Canada to curb inflation. Writing in the late 1980s, Gonick (1987, p. 115) observed: "Now the Bank of Canada would break the cycle of inflationary expectations by imposing strict controls over the supply of money. Henceforth long-term price stability would take precedence over concern with the level of unemployment in the short-to-medium term. Jackson et al. (2000, p. 14) observe that the Canadian government "deliberately gave priority to fighting rising inflation through high interest rates, and abandoned full employment and strong growth as key objectives of macro-economic policy." Therefore, some of the causes of increased numbers of employable people on welfare, child poverty, and the working poor in Canada can in fact be traced to the monetary and fiscal policies of the Canadian government, and the fiscal policies of the provincial and territorial governments. It would therefore appear cynical on the part of governments and social policy commentators to place the blame for increased numbers of poor children on conjectural effects of welfare programming, including the unsupportive arguments of welfare dependency, lack of labour force attachment among the poor, and the deterioration of appropriate job skills from being on welfare. Jackson et al. (2000) comment that in fact there is significant movement between welfare and low-income jobs. They argue that it is a "fundamental" shortage of decent employment that accounts for the able-bodied poor on welfare rather than the argument that welfare creates dependency among its recipients.

Wages and Child Poverty

Although income is not the only factor that influences child poverty, it is key. Most people receive their incomes from paid employment; however, employment income needs to be at an adequate level. One reason for such a large number of Canadian working poor families with children is the large number of low-wage jobs that exist. The *innocenti report card no. 1* (UNICEF, 2000, p. 9) places Canada at thirteenth place out of fourteen rich nations for greatest wage inequality. Table 2.3 puts the low wages paid in Canada into context by providing a comparison to low wages in other rich countries and their poverty levels.

Table 2.3	Child Poverty Rate and Low Wages in Rich Nations	
Country (Rich Nations)	Child Poverty (%)	Low Wages (%)
Sweden	2.8	5.2
Finland	4.3	5.9
Belgium	4.4	7.2
Netherlands	7.7	11.9
France	7.9	13.3
Germany	10.7	13.3
Japan	12.2	15.7
Spain	12.3	19
Australia	12.6	13.8
Canada	**15.5**	**23.7**
Ireland	16.8	18
United Kingdom	19.8	19.6
Italy	20.5	12.5
USA	22.4	25

Source: Innocenti report card no. 1 by UNICEF, 2000, Florence: UNICEF Innocenti Research Centre.

Research on incomes across Canada for 1997 indicates that "growing levels of education and labour force involvement among poor families does not necessarily raise them above the poverty line" (Ross, Scott, & Smith, 2000, p. 80). Child poverty levels in Canada would be even higher if it were not for social income transfer programs.

Social income transfer programs can be considered as a social wage; that is, a program of goods and services provided to the individual by the state, funded by taxes, which are distributed outside of the labour market (Phillips, 1990). Related to the social wage is the surplus wage (Teeple, 1995), which is the room available to governments to use taxation and deferred income from wages and salaries—the largest source of government revenue—for funds that are available to cover social wage programs such as old age pension programs, disability programs, health programs, social assistance programs, or social insurance schemes. The justification of surplus wage taxation is the risk that all people face of having to someday use one or all of these types of social wage programs. Some of the programs assist the poor and working class; they also represent a transfer of benefits to the upper-income earners in Canada as they use proportionally more of the programs (health care, post-secondary education) than their contribution. Additionally, working people contribute more in taxes, premiums, and deferred income for social programs and activities of the state than services they receive because a portion of the transfer of wealth from working people also goes to the corporate sector in the form of grants, loans, subsidies, and concessions.

What are the causes of child poverty?

There is the possibility that the social wage available in Canada will continue to decline. The sizable cuts that have been made to social program spending in Canada and the ongoing demand for tax cuts and tax concessions by certain groups (e.g., business groups, upper-income groups) may endanger more Canadian families and their children facing poverty as funds will not be available to even marginally deliver social programs. Commenting on the effect of program funding cuts made to social assistance and unemployment insurance benefits during the 1990s, Jackson et al. (2000, pp. 37-38) observe that: "The result has been almost no decline in the child poverty rate in a period of recovery, and an increase in depth of poverty. The 'cut-taxes/cut social spending' solution is obviously no solution to the overall social problems of poverty and inequality." The NCW (1999a, p. 5) writes: "The National Council of Welfare believes that the main reason child and family poverty rates have not improved in the years following the last recession is that throughout the 1990s, governments of all levels cut important programs and services that support families." According to the NCW (1999a), the other reason that child and family poverty rates have remained high in Canada is due to governments not addressing the problem of labour market poverty during the 1990s.

Labour market poverty refers to the ability of families to derive a decent standard of living from labour wages and salaries (Ross, Scott, & Smith, 2000). Families that have an income earner and are below some measure of poverty are thought of as not deriving sufficient income from employment to provide a decent standard of living. Market poverty stands in stark contrast to the ideology that jobs are the way to avoid poverty or to get out of poverty, summed up in shallow phrases such as "The best welfare program is a job"

Alleviating
child poverty
and the
Canada Child
Tax Benefit
legislation
(Government of Canada, 1994a, p. 70). The market system is obviously failing the working poor.

Social income programs mitigate some of the income inequality of the market system because these programs serve as a means of income redistribution through funds derived from the social wage. Social programs and a progressive tax system have been used in Canada to reduce inequality of the market system, and have been effective in reducing the level of market income inequality that has been growing in the 1990s in Canada (Jackson et al., 2000). In 1989 the gini coefficient[12] for market income inequality was 0.397 and in 1997 the market income inequality was .425 (Jackson et al., 2000). The increase in the value of the gini coefficient indicates a growth in market income inequality during that period of time. Once the effects of social income transfer programs and the income tax system are included, the gini coefficient is reduced to 0.294 in 1989 and 0.302 in 1997. As can be observed in the data, social income transfer programs and the tax system reduce the level of income inequality generated in the market system. What they do not accomplish, however, is a lowering of the level of income inequality. In other words, social income programs and the tax system reduce the income inequality arising from wages and salaries, but these programs do not reduce the level of income inequality over time.

Alleviating Child Poverty and the Canada Child Tax Benefit Legislation

The major piece of legislation enabling the social income transfer program in Canada designed specifically to eliminate child poverty is the Canada Child Tax Benefit (CCTB). The predecessor to the CCTB (1997) was the New Integrated Child Tax Benefit (CTB) (1993). The social income programs that existed for families with children before the CTB were the universal Family Allowance program and income tax-based measures, including the refundable child tax credit, the non-refundable child tax credit, the equivalent-to-married credit and the child care expense reduction. Under the New Integrated CTB there were three components; the Child Tax Benefit, the equivalent-to-married credit, and the child care deduction. The previous non-refundable and refundable tax credits and the Family Allowance program were aggregated into the income-tested CTB.

The elimination of the Family Allowance program represented a fundamental rethinking about children in Canada. Children were no longer viewed as the responsibility of parents *and* society as a whole through a universal social income program such as the universal Family Allowance program. Rather, children were seen as part of the budget and expenses for family after-tax income spending (Kitchen, 2001, p. 240). Family Allowance allowed all children access to some portion of the social wage; with the CTB program, the social wage was available only to families who were economically vulnerable. The CTB program clawed back benefits as family incomes increased. Additionally, the program did not have scheduled adjustments for inflation.

In 1997, the CTB program was replaced with the CCTB legislation. Both programs are somewhat similar in their underlying values. The major difference between them is that the CCTB includes all the provinces and territories. The provinces and territories were not part of the federal-only CTB program.

The Canada Child Tax Benefit program is divided into two benefits. One is the Basic Benefit, which is provided to all families with children, contingent on their level of income. There are maximum levels of family income after which this benefit is fully phased out. The other benefit is provided under the cost-shared National Child Benefit program (NCB), which the federal government shares with the provinces and territories. The federal contribution to the NCB is the National Child Benefit Supplement (NCBS), which is similar to the previous Working Income Supplement (WIS) program. The WIS program, which replaced the universal Family Allowance program, was a *per family benefit* provided to low-income families with children, while the NCBS is a *per child benefit* provided to low-income families with children. The NCBS has been integrated into the basic allowance component of provincial social assistance programs in the provinces and territories (Kitchen, 2001, p. 241). The NCBS program removes children from the basic allowance component of the provincial welfare rolls, with those payments now coming from the federal government's NCBS contribution to the NCB. The contribution of the provinces, territories and First Nations to the NCB is to provide programs that support low-income working families with children, whether or not the families receive welfare. Programs that can be provided by the provinces to low-income families with children could include pharmacare or dental care, child care services, child credit for low-income families (British Columbia, Quebec), an earned income credit (Alberta), a combination of programs (Saskatchewan, New Brunswick) and early prevention programs for children at risk. The provincial and territorial contributions to the NCB go under various names in the different provincial/territorial and First Nations jurisdictions.[13]

The provincial savings from reduced welfare expenditures under the CCTB are quite substantial. For example:

> By the end of 1999/2000 Saskatchewan will have accrued a National Child Benefit reinvestment pool totaling approximately $19.5 million compared to $11.3 million identified for 1998-99. These reinvestment funds, together with redirected provincial funds and incremental Saskatchewan investment, support a series of major program reforms implemented in July 1998. (Government of Canada, 2000, p. 4)

The federal government estimated that for the fiscal year 1999-2000, Saskatchewan's NCB program spending initiatives would be allotted toward $14.6 million in the Child Benefit/Earned Income Supplement program, $3.5

Alleviating child poverty and the Canada Child Tax Benefit legislation

Alleviating
child poverty
and the
Canada Child
Tax Benefit
legislation

million in the Saskatchewan Child Benefit (a monthly allowance provided for all children of lower-income families), and $1.4 million in the Family Health Benefits program, which provides limited supplementary health benefits to lower-income working families (Government of Canada, 2000, p. 5). These figures suggest that in Saskatchewan most of the reinvestment of funds from savings due to an increase in federal spending under the CCTB has gone into the supplement of low-income wages through programs such as the Saskatchewan Employment Supplement program, which provides an income supplement to lower-income families with children.

In fact, provincial savings on welfare expenditures due to increased federal contributions through the CCTB do not need to go to increased spending on families with children on welfare who have no other source of income, presumably the poorest children in Canada. Rather, the money can be used to fund social income programs for the working poor, as has happened in the provinces. Using the funds saved by not passing on the increase in federal expenditures to the poorest families on welfare with no source of income, and using those funds to support families with low incomes, is entirely in keeping with the intent of the CCTB program. According to the CCTB agreement, provincial savings from decreased welfare expenditures are to go to programs designed to assist low-income families with children. An enriched Canada Child Tax Benefit will "Pave the way for provinces and territories to redirect their resources towards improved child services and income support for low-income working families" (Government of Canada, 1997c, p. 2) and further "To promote attachment to the workforce—resulting in fewer families having to rely on social assistance—by ensuring that families will always be better off as a result of finding work" (Government of Canada, 1997c). The savings incurred by the provinces under the CCTB are to be directed toward children's services and income support programs for low-income families with children.

It should also be noted, however, that the increase in federal spending is not new money. The federal government would have been making these expenditures under the cost-sharing agreement with the provinces under the old Canada Assistance Plan (CAP), which was replaced in 1996 by the block-funded Canadian Health and Social Transfer (CHST). The federal government would have also made further expenditures through the previous Family Allowance program and its successor, the federal CTB program (Pulkingham & Ternowetsky, 1997). Eventually as the CCTB program "matures," the total provincial expenditures for the basic allowance provision for children on welfare will be paid for from the federal contribution to the CCTB program.

As mentioned, the National Child Benefit (NCB) portion of the two-part CCTB is a social income program shared between the federal government and the provinces, territories, and First Nations to assist working poor families with children. Due to the focus of the NCB policy initiative on the workplace attachment of the recipient, there is a fundamental flaw with the NCB portion of the CCTB program. If the program is designed to eliminate child poverty, benefits would increase according to the financial need of families with children (Pulkingham & Ternowetsky, 1997). There is no extra money for families whose only source of income is social assistance. Rather, the federal government has used the CCTB program to alleviate some of the provincial welfare expenditures related to children to gain provincial support for the program.

The provinces agreed to sign on to the CCTB so that they could gain greater control over the low-income support expenditure programs, which would not be possible under a program that was provided only by the federal government. The provinces are resistant to federal government programming in an area they consider under their control. As established in the British North American Act (BNA) (1867) and the Canadian Constitution Act (1982), welfare, health, and education are under provincial, not federal, jurisdiction. However, the federal government has been involved in cost-sharing social programs with the provinces under Section 106 of the Constitution Act of 1982, which allows the Parliament of Canada to appropriate funds for the public service (McGilly, 1998). The motivation for federal involvement is that the provinces cannot afford welfare, health, and postsecondary education programs without federal funds; thus, the federal government can enact national policy initiatives in areas of provincial jurisdiction. Another reason for provincial support of the CCTB is that the provinces are able to retrieve some of their provincial transfer funds lost when the federal government eliminated the Canada Assistance Plan. Estimates suggest that the 1995 federal budget cut up to 40% of transfer funds to the provinces to share the costs of health, postsecondary education, and welfare programs (Clarke, 1998).

An examination of the program criteria and the income effects of the new federal/provincial child poverty program could lead to the conclusion that the new CCTB initiative is not about reducing poverty for the poorest children in Canada. The initiative appears to be designed, within the framework of citizenship theory and right, to make it more attractive to work than to receive assistance. Beyond just distinguishing between worthy and unworthy poor, the program is therefore also entrenching the poor law concept of "less eligibility." It also follows that rather than children being the main benefactor of the CCTB, the business sector will gain the most from the program, because the program tends to subsidize low-wage labour. Research evidence indicates that the consequences of the cuts made during the 1990s to the welfare system in Canada have been to impoverish further the poor on welfare, and to depress the wages of the working poor (Klein & Montgomery, 2001).

Current job growth in Canada is mainly in the service sector, where many of the jobs are low paying with no benefits (Broad, 2000). What the CCTB program has achieved in application is to implement a program that could subsidize employers by distributing small income gains and limited health benefits to their employees. Now there are obviously some businesses that

Alleviating child poverty and the Canada Child Tax Benefit legislation

cannot afford high wages; however, the government could have chosen to help these workers through a more progressive structure in the income tax system. Lower-paid workers in marginal industries and services identified through the income tax system could be taxed at a reduced rate while top-income earners, consistent with the principles of a progressive tax system and a desire to reduce inequality, would be taxed at a higher rate. As well, the program could also be funded from a variety of taxes, which could be placed on business profits (Mackenzie, 1998).

That way, a program to assist paid workers who are vulnerable to job elim-ination and receive lower wages would be funded by a vertical transfer of benefits from the wealthy rather than the horizontal transfer system intro-duced by the CCTB program. Under the current structure of the CCTB any business, including large businesses, can hire taxpayer-subsidized employees at a minimum wage and continue to provide few or no health benefits or decent salaries and wage increases to their employees. Commensurate with neo-liberal ideology, rather than using the tax system in a progressive manner to assist low-income earners, the government has decided to assist busi-nesses by subsidizing low wages and has, therefore, firmly entrenched the concept of less eligibility and worthy and unworthy poor within the welfare system. The CCTB, as it is presently designed and delivered, is not a children's benefit. It is an enriched Working Income Supplement (WIS) program for working poor families with children (Pulkingham & Ternowetsky, 1997). By introducing the Canada Child Tax Benefit in its current form, governments are acknowledging that, for a growing group of people, the economic system will not provide a surplus wage and/or social wage and subsequently inequality of income, inequality of opportunity, and inequality of condition for the poor-est in Canada will continue to grow.

Notes

1 UNICEF uses a relative measure of poverty based upon households with incomes below 50% of the national median. This measure differs from the Low Income Cut-off (LICO) measure used by Statistics Canada, which is based upon the community average spent on essentials.

2 The year 1997 is the last year Statistics Canada produced the *Survey of Consumer Finances*, the data set that has been used on a yearly basis to examine child poverty. The *Survey of Labour and Income Dynamics* (SLID) has replaced it. There are currently strict criteria on access to the SLID data. The longitudinal nature of the SLID data has raised concerns of possible identification of respondents.

3 Statistics Canada defines a family economic unit as all occupants of a dwelling unit who are related by blood, marriage, or adoption, and couples living together in com-mon-law relationships.

4 When using Statistics Canada data, a family's income can be calculated using their income from either wages and salaries or from total income, including government transfers or income after tax. The researcher should identify what income variable was used in the study. In creating the data sets, Statistics Canada does not include families living in First Nations communities (reserves) and children living in institutions.

5 For a more thorough discussion of poverty lines in Canada see Graham, Delaney, & Swift (2000, pp. 48-56); also Ross, Scott, & Smith (2000).

6 In this report Statistics Canada Low Income Cut-Offs (LICO) are used as the benchmark to identify poor children and their families. The data for poor children under eighteen exclude those who are unattached individuals, those who are the major income earner, or those who are the spouse or common-law partner of the major income earner. In creating these survey data sets, Statistics Canada does not include families living in First Nations communities (reserves).

7 Real GDP is the value of all final goods and services produced in Canada for a given year in constant prices. Constant prices, or constant dollars, are used rather than reporting only nominal values so that comparisons can be made across different years, accounting for the rise in prices measured by the consumer price index (CPI).

8 This value is derived by taking the average income gaps for two-parent and single-parent families and multiplying them by the estimated number of families for both groups. The obtained value in this study differs from the *Child poverty in Canada: Report card 2000* (Campaign 2000, 2000) result as they based their calculation on the aggregate number of children. The difficulty is that there may be more than one child in a family and the result could overestimate the monetary value needed to bring children to the LICO (1992) cut-off. This study functions from an understanding that children live in families from which their poverty cannot be separated; therefore, the total number of economic family units with children below LICO (1992) is used rather than the total number of children. The monetary value in this study is calculated by dividing the monetary value required to bring family economic units with children below LICO (1992) by the real GDP for 1998 to obtain a percentage of GDP required. For real GDP values, see Statistics Canada, (2001, p. 3).

9 Real GNP is the value of all final goods and services produced in Canada for a given year by Canadians or by Canadian-owned factors of production (includes net earnings of foreign investment in Canada) in constant prices.

10 Data are from Statistics Canada, (2000, pp. 87-109). The figures are calculated using LICO 1992 total income *after-tax*. The totals are not equal due to rounding estimates provided in the publication.

11 Less than two-thirds of median income.

12 Gini coefficient is a measure of income inequality with a value of 1 representing the most extreme example of income inequality, and a value of 0 representing perfect equality of income. The higher the number, the greater the degree of income inequality.

13 For further information on provincial programs see, Revenue Canada, *Your Canada Child Tax Benefit*, On-line at <www.communication.gc.ca/children-enfants/02_e.htm.>.

References

Broad, D. (2000). *Hollow work, hollow society?: Globalization and the casual labour problem in Canada*. Halifax: Fernwood.

Campaign 2000. (2000). *Child poverty in Canada: Report card 2000*. Toronto: Author.

Clarke, T. (1998). The MAI threat to Canada's social programs. *Canadian Review of Social Policy, 41* (Spring), pp. 64-70.

Dunn, P. (1999). Poverty issues. In F. Turner (Ed.), *Social work practice: An introduction* (pp. 291-305). Scarborough: Prentice Hall Allyn and Bacon Canada.

Durst, D. (1999). Phoenix or fizzle: Background to Canada's new National Child Benefit. In D. Durst (Ed.), *Canada's National Child Benefit: Phoenix or fizzle?* (pp. 11-37). Halifax: Fernwood.

Fellegi, I. (1997, September). *On poverty and low income*. Ottawa: Statistics Canada. On-line at <www.statcan.ca/english/concepts/poverty/pauv.htm>.

Gonick, C. (1987). *The great economic debate*. Toronto: James Lorimer.

Government of Canada. (1994a). *Agenda: Jobs and growth, improving social security in Canada, a discussion paper*.

References   Government of Canada. (1994b). *Agenda: Jobs and growth, improving social security in Canada, discussion paper summary.*

Government of Canada. (1997a). *Investing in a stronger society: Towards a national child benefit system.* On-line at <www.fin.gc.ca>.

Government of Canada. (1997b). *Working together towards a national child benefit System—Budget 1997.* On-line at <www.fin.gc.ca>.

Government of Canada. (1997c). *Budget 1997 fact sheets. Investing in a stronger society: Towards a national child benefit system.* On-line at <www.fin.gc.ca>.

Government of Canada. (2000). *National Child Benefit.* On-line at <www.social union.gc.ca/NCB-2000/prov-terr-reinvest2000.html>.

Graham, J., Delaney, R., & Swift, K. (2000). *Canadian social policy: An introduction.* Scarborough: Prentice Hall Allyn and Bacon Canada.

Hicks, A. (1999). *Social democracy and welfare capitalism.* Ithaca: Cornell University Press.

Jackson, A. (2001). *Low income trends in the 1990s.* Canadian Council on Social Development. On-line at <www.ccsd.ca/pubs2000/lit/>.

Jackson, A., Robinson, D., Baldwin, B., & Wiggins, C. (2000). *Falling behind: The state of working in Canada.* Ottawa: Canadian Centre for Social Policy.

Katz. M. (1989). *The undeserving poor.* New York: Pantheon.

Kitchen, B. (2001). Poverty and declining living standards in a changing economy. In J. Turner and F. Turner (Eds.), *Canadian social welfare* (4th ed.) (pp. 232-249). Toronto: Pearson Education Canada.

Klein, S., & Montgomery, B. (2001). *Depressing wages: Why welfare cuts hurt both poor and working poor.* Ottawa: Canadian Centre for Policy Alternatives.

Krehm, W. (1993). *A power unto itself: The Bank of Canada.* Toronto: Stoddart Publishing.

Mackenzie, H. (1998). Tax relief for those who really need it. In Canadian Centre for Policy Alternatives, *Alternative federal budget papers: 1998* (pp. 335-358). Ottawa: Canadian Centre for Policy Alternatives.

McGilly, F. (1998). *An introduction to Canada's income and health programs: Understanding income and health programs* (2nd ed.). Toronto: Oxford University Press.

National Council of Welfare (NCW). (1999a). *Children first: A pre-budget report by the National Council of Welfare.* Ottawa: Minister of Public Works and Government Services Canada.

National Council of Welfare (NCW). (1999b). *Poverty profile 1997.* Ottawa: Minister of Public Works and Government Services Canada.

Phillips, P. (1990). *Canadian political economy.* Toronto: Garamond Press.

Piven, F., & Cloward, R. (1982). *The new class war.* New York: Pantheon.

Pulkingham, J., & Ternowetsky, G. (1997). The new Canada Child Tax Benefit: Discriminating between "Deserving" and "Undeserving" among poor families with children. In J. Pulkingham and G. Ternowetsky (Eds.), *Child and family policies: Struggles, strategies and options* (pp. 204-208). Halifax: Fernwood Press.

Riches, G. (1997). Hunger and the welfare state: Comparative perspectives. In G. Riches (Ed.), *First world hunger: Food security and welfare politics* (pp. 1-13). London: MacMillan Press.

Riches, G., & Ternowetsky, G. (1990). Unemployment and the work of social work. In G. Riches & G. Ternowetsky (Eds.), *Unemployment and welfare: Social policy and the work of social work* (pp. 13-31). Toronto: Garamond Press.

Ross, D., & Roberts, P. (1999). *Income and child well-being: A new perspective on the poverty debate.* Ottawa: Canadian Council on Social Development.

Ross, D., Scott, K., & Smith, P. (2000). *The Canadian fact book on poverty.* Ottawa: Canadian Council on Social Development.

Ryan, W. (1976). *Blaming the victim* (rev. ed.). New York: Vintage Books.

Shillington, R. (2001). *Newspeak on poverty: Duelling poverty lines offer no comfort to poor kids but generate good PR for governments. Straight Goods*, On-line at <www.straightgoods.com/Analyze/010305.asp>.

Statistics Canada. (2000, November). *Income in Canada 1998*. Ottawa: Statistics Canada, Catalogue No. 75-202-RPE.

Statistics Canada. (2001, March). *Canadian economic observer*. Ottawa: Statistics Canada, Catalogue No. 11-010-XPB.

Statistics Canada. People with low-income before tax. On-line at <www.statcan.ca/english/Pgdb/famil41a.htm>.

Teeple, G. (1995). *Globalization and the decline of social reform*. Toronto: Garamond Press.

Ternowetsky, G. (2000). *Poverty and corporate welfare*. Regina: Social Policy Research Unit, Faculty of Social Work, University of Regina.

Ternowetsky, G., & Thorn, J. (1991). *The decline in middle incomes: Unemployment, underemployment and falling living standards in Saskatchewan*. Regina: Social Policy Research Unit, Faculty of Social Work, University of Regina.

Townsend, P. (1979). *Poverty in the United Kingdom*. Harmondsworth: Penguin.

UNICEF (2000). *Innocenti report card no. 1: The league table of child poverty in rich nations*. Florence: UNICEF Innocenti Research Centre.

Webber, M. (1998, May). *Measuring low income and poverty in Canada: An update*. Ottawa: Statistics Canada, Income Statistics Division, Catalogue No. 98-13.

Williams, F. (1989). *Social policy: A critical introduction*. Cambridge: Polity Press.

Additional Resources

National Council of Welfare. (1998). *Child benefits: Kids are still hungry*. On-line at <www.ncwcnbes.net/htmdocument/reportchild/repchild.htm>.

Pulkingham, J., and Ternowetsky, G. (Eds.). (1997). *Child and family policies: Struggles, strategies and options*. Halifax: Fernwood Press.

Pulkingham, J., and Ternowetsky, G. (1999). Child poverty and the CCTB/NCB: Why most children gain nothing. In D. Durst (Ed.), *Canada's National Child Benefit: Phoenix or fizzle?* (pp. 103-114). Halifax: Fernwood Press.

For a book that presents neo-liberal ideology on the welfare state, poverty lines, etc., see: Paul, E., Miller, F., Jr., and Paul, J. (Eds.). (1997). *The welfare state*. Cambridge: Cambridge University Press.

3

Native Peoples and the Social Work Profession: A Critical Analysis of Colonizing Problematics and the Development of Decolonized Thought[1]

Barbara Waterfall

This chapter is intended to begin a discussion about the relationships between the social work profession, social work education, and Native peoples.[2] This discussion is located within social policy discourse pertaining to the accreditation of social work education in Canada. I am arguing that schools of Social Work have an ethical and professional responsibility to create core curricula that construct colonialism as problematic, centers Native epistemologies and methodologies, and effectively support Native grassroots efforts for self-determined agency. This chapter is not intended to be an exhaustive inquiry but rather to begin to ask critical questions for the purposes of developing decolonized thought. It was originally written for Native peoples who have been working in the Native social work field and for Native social work educators. However, the contents of this discussion have far-reaching implications not just to Native peoples and to Native social workers, but to the profession of social work as a whole, and to the broader objectives of social work education in Canada. It is thus intended that this chapter will influence the development of policy through accreditation criteria for social work education.

It needs to be understood that this discussion does not take place within a vacuum. Any discussion that concerns Native peoples takes place within the context of a history of colonialism, imperialism, and the predominance of Eurocentric thought. Informed by feminist anti-colonial thought I will thus speak to this history, to the implications of Eurocentric thought, and to ongoing imposing colonial processes. In so doing, I will be implicating the profession of social work as colonizing practice. The notion of social work education as a colonizing practice is currently being taken up in my current doctoral research and thus will not be the subject of this text. For the purposes of this chapter I am asking social workers and social work educators to seriously reflect on the problematics embedded within the social work profession. I am also asking the reader, wherever we are located, to seriously question whether social work practice can work toward the objectives of Native peoples' self-determined agency based on Native traditional life-sustaining wisdoms.

The task of writing this chapter is a politicized project. Indeed, the late Howard Adams (1999, p. 55) stated that to offer a critique of hegemonic Native practices is not done without risk. He stated that to offer a critique is a threat to the status quo. Cognizant of the risks I feel that it is imperative that critical questions are raised. The present day situation for many Native peoples is very grave. Addictions and violence are everyday occurrences. Many of our children don't want to live anymore. They don't see any hope. In many communities there are cluster suicides. There is thus a drastic need for change. I therefore feel I have an ethical responsibility to play my part toward the development of decolonized consciousness. It is also important to state that I have been trained as a social worker and have worked within the context of Native communities. I am thus implicating my self and my own past practices when I implicate the profession of social work as a colonizing practice. I have chosen to make use of my middle-class location to help create a space for the many Native voices that have been marginalized and silenced through colonial oppression.

Discursive Framework

I am employing a feminist, anti-colonial discursive framework to guide this discussion on the relationship between the social work profession, social work education, and Native peoples. In accordance with Dei (2000a, p. 23-24) I am identifying this framework as "discursive" rather than "theoretical" to provide space for the reality that academic and political questions are continually changing reflective of "social realities as well as the narration of different histories and experiences." Informed by Adams (1999), Alfred (1999), Allen (1986), Anderson (2000), Dei (2000b), Fanon (1995), Maracle (1996), Puja (2001), Smith (1999), and Trask (1991), I define feminist anti-colonialism as the absence of colonial imposition and colonial influences, as the agency to govern oneself, and the practice of such agency based on gynocentric and gynocratic[3] Native traditional practices. As a starting point a feminist anti-colonial perspective is located outside of the imposed colonial system. The framework that I am proposing assumes that the objectives of the Canadian constitution and the Canadian state are counterproductive to an anti-colonial cause. Hence, this feminist anti-colonial discursive framework also assumes that efforts to assert Native rights for self-determination through the apparatus of the Canadian constitutional agenda are counterproductive to a feminist anti-colonial cause. As such, this framework does not look to the site of the Canadian constitution for legitimacy, or for instruction. That is, the practice of Native self-determined agency is viewed as stemming from outside of the parameters of the Canadian state.[4]

Grounding in Native traditional axiological standpoint feminist anti-colonial thought enables Native traditional values, Native epistemological understandings, Native traditional systems, and Native methodological practices to serve as the foundational framework for Native self-determined agency. However, it is recognized that colonialism has imposed patriarchal values and a patriarchal ordering of social relations within present Native systems. Along with Anderson (2000) I argue that our current understanding of Native "traditions" must be interrogated for patriarchal and other imposed colonial influences. A feminist anti-colonial perspective assumes that most Native cultures were matriarchal, or matri-focal prior to colonization (Allen, 1986). Thus, a feminist anti-colonial discursive framework functions to revitalize Native governance systems based on the values of gynocentric nurturance and gynocratic life-giving principles. It needs to be clearly acknowledged that traditional gynocratic social practices are about meeting the everyday needs of all members of Native societies. Furthermore, systems of accountability are an essential part of gynocratic governance systems. Humanistic, compassionate, or any other grounds do not justify colonial policy imposing foreign, or dominating systems and practices within traditional gynocratic structures. As social workers and social work educators we can be guided by a feminist anti-colonial discursive framework. I contend that only such a framework enables us to map colonialism in all of its guises and to develop strategies that support, rather than hinder the objectives of Native self-determined agency.

Eurocentrism as Rationale for the Colonial Agenda

Battiste and Youngblood Henderson (2000) state that Eurocentric thought informs the theories, the opinions, and the laws that relate to Native peoples. Eurocentric discourses serve the purpose of justifying the colonial agenda. Smith (1999) states that there is a direct relationship between the expansion of knowledge, the expansion of trade, and the expansion of the British empire. The colonial objective on Turtle Island was and continues to be that of gaining access and control of the land's resources. The Native populations were a threat and still are a threat to this objective. In the present day context global economic forces continue to exploit the natural resources of this land such as water, oil, gas, and uranium (Adams, 1999).

Eurocentric theories inform research and policy development concerning Native peoples. In turn, Eurocentric theories inform the nature of the structures which exist in Native communities. They are based on the biased notion that European Peoples are culturally and politically superior to all other Peoples of the world (Adams, 1999). Related to this understanding is the concept of diffusionism. Battiste and Youngblood Henderson (2000) state that diffusionism is based on the premise that most human people are uninventive and those who are inventive should be the permanent centers for cultural change and progress. Eurocentric ideology assumes that Europeans are superior because they are inventive. Conversely this thinking assumes that Native people require the diffusion of European characteristics such as creativity, imagination, invention, innovation, rationality, and a sense of ethics in order for Native peoples to progress (Battiste & Youngblood Henderson, 2000). This theorizing justifies a view of Native peoples as primitive and inferior.

Eurocentrism as rationale for the colonial agenda

I contend that Eurocentrism dominates the profession of social work and thus social work practices. While there are many paradigms for helping and offering social assistance among various cultures, Eurocentrism operates by centering Euro-Western theories and practices as the dominant social work paradigm. Indeed as de Montigny (1995) states, the activities of social work are about engaging in the socially organized practices of power from the stand-point of ruling relations. In the following pages I will speak to the colonial context in which the practice of social work with Native peoples is located. Suffice to say that in spite of Native peoples having our own historic systems and methods of practice Euro-Western case management models are opera-tive within most of today's Native social welfare systems. Thus, the Eurocen-tric social work processes of intake, case recording, clinical assessment, clinical treatment such as individual, group and family therapy, referral, and the termination of case files have become the hegemonic and taken for granted way of managing Native social work practices and Native social wel-fare systems. Indeed Eurocentric assumptions about what counts as legiti-mated case recording and accountability procedures are very operative in what has otherwise been defined as a unique Native cultural perspective (Swinomish Tribal Mental Health Project, 1991).

It is also understood that government audits routinely ensure that the dominant paradigm is carried out in social work systems (de Montigny, 1995; Parada, 2000). The crude reality is that failure to comply with Eurocentric paradigms and methods of practice can often mean the loss of government funding and thus the failure of the government-funded initiative. As a result the need to meet the imposed government objectives can take precedence over meeting the needs of people the social work profession is intended to serve. During my work as a social worker within agency settings I spent 80 percent of my time involved in documenting daily activities and writing reports for the clinical files. De Montigny (1995) states that the socially organ-ized practice of social work case recording silences the actual voices and lived realities of clients. Adding to de Montigny's understanding, I also contend that social work case recording often functions as a dehumanizing and a col-onizing practice. Frustrated by this reality and by the paternalistic power dif-ferential embedded in social work case recording activities I worked with a Native Elder to create a culturally appropriate method for conducting clinical assessments based on the medicine wheel paradigm (Nabigon & Waterfall, 1995.) This effort did facilitate the development of a Native social work prac-tice which respected Native peoples' inherent right to self-determined agency. However, it did little to rupture what was still a dominant Eurocentric sys-temic paradigm.

The
problematic
of historic
and ongoing
colonial
imposition

The Problematic of Historic and Ongoing Colonial Imposition

Colonialism in its imperialist form originally meant the direct control of Native peoples, Native systems, and Native lands by colonial officials. After World War II Native peoples began resisting this direct control. A new colonial system was put in place to appease this resistance. This new system has come to be defined as neo-colonialism (Adams, 1999). Instead of non-Native officials administering programs for Native peoples the system of neo-colonialism enables programs such as income assistance, job training, health, education, and the maintenance of Indian bands and Métis villages to be administered by Native peoples. The major decision making and the control of finances of these programs remained within the hands of colonial forces (Adams, 1999). New to Native relations was the bringing of provincial governments in direct relationship with Native systems. Enforced through the British North America Act (1867), the areas of Native education, social assistance, child welfare, and some justice issues[5] came under the direct control of the provincial governments. Native communities now had to negotiate with both the federal and provincial governments. Battiste (1997) refers to these new provincial relationships as an example of how colonialism continues to reformulate itself.

A new Native middle-class structure was created through the creation of jobs for administrators and workers within these programs. While a few gained jobs through these programs the rest of the people lived in abject poverty. Today many refer to those Native peoples who are given jobs in these programs as the Native middle-class elite (Adams, 1999; Alfred, 1999; Maracle, 1996).[6] This elite class gains economic benefits and social status from these positions. It is thus not surprising that these people are unlikely to develop a critique of the colonial power relations that are embedded within this new neo-colonial schema. Adams (1999) and Alfred (1999) contend that for the most part the Native elite has come to function as collaborators of what are still imperial structures and policies. From a Native community grass-roots perspective, Native peoples not only have to deal with external colonial imposition but also internal collaborative colonial processes. Alfred (1999) helps to explicate this dynamic by stating that there are two value systems at work in Native communities. One value system is rooted in traditional cultural practices while the other has been imposed by the colonial state. He contends that these two value systems create disunity and factionalism in Native communities making it very difficult to effect change.

Adams (1999) and Alfred (1999) further explicate that the Canadian state has created a more subtle form of colonialism through the constitutional agenda. The modern day practices of "First Nations"[7] treaty negotiations take place within the context of the Canadian constitution. The objectives of the Canadian constitution are not and have never been about affording a fair deal to the Native peoples of this land. When Native peoples signed treaties with the colonial government they did not know the details of what were contained in these legal documents. They were verbally told that they would be given a reserve land base to live on so that they could continue to live their lives without interference from the colonial government. From a Native perspective the word "reserve" was understood to come from the French word "reservoir." The reserves were perceived as a place where Native people could protect and maintain their traditional Native way of life.[8] The Native peoples who signed the treaties were not cognizant of the fact that they had signed a legal document which stated that they had agreed "to cede, release, surrender, and yield up to the government of the dominion of Canada, forever, all their rights, titles, and privileges whatsoever" (Adams, 1999). They did not know that the reservation system was to be an institutionalized form of apartheid serving imperial and colonial interests.

We are now living in a time when a rhetoric of Native self-government including Native economic development is being realized. Yet these initiatives are couched within the neo-colonial and constitutional colonial agendas. They are designed to not only serve the interests of colonial governments but also the interests of multinational corporations.[9] Today, this translates as multinational corporations gaining access to the natural resources that exist in Native territories. As indicated above the dominant model of self-government applied today merely grants a few Native elites the right to act as puppets for agendas which serve both the colonial state and multinational interests (Adams, 1999; Alfred, 1999). Furthermore, the rhetoric of Native economic development initiatives merely positions Native peoples as representatives, or stakeholders. Foreign industry inevitably controls the strings making the ability to work within a framework based on Native traditional life-sustaining principles impossible to accomplish (Alfred, 1999).[10] Alfred (1999) states that these supposed self-governing processes do not help Native peoples in Canada. They merely further embed us deeper into colonial structures.

Colonial Imposition and the Disruption of Native Extended Family Systems

There is a great deal of diversity among the varied Native Nations. However, commonalities do exist. I contend that this is particularly true in relation to child rearing practices. Native peoples traditionally believe that children represent the means through which a culture can preserve its tradition, heritage, and language (Thomas & Learoyd, 1990). Traditionally, Native child rearing was valued as a sacred responsibility. Within this context the abuse of children was not problematic. Children were nurtured in a community sense of belonging. Children were encouraged to develop mastery in skills that were needed for survival. They were also encouraged to develop their own unique sense of autonomy while at the same time being taught the value of gen-

[margin note:] Colonial imposition and the disruption of Native extended family systems

Colonial
imposition
and the
disruption
of native
extended
family
systems

erosity (Brokenleg & Brendtro, 1989). Punishment was not a concept that was used traditionally by Native peoples. Rather, techniques such as modeling, group influence, discussion, and positive expectations were employed (Thomas & Learoyd, 1990).

Native communities are made up of extended family systems. Traditionally, families functioned within community systems by being responsible to and for each other. Within this context everyone within the community was responsible for the well-being of the children. Traditionally, Native societies were based on a preventive medicine that focused on maintaining an intricate balance within an ecology that was constantly in flux or change (Battiste & Youngblood Henderson, 2000). These societies were based on a cosmology that understood and respected our connectedness and kinship with all of Creation. Problems and issues that arose traditionally in daily life were immediately dealt with through clan systems of governance.[11] Decision making was based on a consensual paradigm. Citing Mi'kmaw traditional thought the welfare of the group was valued over the individual as was the extended family over the immediate family. This ensured that peace and good order would be preserved within Native community life (Battiste & Youngblood Henderson, 2000). Due to colonial interference the ability to maintain a sense of peace and good order has been difficult to accomplish.

Authorized through the Indian Act (1876) Native children were forcibly removed from their homes and placed in Christian-run residential or day schools. The purpose of these schools was an assimilationist strategy. The children who attended these schools were taught racist ideologies about their own traditional cultures and were encouraged to adopt Euro-Western values and practices. Children were forbidden to speak their own Native languages. If they were caught speaking their own languages, they were punished. The use of physical punishment was very severe and was extensively used (Assembly of First Nations, 1994; Knockwood, 1992). Many survivors of residential schools have reported being tortured by staff within these schools.[12] The principal methods of behaviour management used in these schools were control, domination, shame, and intimidation. As a result we now see these negative uses of power displayed by Native peoples within Native community contexts (Assembly of First Nations, 1994).[13]

The curriculum did not support children learning English and other skills that would help them participate as equals among the mainstream societies. Rather, the curriculum focused on Christian teachings. Most of the time spent in these schools was dedicated to prayer and hard physical labor. The children provided most of the labor to maintain these schools such as laundering, cooking, cleaning, and gardening (Assembly of First Nations, 1994; Knockwood, 1992). However, these students did not receive the benefits of their work. It was the staff in these schools that used the cream separated from the milk in their morning porridge. The staff dined well with three-course meals while the children were not adequately fed. The typical diet for children in these schools was beans, porridge, rancid meat, and rotten potatoes (Assembly of First Nations, 1994; Knockwood, 1992). The experience of seeing first-hand that some live in luxury while others live meagerly taught these children to accept unequal class relations as a taken for granted way of doing things.[14]

The effects of the residential school system severely disrupted the traditional Native way of life. Imagine waking up to a community whose children have all been taken away. The results of the forced removal of Native children were devastating. The adults who were left behind fell into feelings of despair and apathy (Waterfall, 1992).[15] It is not surprising that many of the people picked up alcohol in an effort to cope. In many cases the children in residential schools were only allowed to go home two times during the year. When these children returned to their home communities, they often found family members intoxicated and unable to take care of them. Furthermore, these children were speaking the colonizer's language making it difficult for their communication to be understood. The children no longer felt at home and safe in their own communities (Assembly of First Nations, 1994).

The early 1970s marked the beginning of the end of mandatory residential schooling for Native children in colonial Canada. While these schools are no longer in operation, they remain as vivid memories in the minds of those who attended them. We live with an inter-generational legacy of residential school. I have not met a Native person alive who has not been affected directly or indirectly by these schools. Traditionally, Native peoples possessed profound childcare wisdom. Thomas and Learoyd (1990) documented that the European immigrants might have been better to have adopted this wisdom. Given the distress caused by residential school and the interruption of traditional child rearing practices we now see a multitude of child abuse cases in Native communities (Waterfall, 1992). This is where the social work profession working within the structures of children's aid societies became involved with Native families and Native communities.

Native Peoples and the Profession of Social Work

As indicated above the profession of social work primarily became involved with Native peoples and Native communities through the child welfare system[16] (Alcoze & Mawhiney, 1988; Yellow Bird & Chenault, 1999). The prevalence of Eurocentric discourses about Native peoples prevented a critique of colonialism and a discussion of the adverse effects that colonization had on Native peoples and Native family systems. Of particular significance was the effect of the imposed residential school system. Influenced by Eurocentrism and diffusionism Native people were presumed by these social workers to be unfit to raise their children. A disproportionate number of Native children were apprehended by social workers working within children's aid societies and were placed in white foster homes (Johnston, 1983). The social workers failed to recognize the effects of residential schools on Native families and to respond fairly and appropriately by encouraging the teaching of Native traditional child care practices. Instead, the social workers intervened when incidents of child abuse were reported by taking children from their families and their communities. Many of these children did not return to their home communities and were adopted into white families (Waterfall, 1992).

In the literature this time period is referred to as the "sixties scoop" as it predominantly took place during the 1960s (Johnston, 1983). As indicated above Native residential schools were closing. Native children had returned to their families. It is not surprising thus that there was an increase in the number of reported cases of child abuse in Native communities. This time it was not the federal government, nor the Christian churches who intervened by taking children from their homes. The provincial governments intervened through the legal apparatus of child protection legislation. We thus see another example of how colonization keeps reformulating itself. Indeed Hudson and McKenzie (1980) argued that the child welfare system was an active agent in the colonization of Native peoples. Maracle (1996) stated that the act of apprehending children from their homes is tantamount to kidnapping and inflicts terror on children. It is a violent act and one must wonder how this can be justified in the name of child safety. A social worker who did this dirty work of kidnapping was not well received within Native communities. Indeed, this is still the case. A social worker armed with a child protection mandate from the state is both feared and hated.[17]

One would assume therefore that Native peoples would be hesitant to pursue the practice of social work as a profession, or be specifically interested in working in agencies with a child protection mandate. However, one only needs to look at the predominant neo-colonial context and realize that there are very limited options available. I do admit that Native social workers do a great deal of good for individuals, groups, and families. I also readily acknowledge the many Native social workers who are working against the grain within the confines of government-funded agencies. However, I contend that we must understand that the profession and its relationship to Native peoples is fundamentally problematic for two reasons. These reasons relate to what I have discussed earlier. That is, the characteristics of Eurocentrism and diffusionism make it difficult to bring Native methodologies to the center of a social work practice. Furthermore, the actual practices of Native social work are embedded within a neo-colonial context. I will speak to the case of Native Child Welfare to explicate my point.

Neo-Colonialism and Native Self-Government

Examining the Case of Native Child Welfare Initiatives

In the 1980s Native leaders in the form of elected chiefs, Elders, lawyers, administrators, and social workers were concerned by the interference and devastating impact that the child welfare system had in their communities (Assembly of First Nations, 1989; Native Council of Canada, 1989; Ontario Native Women's Association, 1982). They were primarily concerned with finding ways to control the problem of Native children being apprehended from their communities. A not so surprising correlation existed at this time. That is, provincial governments were changing their legislation enabling Native peoples to inform the direction of foster-care placements for children who were band members within their communities. In 1984 the Ontario Child and Family Services Act was passed, enabling this to take place. Using the Native traditional discourse of "customary care"[18] the Act was amended to enable Native children at risk to be placed with extended family members within their own communities.[19]

This new provision in the Child and Family Services Act was perceived by Native leaders as a window of opportunity to prevent the further interference of Children's Aid Societies in Native communities (Soloman, 1999). In response, some Native territories developed their own child protection agencies. From a Native grass-roots perspective these agencies are often viewed as "brown" children's aid societies. Many of these agencies began with a vision of offering programs based on Native traditional values.[20] Yet, the explicit focus of these agencies was not about ridding Native peoples of colonial imposition. Nor was the focus concerned with revitalizing our Native languages, laws, systems, and cultural practices.[21] Rather, the inevitability of colonial imposition was assumed. Part of the baggage of assuming, or accepting the inevitability of colonial imposition was that of accepting Eurocentric social welfare practices.

I speak from my own experience as a Native social worker and to a dynamic that appeared to be very apparent in the Native contexts where I was employed. That is, many Native peoples who worked within these Native agencies, including me, often accepted the Eurocentric and hegemonic assumption that Native parenting was problematic within Native communities. Native people were thus the problem and the ones who needed to be fixed. Furthermore, the funding criteria for these agencies ensured that standard provincial guidelines were followed. The result was that Native peoples were now doing the dirty work of apprehending Native children from their families. Even though it was now called "customary care" Native children were forcibly removed from their homes and placed in other settings. Furthermore, through time Native workers began placing Native children within White foster homes as they were deemed to be the most appropriate placements.[22] We can see how, although well intentioned, we as Native people can inadvertently end up perpetuating an assimilationist agenda.

It is at this juncture that I believe we must ask a critical question. That is, how can we presume to say that we are offering culturally relevant or appropriate services under a child protection mandate? Being reminded of Maracle's (1996) understanding pertaining to apprehension, where in our Native

Neo-Colonialism and Native self-government

traditions, laws, or values was the terrorizing or kidnapping of children acceptable? We need to seriously reflect on this question. This is not to say that Native peoples who work within these Native agencies do not offer some culturally appropriate services. Indeed Native Healers and Elders are being recruited and funded to offer "culturally appropriate" services such as sweat lodge ceremonies, healing circles, and other Native traditional practices. However, our Native Healers and Elders are usually not positioned as full-time staff within these agencies. Furthermore, there is often a severe discrepancy between what Eurocentric practitioners are paid within these agencies and that of our own traditional Native experts and specialists. That is, the Eurocentric practitioners are given much greater salaries. The prominence of Eurocentrism justifies and ensures that this is so. Therefore, while we may see some "culturally appropriate" programs they are embedded within a neo-colonial bureaucracy where Euro-Western values and methods of practice predominate. I thus contend that we need to seriously take a look at what we have been calling Native self-determined child welfare programs.

I also believe that we need to interrogate our current objectives toward the devolution or transfer of services to Native communities. Indeed we live in a political climate where buzz terms such as devolution and transfer of services are being readily utilized (Browning & van de Sande, 1999; Timpson & Semple, 1997). However, I contend that we need to seriously interrogate how these buzz terms are really being taken up and by whom. That is, we need to question whether we are merely moving what is an essentially Eurocentric service from a main office model to a decentralized Native context. Are we merely allowing the few Native elites such as the elected leadership to be responsible for the administering of these programs while the majority of the people living within the community are alienated from the processes of decision making? If this is indeed the case, we are merely changing the players of what are still bureaucracies.

Alfred (1999) states that the terms "brown" and "bureaucrat" are not compatible. While appearing to be moving toward the objectives of Native peoples' self-determined agency, I contend that these modern day initiatives are merely reformulations of neo-colonial structures. I also contend that Native initiatives will remain essentially colonized structures as long as they are couched within the parameters of the constitutional colonial agenda.[23] In the case of Native child welfare initiatives the provincial governments still ultimately wield the power. The change merely means decentralizing services. It does not change the nature of the services. Native peoples are still positioned to carry out the child protection mandate of the colonial state. We thus must not delude ourselves by what appears to be encouraging discourses about Native self-government, devolution, or the transfer of services.

We also need to seriously reflect on the positioning of Native social workers within neo-colonial schemas. I contend that being positioned as a Native social worker within these contexts presents itself with a very specific and difficult dilemma. If we have accepted Eurocentric practices as a taken for granted way of doing things, we may not feel the dilemma. However, if we are traditionally sensitized to see the great value in our own Native knowledges and methodological practices we find ourselves in a very difficult position. That is, we are being asked to bridge the perspectives, values, and methods used and recommended by their Elders and Healers with the demands imposed by Eurocentric discourses, and Eurocentric social work processes. For Native social workers who have been positioned as full-time staff within these contexts we are automatically put in this position. I contend that Native peoples positioned as social workers within these contexts have been given an impossible task. Let us remember that bridges get walked on and big Mack trucks drive across them. Native peoples positioned as social workers have been presently set up to become very frustrated and angry. Small wonder that there is a high rate of Native social workers burning out in Native communities.

We need to seriously ask ourselves whether when positioned as Native social workers within neo-colonial structures it is possible to work toward the objectives of Native peoples' self-determined agency based upon traditional Native life-sustaining wisdoms. I contend that we will never be able to work toward that self-determined objective without a vision of Native life without colonial imposition. I contend thus that we must envision decolonized possibilities. I also contend that the development of feminist anti-colonial thought is key to developing these envisioned potentialities. Informed by a feminist anti-colonial discursive framework we can more easily disengage ourselves with what deceivingly appears to look like benefits from both neo-colonial and constitutional colonial agendas. Furthermore, we are able to ground our efforts and in the strength and the wisdom of our vibrant Native traditional gynocratic systems. As Alfred stated (1999) neo-colonial structures and processes will not help Native peoples. We are all personally implicated wherever we are located whether we are Native, or non-Native. I contend that we all must dream big dreams and reach for what today may seem impossible.

We must understand that decolonization is a process. We must also recognize that the road toward decolonization is not an easy journey. However, I believe that it is a road we must embark upon. It is imperative that Native peoples stridently work toward the objectives of decolonization and authentic Native self-determined agency. It is also important for social workers and for the profession of social work to disengage from the inherent colonial politic that has been its legacy. I contend that the profession of social work has a responsibility to be informed by feminist anti-colonial consciousness. Guided by feminist anti-colonial thought Schools of Social Work can be one site where we can map the road away from colonial/colonized relations. Rather than teaching predominant social work theories which perpetuate Native peoples' oppression we can develop strategies based on relations of equality and respectful co-existence with "All Our Relations."

Neo-Colonialism and Native self-government

Conclusion

Alfred (1999) states that the primary problem with the profession of social work is that Native peoples' lives continue to be controlled by others. In controlling the lives of Native peoples the profession of social work remains a colonizing practice. This all too often is a sad fact whether we are located as Native, or non-Native social work professionals. Many Native peoples who have been trained in Eurocentric universities have not been given a chance to adequately define what Native helping consists of outside of the parameters of mainstream theories. Even when we do understand what Native helping encompasses the current neo-colonial politic impedes our ability to work with our people based on our own Native foundational understandings. It is imperative thus that the profession of social work develops effective strategies to rupture the dominant colonial paradigm. Alfred (1999) states that colonialism is not an abstract notion. It is a real set of people, relationships, and structures that can be resisted and combated by placing our respect and trust where it belongs in Native peoples, relationships, and structures. As a profession social work can advance its current anti-discriminatory objectives by seriously acknowledging Native peoples' inherent right to self-determination and in so doing problematize colonialism in all of its guises. As Native peoples we are tired of being constructed as the problem. Colonialism and colonial imposition has created the problems that are everyday occurrences in Native communities. Rather than problematizing Native individuals, families, and communities we must be committed to extricating and ridding the roots causes of the problem.

The Canadian Association of Social Workers, CASW (1994) has given a clear direction for the profession of social work to follow. During a presentation to the Royal Commission on Aboriginal Peoples the CASW acknowledged Native peoples' inherent right to self-determination, autonomy, self-sufficiency, and the preservation of culture. At that time they also recognized that social work education must become culturally relevant. As indicated in the introduction of this chapter social work education needs to be involved in three salient tasks. That is, social work theorizing needs to construct colonialism as problematic. Furthermore, the curriculum and pedagogical practices employed within social work education must center, along with other diverse perspectives, Native epistemologies and Native methodological understandings. Finally, the profession has a responsibility to disengage from the current colonial politic. It is thus the job of social work theorizing to develop strategies that rupture the dominant colonial politic and effectively support Native grass-roots efforts for Native self-determined agency. I view the development and inclusion of feminist anti-colonial discourse within social work education as pivotal in the attaining of these ends.

Notes

1   Reprinted with permission from the *Journal of Educational Thought, 36*(3), 2002. Copyright © 1985/1999 by the University of Calgary.

2 I am using the term peoples here as intended by Smith (1999: 114) to acknowledge Native peoples' rights to self-determination and also to acknowledge the reality of Native peoples as diverse.

3 The terms gynocentric and gynocratic were used by Allen (1986: 2) to refer to traditional Native systems as matriarchal, or woman-centred.

4 While a discussion of the Canadian government's newly proposed First Nations Governance Act is not the intent of this chapter one can critique the federal government's proposal as not acknowledging Native peoples' inherent, Creator-given right to autonomous self-government outside of the parameters of the Canadian state.

5 Within the structures of colonial Canada the provincial governments are responsible for judicial convictions and sentencing of two years less a day. Other sentences are within the jurisdiction of the federal justice system.

6 The author acknowledges that she is part of the middle class within Native societies.

7 The term First Nations is prominently used by treaty chiefs to refer to Native communities that fall under the jurisdiction of the Indian Act. People such as Adams (1999) contend that it is an exclusionary term that serves a constitutional colonial agenda where Non-status Indians and Métis have been left out of the politic. Adams (1999: 64) refers to this as a problematic which serves colonial interests of dividing and conquering Native peoples. For this reason I am not using the term First Nations in this text in favour of using the inclusive term of Native peoples.

8 As told by a very respected Anishnabe Elder. Due to Anishnabe protocol and the expressed wishes of this Elder I will not cite his name. Many Anishnabec who read this text will easily be able to identify the origins of this statement.

9 The recent deal signed between Hydro-Québec and the James Bay Cree is an example of corporate interests superceding the interests and values of traditional Cree land-based people. Through this deal the James Bay Cree relinquished their rights to their land and the land's resources.

10 This is a very sad reality given the nature of how Native peoples feel about the land. Traditionally, the land is understood to be our Mother. As Indigenous peoples of this land we believe that we have been given the responsibility from the Creator of Life to be stewards and thus caretakers of the land. Multinational interests will prevent us from being able to continue to act in this capacity. Alfred (1999: 97) contends that the choices for Native peoples today are two-fold. Either they are about gaining immediate economic benefits, or refusing to comply with imposed corporate and neo-colonial structures in favour of preserving the long term goal of Native self-determination on terms which are based on our own cultural values. This is not an easy choice given the nature and extent of poverty in Native communities.

11 This information has been obtained through our Native oral tradition. It has been precisely passed down to me through my associations with many respected Native Elders and traditional teachers.

12 I became aware of this through my practice as a social worker in Native communities.

13 Traditionally the notion of power over was never used. Rather the model of power traditionally used is that of power from within. One gains power and holds power through life experience and from directed learning from Elders. If a convincing argument needs to be employed it can be achieved by way of oration or verbal persuasion (Alfred, 1999: 48-51; Maracle, 1992: 87)

14 I contend that this is one reason why the Native middle class does not speak out in outrage concerning the deplorable conditions that the majority of Native people live in.

15 This information was obtained by interviewing survivors of residential schools.

16 It is also recognized that social workers became involved with Native peoples through the mental health system.

17 I am aware of this perception from my own experience of working as a social worker in a Native agency that had a child protection mandate. While the work that I did was essentially clinical my clients were very aware that I carried a big stick and could report child abuse cases to the investigation unit within this agency.

18 The term customary care refers to the extended family as the locus of support for children within the community. It was thus not unusual for children to live with extended

family members. This notion does not equate easily within the context of the Euro-centric nuclear family system where one would go to live with extended family members in times of extreme need. Traditionally everyone within the community was responsible for the care giving of all the children in the community (Thomas & Learoyd, 1990: 21-22). Colonial interference through residential school and the imposition of Christian marriages changed the fabric of Native community life (Allen, 1986: 41-42). Based on my own observations of Native communities I can see that today there is the hegemonic assumption that if children go live with extended family members it is defined as symptomatic of there being a problem.

19 My thinking about this has been influenced by Dennis McPherson, a Native lawyer who was one of the people whose work enabled the term customary care to be included in the amended Ontario Child and Family Services Act. From a Native perspective, the motivation to have the provision of customary care included in the Act was for the purpose of enabling Native communities to deal with incidents of child abuse in a traditional Native, or a customary fashion. In practice, the new provision merely provided an opportunity to place Native children at risk in other Native homes. It did not enable Native peoples to deal with the problem of child abuse in Native communities according to their own traditional laws, cultures and values. That is, the area of Native child welfare was still bound by the legislation of the Eurocentric Child and Family Services Act.

20 I am purposefully not including the names of these agencies for the following reasons. That is, I do not have the expressed permission of these agencies nor do I intend to create any kind of harm for these agencies, or for the people who work within them.

21 In fairness I must say that the interventions used in a Native agency where I was employed were very much leading edge in terms of going beyond the surface of the observable dysfunctional behaviours by dealing with internalized pain and trauma.

22 Provincial foster care guidelines found many Native homes unfit for foster care placements. One reason was that a foster home could not contain firearms. Yet hunting is a very common practice in Native communities. Thus guns are often found in Native homes. Another issue was that the impoverished conditions that Native peoples lived in were deemed to be unacceptable for foster care placements.

23 The First Nations and Inuit Home and Community Care Program (2000) funded by the federal government's First Nations Indian Health Branch is a very concrete example of how Indigenous self-governed initiatives are being organized and structured according to Eurocentric standards. St. Germaine (2001) indicates that the rhetoric of this program is one of being "community-based" and "community-paced." However, she also states that, "First Nations are subject to Eurocentric/hegemonic thought, through the imposition of contribution arrangements that include goals & objectives, deadlines, work plans and budgets." She also says, "to add insult to injury a policy template has been developed for ease of implementation by First Nations without regard for culture or community ownership of the document" (See Saint Elizabeth Health Care, 2000, for a copy of the template.)

References

Adams, H. (1999). *Tortured people: The politics of colonization*. Penticton: Theytus Books.

Alcoze, T., & Mawhiney, A.M. (1988). *Returning home. A report on a community-based Native human services project*. Sudbury: Laurentian University.

Alfred, T. (1999). *Peace power righteousness: An indigenous manifesto*. Don Mills: Oxford University Press.

Allen, P.G. (1986). *The sacred hoop: Recovering the feminine in American Indian traditions*. Boston: Beacon Press.

Anderson, K. (2000). *A recognition of being: Reconstructing Native womanhood*. Toronto: Secondary Press.

Assembly of First Nations. (1989). *National inquiry into First Nations child care.*   **References**
Ottawa: Author.

Assembly of First Nations. (1994). *Breaking the silence: An interpretive study of residential school impact and healing as illustrated by the stories of First Nations individuals.* Ottawa: Author.

Battiste, M. (1997). Enabling the autumn seed: Framing a decolonized curricular approach toward Aboriginal knowledge language and education. Paper presented at the CSAA Learned Society Conference, St. John's, Newfoundland, June 8-11.

Battiste, M., & Youngblood Henderson, J.S. (2000). *Protecting indigenous knowledge and heritage: A global challenge.* Saskatoon: Purich Publishing.

Brokenleg, M., & Brendtro, L. (1989). The circle of caring: Native American perspectives on children and youth. Paper presented to the Child Welfare of America International Conference, Washington, DC.

Browning, R., & van de Sande, A. (1999). Long-term evaluation of health-transfer initiatives: Major findings. *Native Social Work Journal 2*(1), 153-62.

Canadian Association of Social Workers (1994). The social work profession and the Aboriginal peoples: CASW presentation to the Royal Commission on Aboriginal Peoples. *The Social Worker,* December, 158.

Dei, G.J.S. (2000a). Towards an anti-racism discursive framework. In G.J.S. Dei (Ed.), *Power, knowledge and anti-racism education: A critical reader,* (pp. 23-40). Halifax: Fernwood.

Dei, G.J.S. (2000b). Rethinking the role of indigenous knowledges in the academy. *International Journal of Inclusive Education 4*(2), 111-132.

De Montigny, G. (1995). The power of being professional. In M. Campbell & A. Manicom (Eds.), *Knowledge, experience and ruling relations,* (pp. 209-220). Toronto: University of Toronto Press.

Fanon, F. (1995). National culture. In B. Ashcroft, G. Griffiths, & H. Thiophene (Eds.), *The post-colonial studies reader,* (pp. 153-57). New York: Routledge.

First Nations and Inuit Health Branch. (2000). *First Nations and Inuit home and community care: Planning resource kit.* Ottawa: Government of Canada.

Hudson, P., & McKenzie, B. (1985). Native children, child welfare and the colonization of native people. In K. Levitt & B. Wharf (Eds.), *The challenge of child welfare* (pp. 125-141). Vancouver: University of British Columbia Press.

Johnston, P. (1983). *Native children and the child welfare system.* Ottawa: Canadian Council on Social Development.

Knockwood, I. (1992). *Out of the depths: The experiences of Mi'kmaw children at the residential school at Shubenacadie, Nova Scotia.* Lockeport: Roseway Publishing.

Maracle, L. (1996). *I am woman: A Native perspective on sociology and feminism.* Vancouver: Press Gang.

Nabigon, H., & Waterfall, B. (1995). An assessment tool for First Nations individuals and families (p. 32). Cited in Francis Turner (Ed.) *Social work treatment: Interlocking theoretical approaches,* (4th ed.) New York: Free Press.

Native Council of Canada. (1989). *Report on the National Day of Native child care: Challenges into the 1990s.* Ottawa: Author.

Ontario Native Women's Association. (1982). Remove the child and the circle is broken: A response to the proposed Children's Act Commission paper. Thunder Bay: Author.

Parada, H. (2000). The social organization of power within Children's Aid Societies. Paper presented at the May 2000 Institutional Ethnography Conference, Ontario Institute for Studies in Education of the University of Toronto, Toronto.

References   Puja, G.K. (2001). Moving against the grain: Expectations and experiences of Tanzanian female undergraduates. Unpublished doctoral thesis. Toronto: OISE / University of Toronto.

Saint Elizabeth Health Care. (2000). *First Nations and Inuit home and community health care policies template manual.* Markham: Author.

Smith, L. (1999). *Decolonizing methodologies: Research and indigenous peoples.* New York: Zed Books.

Soloman, A. (1999). Interview notes, Toronto, 15 November.

St. Germaine, J. (2001). Home and community care policy development. Unpublished paper. Sudbury: Native Human Services, Laurentian University.

Swinomish Tribal Mental Health Project. (1991). A gathering of wisdoms: Tribal mental health: A cultural perspective. Swinomish Tribal Community: LaConner.

Thomas, L., & Learoyd, S. (1990). Native child care: In the spirit of caring. Unpublished masters thesis. Ottawa: Carleton University.

Timpson, J., & Semple, D. (1997). Bringing home Payahtakenenmowin (Peace of mind): Creating self-governing community services. *Native Social Work Journal* 1(1), 87-101.

Trask, H.K. (1991). Natives and anthropologists: The colonial struggle. *The Contemporary Pacific 3*(1), 159-167.

Waterfall, B. (1992). Mending the circle: Healing from the effects of family violence. Unpublished masters' thesis. Ottawa: Carleton University.

Yellow Bird, M.J., & Chenault, V. (1999). The role of social work in advancing the practice of Indigenous education: Obstacles and promises in empowerment-oriented social work practice. In K.G. Swisher and J.W. Tippeconnic III, (Eds.), *Next steps: Research and practice to advance Indian education.* Chareston: ERIC Clearinghouse on Rural Education & Small Schools.

Additional Resources

Antone, B., Miller, D., & Myers, B. (1986). *The power within people: A community organizing perspective.* Deseronto: Peace Tree Technologies.

Dei, G.J.S., & Asghardzadeh, A. (2000). The power of social theory: The anti-colonial discursive framework. *Journal of Educational Thought 35*(3), 297-323.

Graveline, F.J. (1998). *Circle works: Transforming Eurocentric consciousness.* Halifax: Fernwood.

McIvor, S.D. (1999). *Self-government and Aboriginal women.* In E. Dua & A. Robertson (Eds.), *Scratching the surface: Canadian anti-racist feminist thought* (pp. 167-186). Toronto: Women's Press.

Monture-Angus, P. (1995). A first journey in decolonized thought: Aboriginal women and the application of the Canadian Charter. In P. Monture-Angus (Ed.), *Thunder in my soul: A Mohawk woman speaks* (pp. 131-151). Halifax: Fernwood.

Monture-Angus, P. (2001). In the way of peace: Confronting "whiteness" in the university. In R. Luther, E. Whitmore, & B. Moreau (Eds.), *Seen but not heard: Aboriginal women and women of colour in the academy* (pp. 29-49). Ottawa: CRIAW.

Stevenson, W. (1999). Colonialism and First Nations women in Canada. In E. Dua & A. Robertson (Eds.), *Scratching the surface: Canadian anti-racist feminist thought* (pp. 49-80). Toronto: Women's Press.

Ricks, F., Wharf, B., & Armitage, A. (1990). Evaluation of Indian child welfare: A different reality. *Canadian Review of Social Policy* (25), pp. 41-47.

Royal Commission on Aboriginal Peoples. (1996). Report of the Royal Commission on Aboriginal Peoples. Vol. 1: Looking forward, looking back; Vol. 2: Restructuring the relationship; Vol. 3: Gathering strength; Vol. 4: Perspectives and realities; Vol. 5: Renewal: A twenty-year commitment. Ottawa: Canada Communications Group.

4

Lea Caragata

At some level, homelessness touches the lives of many Canadians. Most urban Canadians have some direct experience with homeless people, even if it's just passing a homeless person on a street corner, or exchanging an occasional word with a panhandler. Current levels of homelessness also mean that those on the streets or without adequate housing are increasingly likely to be the brother, sister, son, or daughter of someone you know. Research done in Kitchener-Waterloo found a surprisingly high rate of personal connections to the homeless among those randomly selected to participate in a focus group on the issue (Jeffrey, 1999). It is widely acknowledged that there are homeless people and that they are in greater numbers than ever. This is perhaps the limit of a common understanding of the issue. Why homelessness occurs and its causes are a matter of intense debate with important implications for public policy. This chapter will discuss these issues and their policy ramifications.

Notwithstanding a debate about cause, there has been strong societal agreement that homelessness *is* a social problem. This accord probably stems from the frequency of contact between those who are homeless and the rest of the population. The Canadian public is unused to being confronted with our social ills—the problems of the poor, domestic violence, slum housing—as they are usually removed from our everyday world. Because contact with the homeless is largely unavoidable, public discomfort may explain the consequent public concern. This, as we shall further discuss, does not necessarily translate into the policy responses that might address the problem. There is an unusual level of agreement among the public, governments, and the homeless themselves that homelessness is a problem. Given the nature of such accord, one might justifiably ask why so little has been achieved in resolving the issue since it first came to the public's attention over fifteen years ago (Burt, 1992; City of Toronto, 1995; Dear & Wolch, 1987; Greve, 1971; McLaughlin, 1987). This query returns us to the question of cause, because our understanding of the nature and severity of the problem determines the scope and nature of the policy response. If we incorrectly assess the cause, if our commitment is limited and/or our willingness to spend is weak or incon-

sistent, we will have (as in the case of homelessness) policies and programs at
every level of government *and* a continuation of the problem. Such is the
policy minefield related to those who are homeless.

Social Problems as Social Constructions

Before identifying the homeless, a point about how we construct and define
a social problem is in order. Blanco (1994), Hacking (1999), and many others
have discussed the social construction of social issues so these debates will
not be replicated here. But it is important to note that disagreement over who
counts among the homeless are not mere quibbles over numbers but says
much about our social expectations and the ideologies on which they are
based. Our constructions include more than the "facts" of the issue. Facts are
determined by the nature of the inquiry into a problem, which is in part determined by our suppositions about it. In our suppositions, we have various
ideas or notions about an issue that may or may not be strictly relevant. Over
time, a framework of associations, images, and attitudes cluster around a
term and reinforce its ideological reproduction. In this way, social problems
become "metaphors" (Blanco, 1994). We think we know what we mean by
homelessness, and this causes, as Blanco suggests, "goals and strategies for
action to be quickly accepted, often by-passing a comparison of causal structures, functional, temporal and other aspects of the situations" (Blanco, 1994,
p. 185). Because a term comes to have a varying and often pejorative subtext,
the term "deconstruction" has come to signal a delayering or unmasking of
these other meanings.

As an illustration of the social (and political) significance of our definitions, if we include among the homeless welfare recipients who spend more
than 30% of their incomes on housing (and are therefore at least statistically
at risk of homelessness), we acknowledge that such a level of impoverish-
ment is a social issue and therefore a matter of public, rather than individual
or private, concern. The kind of definition we employ directs us toward certain kinds of policy choices and obscures others. For example, it appears that
street homelessness causes greater public concern than "doubling up," that is,
people sharing accommodation. Why? Is our concern only for the welfare of
those on the street? Or is there a mixture of concern for them and middle-
class self-interest in not wishing to confront beggars as we leave a store or
restaurant? Making efforts to genuinely appraise what drives the identification
of an issue as a social problem helps to deconstruct or tease out unspoken
associations, such as that between street homelessness and alcoholism or—
in another social policy area—associations between teenage pregnancy and
welfare dependency. Such associations affect our policy choices; if we think
young women are having babies in order to be eligible for welfare, we will
put in place a different set of welfare regulations (as has occurred in the
United States) than we would if we believed that teen pregnancies are
unplanned. If we think that the street homeless are alcoholics, we may decide

that these people are undeserving and offer fewer services or even a punitive response such as vagrancy laws. On the other hand, the services may be oriented to treatment (which assumes individual pathology) rather than the addressing of structural failings. While the evidence of a linkage between alcoholism and homelessness is not so obvious in the Canadian case, in Finland the word for "homeless" combines two other Finnish words meaning "lacquer" (drunk by people on the street) and "man" (Glasser, 1994). Aware of the problems engendered by such language, the Finnish government made an attempt to de-label the homeless. Summa (as cited in Glasser, 1994) refers to the new language as "coded." The associations with alcoholism are no longer explicit but still endure, which likely remains the case in Canada as well as in the United States.

Who is homeless and why?

Both underpinning and deriving from these associations are our notions of the deserving and undeserving poor. These distinctions are especially influential in policy choices with regard to the homeless. Given the presence of shelters and other services (but not housing), the street homeless are often perceived as "choosing" to stay on the streets, even though there are hostels where there are services available. The structuring of the debate is falsely based on the notion that the choice to be on the street was freely made, whereas in fact the "choice" is severely constrained by the very limited range of available options. The following is illustrative of the policy direction that can result when homelessness is viewed as self-caused, a matter of "choice": "We have travelled in the wrong direction for far too long. We must face the reality that vagrancy is against the law and proceed accordingly with formulating public policy. People do not have a right to live on our street and in our parks" (San Francisco mayoralty candidate as cited in Daly, 1996, p. 179). The government of Ontario provides another example of a punitive policy response in introducing the Safe Streets Act. The Act banned panhandling in certain circumstances and also prohibited "squeegee" kids from approaching motorists at busy intersections (Government of Ontario, 1999). These policies (and there are similar ones in place in Winnipeg and Vancouver, all currently facing challenges under the Canadian Charter of Rights and Freedoms) acknowledge more directly that part of the policy goal is saving "taxpayers" from the nuisance of beggars and homeless people. Policies of this nature are in stark contrast to those facilitating social housing construction (which acknowledge structural or at least market failures).

Who Is Homeless and Why?

Definitions

Canadian governments and other key housing players utilize "core housing need" as a common measure of the number of people in Canada who have a housing "problem" of significant severity. Core housing need measures the *adequacy* of the household unit (having a full bathroom and not in need of major repairs); its *suitability* (having sufficient bedrooms, generally no more than two people per room and no sharing of bedrooms between opposite sex children or between a parent and a child older than twelve years); and *affordability* (shelter and utility costs are not more than 30% of household income) (Canada Mortgage and Housing Corporation, 1996). Households whose housing does not meet one or more of these standards and whose income is insufficient to obtain housing without such deficits are considered to be in core housing need. The definition and its application are generally considered adequate for assessing housing need in Canada. As will be evident, it is possible to have an adequate government-sanctioned assessment tool and still experience the sort of definitional debate revealed below. Such disjuncture is a consequence in part of the many players who are involved in problem definitions, technical specifications, needs assessments, treasury allocations, policy development, and the raw politics that inform all of these decisions.

In spite of the seemingly clear determination of "core housing need," an enormous debate continues over where to draw the definitional line. The British literature makes such distinctions as single homelessness or "sleeping rough," which means street homelessness (Pleace, 1998), while the Canadian and American literature (Daly, 1996; Springer, Mars, & Dennison, 1998) identifies categories like hostel users, people who live on the street, and those "at risk" to describe who is being spoken of among the homeless. People who live on the street are one of the most difficult groups to count. They are neither generally amenable to being counted, nor is it easy to determine real numbers. A significant number of people whom many would regard as homeless live in shelters for what are usually two-week residencies. While most engaged in defining the homeless include hostel users among that group, there is a neo-conservative view that hostel users are not without shelter and are already in receipt of services. Even more contentious and hard to count are those who are "doubling up," staying with friends or family, often on a rotational long-term basis. One such family of six reported staying with friends on this basis for several months, although they acknowledged, "it can't last" (Caragata & Hardie, 1999). Another group that homeless advocates claim must be counted are those at imminent risk of homelessness. To be assessed as "at risk," one must meet the federal government's own definition of core housing need. Risk is assessed on the basis of the cost of the housing relative to the family income, in situations of a pending eviction, or where there are significant rent arrears. Advocates argue that people in these "at risk" situations have often been homeless before, and periods of housing and homelessness become cyclical as each housing situation is likely to be unaffordable or inadequate in the long run, triggering a further incident of homelessness. Clearly, this definitional move dramatically increases the numbers identified as homeless. Another group sometimes included in this "at risk" category are those who have qualified to be on waiting lists for subsidized housing but have not yet received a housing unit. Advocates argue that because such applicants must demonstrate both financial and housing need, they are at risk of homelessness until they obtain secure, affordable housing. Recent data confirm that a high percentage of social housing applicants are currently homeless, have been homeless before, and/or have housing situations that put them at imminent risk (Caragata & Hardie, 1999). Thus, social housing waiting lists are a reliable way to tally at least a portion of the "at risk" group.

Given these debates about whom to include among the homeless and the persuasive arguments made by advocates for the homeless and those disinclined to see the problem as particularly great, a broader way of conceptualizing the issue is useful. Oberlander and Fallick suggest that:

> homelessness involves more than simply the presence or absence of shelter. The search for the nature and scale of homelessness in Canada rests on the definitional problems. Is homelessness an issue of poverty? Or employment? Is it an issue of discrimination? Or of location? Of education? Or is it primarily an issue of measurement? Varied evidence increasingly points to the answer: It is all of these factors and more; no single causal factor can be used to define homelessness exclusively or successfully. (As cited in Layton, 2000, p. 32)

This view, while instructive (and to which we will return), has not resolved questions of who is homeless and how many people are indeed homeless (using whatever definition might be in vogue) in any region at a given time. Reliable estimates of the numbers of homeless are difficult to obtain because of potential double counting and the logistical issues of counting those who are doubling up and living on the streets. However, many efforts have been made to profile the homeless in Canada, and a brief summary of these data will follow.

Much of what follows in this review of homelessness in Canada will be, if not familiar, then at least not surprising. The category of homeless people encompasses the full range of human needs in all their variation. Perhaps the only constant among the homeless is an income level inadequate for renting housing in the marketplace. Most homeless people are poor; as a group they are less well educated, sometimes they have histories of abuse, some have addictions or mental health issues, while others may have been in trouble with the law. These issues act *in combination* with Canada's largely private housing market and very limited availability of low-end rental accommodation to explain most homelessness in Canada. This is a critical point: many people with personal or behavioural issues or problems do not become homeless if their housing is secure and readily affordable for their income level. Rather, competition in a tight housing market renders many individuals who were already vulnerable unable to compete. In the absence of a housing safety net,[1] homelessness results.

More Definitions and Categorization: Attempts to Understand

A number of major studies have been done recently across Canada that provide a picture of homelessness. In Toronto, the Mayor's Action Task Force on
Homelessness submitted a report in 1999 and funded several research studies. Also in Ontario, the Ontario Non-profit Housing Association (ONPHA)
and the Co-operative Housing Federation of Canada, Ontario Region (CHF),
have just released a study called "Where's Home?" British Columbia has just
completed a large review of issues related to homelessness, and the cities of
Ottawa and Edmonton have also done studies. Nationally, the Federation of
Canadian Municipalities (FCM) also completed a report on homelessness.
The number of studies (and these are only the recent ones) supports the
assertion that the problem is one of significance and concern to a broad range
of interests.

As of October 1998, there were at least 200,000 homeless people in
Canada—people with no private spaces in which to live, people existing day
to day, twenty-four hours a day, in public places. And the situation is getting
worse. In Ontario, rental housing construction has virtually stopped, falling
from 27% of new construction in the period 1989-1993 to only 2% in 1998
(Layton, 2000, p. 79). In Toronto, 170,000 different individuals used shelters
in Toronto over the period 1988-1996 (Golden, Currie, Greaves, & Latimer,
1999, p. 26). The fastest-growing groups of homeless in Toronto are women
and children. There were more than 5,000 children homeless in 1996 and
over 100,000 people on the waiting list for social housing (Caragata & Hardie,
1999; Golden et al, 1999). In Montreal, estimates suggest there are more than
15,000 homeless people. Almost 25% of tenant households in Montreal are
paying more than 50% of their income in rent. Calgary is one of the only
Canadian cities to do an annual count of the homeless. From 1996-1998 there
was an increase of 61% in the number of homeless. Rental housing in Calgary is disappearing at an alarming rate. In Vancouver, 1,000 people a night
sleep on the street—these are the absolute homeless and this level of homelessness occurs in a province that has maintained social housing provision
even in the wake of complete federal retrenchment. In private market accommodation, one in four tenant households in Vancouver pay more than 50% of
their income on rent (Layton, 2000). A partial explanation of Vancouver's
homelessness is provided by Layton (2000): in the three-year period 1995-
1998, 3,500 rental units were converted to condominiums, while in 1998 only
fifty-eight new rental units were completed.

Homelessness is generally higher in urban settings, although it is not only
a big city problem. Barrie, Ontario, is a case in point. An hour north of
Toronto, Barrie has become a commuter town and the fastest-growing community in Ontario. Having a vacancy rate of only 1%, "Barrie has experienced
a ten-fold increase in the number of people seeking shelter over the last five
years" (Layton, 2000, p. 80). The small city of Peterborough east of Toronto
has, over the last five years, had a 100% increase in people occupying shelter
beds. Estimating the numbers of homeless is, of course, subject to the variety

of issues previously discussed. Homelessness is often hidden. If there is less social tolerance, homeless people are more likely to stay out of busy commercial areas. If, on the other hand, there is tolerance and even sympathy, the prospect of handouts make it more likely that homeless people will be visible in busy neighbourhoods. The absence of obvious street sleepers is not an indication that a community does not have a homelessness problem.

Keyes (as cited in Mulroy & Lane, 1992) classifies the homeless population into a continuum of three major groups that accord with most analyses of homelessness and identification of who is homeless. The first group is "needs housing only," the economic homeless, those who cannot compete in a private rental market to secure adequate affordable housing. Homelessness in this case derives from both an income and a housing stock problem. Increasing the income of one individual will enable him or her to compete, but overall the presence of a group of economically homeless suggests that there is not enough rental housing at the low end of the market. Developers concede that this is a group for whom they have little interest (Daly, 1996, p. 184), because the profitability of low-end market rental properties is poor. For this reason, all of the industrialized countries have had some level of postwar government intervention in the housing market for low-income people.

The second group Keyes identifies are the "situational homeless," who require housing, but also face additional difficulties such as domestic violence or medical problems. For some members of this group, homelessness was likely triggered by an acute incident, and so may not fit the profile of those we usually associate with homelessness. During some previous research (Caragata & Hardie, 1999), I interviewed a sixty-five-year-old grandmother who had lived all her married life in a home owned with her now-deceased spouse. He had died suddenly and she had no financial competence ("I could always rely on him"). By accepting the well-meaning but ill-advised help of a neighbour, she lost her house and was living in a shelter. She was too humiliated to make contact with her family. Such stories are more common than might be imagined. There are many people who cope quite well as long as nothing extreme happens, but when and if it does, they have few resources—personal, social, or financial. For many members of this group, once homeless, the resources necessary to secure and return to permanent housing are difficult to marshal. In a very tight rental market, these individuals can find it very difficult to escape from homelessness as landlords can be in a position to pick and choose among prospective tenants and will inevitably select those with more resources. (The targeted services discussed later are useful for this group. However, the availability of housing stock remains an issue.)

Keyes's third group is the "chronic homeless," who include those with chronic mental health and substance abuse issues. As Mulroy and Lane (1992) point out, this latter group's presence among the homeless is quite directly attributable to state deinstitutionalization policies and the lack of viable community-based alternatives. They are often the very visible street homeless.

Who is homeless and why?

Burke's categorization of homelessness acknowledges homelessness as a socially constructed term (as cited in Hallebone, 1997):

Table 4.1	Categories of Homelessness
Third-degree relative homelessness; inadequate housing; incipient homelessness	Housed but without conditions of "home," e.g., safety, security, other standards of adequacy.
Second-degree relative homelessness	People constrained to live permanently in single-room occupancy hotels or boarding houses.
First-degree relative homelessness	People moving between various forms of temporary shelter— hostels, friends' homes, boarding houses.
Absolute homelessness	People living on the streets, deserted buildings.

Source: E. Hallebone (1997). Homelessness and marginality in Australia: Young and old people excluded from independence. In M.J. Huth & T. Wright (eds.), International critical perspectives on homelessness (pp. 69-106). Westport: Praeger, p. 72.

Burke's categories are inclusive and make clear the boundaries that determine the various and often disputed definitions. The fact that homelessness is a continuum where the severity of both housing issues and other problems exist across a range is also made clear.

Profiles of the Homeless

Following are brief summary descriptions of some population groups who together comprise the homeless. Hundreds of books and journal articles provide in-depth analyses of each subgroup. These descriptions are meant to show the scope of homelessness and to highlight some of the less-visible populations (Glasser, 1994). I have not provided more detail on the single homeless because most often they are who we assume the homeless to be. As discussed, our constructions of homelessness and the associations we have on hearing the word usually evoke a picture of a homeless man, often with substance abuse issues. Appreciating the pervasiveness and scale of the issue requires a fuller understanding of its impact on other sectors of the population.

People of colour

In Canada, which prides itself on being multicultural and at least quasi-egalitarian, homelessness is not colour-blind. As in most industrialized countries, people of colour make up a disproportionate percentage of the homeless population. In the United States, Blacks and Hispanics are disproportionately represented. This correspondence between homelessness and people of colour is also apparent in the countries of Western Europe, although there it is an immigrant (largely from the countries of North Africa) rather than native-born population who are homeless and marginalized. In Canada, most of the people of colour disproportionally affected are Aboriginal, but the degree of racialization is much the same. Utilizing Canadian Mortgage and Housing Corporation's (CMHC) definition of core housing need, 52% of Aboriginal households fall into this category compared to only 32% of non-Aboriginal households (CMHC, 1996). One quarter of on-reserve households lack a functioning bathroom. In urban areas, Aboriginal households are almost twice as likely as non-Aboriginal households to be in core need (CMHC, 1996, p. 2). Aboriginal peoples are part of that same stream of rural-urban migration that is occurring worldwide. In 1961, only 14% of all Aboriginals in Canada were urban dwellers; by 1981 it was more than half. Because of the poverty endemic in Native communities, most of those relocating to Canada's urban centres (primarily the prairie cities) are poor. Consider, for example, the 50,000 Aboriginals in Winnipeg. According to Murphy (2000), they have the worst housing (three-quarters have problems with housing conditions), the lowest incomes (of which half is spent on rent), and are frequent victims of discrimination by landlords. Estimates suggest that half of Winnipeg's homeless are Native. In all of Canada's prairie cities, night after night, Aboriginal peoples are dramatically overrepresented among the homeless.

> Who is homeless and why?

It is not only Aboriginal peoples who experience discrimination based on notions of "race." In recent research examining social housing waiting list applications, immigrants felt they experienced discrimination in trying to obtain market housing. One man said: "No matter whether I see the apartment first, [or] how I fill in the application, they always call back and say 'Sorry' the apartment has gone to another applicant." While many applicants appeared reluctant to claim that they felt discriminated against, one man said gently, "It's the same in my country—we put my country's people first" (Caragata & Hardie, 1999). The need for larger units and the desirability of living in a community with others from their native country create further obstacles for many immigrants and refugees in the housing market. These issues are in addition to the struggle they face as a result of differences in language, customs, and culture (such as family size), as well as discrimination.

Further data has been well presented by Murphy (2000) and Daly (1996), as well as the more extensive work on issues of "race" and poverty. In summary, in most White-dominated societies a disproportionate number of those experiencing homelessness are the racialized "other."

Families with children
Caplow, Bahr, and Sternberg (as cited in Glasser, 1994) cite a classic conception of homelessness as a "detachment from society." Glasser (1994, p. 84) contrasts this with the notion of family: "the very act of being a family is an affirmation of the ability to bond." Glasser's view and the data on homeless families confirm that the issue of family homelessness derives from poverty and inadequate, affordable housing. Homeless families have reason to remain less visible. In addition to trying to ensure some level of safety and security for

their children—which is not usually possible on busy thoroughfares—they also face the constant threat of losing their children to the child protection authorities (Caragata & Hardie, 1999; Glasser, 1994). In the United States, the phrase the "new homeless" is often used to distinguish homeless families from the "old" or traditional skid-row homeless male (Glasser, 1994). There is widespread agreement that the cause of homelessness for families with young children is primarily attributable to the increased numbers of poor, usually women-headed households and to the lack of affordable low-income housing (Blau, 1992; Choi & Synder, 1999; Rossi, 1989). Thus, families remain largely in the category of the "deserving" poor, and we are more likely to suggest macro-level issues as the causes of this widespread and growing rupture in family life. This macroanalysis, if it might be called that, is very superficial as our approaches to family homelessness have differed only marginally from programs for singles.

In all three of Keyes's categories of homelessness (as cited in Mulroy & Lane, 1992), the numbers of mothers with children are increasing. Recent Canadian studies found this to be the fastest-growing group among the homeless (Caragata & Hardie, 1999; Golden et. al., 1999). In a review of social housing waiting list data in Toronto, 48% of all applicants were families with children. The number of applicant households tripled between the periods 1991-93 and 1994-96. These were years during which Toronto struggled out of a recession, and a newly elected Conservative government cut welfare rates by over 21%. These data from Toronto mirror the circumstances of low-income families across Canada, in the United States, and to a lesser degree, in Western Europe. In Canada, the income levels of Canadian women show that for single-mother-led families, obtaining affordable housing and other necessities of life will be extremely difficult. Over 98% of single parents are women (Freiler & Cerny, 1998) and almost 40% of poor children in Canada live in a single-parent, mother-led family. This number has grown from 31% in 1980. Together, women and children account for 70% of Canada's poor (Canadian Centre for Policy Alternatives, 1998, p. 33).

These statistics have both a personal face and enduring implications. Children suffer from homelessness in ways that will affect their adult lives through poor nutrition, stress, transience, and poor school attendance. As well, their lives tend to be less carefully supervised, thus putting them at greater risk of accidents and abuse. One single mother reported having to leave her children alone while she attended a community college program. She had asked for help and been refused because her program was "too intensive" (Caragata & Hardie, 1999). A family who, while homeless, lived in a shelter, reported that:

> the whole family found it easier—no constant worry over rent. We could just live. There was no space, we were on top of each other, but there was less stress. I knew I'd get the money for food and we could spend it on

food....When I [have] got a place, like now, I always worry, "Don't buy so much, don't buy meat, save the money for the rent," and there's never enough [money] for both [food and rent]. I feel like I'd rather die than tell my kids there isn't any more [food].

Who is homeless and why?

Deprivation also extends to homeless parents as they routinely give up things—including food—for the sake of their children. Burt and Cohen (as cited in Burt, 1992) report that adults in homeless families consistently eat less and less well than single homeless people. In their study a full 88% of the homeless adults with children were women.

Two additional subgroups among the homeless warrant mention. Due to space limitations, it is not possible to describe appropriately the growing numbers of seniors and youth who are homeless.[3] Welfare state retrenchment, combined with a very tight housing market, have forced seniors into unprecedented levels of homelessness. In the case of youth, causal factors also include welfare state retrenchment; most provinces deny benefits to those under eighteen and to "single employables" beyond that age. Family breakdown—fleeing violence or abuse—is often cited as the reason youth leave home. A possible explanation for the increasing numbers of youth on the street is that low-income families face heightened stress from their increased poverty—an eerie and not-too-distant parallel with poor families in Brazil or India.

Money and Housing Stock

Whatever the divergence of opinion about the causes of homelessness, there is agreement that homelessness is a problem of, in part, affordability related to housing stock and the housing market, which determines what "stock" is available and for how much money. A number of factors combine to make rental housing beyond what is affordable for many people.

Declining incomes for those at lowest income levels

As we have seen, in Vancouver one in four tenants pays more than 50% of their income on rent (Layton, 2000). In 1996, 44% of Ontario tenants had an affordability problem (defined as those paying more than 30% of their income on housing). This situation has worsened continually over the past four census periods (Canada Mortgage and Housing Corporation as cited in ONPHA & CHF, 1999). An impact of the "new economy" has been the much-reported polarization of jobs and incomes (Sassen, 1998). For those with low incomes, these changes have occurred in combination with significant welfare benefit cuts (Yalnizyan, 1997), further reducing the incomes of the already poor.

Rising rents

Rents go up with increased demand when there are fewer rental units on the market and more people wanting them, which happens when potential buyers can't afford to buy and there is an influx of new residents (growth and new household formation). Average rents in Ontario have increased about 20% since 1995 (Shapcott, 2001).

Reduced vacancy rates

Vacancy rates are very low in many urban centres across Canada because of a combination of high demand and limited supply. They are particularly low in Ontario—below 3%—which is usually a marker of a healthy rental market. In Toronto, Canada's largest city, the vacancy rate is only 1% (ONPHA & CHF, 1999).

High prices for purchased homes

If the price of home ownership goes up because house prices, interest rates, and the costs of borrowing rise, fewer people leave the rental market. Thus, the rising cost of home ownership affects the rental stock available. Because landlords discriminate against the poor, especially those on social assistance, middle-income earners do better in a tight rental market; landlords will choose tenants with more resources. Builders cite increasing building code standards as one reason for increased housing costs. They query whether we can really afford the construction standards now in place (Murphy, 2000).

Declining rental stock construction

In Canada, 30,000 rental units were begun in 1986. By 1999, only 7,000 units were built in all urban centres across the country (Murphy, 2000, p. 104). In Ontario, rental housing construction comprised 27% of all housing starts in 1989 and only 6% in 1998 (ONPHA & CHF, 1999). The reasons for this dramatic decline are complex. Murphy likens it to a strike, private sector developers citing income tax changes, lot levies, property tax issues, rent controls, and increasing building code variance and standards as all contributing to an environment in which investment in rental accommodation is simply not profitable. In reviewing these issues, Murphy concludes that although the building industry's lobby group, the Canadian Homebuilders Association, is pressing for government reductions in regulation and taxation, they make no promises about the private sector's ability to provide rental housing for low-income people (Murphy, 2000).

Non-profit housing construction stops

The year 1945 marked the beginning of the construction of public housing in Canada with the Wartime Housing Act. Thousands of small "wartime houses" can be found in cities across the country. These were followed by the now infamous large-scale public projects such as Regent Park in Toronto. In 1973 there was a further change to the National Housing Act to enable the construction of non-profit housing co-operatives. The 1970s and early 1980s saw the development of many municipal non-profit housing developers and the growth of small non-governmental organizations (NGOs) building specialized social housing. Overall, there has been small but continuous growth

of housing stock specifically geared for those tenant households who might
otherwise be at risk in a competitive rental market. Social housing has
ensured housing security to those outside the home ownership market. In
Canada, state intervention in the housing market effectively ended in 1993
when the federal government withdrew all new funding; Ontario and other
provinces followed this federal lead. In Britain, Margaret Thatcher
was well known for her contentious selling off of many "council houses" or
municipally owned non-profit stock. In this same period—during which the
Canadian federal government stopped funding social housing—other industrialized countries did the same. In much of Western Europe and, to a
lesser extent, even in the United States, this policy has now been reversed
and governments have re-entered the social housing arena.

> Policy
> responses

Canada has also recently witnessed a modest reversal, with the federal
government committing limited matching funds on a province-by-province
basis. In Ontario, subject to the requisite matching dollars being found, up to
10,000 new housing units could be built over the next five years. This initiative is open to both non-profit and for-profit developers although the former
will find it difficult to obtain matching funding without a more significant
provincial response than the $2,000 promised by the province of Ontario for
each $25,000 maximum per unit of federal funding (News Release, May 30,
2002). This initiative is encouraging, because it brings senior government
back into the development of social housing. Its more tangible impact in
enabling the construction of affordable housing remains to be seen.

Policy Responses

Jobs

Policies of "full employment," increases in the minimum wage, and public
sector employment were, over the past forty years, the labour market policies
that helped Canadians avoid unemployment and poorly paid employment
that contributes to homelessness. These were, of course, augmented by a
social safety net without the gaping holes of today. Unemployment insurance and welfare programs combined to keep most people out of extreme
poverty when labour market solutions were unavailable. In both of these
areas, benefits have been cut and eligibility narrowed. For example, from
1989 to 1994 the number of unemployed parents without Employment Insurance protection increased from 28% to 41% (Novick & Shillington, 1996), and
average weekly benefits fell by $6 (Battle, 1996). Most significant perhaps is the
change in our attitudes to unemployment. While we talked of full employment, it was always acknowledged that the capitalist marketplace requires
some level of "structural unemployment," by which is meant a mismatch
between the needs of employers and the skills and training of the labour
force. Beginning most acutely in the late 1970s with the federal introduction
in Canada of wage and price controls, and continuing through the 1980s,

higher levels of unemployment were seen as essential to preventing inflation.[4] Canada, like other industrialized countries began to target acceptable
unemployment in the low double digits. These and other labour market
changes provided the first swelling of the ranks of the permanently unemployed, generally people with the lowest skill levels.

Housing

A variety of models are in place around the world whereby governments support the construction of housing units for the poor. These models vary from
direct government construction and ongoing ownership to funding of non-
governmental organizations to build and manage units, to support for the
private market to build housing for this constituency. Early manifestations of
"public" or government-developed housing tended to be large projects that
congregated the poor and gave such interventions a bad name. Later, many
Canadian municipalities began to develop housing, usually on a smaller scale
and in better-integrated forms. Funding for these developments was shared
and reliant on high levels of federal support. Although there were real issues
of scale and lack of integration with some government-developed housing,
even these provided stable, affordable housing for many tenant households
who might otherwise be on the street. Co-operative housing and supported
housing developed by religious organizations and NGOs (usually for seniors or
special-needs groups) are models of housing construction that remain non-
profit and are an enduring part of Canada's housing stock. A number of such
projects were built on a small scale specifically to house the homeless and
have been very successful.

The private sector also used to build housing for low-income Canadians
supported by public programs, including mortgage subsidies, tax breaks, tax
shelters, and loan agreements wherein some percentage of the rental units
would be available at lower rents for a given number of years. Private sector
developers claim that the end of these incentives and overregulation, municipal lot levies, increasing building code standards, and rent controls drove
them from building rental accommodation (Murphy, 2000).

The advantage of these federally initiated new construction programs is
that they produced new housing stock that some twenty to forty years later,
continues to house low-income households. While some of these programs
were expensive, they produced a good of lasting value. Unfortunately, both
governments and the private sector increasingly plan on short-term cycles—
the upfront costs are assessed at the expense of considering the long-term
benefits.

The major policy competitor to public or social housing construction has
long been the shelter allowance. Simply put, the shelter allowance gives extra
money to eligible individuals so that they can afford private market rents.
The arguments for and against shelter allowances can be complex and are
well detailed (Murphy, 2000) and thus only briefly discussed here. A benefit
of the shelter allowance is its portability, which enables the tenant to choose

where he or she wishes to live. The subsidy can be given directly to the tenant so that the landlord need not know that the household is being subsidized. The program is easily expandable in tight housing markets, and can be readily contracted when markets ease. The level of subsidy too can be easily adjusted to take account of changes in household income or average market rents. The downside of shelter allowances is that they do not add any housing units to the marketplace. Thus, they tend to have an escalating effect on rents as more tenants compete for the same rental units. The benefits of a tight housing market and low vacancy rates continue to accrue to private market landlords. Proponents of expanded[5] shelter allowance programs have become very active as pressure to deal with homelessness increases.

The "new" focus: Services

The "New" Focus: Services

As homelessness has become both widespread and accepted, there has been a range of new policy measures directed to it. These interventions, as we have seen, have done little to ameliorate the numbers of homeless people. What has developed, in fact, is an industry of services for homeless people that do little, if anything, to address the problem of homelessness itself. If one subscribes to a macro or structural view, this will be of little surprise as real structural change confronts the ideology of the marketplace. What has been put in place are a range of extensive—but still inadequate—secondary or emergency services. The US McKinney Act (1987) is a useful illustration. It represented a national commitment to homelessness and was wide ranging, providing fiscal incentives and planning requirements for state implementation. "Unfortunately, however, most programs funded by the *McKinney Act* were meant only as short-term, emergency responses and were directed at ameliorating or managing the symptoms instead of ending homelessness by addressing systemic causes of homelessness, poverty and the lack of low income affordable housing" (Choi & Snyder, 1999, p. 26). In 1997, there was a modest amendment to the Act directed to permanent housing, but the primary emphasis remained emergency services (Choi & Snyder, 1999).

Canada has no national policy on homelessness. Instead we once had a modest national program of social housing construction. After the federal government withdrew funding for new social housing construction and most provinces followed suit, homelessness became a matter largely for municipalities to deal with using their limited resources. The downloading of this responsibility has caused policy on homelessness in Canada to mirror that of the United States. Where there are policies and programs to address the needs of the homeless, they are emergency services. Over the course of the 1980s, the US Department of Housing and Urban Development (HUD) reduced housing expenditures by over 70% (Daly, 1996, p. 174).

In Canada, Layton (2000), a Toronto city councillor and now (2003) leader of the New Democratic Party, discusses his response and strategy prompted by the death of a homeless man who froze near his own home. Layton and

The role of
theory in
understanding
homelessness

Two major
and
competing
theories

others sought city council support for an emergency phone line for homeless people in trouble, expanded cold night street patrols, expanded drop-ins and shelter beds, and formed a committee to work to prevent freezing deaths (Layton, 2000, p. 11). Other new services for homeless people support their job and apartment hunting. These services are useful, but unlikely to make a difference as adequate responses to homelessness. The housing market and vacancy rates are such that if one low-income person manages to find an affordable apartment with the aid of such support services, that person is better off, but another low-income person has lost the opportunity to occupy that unit. The funding of emergency services may also give the public a sense that government is responding and may even minimize the number of homeless people visible on the streets.

The Role of Theory in Understanding Homelessness

The theory of why people are homeless is, of course, critical to developing an adequate policy response. While some would argue that all levels of government in Canada have failed to substantively address the problem of homelessness, imagine that government was committed to eliminating homelessness in Canada. What might the "right" policies be to eradicate homelessness in Canada? An adequate answer requires research that can build theory, or (depending on one's level of adherence to positivism) the testing of theory through research. This has, of course, given rise to much research on homelessness—how many people are homeless and who they are (Burt & Cohen, 1989; Golden et al., 1999; Kozol, 1988); what causes or triggers homelessness (Golden et al., 1999; Layton, 2000; Marcuse, 1987; Rossi, 1989); the behaviours of homeless people (Carlen, 1996); their health and health histories (Bines, 1994; Pleace & Quilgars, 1996); and their stories (Kozol, 1988; Ralston, 1996). This research has produced what are seemingly quite thorough studies, but most findings have remained focused on some combination of the two theoretical perspectives described below.

> To most observers, poor people, particularly men and women not attached to family constellations, are either the "undeserving" or "unworthy poor" of old or (using the new "medicalized" vocabulary of the late twentieth century) people with severe personal pathologies. (Wagner, 1997, p. 55)

Two Major and Competing Theories

It's Their Fault

This view includes a wide range of perspectives, including the most extreme and largely ideological conviction (emanating from a liberal world view) that we are individuals responsible for our own well-being, to the extent that we are able to make choices about it. Thus, if we are hit by a car or severely disabled, our level of responsibility for the consequences will be tempered by society accepting some responsibility. However, if someone is unable to find work (and there are deemed to be jobs available) or doesn't want to work at these available jobs, the economic and social consequences facing them are seen to be of his or her own making. The extreme liberal view of absolute self-reliance has been tempered over time by extending public responsibility but usually only to those perceived as needy and/or deserving of public help. The critical question is how far such public or social responsibility extends and to whom. Usually such need is established on the basis of the vulnerability or helplessness of the claimant—the notions of the "deserving" and "undeserving" poor. Historically the "deserving" poor included children and single parents, although this view has begun to change, and those with indisputable illness or disability. Thus, the person who is ill may warrant some form of social support, while the person who does not want to work would warrant none. This range of views is associated with characterizing homelessness as deriving from individual pathology, i.e., it is the individual's fault that he or she is in this circumstance. Because no rational person would voluntarily opt for such circumstances, he or she therefore must have some deficit or shortcoming that, as Wagner in the above citation suggests, is often now medicalized. Thus, it follows, for some, that the homeless are made up of two groups: those who have some personal problem that makes them unable to function "properly," and those who are on the streets by choice. For the former group, services are already in place, although they may need some adjustment to make them better suited to the particular kinds of problems the homeless have. The basic belief is that help is available to those who really want help. The notion of choice or intentionality is given legal status in Britain where the Housing (Homeless Persons) Act of 1977 mandates local governments to provide housing for homeless people except those who are homeless as a result of "intentionality." This notion is variably interpreted sometimes to include those who lose their housing because of rent arrears, that is, they have become homeless by "intention" (Daly, 1996).

Two major and competing theories

Structural Failing

The other widely held view can be classified as the structural view: homelessness is caused by failings in our economic and social systems that leave some people without adequate money to "purchase" housing in the marketplace in which it is a commodity like any other. Our economic system needs what Galbraith (1992) refers to as the "functional underclass." "All industrial countries have one....As some of its members escape from deprivation and its associated compulsions, a resupply becomes essential" (Galbraith, 1992, p. 412). The holders of these structural views may argue about whether a first priority in addressing the issue is jobs, or the level of public assistance, or the construction of non-market housing. They are, however, in general accord that homelessness is a function of the capitalist marketplace, and that increasing neo-conservatism has slowed our collective willingness to intervene in the market. Because our housing system is a "market" system, we have an insufficient supply of specialty housing—public or social or supported housing—to meet the needs of all those who can't function sufficiently well in the marketplace to afford the market rates for housing.

These two views are, of course, not mutually exclusive and there are many subscribers to some mix of the two perspectives. More recently, there are some who have begun to contend that neither of these theories adequately and satisfactorily accounts for the problem.

An Alternative or Modified Theory: Social Exclusion

In the European literature (Pitts & Hope, 1997; Pleace, 1998; Smith & Stewart, 1997) there is a broadening acknowledgement of a phenomenon, or a set of phenomena, that have been labelled social exclusion. Perhaps the use of this term might come about only in a European context where there remains at least a history (if not more) of expectation that at some level, the homeless population was to be *included* as part of the public realm. Thus, when evidence suggests that there is a systematic, classifiable process of exclusion, it comes to society's attention. The theory being developed to explain these phenomena argues that homelessness is not a problem that requires a policy response but is a symptom of another more complex dilemma. Thus, we hearken back to Blanco's (1994) notion of social problems as social constructions and the need to deconstruct or tease out what the "real" problem might be.

In a North American context, the focus of policy attention is more narrowly on homelessness and tends toward the individual pathology end of the spectrum—the increasing number of services already described. What is meant by the phrase "social exclusion"? Does it have merit as a way of thinking about what we call homelessness?

Bryne (1995, p. 95) suggests that the term "underclass"—used to characterize a broad group that would include the homeless—has increasingly been utilized (to explain both the phenomenon and the particular people in it) to infer a "combination of the 1960s concept of the culture of poverty and the identification of the dependence-inducing character of income maintenance programmes." This usage by the new right has caused others to abandon the term, not wishing to invoke these same associations. In querying the term and what it signifies, Bryne and others do not wish to suggest that this phenomenon—a group seemingly without critical ties to the social and economic system, often even without enduring personal ties—is not real or in need of research. Quite the contrary. The change in our social and economic structures—that there is a large, seemingly permanent group relegated not only to the economic sidelines but the social and political as well—has warranted further scrutiny. The European literature has settled on "social exclusion" as a descriptor that is now utilized by governments as well as academics and activists.

What does such exclusion look like? What are its implications? There have always been people who don't work, for whom jobs are difficult to get or hang on to. Some of these people—largely men, as for most of the period of industrialization women were not expected to work outside the home—were the traditional inhabitants of skid row, occupying the offices of casual labour pools when economic necessity required it. Most often, such people drifted in and out of work. They may have been, in the "medicalized" parlance of today, "poorly attached," usually single and sometimes without permanent housing. Others, though, followed these same work patterns, but were strongly established in their working-class neighbourhoods where they may have boarded or rented a room. Except during the Depression of the 1930s, they were in relatively small number. What appears to have happened now is that such minimal attachment, the lack of a meaningful stake in the community, is experienced by a diverse range of people of all ages, many different backgrounds, and even levels of education (Choi & Snyder, 1999). This exclusion is not just from the labour force; it is pivotal. Much of our social engagement stems from having money—it affects the neighbourhood we live in, the schools our children attend, where we shop and what we buy—all of these things are more spatially segregated by income than was the case fifty years before. (In the cities of forty and even thirty years ago, we all shopped, for example, in the stores located "downtown." Think now of the strategically located shopping malls and the stores in them which target the neighbourhood income level. No dollar stores will be found in the malls of exclusive neighbourhoods. Our jobs also determine our social locations, which in part, because of this spatial separation, are much less integrated. Our social networks are very likely to be based in these residential or work communities and these have been demonstrated to be important in helping us maintain our social and economic position—staying "included." Our social activities too are more market-based. Thus, those describing social exclusion claim that it is both powerful and self-reinforcing (Caragata & Skau, 2001). Central to the notion of social exclusion are social and spatial separation—not only by class, money, status, etc., but also a more profound exclusion from the social order of things. "It is not simply a matter of the group being poor but it is separated from mainstream society so that it cannot access general social life and crucial social goods, especially education in schools, on the same terms as the rest of us" (Bryne, 1995, p. 97). As education has historically been the door to upward mobility (Kaus, 1992), without such access the permanence of these divisions is reinforced.

Concluding thoughts: Combined, multilevel responses

Concluding Thoughts: Combined, Multilevel Responses

We must consider what might be adequate policy solutions. They must address the structural elements—housing and income—but also pay atten-

Concluding
thoughts:
Combined,
multilevel
responses
tion to social *in*clusion, social engagement. Because this, too, has become structurally and spatially shaped, it will not be an easy task.

Continued demands must be made of the federal government in Canada to resume its leadership role in supporting the construction of affordable housing. Part of this role must be creating incentives for provincial involvement. All types of housing models should be explored; many NGOs have developed innovative, cost-effective examples. Private sector involvement should also be encouraged and building codes must be re-examined. In the postwar housing crisis, many families built their own homes and were given time to bring them up to building code standards.

Job creation is critical and the role of job creation programs and public sector employment should be re-examined. Many of those who are currently homeless do work or have worked when other support services were in place to facilitate their getting to work. A national daycare policy, such as was once envisioned for Canada, would do much to enable families, including those who are mother-led, to earn incomes.

Social assistance levels must be high enough to enable recipients to secure housing that will be sustainable in the long run. A single mother of three I interviewed paid over $900 per month for rent out of a benefit cheque of under $1,400 (Caragata & Hardie, 1999). She had been homeless before, and with that percentage of expenditure on rent, it was clear she would be again.

An emergency service in Vancouver caught my attention recently because it offered courses to its users—not in life skills or resumé preparation—but in philosophy and the classics, taught voluntarily by university professors. These are unlikely offerings because we assume a hierarchy of human needs—that those on the streets are unlikely to want intellectual engagement. Such assumptions reinforce the exclusion of the already marginalized. If living on the street is now part of one's ongoing expectations, then every possible enrichment would seem in order. The Vancouver experience seems successful, as are other diverse efforts at re-engaging those who are excluded. These include political and social action (an Ontario example is Low Income Families Together (LIFT), which demonstrates the impact of such activity on the participants as they gain voice and confidence and focus attention on the needs of low-income families). Other efforts include neighbourhood associations that have been successful in regaining control of what were once violent or unsafe areas, and various self-help housing associations in which homeless people contribute their skills to developing their own housing solutions.

Many other examples could be provided, but instead I will reiterate the principle issue. If we recognize homelessness to be symptomatic of this larger problem of social exclusion, then we have a new set of considerations to undertake in planning a policy response.

Notes

1 Hostels, or indeed welfare, might be seen to fulfill this safety net function, but they do not. In the first case, because hostels are not housing (i.e., they are temporary, crowded, and without personal space), many homeless people would rather avoid them, even if it means "sleeping rough." Welfare rates may technically be high enough to enable the client to obtain rental housing (although they are often inadequate, even technically), but they do not factor in competition for the small number of affordable units and the likelihood of welfare clients systematically losing out to more affluent applicants for a rental unit.

2 About 17% of all Canadians live below the poverty line—a shocking statistic. For Native peoples, the number doubles; over one-third of Canadian Aboriginal peoples live below the poverty line (Murphy, 2000).

3 For more information on homeless youth and an excellent bibliography, see van der Ploeg and Scholte (1997). For information on homeless seniors, see Rich, Rich, and Mullins (1995).

4 For a more complete discussion of these issues, see McQuaig (1995).

5 The reference to the expansion of such programs acknowledges that many welfare programs in effect operate a shelter allowance by varying the benefit level up to a certain maximum depending on the actual rent paid by the client.

6 The US welfare changes are an illustration of such change as with time-limited eligibility, some women and their children will simply run out of public support.

7 Space limitations prevent an expanded discussion on this important point. For an excellent discussion of this issue, see Kaus (1992).

8 On the notion of social networks and how they support our social position, see the extensive work of Barry Wellman.

References

Battle, K. (1996). *Precarious labour market fuels rising poverty.* Ottawa: Caledon Institute.

Bines, W. (1994). *The health of single homeless people.* York: Centre for Housing Policy, University of York.

Blanco, H. (1994). *How to think about social problems.* Westport, CT: Greenwood Press.

Blau, J. (1992). *The visible poor: Homelessness in the United States.* New York: Oxford.

Bryne, D. (1995). Deindustrialization and dispossession: An examination of social division in the industrial city. *Sociology, 29*(1) (February), 95-15.

Burt, M. (1992). *Over the edge: The growth of homelessness in the 1980's.* New York: Russell Sage Foundation.

Burt, M.R. & Cohen, B.E. (1989). *America's homeless: Numbers, characteristics, and the programs that serve them.* Washington, DC: Urban Institute Press.

Canada Mortgage and Housing Corporation (CMHC). (1996). *Research and Development Highlights, 27*(August).

Canadian Centre for Policy Alternatives. (1998). *Alternative federal budget papers 1998.* Ottawa: Author.

Caragata, L., & Skau, B. (2001). A chip in the Canadian veneer: Family and child poverty as social exclusion. *Social Work and Social Science Review, 9*(1), 36-53.

Caragata, L., & Hardie, S. (1999). *Social housing waiting list analysis: A report on quantitative and qualitative findings.* Prepared for Mayor's Action Task Force on Homelessness, City of Toronto.

Carlen, P. (1996). *Jigsaw: A political criminology of youth homelessness.* Buckingham, UK: Open University Press.

Choi, N.G., & Snyder, L.J. (1999). *Homeless families with children.* New York: Springer.

City of Toronto. (1995). *Report of the alternative housing subcommittee.* Toronto: Author.

References   Daly, G. (1996). *Homeless.* New York: Routledge.

Dear, M., & Wolch, J. (1987). *Landscapes of despair: From deinstitutionalization to homelessness.* Cambridge: Polity Press.

Freiler, C., & Cerny, J. (1998). *Benefitting Canada's children: Perspectives on gender and social responsibility.* Ottawa: Status of Women Canada.

Galbraith, J.K. (1992). The functional underclass. *Proceedings of the American Philosophical Society, 136*(3), 411-415.

Glasser, I. (1994). *Homelessness in global perspective.* Toronto: Maxwell Macmillan International.

Golden, A., Currie, W., Greaves, E., & Latimer, E.J. (1999). *Taking responsibility for homelessness: An action plan for Toronto.* Report of the Mayor's Homelessness Action Task Force. Toronto: City of Toronto.

Government of Ontario. (1999). *Safe Streets Act.* Toronto: Author.

Greve, J. (1971). *Homelessness in London.* Edinburgh: Scottish Academic Press.

Hacking, I. (1999). Teenage pregnancy: Social construction? In J. Wong & D. Checkland (Eds.) *Teen pregnancy and parenting: Social and ethical Issues* (pp. 71-80). Toronto: University of Toronto Press.

Hallebone, E. (1997). Homelessness and marginality in Australia: Young and old people excluded from independence. In M.J. Huth & T. Wright (Eds.), *International critical perspectives on homelessness* (pp. 69-106). Westport: Praeger.

Jeffrey, H. (1999). *The construction of homelessness as a social problem: Linking contributing factors, mediating factors, and interventive strategies.* Unpublished MSW thesis.

Kaus, M. (1992). *The end of equality.* New York: Basic Books.

Kozol, J. (1988). *Rachel and her children: Homeless families in America.* New York: Crown.

Layton, J. (2000). *Homelessness: The making and unmaking of a crisis.* Toronto: Penguin/McGill Institute.

McLaughlin, M.A. (1987). *Homelessness in Canada: The report of the national inquiry.* Ottawa: Canadian Council on Social Development.

McQuaig, L. (1995). *Shooting the hippo.* Toronto: Penguin.

Martin, C. (1996). French review article: The debate in France over social exclusion. *Social Policy and Administration, 30*(4), 382-392.

Marcuse, P. (1987). Why are they homeless? *The Nation,* (April 4), 426-429.

Mulroy, E.A., & Lane, T.S. (1992). Housing affordability, stress and single mothers: Pathway to homelessness. *Journal of Sociology and Social Welfare, 19*(3), 51-64.

Murphy, B. (2000). *On the street: How we created the homeless.* Ottawa: J. Gordon Shillingford.

News Release. Canada and Ontario sign affordable housing program agreement. (2002, May 30). Online at <www.johnmanley.ca/en/newsroom/p_affordable_may30.htm>.

Novick, M., & Shillington, R. (1996). *The progress of Canada's children.* Ottawa: Canadian Council on Social Development.

Ontario Non-profit Housing Association (ONPHA) & Co-operative Housing Federation of Canada (CHF). (1999). Where's home? A picture of housing needs in Ontario. Toronto: Ontario Non-profit Housing Association.

Pitts, J., & Hope, T. (1997). The local politics of inclusion. *Social Policy and Administration, 31*(5), 37-58.

Pleace, N. (1998). Single homelessness as social exclusion: The unique and the extreme. *Social Policy and Administration, 32*(1), 46-59.

Pleace, N., & Quilgars, D. (1996*). Health and homelessness in London: A review.* London: King's Fund.

Ralston, M. (1996). *Nobody wants to hear our truth.* Westport, CT: Greenwood.   **References**

Rich, D.W., Rich, T.A., & Mullins, L.C. (1995). *Old and homeless—double jeopardy.* Westport, CT: Auburn House.

Rossi, P.H. (1989). *Down and out in America: The origins of homelessness.* Chicago: University of Chicago Press.

Sassen, S. (1998). *Globalization and its discontents.* New York: Free Press.

Shapcott, M. (2001). *Housing and the 2001 Ontario Budget.* Toronto: Co-operative Housing Federation of Ontario.

Smith, D., & Stewart, J. (1997). Probation and social exclusion. *Social Policy and Administration, 31*(5), 96-115.

Springer, J.H., Mars, J.H., & Dennison, M. (1998). A profile of the Toronto homeless population. In A. Golden et al. (Eds.), *Background Papers, Vol. II.* Toronto: City of Toronto.

van der Ploeg, J., & Schlote, E. (1997). *Homeless youth.* London: Sage.

Wagner, D. (1997). Reinterpreting the undeserving poor. In M.J. Huth & T. Wright (Eds.), *International critical perspectives on homelessness* (pp. 55-68). Westport, CT: Praeger.

Yalnizyan, A. (1997). *The growing gap.* Toronto: Centre for Social Justice.

5

Single Motherhood in the Canadian Landscape: Postcards from a Subject[1]

Iara Lessa

Motherhood carries such consensual approval that the word is commonly used to represent issues that convey undisputable support and acceptance. But what does this consensual approval bring with it? A recent study (Save the Children Foundation, 2001, p. 4) shows important differences underneath the superficial consensus by classifying ninety-four countries according to their treatment of "the women who are raising the world's future generations." Although studies like this one, using average indicators, tend to make invisible the detail of how different groups fare within a country, they are important for highlighting some general trends, brief messages that fit in a postcard. For example, Canada was placed in seventh place behind Sweden, Norway, Denmark, Finland, the Netherlands, and Switzerland. Rich countries such as the United Kingdom and the United States ranked tenth and eleventh, pointing out the fact that national wealth alone does not guarantee the health and well-being of mothers and children. The treatment of mothers depends, no doubt, on the resources available, but it is, above all, one of the clearest indicators of a country's commitment to equity, social justice, and well-being of its populations. Furthermore, importance and meanings of motherhood vary not only with national boundaries but also with the different groups in which the mother may be classified; that is, for example, according to her racialized location, social class, sexual preference, and mental or physical abilities.

A detailed look at motherhood in Canada, as in other parts of the Western world, requires a careful examination of their most vulnerable group of mothers: the single mothers. Changes in the family form and the redefinition of the family as an institution have been at the core of the discussions regarding the nature of these societies. Single mothers are, in these locations, widely studied and highly polemicized, prompting many of the debates regarding their social welfare traditions. As enduring and controversial as the welfare system itself, the single mother is one of its most popular images. As the single mother is a threat to the assumptions of the traditional family or a promise of women's independence from male control or, even because of the challenges single motherhood poses to the universalization of the wage-

worker subject, social interventions addressing single mothers, directly or
indirectly, have been at the centre of a discussion regarding the public management of a future society and the socialization of its members.

In this chapter I will discuss not the single mother as a given and independent being but the formation of a group of women called single mothers,
and its changing meanings and sustenance as it is manifested in Canada.
Although these women come from a variety of social locations and life circumstances, through many processes, their social identity becomes essen-
tialized as mothers raising children alone. This discussion calls attention to
the nature of single motherhood and its relationship with social welfare, and
focuses on the ways society problematizes certain population groups and
makes them the object of collective provision. Its conceptual underpinnings
can be situated in a body of literature inspired by Foucault's work and loosely
called governmentality for its interest in exploring the contexts in which
government of self and others take place (see Dean, 1999). The chapter
starts with a classification of the various issues associated with single mothers to arrive at a rather broad definition of this group. It then proceeds to
examine the several policies that contributed to shaping and defining single
motherhood in Canada. Finally, it will describe and discuss contemporary
policies and issues associated with single mothers and their relationship with
the dignity, social justice commitment, and equitable resources distribution
in society.

Defining perspectives (margin note)

Defining Perspectives

The term "single or lone mother" gained currency during the 1960s, unifying
a variety of situations that until then were understood as different and isolated, for example: the death of the father, the abandonment of the family
by the husband, a birth out of wedlock, a divorce or a separation. The term
consolidated within one group the war widow with young children, the
deserted mother, the divorced mother, the separated or married mother with
absent husband, the displaced homemaker, the battered wife, the adolescent mother, and multiple other characterizations of many women's lives,
which have been, throughout the twentieth century, the focus of particular
social policies and strategies. This large group of women, independent of
their class, race, religion, sexual preference, country of birth, physical and
mental abilities, or any other descriptor, became defined by one sole aspect
of their lives: the absence of a father in their family unit. While in the United
States the term is also highly racialized, in Western societies in general,
single motherhood in itself implies a set of social attributes and makes the
lives of poor women raising children alone the subject of public scrutiny and
attention.

The ideal of the male breadwinner, dependent wife, and children as the
basic unit of society has inspired a system that reproduces and reinforces
this form of family through a complex of ideas and practices (e.g., Gordon,

1990). The social organization of Western societies and the functioning of their capitalist economic systems assumes a basic family unit that has been shaped according to specific class, race, gender, and heterosexual assumptions as the core of production and reproduction of resources (e.g., Cossman, 1997). Families that deviate from it, such as the one constituted by the woman who is raising children alone, are considered incomplete and problematic. Single mothers become the feared others, outside the normality of the ideal, problematized through reference to social norms regarding the private family responsibility for maintenance, care, and upbringing of their children (see Gordon, 1994).

In the face of this normalized family ideal, the mention of single mothers in the Western world invokes a variety of tightly woven social expectations, values, and judgments. These are both echoed and fuelled by professional and scientific discourses that cast this group of women as a social problem (see Harding, 1993a, 1993b). The problems they seem to represent are as diverse as the many individual portraits of single mothers themselves. They seem, nevertheless, to converge around three general arguments—individual characteristics, structural circumstances, and moral imperatives (see also Seccombe, James, & Walters, 1998)—which, although not mutually exclusive, characterize the common discourses regarding single motherhood.

A first set of arguments sees single motherhood as a problem characteristic of particular individuals or groups, such as Blacks in the United States, who, as argued by Amott (1990), were forced into a tradition of customary family separations under slavery. This association persists despite the fact that in 1996 African Americans constituted only 36% of welfare recipients (Seccombe, James, & Walters, 1998, p. 850). Another group currently associated with single motherhood is comprised of teenage unwed mothers and young divorcees. In Canada there are reports that this group is growing, and increasingly these mothers are choosing to raise their children themselves rather than pursuing adoption or abortion (Clark, 1993). This group is widely assumed to be unprepared for motherhood and doomed for dependency on state support despite evidence to the contrary (Davis, McKinnon, Rains, & Mastronardi, 1999). They are commonly pathologized (see Horowitz, 1995) and portrayed in the media as deviant and as symbols of the decline of social order and discipline (e.g., Hewlett, 1986; Schamess, 1990). As part of these arguments some authors have constructed an explanation of single motherhood in which certain families have developed a set of "sub-cultural"(see Seccombe, James, & Walters, 1998) or "underclass" values (see Leung, 1998) as a result of living for prolonged periods in social marginalization. Therefore, single-mother families are not only a problem for the present but also a reminder of the exponential growth of these problems with their intergenerational consequences for the future: some arguments propose that offspring from single-mother families are "more likely to drop out of school, be unemployed, and themselves form mother only families than are children who grow up with two parents" (Garfinkel & McLanahan, 1986, p. 11-12).

The structural argument invokes the prevalence of poverty and associ-   **Defining**
ated stresses among single mothers (e.g., Lero & Brockman, 1993; McDaniel,   **perspectives**
1993). Although not all single mothers are poor, a large group of the poor
seem to be single mothers. For example, in 1998, 54% of all single mothers in
Canada were poor, with the rate for those under twenty-five reaching 85%; for
single mothers with two children under seven years old it was 87% (National
Council of Welfare, 2000). Resting on feminist and political economy explanations, authors using this argument (e.g., Kitchen, 1992) discuss the structural barriers to women obtaining stable, well-paid jobs; the demands of
contemporary standards of living that require, most often, two incomes per
family; the domestic division of labour; and women's disadvantaged situation in the labour market. Consequently single mothers are associated with
low income, housing difficulties, and dependency on state support (e.g., Milar,
2000). Single mothers' poverty is also seen as significantly affecting their children's academic, behavioural, and emotional situation (e.g., Hetherington,
Camara, & Featherman, 1983), as well as being a risk to adolescents' health
and adaptation (Hamburg, 1993; Russell & Ellis, 1991). These arguments are
variously explained by a combination of less parenting time, extreme stress
and duress, absence of father figure, impoverished living environment, and
less than adequate housing situations (Amato, 1999; Gringlas, 1995).

The third set of general arguments regarding the problematics of single
motherhood—the moral arguments—proposes that fatherless families are
a problem to the institution of the family, threatening to break down and dis-
organize this basic unit of society (Morgan, 1995). In the United Kingdom,
Green (1993, p. vi) suggests that the traditional family is the foundation of
freedom because in it children "learn voluntary restraint, respect for others
and sense of personal responsibility." Reflecting the deep patriarchal roots
of Western society, single-mother families, in this argument, embody the fears
and concerns about the changes in the family and the relationships between
the genders (see discussion in Eichler, 1997). In this sense lone mothers are
portrayed as a growing threat to the foundation of liberal societies and constitute the preferred target for groups advocating the return to traditional
ways (e.g., Richards, 1997). Single motherhood, thus, has been used as one
of the reasons to attack sex education, divorce laws, abortion, obscenity,
homosexuality, and contraceptives (see Somerville, 1992).

These understandings of single motherhood as a problem for social
organization have generated an urgency for change and heated discussions
throughout the affluent West. These discussions have profoundly linked single motherhood with the welfare state, and hence accorded particular roles
for the state and the market in the allocation of resources and in the formulation of solutions to the problems associated with it. For the Western idea of
welfare, single mothers embody a particularly conflicting combination of
roles in modern societies: they are responsible for children's upbringing and
socialization, but, at the same time, they are also responsible for supporting
the family. In other words, they are mothers and workers or caregivers and

breadwinners (Evans, 1992). On one hand, as mothers raising the future generation, they should be supported in order to adequately carry out their social
reproduction functions. On the other hand, they must be socially discouraged in order to discourage the numbers of those entering single motherhood and to limit the costs to the system. Ellwood (1988) has argued that
availability of financial and other benefits tends to encourage single parenthood and consequently just increases the problem. More conservative commentators have charged that the support of single mothers is a disincentive
to marriage and family life (Gilder, 1982; Murray, 1984) and actually causes
single motherhood (Richards, 1997). Many feminist authors argue in favour of
an extensive web of supports for single motherhood, citing evidence that as
many as 40% of Canadian women may experience single motherhood at
some time in their lives (Desroisiers, le Bourdais, & Lehrhaupt, 1994) and that
income support is usually a transitional state: 41% of the women who received
social assistance income in 1994 also had paid employment at some point
during the year (Scott, 1998). To map the nature of what we call single mother
is, hence, to touch on the very processes that constitute the complex set of
relations and interactions embedded in the implementation of social care—
the welfare system and our society as a whole.

I propose that we approach single motherhood as an assemblage of ideas,
knowledges, expectations, beliefs, judgments, and assumptions about women
raising children without a male partner. This assemblage represents relations
of power; that is, it represents ways of acting upon these women that bring
about relations among individuals. Some women become socialized into single motherhood through a series of rationalities and practices directed at
poor women raising children alone but also aimed at the well-being of the
population of a nation as a whole. As such single mothers are not a given,
ahistorical or universal. They are located in a specific time and place, in constant change, and profoundly bound to collective values, social policy, and
practices.

Thus, discussing single motherhood in Canada necessarily involves
reviewing the social policies that help to create a variety of power relations to
produce a concrete group of women who, despite their various circumstances, represent a challenge to the social understandings of the family. This
discussion involves not only the actual policies but also their motivations
and intentions, as well as the contexts and practices that help to translate
those into actions. The next section proposes a broad periodization of policies
addressing single motherhood in Canada and discusses how they shaped
contemporary understandings of women who raise children alone. Its starting point is not who single mothers are or what their needs are but how they
were made to be; how it became thinkable to support mothers in their child-
raising activities; and what forms these practices took. The focus, hence, is not
on a coherent and simplified statistical profile but on an intricate way of governing social well-being that creates particular ways of life with implications
for society as a whole.

Three Broad Periods

Three broad
periods

Paying for Mothers' Caring Work

While single motherhood is not specific to an economic class, it is primarily the poor ones who became a social concern and in need of financial support. Support to mothers constituted, both in Canada and in the United States (see Gordon, 1994), the first experience with direct public financial aid for a group. Previously there was no concerted social policy addressing women who raised children without a male partner, but a series of traditions and conventions with old roots undertaken by individuals, institutions, organizations, and local governments. In Britain, the Poor Laws called for different treatment for widows, deserted, and unmarried mothers, and these traditions, although not implemented throughout Canada, influenced the charitable approaches to these women during the nineteenth and early twentieth century until the institution of Mother's Allowance by the provinces after World War I.

Many factors contributed to the widespread acceptance of supporting poor mothers. Paid motherhood was one of the various reforms advocated by the late nineteenth- and early twentieth-century women's movement across Western nations, which also included women's suffrage, birth control, sexual freedom, child welfare, labour reform, civil rights, and other demands (Comacchio, 1999; Gordon, 1994). Paid motherhood was proposed as a way of preventing the dissolution of family ties and attending to the plight of dependent poor children. It stressed the importance of enabling women to dedicate themselves to child socialization. As articulated at the time, these arguments implied support for a gender division of labour with the male worker being paid a family wage, and defined motherhood by White middle-class standards of citizenship, class relations, gender differences, race, and national identity (Little, 1995).

By World War I in Canada, the growth of slums, infant mortality, crime, and disease became increasingly associated with the instability of the family and support for motherhood received widespread sanction. Suffragists, such as Nellie McClung, argued for greater appreciation of women's maternal qualities and more humane values, while Leacock, for example, emphasized female weakness, questioning women's ability to support themselves and their families on their own (Strong-Boag, 1979). Mother's Allowance legislation in Canadian provinces was also influenced by events during the 1914-1918 war: the images of poor widows and their children popularized the need for the propagation of a physically and morally fit generation to inherit the nation. Examples of public interventions were provided by the implementation of the mothers' aid programs in some of the American states and, as well, by support provided by the Canadian Patriotic Fund and local experiments by Local Councils of Women.

Three broad
periods **Mother's Allowance (1916-1964)**

Mother's Allowance was the first instance of provincial governments accepting responsibility for the welfare of a specific group of people and committing themselves to their support (Struthers, 1994). Manitoba (in 1916) was the first province in Canada to pass legislation granting an allowance to poor widows. By 1920 the western provinces and Ontario had similar legislation in place, and by the 1950s all provinces had some form of support for these mothers (Little, 1998). Particularly important is the fact that provinces and municipalities were paying mothers without means of support to stay at home to look after their children, thus supporting caring work and family life, and recognizing the importance and value of motherhood and its effects on a healthy citizenship. From the onset, as we shall see next, they were characterized by restricted domestic supervision, categorical eligibility, stringent moral requirements, and meagre financial support.

Grounded in their White, middle-class Protestant origins, women's organizations and social service leaders, who came to dominate the Mother's Allowance campaign, modelled the program on their own charitable initiatives, insisting on stringent eligibility criteria and enforcing their own values as standards. While supporting poor mothers, women in these organizations also saw for themselves a role in the public world defined by a career in family management using professional tools for the direction of mothers of the lower classes, whom they regarded as deviant and distressed. The programs were organized around arguments about individual or group characteristics separating selected categories of mothers from all other mothers and making their private family matters a public concern. They initially supported primarily poor widows with at least two dependent children, but gradually eligibility criteria were extended to include various categories of excluded poor mothers alone: wives of incapacitated men, deserted women, foster mothers, mothers with only one child, divorcees and officially separated mothers, wives of criminals in prison, unmarried mothers, as well as previous residents of other provinces and immigrants. These sequential enlargements of eligibility criteria were the result of struggles by the excluded group and those who spoke for them (social workers and women's groups). This process of negotiation left its mark on the program by simultaneously maintaining its categorical nature and increasing the total number of beneficiaries. By the 1960s most provinces did not place restrictions on the causes of single motherhood, but arguments regarding fathers' or male partners' responsibility for their families continued to be important mechanisms of exclusion from benefits.

In addition, mothers were subjected to stringent tests of destitution and thriftiness, as well as moral investigations in order to be admitted and to continue in the program (Strong-Boag, 1979). Supervision of mothers regarding their motherhood expertise, their household management, and their moral fitness were central characteristics of Mother's Allowance programs through-

out their existence. They incorporated an understanding of individual cir-   **Three broad**
cumstances of the families, but imposed on them a grid of priorities elected   **periods**
by the program values and objectives: healthy habits, children's upbringing,
satisfactory home environment, budgeting and management, and moral fitness (Lessa, 1999). In so doing the programs defined these priorities as indicators of good motherhood, shaping it according to the class, race, religion,
sexuality, and gender of investigators and administrators.

The type and amount of support varied, but, with the caseloads soaring,
financial support maintained one constant aspect: provincial obsession with
cost containment. The provinces only reluctantly accepted the responsibility
for the well-being of families with a female head, and the programs were
residual and partial. The women and their families were kept in the most
abject poverty. In-kind and tagged benefits consisted of medical and dental
assistance, support for fuel and winter clothing, and, in some cases, emergency funds were incorporated into the allowance as a discretionary practice resulting from advocacy and the recognition of inadequacy of benefits.
Financial support, reflecting a fear of discouraging industriousness, was contingent on assessments of need and constrained by strict ceilings. The
allowance was never sufficient to raise a family, even by the most modest
standards, and women were expected, initially, to supplement it with
approved work. The major real supplementation to Mother's Allowance, however, was the Family Allowance, a universal benefit established by the federal government in 1944 (Kitchen, 1987).

In sync with the development of Western capitalism, a focus on work,
during the Mothers' Allowance period (1916-1964), grew to dominate the discourse of the programs, gradually eroding their initial valuing of caring activities. In the process of building the Canadian post-World War II welfare state,
transfer of federal funds for provincial social programs became contingent on
the employable-unemployable dichotomy (Hum, 1987), and existing provincial programs addressing subjects under different deserving categories
changed to benefit from these funds. Mothers raising children without men
were recast under this dichotomy: these women, rather than being seen as
important to the nation because of their motherhood role, started to be
defined (in the different policy proposals of the time) primarily in relation to
their participation in the labour market. Their motherhood duties were rein-
terpreted as an obstruction to entering the labour force rather than as a necessary job, as previously articulated. These were important transformations in
the meaning of motherhood within the welfare system in Canada: poor mothers' activities and duties became understood differently from those of other
mothers. Although in earlier periods, the Mother's Allowance beneficiary was
prompted to work to supplement the allowance, in the postwar period she
gradually become a category of the unemployable because of her family
responsibilities. Her unemployability started to be rigidly defined by the programs through a limit in the number of hours she was permitted to work. In

Three broad
periods
this sense Mother's Allowance ceased to be primarily a reward for an *ability* to do child raising with employment supplementation and supervision, and became essentially a provision attending to a *deficiency* impeding full-time employment (Lessa, 1999).

Canada Assistance Plan (1966-1996)

The introduction of the Canada Assistance Plan (CAP) in the mid-1960s is a marker for the consolidation of the transformations in social policy approaches to poor women raising children alone. These transformations provided the possibility for integrating the provincial Mother's Allowance programs within a national welfare system and its financing. CAP marks the maximum expansion of the Keynesian postwar welfare state in Canada. It captured and crystallized a change in the understanding of the importance of motherhood reflected in Mother's Allowance and the emergence of a different attitude toward women raising children alone. Their eligibility for social support was rationalized through the perception that their caring work constituted an obstacle to their participation in the labour force. Many of these mothers were, in fact, "unemployable" not only because of motherhood obligations but also because of their lack of paid work experience, limited skills, the cumulative effect of living in poverty for years, and the structural results of devaluing traditional women's jobs. While some of these trends also affected married women, who by the 1960s began to enter the labour force in large numbers, in the two-parent family, the mother's income from work was but a complement to her husband's. Within the families of women raising children alone, earnings from work were the sole source of support, and when they supplemented the allowance, these earnings were controlled and deducted from the benefit received. Faced with benefits eroded by inflation, an economic recession that made supplementation through paid work very difficult, and extremely high shelter costs, women raising children alone became the main image of the newly discovered feminization of poverty.

Under the CAP umbrella, provincial Mother's Allowance programs were integrated into the national system of welfare, consolidating a number of federal and provincial programs—Unemployment Assistance, Old Age Assistance, Blind Person's Allowance, Disabled Person's Allowance, and Mother's Allowance—into a single 50/50 cost-sharing arrangement between the governments. Provincial residency requirements were dropped and standard responsibilities were imposed on all provinces. Reflecting contemporary progressive discussions regarding poverty amid the postwar wealth (see Struthers, 1994), benefits were proposed in terms of human rights and their calculation conditioned to a particular definition of needs. CAP gave women who raise children alone the legal right to benefits, thus empowering different groups of mothers and individuals to demand dignity and adequate living standards (Evans, 1996).

The discourse of needs and rights, however promising, carried only a **Three broad periods** rhetorical weight. CAP turned away from the causes of poverty as the justification for support, implying that women who raise children alone were no longer among the categories of deserted, widowed, wives of incapacitated men, unwed mothers, and others, performing the valuable caring work under acknowledged difficult circumstances. They would be supported under the generic financial need of the unemployable subject, which reflects a more universal formulation of deservedness than the previous categories could. Implementation of the program, however, maintained the traditions of the Mother's Allowance program: eligibility under categorical definitions, similar definition of needs, and emphasis on supervision of mothers. The discourse of rights was further eroded when considering the promised mechanisms of appeal, which were not consistently or independently established in all provinces.

Paradoxically, accompanying the discourse of rights and dignity of the poor, the implementation of programs for poor single mothers under CAP was marked by low levels of benefits and increasingly intrusive practices. The provincial programs showed a complete dissociation between the expectations levied and the means provided by the benefits, which were below the poverty line in all provinces. The paltry amounts of the benefits (constantly eroded by inflation) and the regulation (not only of home life but also of the type and hours of work) maintained single mothers' marginal status in society. As the number of divorced mothers increased with the Divorce Act of 1968, Little (1998) points out, the lives of women raising children alone were scrutinized, their contact with men was carefully monitored, and cohabiting mothers became the target of extreme regulations. The racial and class assumptions embedded in the education and supervisory activities of Mother's Allowance, as well as judgments regarding morality and respectability of the recipients, were incorporated into the new practices under CAP through home visiting by welfare caseworkers (Little, 1994).

Under CAP preventive services and employment training also received federal cost sharing, and the social services sector expanded enormously through the provision of personal services to poor mothers. Preventive services, provided primarily by a variety of dispersed, private, non-profit social services agencies, delivered what is known as personal services in a model that made integration and coordination difficult. In addition, many of these services were conceptualized through individualistic assumptions, which dissociated them from general poverty measures and drove a wedge between financial and personal needs of poor mothers. Furthermore, professional discourses, as well as the increased costs in standards of living and consumption of goods, created additional barriers to poor mothers' ability to care adequately for their children by raising child rearing requirements and developmental knowledge (Callahan, 1991). These circumstances—hopeless poverty, intrusiveness of benefits, the individualistic nature of preventive services and

Three broad periods

the changes in child rearing practices—combined to establish a common set of individual characteristics attributed to mothers receiving preventive services funded under CAP: low self-esteem, anxiety, guilt, and inability to manage their families under increasingly demanding child care requirements.

CAP also emphasized employability, which constituted, perhaps, its most striking legacy for single motherhood. Provincial governments seized upon this opportunity and experimented with a variety of different training and support programs varying from education advice to significant supports for voluntary participation in employment schemes (Evans, 1992; Snyder, 2000). The latter could include providing benefits such as housing subsidies, dental care, and daycare, which were substantial contributions to poor women's standard of living and gave strong encouragement to join the labour force. By the end of the 1980s, these programs occupied an increasingly central place in the government agenda in an attempt, as discussed by Evans (1996), to transform the single mother into a worker modelled after the ideal of the independent male breadwinner. They overlooked the structural forces that locked women in low-paying jobs and, in fact, few poor mothers could escape poverty even with full-time employment. These women were in a weak position in the marketplace since the already low salaries, and the number and quality of entry-level jobs were declining, as well as the chances for improvement through training, individual mobility, or collective bargaining. In addition, the absence of a childcare program made it impossible for women to work for the low wages offered to the abundant pool of unskilled labour. The possibilities for training were reduced due to devaluation of professions and tasks traditionally dominated by women, which were performed under deteriorating conditions. While employment constituted a banner of the women's movement and has substantially improved the lives of middle-class professional mothers, their sisters raising children alone in poverty found in the banner of employment just another mechanism for transferring the responsibility for structural inequalities to them.

The failure to transform poor single mothers into self-sufficient workers resulted in them being further pathologized and blamed. They were increasingly seen under the influence of neo-conservative arguments as difficult to employ, incompetent learners, and unable to keep a job for a lengthy period. However, as of the mid-1980s, despite the failure of the employment programs, work requirements grew increasingly mandatory and the amount of time women could stay on benefits was reduced (Baker, 1997). Conditions for single mothers deteriorated even further with an economic depression that devalued benefits through inflation and a cutting of expenditures that followed a wave of government reforms. In addition the universal Family Allowance, which, since World War II, had complemented Mother's Allowance, was, in 1993, replaced by the Child Tax Benefit, which functions as a work incentive for the working poor. After a variety of cuts, CAP was finally eliminated in 1996 and replaced by the Canada Health and Social Transfer (CHST).

The CAP period generated small material improvements for women rais- **Possibilities**
ing children alone: a right to benefits based on needs, but implemented **for the**
through regulations and practices derived from Mother's Allowance; attention **present**
to labour market issues through employment programs, which transferred
to poor mothers much of the burden of curbing gender inequities; and expansion of preventive personal services grounded in individualistic assumptions.
Nevertheless, the mothers' own understanding of themselves and their situation was radically changed from the supplicant and grateful widow of the
early twentieth century. Single mothers, living in public housing projects,
receiving benefits as a single category of unemployable for family reasons,
and bombarded with a professional and media discourses that harmonized
their predicaments, gained a sense of group identity and were the object of an
intensified level of feminist action regarding women's needs. In a variety of
settings and occasions they were vocal in demonstrating the impossibility of
their situations and their image became the symbol of society's unfairness
toward the deserving subject. They achieved priority in public housing waiting lists (Lessa, 1999), consultation status in support services, a voice in the
movements against injustices and inequality, and leadership roles in organizations and campaigns (Andrew & Rodgers, 1997). While the women grouped
under this category developed an agenda of rights and demands under different groupings, they have also defined alternative directions for society as
a whole. In this sense they are used, by some (see Orloff, 1993), as a catalyst for
struggles regarding the issues of social citizenship and the right to form an
independent household without the risk of poverty, violence, or marginalization.

Possibilities for the Present

The new federal program, the CHST, comes in the form of block funds for
health, postsecondary education, and social assistance, while continuing the
trend of reducing federal contributions to social programs (Carniol, 2000). It
belongs to a much changed political landscape from that of the 1960s, which
created CAP. The postwar welfare state and its commitment to full, White
male employment are no longer in place, and a neo-conservative political
agenda has promoted the dynamics of economic recessions, the mobility of
capital and labour, global competition and technological innovations to
implement radical changes on the nature and management of the national
state. Neo-conservative emphasis is on efficiency of service delivery and har-
monization of the social and political conditions within national barriers to
facilitate trade, as well as reinforcement of the traditional institutions of society such as the two parent, heterosexual family. CHST gives the provinces the
leeway to spend federal funds without central standards, allowing criteria for
receiving social benefits to be established by the provinces themselves. The
new program eliminates the previously required rights of appeal, and in most
provinces benefits to single mothers became conditional upon acceptance of

specific types of training, low-paying, unattractive work or workfare. The result was a profound change in the social and political life of Canada (Day & Brodsky, 1998), entrenching the punitive and rash measures many provinces had been experimenting with and eliminating the discourse of rights based on needs. CHST marks a new recasting of single motherhood in Canada.

In 2001 women headed 83.6% of all lone-parent families, representing 13% of all census families in Canada. Their total number (1,111,116 families) grew by 3.1% in 2000-2001 compared to 0.9% for all census families (Statistics Canada, 2001). In this same year, the welfare income of single-parent families as a proportion of the poverty line was a low of 48% in Manitoba to a high of 73% in Newfoundland and Labrador. In Ontario this proportion was 59% for a single parent with one child (National Council of Welfare, 2002). These drastically low incomes reflect the harsh treatment of provincial income policies. Policies and initiatives during the CAP years had consolidated the departure from the assumptions of caring for children as reason for entitlement in itself and streamlined social support under the universal deserving subject: the worker. Under the CHST a mother who was a sole breadwinner continues to face bleak employment prospects (Schellenberg & Ross, 1997), her benefit levels were cut, eligibility was restricted, work was made compulsory (Shragge, 1997), and, rather than social transfers or programs, staying married became the best guarantee against poverty for women (Lochhead & Scott, 2000). And entering into a marital relationship is the best chance single parents have to lift their children out of poverty (*The Daily*, 1999). As conditions in the labour market continue to deteriorate, cuts to social assistance programs have had the biggest impact on lone parents (Scott & Lochhead, 1997) who were made increasingly dependent on the separated or divorced partner's support payments (Baker, 1997; Hunsley, 1997). In addition, under the banner of preventing crime and violence, children and youth came under increased surveillance, bringing to the fore an emphasis on effective parenthood, which further blamed mothers for the lack of options society offers for its future generations (Chen, 2000).

These changes were accompanied by the institutionalization of demeaning everyday practices, such as Ontario's snitch line, decreasing support for housing and daycare, and forced disclosure of the father's name, along with public discussion of the cost of single motherhood to the public purse (Little, 1999). All of these are damaging to a person's dignity, self-esteem, and public image and characterized these women as incompetent mothers who produce children costly to society. Their treatment by social systems is permeated with suspicion, disrespect, and the utmost contempt. The press documents single mothers being taken to court over minor rent issues (Philp, 2001a), complete denial of any benefit (Philp, 2001b), and being placed in out-of-town motels rooms (Sarrick, 1999). "One third (32%) of all single mother households were food insecure to some extent and 28% reported their diet had been compromised." (*The Daily,* 2001). Their lives are made miserable: single mothers have debts, restricted expenditure on basic items, lack of choice in housing and neighbourhood, and are unable to have things that other families take for granted, such as holidays, toys, new clothes, and sports equipment. These women have feelings of shame, concealment, and chronic depression.

Possibilities for the present

As a result, the single mother is no longer seen as a special worker who needs supports to re-enter the job market but as someone trying to cheat society's goodwill and the universal requirement of work, a marginalized outcast, a scourge who causes trouble and suffering. Negative stereotypes are frequently associated with them: they are alleged to be lazy, unmotivated, and dependent; they are accused of getting pregnant to qualify for benefits and sitting idly at home (Little, 1998). Further, social policy interventions have attempted to address the problems of single mothers through the subjectivity and body of the women raising children alone: reformation of the self, emotional support, and parenting training are the urgent activities accompanying limited financial support. Such derogatory treatment suggests that women raising children alone, as scourges, have been made a humiliating example to the social body, illustrating the price to be paid for non-compliance with normality. They are used to legitimize the idea that only integration in the labour market can prevent poverty and marginalization. From their confined social location, women raising children alone are used as postcard images for the rest of society: they generate an effect of chill and surveillance, enforcing and normalizing assumptions about individual opportunities, eroding commitment to collective responsibility, and discouraging demands that challenge a social organization based on the nuclear family, a gendered division of labour, and income exclusively based on employment.

They have, therefore, a paradigmatic importance for social policies: talking about single mothers is also talking about the very fabric and workings of the social organization. Understanding single motherhood not as the problematic condition of a group of people but as a web of relations of power allows for an analytical emphasis on the social policies and practices that shape the lives of women in this marginalized location. Addressing single motherhood involves, hence, combining ways to confront the ingrained effect of structural forces, with prioritizing the value of caring work and the different situations, preferences, and concerns of these mothers. Some alternatives have urged the definition of a new citizenship (Lister, 1997) or of entitlement based on human rights (Pearce, 2000), which, having the single mother as a barometer, encompassed not only work issues—jobs, education and training articulated with a wage policy—but a variety of conditions to care for children and a diversity of housing options. While these calls may be ambitious and fixed in face of the fluidity and changing nature of single

Note

References

motherhood, they may prompt alternatives in the form of programs and supports that, as proposed by Lister (1997), promote women's independence, in the context of relationships of interdependence, allowing women raising children alone to signal welcome news of the ethics of collective care and social justice.

Note

1 Research for this chapter was supported by a National Welfare Fellowship from the government of Canada and by the dean of the Faculty of Community Services at Ryerson University. Colette Agaliotis has worked on compiling material on CHST. My work has benefited from the comments and support of innumerable colleagues, among whom I would like to thank Akua Benjamin, Ben Carniol, Cynthia Comacchio, Henry Parada, Ian Skelton, and Anne Westhues in particular.

References

Amato, P.R. (1999). Parental involvement and children's behaviour problems. *Journal of Marriage and the Family, 61*(2), 375-385.

Amott, T.L. (1990). Black women and AFDC: Making entitlement out of necessity. In L. Gordon (Ed.), *Women, the state, and welfare* (pp. 280-98). Madison: University of Wisconsin Press.

Andrew, C., & Rodgers, S. (Eds.). (1997). *Women and the Canadian state.* Kingston: McGill-Queen's University Press.

Baker, M. (1997). Women, family policies and the moral right. *Canadian Review of Social Policy, 40,* 47-64.

Callahan, M. (1991). A feminist perspective on child welfare. In B. Kirwin (Ed.), *Ideology, development and social welfare: Canadian perspectives* (pp. 137-156). Toronto: Canadian Scholar's Press.

Carniol, B. (2000). *Case critical: Challenging social services in Canada* (4th ed.). Toronto: Between the Lines.

Chen, X. (2000). Is it all neoliberal? Some reflections on child protection policy and neo-conservatism in Ontario. *Canadian Review of Social Policy, 45-46,* 237-247.

Clark, S.M. (1993). Support needs of the Canadian single parent family. In J. Hudson & B. Galaway (Eds.), *Single parent families: Perspectives on research and policy* (pp. 223-237). Toronto: Thompson Educational Publishing.

Comacchio, C.R. (1999). *The infinite bounds of family: Domesticity in Canada, 1850-1940.* Toronto: University of Toronto Press.

Cossman, B. (1997). Family inside/out. In M. Luxton (Ed.), *Feminism and families: Critical policies and changing practices* (pp. 124-141). Halifax: Fernwood

The Daily (24/04/1999). *Low income among children.* Ottawa: Statistics Canada

The Daily (15/08/2001). *Food insecurity in the Canadian household.* Ottawa: Statistics Canada.

Davis, L., McKinnon, M., Rains, P., & Mastronardi, L. (1999). Rethinking child protection practice through the lens of a voluntary service agency. *Canadian Social Work Review, 16*(1), 103-116.

Day, S., & Brodsky, G. (1998). *Women and the equality deficit: The impact of restructuring Canada's social programs.* Ottawa: Status of Women Canada.

Dean, M. (1999). *Governmentality: Power and rule in modern society.* London: Sage

Desroisiers, H., le Bourdais, C., & Lehrhaupt, K. (1994). *Vivre en famille mono parentale et en famille recomposée: Portrait des Canadiennes d'hier et d'aujourd'hui.* Montréal: Institut National de la Recherche Scientifique.

Eichler, M. (1997). *Family shifts: Families, policies, and gender equality.* Toronto: Oxford University Press.

Ellwood, D.T. (1988). *Poor support: Poverty in the American family.* New York: Basic Books.

Evans, P. (1992). Targeting single mothers for employment: comparisons from the United States, Britain, and Canada. *Social Services Review, 66*(3), 378-398.

Evans, P.M., & Wekerle, G.R. (Eds.). (1997). *Women and the Canadian welfare state: Challenges and change.* Toronto: University of Toronto Press.

Evans, P. (1996). Single mothers and Ontario's welfare policy: Restructuring the debate. In J. Brodie (Ed.), *Women and public policy* (pp. 151-171). Toronto: Harcourt.

Garfinkel, I., & McLanahan, S. (1986). *Single mothers and their children.* Washington, DC: Urban Institute Press.

Gilder, G. (1982). *Wealth and poverty.* London: Buchan & Enright.

Gordon, L. (Ed.). (1990). *Women, the state, and welfare.* Madison: University of Wisconsin Press.

Gordon, L. (1994). *Pitied but not entitled.* New York: Free Press.

Green, D.G. (1993). Editor's foreword to the second edition. In N. Dennis, & G. Erdos (Eds.), *Families without fatherhood* (2nd ed.), (pp. vi-vii). London: IEA Health and Welfare Unit.

Gringlas, M. (1995). The more things change: single parenting revisited. *Journal of Family Issues, 16* (1), 29-53.

Hamburg, D.A. (1993). The American family transformed. *Society, 30* (2), 60-69.

Harding, L.F. (1993a). "Alarm" versus "liberation"? Responses to the increase in lone Parents—part 1. *Journal of Social Welfare and Family Law, 2,* 101-112.

Harding, L.F. (1993b). "Alarm" versus "liberation"? Responses to the increase in lone parents—part 2. *Journal of Social Welfare and Family Law, 2,* 174-184.

Hetherington, E.M., Camara, K.A., & Featherman, D.L. (1983). Achievement and intellectual functioning of children in one parent households. In J. Spence (Ed.), *Achievement and achievement motives* (pp. 205-284). San Francisco: W.H. Freeman.

Hewlett, S.A. (1986). *A lesser life: The myth of women's liberation in America.* New York: William Morrow.

Horowitz, R. (1995). *Teen mothers: Citizens or dependants?* Chicago: University of Chicago Press.

Hum, D. (1987). Working poor, the Canada Assistance Plan, and provincial response in income supplementation. In J.S. Ismael (Ed.), *Canadian social welfare policy* (pp. 120-138). Kingston: McGill-Queen's University Press.

Hunsley, T. (1997). *Lone parents' incomes and social policy outcomes.* Kingston: School of Policy Studies, Queen's University.

Kitchen, B. (1987). The introduction of family allowance in Canada. In A. Moscovitch & J. Albert (Eds.), *The benevolent state* (pp. 222-241). Toronto: Garamond Press.

Kitchen, B. (1992). Framing the issues: The political economy of poor mothers, *Canadian Woman Studies, 12* (4), 10-15.

Lessa, I. (1999). Restaging the welfare diva: Case studies of single mothers and social policy. Unpublished PhD dissertation, Wilfrid Laurier University.

Lero, D., & Brockman, L.M. (1993). Single parent families in Canada: A closer look. In J. Hudson & B. Galaway (Eds.), *Single parent families* (pp. 91-114). Toronto: Thompson Educational Publishing.

Leung, L.C. (1998). *Lone mothers, social security and the family in Hong Kong.* Aldershot, UK: Ashgate Publishing.

Lister, R. (1997). *Citizenship: Feminist perspectives.* London: Macmillan Press.

References   Little, M.H. (1994). "Manhunts and bingo blabs": The moral regulation of Ontario single mothers. *Canadian Journal of Sociology, 19*(2), 233-247.

Little, M.H. (1995). The blurring of boundaries: Private and public welfare for single mothers in Ontario. *Studies in Political Economy, 47* (Summer), 89-109.

Little, M.H. (1998). *No car, no radio, no liquor permit: The moral regulation of single mothers in Ontario, 1920-1997.* Toronto: Oxford University Press.

Little, M.H. (1999). Limits of Canadian democracy: The citizenship rights of poor women, *Canadian Review of Social Policy, 42,* 59-76.

Lochhead, C., & Scott, K. (2000). *The dynamics of women's poverty in Canada.* Ottawa: Status of Women Canada.

McDaniel, S.A. (1993). Single parenthood: Policy apartheid in Canada. In J. Hudson & B. Galaway (Eds.), *Single parent families* (pp. 203-212). Toronto: Thompson Educational Publishing.

Milar, J. (2000). Lone parents and the new deal. *Policy Studies, 21*(4), 333-345.

Morgan, P. (1995). *Farewell to the family?* London: Institute of Economic Affairs.

Murray, C. (1984). *Losing ground.* London: Basic Books.

National Council of Welfare. (2000). *Poverty profiles, 1998. National Council of Welfare Reports, 113.* Ottawa: National Council of Welfare.

National Council of Welfare. (2002). Welfare incomes, 2000 and 2001. *National Council of Welfare Reports, 116.* Ottawa: National Council of Welfare.

Orloff, A.S. (1993). Gender and the social rights of citizenship: The comparative analysis of gender relations and welfare states. *American Sociological Review, 58* (June), *303-328.*

Pearce, D. (2000). Rights and wrongs of welfare reform: A feminist approach. *Affilia, 15* (2), 133-152.

Richards, J. (1997). *Retooling the welfare state.* Toronto: C.D. Howe Institute.

Russell, C.D., & Ellis, J.B. (1991). Sex-role development in single parents households. S*ocial Behavior and Personality, 19*(1), 5-9.

Save the Children Foundation. (2001). *State of the world's mother.* Westport: Author.

Schamess, G. (1990). Toward an understanding of the etiology and treatment of psychological dysfunction among single teenage mothers: Part 1, a review of the literature. *Smith College Studies in Social Work, 60* (2) (March), 153-168.

Schellenberg, G., & Ross, D.P. (1997). *Left poor by the market: A look at family poverty and earnings.* Ottawa: Centre on International Statistics, Canadian Council for Social Development.

Scott, K. (1998). *Women and the CHST: A profile of women receiving social assistance in 1994.* Ottawa: Canadian Council on Social Development and Status of Women.

Scott, K., & Lochhead, C. *(1997). Are women catching up in the earning race?* Ottawa: Canadian Council on Social Development.

Seccombe, K., James, D., Walters, K.B. (1998). "They think you ain't much of nothing": The social construction of the welfare mother. *Journal of Marriage and the Family, 60*(4), 849-865.

Shragge, E. (Ed.). (1997). *Workfare: Ideology for a new under-class.* Toronto: Garamond Press.

Somerville, J. (1992). The new right and family politics. *Economy and Society, 21*(2), 100-20.

Snyder, L. (2000). Success of single mothers on social assistance through a voluntary employment program. *Canadian Social Work Review, 17*(1), 49-68.

Statistics Canada. (2001). *Annual demographic statistics* (catalogue no. 91-213). Ottawa: Statistics Canada.

Strong-Boag, V. (1979). "Wages for housework": Mothers' allowances and the beginnings of social security in Canada. *Journal of Canadian Studies, 14*(1), 24-34.

Struthers, J. (1994). *The limits of affluence: Welfare in Ontario, 1920-1970.* Toronto: University of Toronto Press.

References

Additional Resources

Comacchio, C.R. (1997*). The infinite bonds of family, domesticity in Canada 1850-1940.*Toronto: University of Toronto Press. From a historical perspective, this book provides an important summary of the changes in ideas and roles of the family in early 20th-century Canada.

Gordon, L. (1994). *Pitied but not entitled.* New York: Free Press. Constitutes an exceptional analysis of single motherhood in the United States.

Little, M.J.H. (1998). *"No car, no radio, no liquor permit": The moral regulation of single mothers in Ontario, 1920-1997.* Toronto: Oxford University Press. This book provides a comprehensive description of the Mothers Allowance program in Ontario, providing extensive documentation about the lives of women raising children alone.

<http://www.statcan.ca>: Statistics Canada's Web site is the most important source of empirical data about single mothers in Canada. In addition to census data they publish periodical booklets addressing specific groups among which single mothers figure prominently.

<http://www.canadiansocialresearch.net>: This site offers a comprehensive array of links to policy and discussions about children, families, and youth in Canada.

6

Workfare

Linda Snyder

Workfare is a relatively new and highly controversial policy alternative in Canada. The term "workfare" is a contraction of "work for welfare" and refers to programs that require welfare recipients to participate in work and related activities in order to receive financial assistance (Evans, 1993). Welfare attempts to address the problem of insufficient income for individuals and families to meet their basic needs. Workfare, as a contemporary form of welfare tied to work, has arisen from a neo-conservative ideology that reformulates welfare assistance as a disincentive to employment. Controversy has arisen precisely because of this shift away from the problem of meeting people's basic needs to addressing what some policy makers believe is a pervasive disincentive to work. Ontario, in 1997, was the first Canadian province to formally introduce workfare; Quebec's practice, since the early 1990s, of providing lower benefits to recipients not participating in employment programs, as well as Alberta's rate reductions in 1993, were, however, earlier examples of the same eligibility restriction policy.

Key Concepts

Several concepts important to an understanding of the topic of workfare need to be clarified at the outset.

Social assistance, more commonly known as "welfare," is the government program that provides a minimal income to people "in need." Eligibility requirements are specified in relation to reasons for being "in need"—reasons such as lack of employment, family breakdown, and inability to work. For example, employable people applying for assistance due to lack of employment have always been required to actively seek employment and to accept any work that they are physically capable of doing. Social assistance is an important component of Canada's social safety net along with universal programs (such as Old Age Security) and insurance programs (such as Employment Insurance). However, it is the "program of last resort" after recourse to the market and all other legitimate sources of income have been sought. Provincial and territorial governments are responsible for the provision of social assistance, although in some provinces this responsibility is delegated to municipalities and First Nations' councils.

Employment strategies to reduce welfare expenditures have been conceptualized by Martin Rein (1974) as comprising three fundamental approaches. The income incentives strategy promotes employment by exempting a portion of earned income in the calculation of social assistance benefits. The service strategy encourages independence through direct services such as job search assistance and training programs and through indirect supports such as help with child care and transportation costs. The third strategy of eligibility restrictions, which uses sanctions such as loss of benefits for non-compliance, is the strategy underlying workfare. More recent conceptualizations distinguish between "carrots" and "sticks." The carrots are human resources strategies, sometimes called human capital development models, that parallel Rein's incentives and services strategies; the sticks are workfare programs, sometimes referred to as labour force attachment models, that parallel Rein's restrictive strategies (Finnie, 2000; Torjman, 1996).

The term "workfare" has come to have a very elastic meaning (Peck, 2001). Its strictest definition is "work for welfare" referring to programs that require welfare recipients to perform unpaid work for designated organizations in order to receive financial assistance (Gorlick & Brethour, 1999). A broader definition is commonly used, however, which implies mandatory participation in a range of designated employment-related activities along with sanctions, such as reduced assistance, for non-compliance (Pulkingham & Ternowetsky, 1998; Torjman, 1996).

The notions of the "deserving" and the "undeserving poor" have their origins in the British Poor Laws, which distinguished between the "deserving" poor who were unable to work due to age or infirmity, and the able-bodied "undeserving" poor, who were set to work as a condition of relief. The principle of "less eligibility" has the same historical roots and refers to the stipulation that those in receipt of public relief be less well off than those earning minimum wages in the paid labour market.

The "employable" category of social assistance eligibility refers to able-bodied, working-age recipients who must actively seek employment in order to qualify for assistance. The definition of "employable" is particularly relevant to single parents receiving social assistance who, in earlier days, were exempt from job search requirements because of their child care responsibilities but, with the advent of eligibility restriction strategies such as workfare, are now considered employable unless they have young or disabled children.

Social Assistance Recipients and Their Realities

The number of people across Canada who were receiving social assistance in 2000 is estimated to be slightly over two million (Canada, Human Resources Development Canada [HRDC], 2001). However, the total numbers include dependent children, disabled people, and others who would not be categorized as "employable" and, therefore, should not be included in a count of Canadians subject to workfare expectations. The "other" category includes people with temporary medical conditions that prohibit employment, foster parents, elderly people who don't meet residency requirements for Old Age Security, and refugees who have not been granted permission to work in Canada. In March 1997, the composition of the welfare caseload according to reasons for assistance was: job-related 45%, disability 27%, single parent 14%, and other 14% (National Council of Welfare, 1998).

Employable recipients without work or without full-time work at a level of earnings to meet their families' needs must continue to search for gainful employment in the competitive labour market. Income from social assistance varies by province and other factors such as family size, but, in all cases, leaves people living well below Statistics Canada's Low Income Cut-Off (LICO). For example, the 1998 median annual income (including basic assistance plus other "income-tested" benefits provided through the tax system such as the federal Child Tax Benefit, the GST credit, and provincial tax credits) for a single employable person was $5,533 and for a single parent with a two-year-old child was $12,588; in comparison, the 1998 Statistics Canada LICO, for a city with a population of 500,000 or more, for a single person was $16,472 and for a family of two was $22,327 (National Council of Welfare, 1999).

In addition to the economic assaults of poverty, people living on social assistance must live with the stigma and stereotypes associated with receipt of welfare. This stigma has been heightened through the public vilification of the poor by politicians attempting to persuade the electorate of the necessity of the workfare policy. Two of the most popular myths propagated are the misconception of laziness and the fallacy of dependency. Providers of employment services, meanwhile, have been well aware of clients' desire to find work and become independent of social assistance and of the reality that employment programs are usually oversubscribed (Lalonde, 1997). Furthermore, increases in social assistance caseloads are more closely related to levels of unemployment than to social assistance rates—applying for social assistance is a matter of need, not choice (Mitchell, 2000b).

These stresses affect physical and emotional well-being, relationships within the family, child development, and opportunities to participate fully as citizens within the social and political life of the community.

Social Values at Stake

Judgments concerning what values are at stake depend upon one's ideological perspective. Mullaly (1997) has illuminated the core values in the various paradigms (neo-conservative, liberal, social democratic, and socialist) across the ideological spectrum.

The dominant ideology, evident globally in the discourse concerning international trade and locally in policy decisions favouring workfare, is the neo-conservative perspective. The neo-conservative position upholds the

values of freedom, individualism, and inequality, and it advocates a mini- **Social values**
malist role for the state (Mullaly, 1997). Freedom is held to be a natural right **at stake**
and an absolute principle, more important than other ideals such as distributive justice. Individualism leads to the conceptualization of many conditions, which would otherwise be considered social issues, as problems with
individual causes that are best managed through self-reliance and family
responsibility. Inequality is considered an essential incentive for innovation
and effort. The most important role of the state, in this perspective, is to
ensure the freedom of the market.

From the neo-conservative ideology emanate the neo-liberal economic
policies which include elimination of trade barriers, decreased public spending, and deregulation (World Bank, 1995). Transnational corporations and
international investors benefit enormously, under the "free-market" model,
from this reduction in both the costs and constraints to their operations.
Through their relocation and investment leverage, they have pressured governments worldwide to adopt the neo-liberal policies. Thus, we find, in many
of the nations that had developed advanced welfare state programs in the
postwar period, the imposition of workfare programs and the residualizing of
welfare (Peck, 2001).

The emphasis of the neo-conservative perspective upon individual
responsibility and culpability is unmistakable in the rhetoric promoting workfare. As Peck notes in his cross-national study:

> Discourses of "welfare dependency" that construct the causes of poverty
> and un(der)employment in terms of individual failings and that legitimate
> distinctively antiwelfare restructuring strategies are fast becoming staples
> of the political orthodoxy...particularly where neoliberal economic ortho-
> doxies are most heavily entrenched. (Peck, 2001, p. 11)

In Canada, Jim Struthers (1996) finds the same emphasis in four recurring
themes throughout workfare's history: that workfare follows major structural
change in the economy, that it occurs in response to high welfare caseloads,
that it is "part of a wider campaign of suspicion and punitive administrative
practices directed against those on welfare," and that it

> represents an attempt to shift the causal location of persistently high lev-
> els of unemployment away from structural changes within the economy
> and towards the inner moral character or values of the victims of these
> changes. Simply put, workfare seeks to return to the oldest distinction in
> social policy history—between the deserving and undeserving poor.
> (Struthers, 1996, p. 7)

Similarly, in relation to the United States, Nancy Rose (1995, p. 1) identifies
the rationale for the workfare initiatives as: "drawing on negative stereotypes
of recipients...and justified by arguments that 'welfare dependency' should
be replaced by the 'independence' that comes from working for wages."
Describing the 1990s as an intensification of processes begun in the 1980s,

Rose (1995, p. 150) writes: "Ignoring structural causes of poverty, a 'culture of poverty' analysis diagnosed 'welfare dependency' as a disease that could be cured by absorbing American values of 'work, self-reliance, and family.'" Even the naming of the 1996 legislation, the Personal Responsibility and Work Opportunity Reconciliation Act (PRWORA) is very telling.

The "work ethic" and "family values" are central to the neo-conservative emphasis on individual responsibility. The preservation of the "work ethic" has been paramount in social assistance policies since their origin in the Elizabethan Poor Laws. The principle of "less eligibility" ensured that social benefits remained lower than remuneration from paid work. However, in recent years, maintaining this principle has become increasingly difficult with the low level of wages and the hefty work-related costs of child care and transportation. Thus, Rose (2000) suggests, the more punitive workfare requirements have become necessary. Mink (1998, p. 4) similarly documents that, in the United States, "the broad support for disciplinary welfare reform is rooted in the view that mothers' poverty flows from moral failing." She finds the reforms that followed Clinton's promise to "end welfare as we know it" an outrageous assault on women's equality and citizenship rights, and claims, "We do indeed need to end welfare—but as poor single mothers experience it, not as middle-class moralizers imagine it" (Mink, 1998, p. 134).

Social democracy, with its emphasis on the values of equality, freedom, and collectivism (Mullaly, 1997) stands in stark contrast to the ideology of neo-conservatism. It is the paradigm that is most closely aligned with the values of the social work profession and its fundamental principles of humanitarianism and egalitarianism (Canadian Association of Social Workers, 1994). Social work responsibilities, flowing from these principles, include respecting human dignity and people's right to self-determination. Clearly, workfare policies that are based on negative misconceptions of social assistance recipients and that enforce compliance with mandatory participation requirements through sanctions are at odds with social work principles and responsibilities. An examination of outcomes of various employment strategies including workfare will reveal, as Lightman (1995, p. 153) has pointed out, that the promotion of workfare "has more to do with values, norms, and ideology than any rational or empirical assessment."

Alternatives Attempted

Policy alternatives to encourage independence from social assistance through employment have been attempted as voluntary programs emphasizing incentives and services and as mandatory programs using the eligibility restrictions of workfare. Examples of voluntary programs in Canada will be described before looking at examples of workfare programs in Canada and other countries.

Voluntary Employment Programs

In Canada an extensive social safety net was woven during the twentieth century. Numerous social and economic rights ratified by the United Nations were enshrined in Canadian legislation such as the Canada Assistance Plan, which guaranteed the right to income when in need and the right to work that is freely chosen (Morton, 1998). Workfare strategies were ineligible for federal cost-sharing until the repeal of the Canada Assistance Plan in 1996. Thus, from 1966 to 1996, primarily incentive and service strategies were prevalent.

Incentive strategies are currently being examined in British Columbia and New Brunswick in a federally funded experiment managed by the Social Research and Development Corporation (SRDC). The Self-Sufficiency Project provides a substantial supplement (equal to half the difference between the participant's earnings and approximately $35,000) for up to three years to single parents who leave social assistance for full-time employment. Results thirty-six months after participants entered the study show a continued greater likelihood of employment for program participants, a 68% increase in the proportion of program participant families with incomes above the Statistics Canada LICO, and no net cost to government (Social Research and Development Corporation, 2001). Incentive strategies have been utilized in other Canadian provinces, although none to the scale of the Self-Sufficiency Project. In fact, the Supports to Employment Program (STEP) introduced in Ontario in the 1980s is currently being downscaled under Ontario Works—the "variable exemption" which allowed recipients to retain 25% of earnings above the "flat rate exemption" has been reduced to 15% after one year and to 0% after two years (Mitchell, 2000a).

Service strategies were abundant in Canada prior to the implementation of workfare. Ontario's Employment Support Initiative (ESI), a voluntary program begun in 1983, assisted single parents with a range of pre-employment programs and with the cost of child care and transportation. A provincial evaluation in 1988, using matched comparison groups, found that ESI participants were less likely to be on social assistance, more likely to be in school or job training, more likely to work full-time, and received higher hourly rates of pay than the comparison group (Ontario, Ministry of Community and Social Services, 1988). A later evaluation of ESI conducted a four-year follow-up of clients who entered the program in 1985-1986 and found a small but positive impact: "57.6% of ESI clients were off [social assistance] by December 1989 compared to 54.3% of the adjusted comparison group—a net impact of +3.3%" (Porter, 1991, p. 39). The researcher makes a very interesting comparison with seven US studies, where mandatory elements were being introduced, which also found a net impact of 3.3%.

In one Ontario municipality, a longitudinal study was conducted of a voluntary employment program that assisted single parents with employment preparation as well as child care and employment-related expenses.

Alternatives
attempted
Outcomes of participants who completed up to five years by 1995 were examined. The study found that involvement in the program and, in particular, participation in the program's career planning and job search components, along with the clients' previous employment experience, were more significant in predicting employment and/or exiting social assistance than personal demographics or child factors (Snyder, 2000).

Workfare Strategies

An international survey completed under the auspices of the Organisation for Economic Co-operation and Development (OECD) identified the introduction of welfare-to-work programs in several member countries during the 1990s with considerable differences in the measures introduced:

> On the one hand the United States, the United Kingdom and Australia have each introduced compulsion to certain parts of their welfare-to-work programs. This involves imposing a requirement on unemployed people to undertake activities to improve their employability or to carry out work of community benefit in return for welfare payments. The term "workfare" is sometimes used to describe this approach. On the other hand, many of the continental European countries in particular are quite strongly opposed to the idea of suppressing existing welfare benefits in order to induce a person to take work. They nonetheless share a focus on the "activation" of support. For example in France and Italy there is a strong emphasis on job creation measures through social enterprises and the creation of new activities of community benefit. (OECD, 1999a, p. 11)

Australia has established a principle of a "mutual obligation," requiring employable people who receive public assistance to participate in an additional activity such as training or volunteer work while they search for employment (OECD, 1999a). In Switzerland, as well, social assistance clients in some jurisdictions must now meet workfare requirements (OECD, 1999b). Thus, Peck (2001, pp. 74-75) notes that: "In the 'liberal' welfare states, such as the United States, Canada, Australia, Switzerland, and the United Kingdom, where means testing and limited social transfers reflect a vision of welfare as necessarily subordinate to market allocation, workfare strategies have been at their most developed."

The United States introduced mandatory participation in employment services in the 1980s and work-for-welfare expectations in the 1990s. However, the most radical reform to date is found in the Personal Responsibility and Work Opportunity Reconciliation Act (PRWORA) of 1996 (Straits, 1999). It ended the Aid to Families with Dependent Children (AFDC) program as well as the federal entitlement to welfare and replaced it with a system of block funding to the states under the new Temporary Assistance to Needy Families program (Rose, 2000). President Clinton had campaigned in 1992 on a platform to "end welfare as we know it," but found himself facing a Republi-

can Congress who wanted to end welfare altogether (Abramovitz, 2000). The
PRWORA is the harshest of restrictive eligibility strategies, combining the
existing workfare requirements with a lifetime limit of sixty months of social
assistance.

In Canada, the implementation of workfare strategies became more frequent with the repeal of the Canada Assistance Plan and its replacement with
the Canada Health and Social Transfer block funding regime in 1996. Although
there are some parallels with the legislative and funding changes in the United
States in the same year, it is important to discern that while Canadian legislation now permits workfare, US legislation now requires it.

The current strategies in place across Canada have been documented by
Gorlick and Brethour (1998a, 1999). In their overview document, Gorlick and
Brethour (1998b) distinguish between "welfare-to-work" and "workfare" programs, indicating that the provinces and territories appear to have defined
workfare as requiring a recipient to work in an unremunerated job (not primarily intended as on-site training) in order to continue receiving social assistance. The researchers note that most of the provinces and territories insist
that their welfare-to-work programs are not workfare programs, with the
exception of Ontario, which describes its Community Participation component as workfare. However, across the country, a much more coercive
approach is apparent than was evident in the earlier employment programs.
Most of the provinces and territories now have active employment strategies, emphasizing "the shortest route to paid employment," based on the
belief that "any job is a good job," with requirements for mandatory participation and sanctions for non-compliance (Gorlick & Brethour, 1998b, pp. 6-
7). The more restrictive strategies were frequently accompanied by substantial
cuts to social assistance benefits rates—19.0% for single, employable Alber-
tans in 1993 (Boessenkool, 1997) and 21.6% for all non-disabled recipients in
Ontario in 1995 (National Council of Welfare, 1997). Table 6.1 provides a
synopsis of the work-to-welfare programs across Canada, constructed from
the inventory and provincial summaries prepared by Gorlick and Brethour
(1998a, 1999).

Pulkingham and Ternowetsky (1998, p. 6) who define "workfare or trainfare" as programs "where work or training is a requirement for social assistance," consider mandatory workfare or trainfare programs to be operational
in Quebec, Ontario, Manitoba, Saskatchewan, Alberta, and British Columbia. In most Canadian provinces, single parents with dependent children are
now considered employable depending on the age of their youngest child.
The age of youngest child criterion varies considerably across the country.
British Columbia sets this age at seven years; Manitoba, similarly, uses the
age of six years; Ontario exempts single parents with preschoolers; Saskatchewan, the Yukon, and Newfoundland set the age at two years; Alberta, however, considers single parents employable when their child reaches six months
of age (Gorlick & Brethour, 1998b).

Alternatives
attempted

Table 6.1	Welfare-to-Work Programs across Canada	
Prov./Terr.	**Title of Program**	**Program Description**
Newfoundland	• Supports to Employment Program, 1996	• Continuum of services • Incentives, rather than requirements
Prince Edward Island	• Employment Enhancement Program and Job Creation Program, 1995	• Participation expected of employable people • Sanctions for non-compliance
Nova Scotia	• Employment Support Services, 1997	• Array of services, including work placements • Participation mandatory or benefits discontinued
New Brunswick	• New Brunswick Works, 1992-1998 • New strategy being developed, 1999	• Extensive voluntary training and education • New strategy unknown
Quebec	• APTE (Positive Action for Work and Employment) since 1989 • Dept. of Employment and Solidarity, 1997	• Provision of higher benefits to participants
Ontario	• Ontario Works, 1997	• Employment supports • Employment placement • Community placement (workfare) • Mandatory participation or sanctions imposed
Manitoba	• Employment First, 1996	• Variety of training and employment programs • Mandatory participation by employable people
Saskatchewan	• Saskatchewan Assistance Plan, 1997	• Plan for independence by employable people • Benefits withheld for non-compliance
Alberta	• Supports for Independence, 1990 • Welfare Reform, 1993	• Employable people must seek or prepare for work • Refusal may result in loss or reduction of benefits • Initial applications "diverted"
British Columbia	• Welfare-to-Work, 1996	• Job search assistance—mandatory participation • Employment preparation—voluntary • Employment-based activities—voluntary
Yukon	• Employment Training Services Head Start, 1993	• Program participation—voluntary • Self-sufficiency Plan—mandatory
Northwest Territories	• Productive Choices, 1997	• Participation required • Self-employment and volunteerism accepted

Source: C. Gorlick & G. Brethour. (1998a). Welfare-to-work programs: A national inventory. Ottawa: Canadian Council on Social Devleopment; C. Gorlick & G. Brethour. (1999). Welfare-to-work—Provincial Summaries. Ottawa: Canadian Council on Social Development.

The OECD's (1999b) comparative study of Canada and Switzerland re-
ported that Ontario was the only province of the four Canadian provinces studied that had a workfare program. New Brunswick and Saskatchewan were specifically cited as emphasizing a long-term reintegration strategy to improve clients' employability, holding the view that as long as job search expectations were met, forcing recipients into employment programs would be counterproductive. Although Alberta is similar to Ontario in its political tone and in the use of a retrenchment strategy such as cutting benefit rates, Alberta policy makers stressed that the workfare strategy is not used.

In Ontario, the Progressive Conservative (PC) party, elected in June 1995, reversed the direction of the earlier reform. As Mike Harris (1995, p. 36), former leader of the PC party stated: "Our proposals are intended to mark a fundamental change in the direction of the welfare system ... an acknowledgement of mutual responsibility through the mandatory requirements of workfare." The Ontario workfare strategy is detailed in the initial government publication (Ontario, Ministry of Community & Social Services, 1996) and on their Web site. As noted above, it is the Community Participation component placing social assistance recipients in not-for-profit organizations where they "work for welfare" that distinguishes Ontario Works as fitting the strict, formal definition of workfare. The sanctions for non-compliance—reduction or cancellation of social assistance for refusing to participate in any component of Ontario Works—are consistent with broader definitions of workfare. The Social Assistance Reform Act (Bill 142), which enacted the Ontario Works and the Ontario Disability Support Program legislation, replaced the General Welfare Assistance Act and the Family Benefits Act, both of which had been in place since 1966. Work-related obligations are now stipulated as a condition of eligibility for social assistance, and there is no longer an exemption from employment expectations for single parents in recognition of their child care responsibilities (Ontario, Legislative Assembly, 1997). By the end of 1999, as a condition of eligibility, sixteen- and seventeen-year-old mothers were required to attend school without regard for the age of their children—within the Learning, Earning, and Parenting (LEAP) program and, more recently, drug testing and literacy testing as additional mandatory elements of social assistance eligibility have been introduced (Ontario, Ministry of Community & Social Services, 2001).

Outcomes of Workfare Strategies

Results, thus far, suggest reason for concern about the current primacy of workfare strategies. In the United States, with its longer history of workfare, there is clear evidence that mandatory unpaid work programs do not improve people's skills or their employability (Gueron, 1996). Although caseload declines are evident, and particularly so since the implementation of PRWORA, a large proportion of those leaving welfare are still left living in poverty (Besharov & Germanis, 2000; Loprest, 2001). Income inequality is greater than ever, with mother-led, single-parent families in the lowest decile experiencing an income drop of 14% between 1995 and 1997 (Primus, Rawlings, Larin, & Porter, 1999; Straits, 1999).

Canadian data is now available that is beginning to show some of the impacts of workfare and other eligibility restriction strategies. The National Anti-Poverty Organization (1998, p. 3) noted that the erosion of social assistance had meant "real suffering and increased hardship for a growing number of poor Canadians." Data from the National Council of Welfare (1998) show that since welfare reform measures including workfare programs began in Canada, the numbers of social assistance beneficiaries decreased (from 3,100,200 in 1994 to 2,937,100 in 1996, or 5.3%) while the number of poor people under the age of sixty-five increased (from 4,408,000 to 4,535,000, or 2.9%). In Ontario, the pattern is even more dramatic with an 11.9% decrease in social assistance beneficiaries and a 14.1% increase in poor people.

The Ontario Works program has now been the subject of some preliminary reviews. Ekos Research Associates (1998), contracted by the provincial government to survey a sample of people who left social assistance in November 1997, found that 58% of respondents withdrew because they found jobs. A study completed by the Regional Municipality of Waterloo (1999) surveyed clients one year after leaving social assistance and found that 56% of respondents were employed (with one-third of those in part-time jobs), but that 29% of the respondents were back on social assistance. These results suggest caution in interpreting exits from social assistance as an economically beneficial or long-term change. A federally funded study that looked specifically at the impact of Ontario's welfare reforms on single parents found that "while the proportion of lone mothers with paid work went up, some of those who found jobs may have been financially better off in 1994 than they were in 1996" (Canada, [HRDC], 1998). Without policy measures such as access to affordable housing, quality child care, and improved employment standards including an increased minimum wage, Mayson (1999) suggests that the Ontario Works program is unlikely to foster economic independence. In his cross-national study of workfare, Peck takes notice of the grandiose claims made regarding Ontario Works (OW), and the deficiencies in terms of results or objective data:

> While the headlines proclaim that workfare has driven more than 400,000 people off welfare—and supposedly into work—numbers on the workfare component of OW remain tiny in comparison, at just six thousand in July 1999…[and] for all the great claims that are being made for OW, there are no plans to commission an independent evaluation. (Peck, 2001, p. 248)

Some useful information is also available now regarding the results of the eligibility restriction strategy in Alberta. A study by Boessenkool (1997) for the C.D. Howe Institute, which is generally known for its pro-business stance, notes that the number of social assistance beneficiaries in Alberta was nearly halved (in rounded numbers, from 95,000 to 50,000) between 1993 and 1996. The greatest reduction was a result of the decrease in first-time applicants— generally young people who were refused access to assistance. Many of those potential clients, as well as some existing clients, were diverted to employability enhancement and skill-training programs as well as job-creation projects. These human resources strategies were expensive, with an average annualized cost per participant of over $10,000 for university education and over $18,000 for job creation. Job growth in a robust economy is also acknowledged as contributing to the caseload reduction. Concern is raised about the evidence that some people may have returned to primary relationships, some of which may have been abusive. A further question is posed as to whether the low caseload levels can be maintained in the next economic downturn.

A separate evaluation of outcomes in Alberta was completed by Elton, Sieppert, Azmier, and Roach (1997) for the Canada West Foundation. They conducted a follow-up study of people who left social assistance between September 1993 and October 1996. Although they found that about two-thirds had found either full-time or part-time work, an equivalent proportion reported "not having enough money to meet their basic needs (food and shelter) at least once since leaving welfare" (Elton et al., 1997, p. 86). As in many other applications of eligibility restrictions, the concern remains that although people are exiting social assistance, many are not escaping poverty.

Considerable new knowledge about poverty in Canada is contributed by a study completed by Ross Finnie (2000) using the new Longitudinal Administrative Database (a 10% sample of Canadian tax filers, followed over time as individuals and families). Despite the study's sponsorship by the C.D. Howe Institute, it provides strong empirical evidence for progressive policies. The analysis confirms the distinction between people whose experience of poverty is a transitory one and those who experience longer-term poverty. Finnie (2000, p. 29) suggests policy responses such as short-term income support and brief assistance with skill development and job search for the transitory poor and more fundamental assistance "such as developing essential labor market skills, making work a more feasible option (for example, by facilitating child care), helping with job search, and providing longer-term income support" for people experiencing longer spells of poverty. Although over 80% of the long-term poor are not single mothers, Finnie points out the high incidence of poverty, the greater length of time spent in poverty, and the frequent re-entry into poverty for this group. Measures to address underlying factors such as women's lower earnings are suggested along with employment supports. More generally, Finnie proposes "carrots" that include what Rein (1974) would have called services and incentives, "sticks" that Rein would have considered eligibility restrictions—but only to prod people from loss of hope to programs with promise—and, lastly, a strong labour market. Specific initiatives, Finnie (2000, p. 32) advocates, "should increase both work *and*— in contrast to certain workfare programs—the economic well-being of those at the bottom end of the income distribution." Such measures, he notes, will be more expensive than social assistance initially, but will be cost-effective investments in the long term.

To conclude the discussion of policy alternatives attempted and work-fare strategy outcomes, it is instructive to look at an international review encompassing a broader range of strategies. Maureen Baker (1996) examined the relationship between work and welfare in relation to mothers. Sweden, which requires single mothers with preschool children to seek employment in order to qualify for social assistance, has a commitment to job creation and child care provision, making workfare largely irrelevant. Not all industrialized countries, however, are following this policy direction; the Netherlands, for example, allows single mothers to care for their children at home while receiving social assistance. Baker found government support and statutory protections to be more important in alleviating poverty than strategies that focus on employment requirements for mothers:

> Instead of being influenced by the employability of mothers, family poverty is influenced by the generosity and scope of government benefits (including the level of cash benefits and tax concessions for families with children), the availability of jobs with statutory protection (such as pay equity, parental benefits, and leave for family responsibilities), the availability and affordability of child care, and the existence of universal social programs such as health insurance and unemployment insurance. (Baker, 1996, p. 486)

Whose Problem Definition?

The governments implementing workfare strategies generally hold a neo-conservative political philosophy consistent with the view of the business communities and social elites that support them. From their perspective, lack of income and lack of employment are seen first and foremost as responsibilities of the individual and not of the government. The problem of insufficient individual or family income is considered to be best remedied through earnings from employment or through support from one's primary community; government expenditures and resultant taxes are thought to be a hindrance to business competitiveness in the global market. Unemployment and underemployment are seen as the fault of the individual and not related to structural problems in the economy and the labour market; the market is thought to be best left "unfettered." In addition, provision of social assistance is believed to be a serious disincentive to seeking employment. The primacy of the political agenda, despite evidence from research about the ineffectiveness of workfare strategies, was clear in the government choices made during the design of Ontario Works (Gorlick & Brethour, 1998a) and remains apparent in subsequent decisions such as the increase in Community Participation targets (Mitchell, 1999).

The social work profession, as well as other humanitarian groups and **Problem context** individuals operating from a more social democratic philosophy, see the problem of inadequate income as stemming from structural flaws. Unemployment and underemployment are related to global changes in the economy and the nature of work as well as to systemic disadvantages for particular groups. From this perspective, the workfare strategy itself is seen as a problem that further punishes those who are the victims of larger forces.

Problem Context

My analysis of the problem and its context are situated within the framework of a social democratic ideology. Thus, consistent with the humanitarian and egalitarian values of the social work profession and many other progressive social organizations, I see the problem as one of insufficient income rather than insufficient effort on the part of social assistance recipients. Lack of sufficient income is related to inequitable distribution of wealth, a decrease in the number of stable well-paying jobs, and barriers to employment for marginalized groups. Economic, political, and social factors contribute to the creation and maintenance of these problems.

The primary economic force is the globalization of the market through advances in communications and transportation technology, resulting in heightened competition for best product prices and increased mobility of production. In this environment, producers seek a low-cost, flexible labour force and are able to relocate in order to find it. Wages remain low and jobs become more precarious (e.g., part-time, limited-term) while wealth becomes concentrated among the owners of capital and the means of production (Swift, 1997).

Political decision making is strongly influenced by the business elites who hold considerable leverage in their ability to move their revenue-producing operations to other jurisdictions. The political policies that favour business are the neo-liberal (free market) economic measures, which minimize costs and constraints to production. These include low taxation and minimal government spending, limited regulations (e.g., employment standards, environmental controls), and freedom for trade. The congruent neo-conservative philosophy, with its emphasis on individual responsibility for one's own well-being, promotes a break from Canada's historical development of programs expressing a collective sense of responsibility. One example of this is the alteration of unemployment insurance in Canada from a program that provided insurance-based benefits to 88% of unemployed workers in 1990 to the new Employment Insurance Act, which covered only 43% of unemployed workers by mid-1997 (National Council of Welfare, 1997). Hence, consistent with policies favouring lower government costs and the location of culpability with the individual, we witness in the workfare strategy the current preference for labour force attachment programs, rather than human capital development strategies (Peck, 2001).

Implications
for oppressed
groups

Some of the social factors that have contributed to more restrictive social assistance policies are the increases in numbers of people receiving social assistance, the high rate of poverty among female-headed, single-parent families, and the general increase in women's participation in the labour force. The number of Canadians receiving social assistance climbed from 1,334,000 in 1980 to a high of 3,100,200 in 1994; the numbers continued to climb even after the end of the recession in 1991 because of persistently high unemployment (National Council of Welfare, 1998). The 1996 census identified over 1.1 million single-parent families, which represents over one fifth of families with children in Canada (Canada, Statistics Canada, 1997). Over 80% of single-parent families are headed by women; the majority of them (56% in 1997) have incomes below the Statistics Canada LICO and 42% reported some social assistance in 1994 (Canada, Statistics Canada, 1999; Scott, 1998). Finally, the increase in women's participation in the labour force (from 30% in 1961 to 58% in 1996) has been a factor in the redefinition of women on social assistance as employable (Scott & Lochhead, 1997).

Implications for Oppressed Groups

The workfare strategy has particularly poignant impacts for members of groups that have already been marginalized through the historical processes of patriarchy, capitalism, and colonialism. Nancy Rose (1995), in her historical overview of women, welfare, and government work programs, uses a conceptual framework based on the importance of gender, class, and race.

Abramovitz, in the 1988 edition of *Regulating the Lives of Women*, was one of the first feminists to highlight the imposition of the family ethic and the maintenance of patriarchy through social welfare policy. Gender biases are more evident in the social assistance policies of the United States since their programs were constructed to assist single-parent families only, and were extended later to assist two-parent families in very restricted circumstances, such that in 1996 two-parents families represented only 7% of the caseload (Sorensen, Mincy, & Halpern, 2000). Hence, it is not surprising to find that the PRWORA and the Temporary Assistance to Needy Families (TANF) program explicitly promote marriage to end dependency on social assistance (Rose, 2000).

In Canada, where single mothers comprise a much smaller portion of the welfare caseload (27% in 1997; National Council of Welfare, 1998), there is a similar redirection of single mothers to "become either economically self-sufficient or the responsibility of any 'male bread-winner" (Mayson, 1999, p. 107). Single mothers are expected to participate in welfare-to-work programs with exemptions only for parents of young or disabled children (Gorlick & Brethour, 1998a). In addition, single mothers cohabiting with unrelated males are considered to be in a spousal relationship and are no longer eligible for social assistance in their own right.

An important change in the conceptualization of employability has occurred with the advent of workfare programs. From the initiation of Mother's Allowance in Manitoba in 1916 to the end of the 1950s, women's labour market participation was considered "incompatible with their duty to their children" (Evans, 1996, p. 153). Women on social assistance in Ontario during this period were fearful of losing their children to the child welfare authorities if they sought employment in order to improve their economic well-being (Strong-Boag, 1979). The traditional view began to give way in the 1970s and 1980s in response to both feminist pressures for greater choices for women and economic pressures for additional income in two-parent families. Women's choices regarding parenting or work outside the home and regarding their economic dependence on male friends are more circumscribed under workfare regimes.

According to a Marxist analysis of capitalism, the owners of capital and of the means of production have higher profits when there is a ready supply of cheap labour. The cost of labour is reduced through the application of workfare policies, as Rose explains:

> Workfare programs are congruent with the logic of production-for-profit. In fact, they lower wage costs and boost profits in the short run by channelling the poor into low-wage labor markets, where the increased supply of labor makes it more difficult for workers to demand higher wages and better working conditions. (Rose, 1995, p. 14)

Workfare and other restrictive eligibility policies in Canada similarly fit the strategy of present-day "owners of capital" who seek a flexible, low-cost labour market (Broad, 1997). Peck, (2001, p. 6) who describes workfare as a labour force regulator, notes that "workfare is not about creating jobs for people who don't have them; it is about creating workers for jobs that nobody wants."

The reality of oppression based on race in Canada has been documented by Christensen (1999). Discrimination in employment keeps non-White workers in lower paying, less secure employment and, therefore, at greatest risk of needing social assistance and facing workfare measures—which, in turn, ensures their ties to an unrewarding job market. The triple jeopardy of being a non-White woman on social assistance in the present age of workfare is ominous indeed. Cummings (1997) describes the intersection of gender, class, and race in the experience of workfare programs and decries the failure of feminism to bridge the class and race differences that prevent women of the dominant culture from joining forces with poor women and women of colour to challenge workfare policies.

Conclusion

Workfare has reformulated the problem of insufficient income, formerly addressed (albeit only partially) by welfare programs, into an ill-founded fear of pervasive disincentives to work, which purportedly must be addressed through restrictive strategies. It is a social policy that is firmed rooted in neo-conservative ideology, holding individuals and families responsible for the causation and solution of their poverty. Workfare meets the neo-liberal economic objectives of limiting government spending and maintaining a ready supply of workers for a flexible, low-cost labour force. Thus, many advanced welfare states, yielding to the pressures of globalized capitalism, have chosen to impose workfare programs.

Although much of the political rhetoric attempts to suggest that workfare gives "a hand up" to social assistance recipients, empirical evidence reveals that, while social assistance caseloads have decreased, poverty concurrently has worsened. Many people are no longer eligible for social assistance and have found employment in the low-paying, part-time, and seasonal precarious job market. Their earnings and benefits, minus their employment-related expenses for such costs as child care and transportation, frequently provide less than what they were receiving earlier in welfare benefits. The social consequences of this poverty are borne disproportionately by groups already experiencing oppression due to gender, race, and class. Women are particularly disadvantaged in the provisions that require them to work, but that do not recognize the realities or the importance of their child care responsibilities.

Clearly, economic objectives take precedence over social goals in the neo-conservative world of workfare. Government spending on social assistance has been reduced and a more flexible workforce has been created. Poverty, with its disabling consequences for people and society, has increased. An ideology congruent with the interests of the architects of global capitalism undergirds workfare strategies, an ideology that is not in keeping with Canada's tradition of liberalism and collective concern for well-being.

References

Abramovitz, M. (1996). *Regulating the lives of women: Social welfare policy from colonial times to the present* (Rev. Ed.). Boston: South End Press.

Abramovitz, M. (2000). *Under attack: Fighting back.* Boston/New York: Monthly Review Press.

Baker, M. (1996). Social assistance and the employability of mothers: Two models from cross-national research. *Canadian Journal of Sociology, 21*(4), 483-503.

Besharov, D. & Germanis, P. (2000). Welfare reform—four years later. *The Public Interest, 140,* 17-35.

Boessenkool, K. (1997, April). Back to work: Learning from the Alberta welfare experiment. *C.D. Howe Institute Commentary, 90,* 1-29.

Broad, D. (1997). The casualization of the labour force. In A. Duffy, D. Glenday, & N. Pupo (Eds.), *Good jobs, bad jobs, no jobs: The transformation of work in the 21st century* (pp. 53-73). Toronto: Harcourt Brace.

Canada, Human Resources Development Canada (HRDC). (1998). Welfare cuts may lead to more paid work for lone mothers—But not necessarily to higher incomes. *Applied Research Bulletin, 4*(1), 25-26.

Canada, Human Resources Development Canada (HRDC). (2001). *Number of beneficiaries (including dependants) of provincial and municipal social assistance, by Province and for Canada, as of March 31, 1997 to 2000*. Ottawa: Online at <www.hrdc-drhc.gc.ca/stratpol/socpol/statistics/75-76/tab35.shtml>

Canada, Statistics Canada. (1997). *Census families in private households by family Structure*. Online at <www.statcan.ca/english/census96/oct14/fam2.htm>

Canada, Statistics Canada. (1999). *Low income persons, 1980-1997*. Catalogue 13-569-XIB. Ottawa: Author.

Canadian Association of Social Workers. (1994). *Social work code of ethics*. Ottawa: Author.

Christensen, C. (1999). Multiculturalism, racism, and social work: An exploration of issues in the Canadian context. In G. Lie & D. Este (Eds.), *Professional social service delivery in a multicultural world* (pp. 293-310). Toronto: Canadian Scholars Press.

Cummings, C. (1997). "Welfare (d)eform: A call to arms." *Sojourner, 22*(12), 16-20.

Ekos Research Associates. (1998). *Survey of individuals who left social assistance*. Toronto: Ministry of Community & Social Services.

Elton, D., Sieppert, J., Azmier, J., & Roach, R. (1997). *Where are they now?: Assessing the impact of welfare reform on former recipients*. Calgary: The Canada West Foundation.

Evans, P. (1993). From workfare to the social contract: Implications for Canada of recent U.S. welfare reforms. *Canadian Public Policy, 19*(1), 54-67.

Evans, P. (1996). Single mothers and Ontario's welfare policy: Restructuring the debate. In J. Brodie (Ed.), *Women and Canadian public policy* (pp. 151-172). Toronto: Harcourt.

Finnie, R. (2000). The dynamics of poverty in Canada. *C.D. Howe Commentary*, (145), 1-37.

Gorlick, C., & Brethour, G. (1998a). *Welfare-to-work programs: A national inventory*. Ottawa: Canadian Council on Social Development.

Gorlick, C., & Brethour, G. (1998b). *Welfare-to-work programs: An overview*. Ottawa: Canadian Council on Social Development.

Gorlick, C., & Brethour, G. (1999). *Welfare-to-work—Provincial summaries*. Ottawa: Canadian Council on Social Development.

Gueron, J. (1996). A research context for welfare reform. *Journal of Policy Analysis and Management, 15*(4), 547-561.

Harris, M. (1995). Welfare should offer a hand up, not a hand-out. *Policy Options, 16*(4), 33-36.

Lalonde, L. (1997). Tory welfare policies: A view from the inside. In D. Ralph, A. Regimbald, & N. St-Amand (Eds.), *Mike Harris's Ontario: Open for business. Closed to people* (pp. 92-102). Halifax, Fernwood Press.

Lightman, E. (1995). You can lead a horse to water, but...: The case against workfare in Canada. In J. Richards et al. (Eds.), *Helping the poor: A qualified case for workfare* (pp. 151-183). Toronto: C.D. Howe Institute.

Loprest, P. (2001). How are families that left welfare doing? *The Urban Institute, B*(B-36), 1-7.

Mayson, M. (1999). Ontario Works and single mothers: Redefining "Deservedness and the social contract." *Journal of Canadian Studies, 34*(2), 89-109.

Mink, G. (1998). *Welfare's end*. Ithaca: Cornell University Press.

Mitchell, A. (1999). Workfare: Symbolic purposes at the expense of substantive benefits. *Workfare Watch Bulletin, 1*(9), 1-5.

Mitchell, A. (2000a) A backwards STEP. *Workfare Watch Bulletin, 1*(10), 1-6.

Mitchell, A. (2000b). Welfare and the myth of dependency. *Workfare Watch Bulletin, 1*(11), 1-5.

References   Morton, B. (1998). No CAP in hand: The government has virtually eliminated universal social programs. *Briarpatch, 26*(10), 9-10.

Mullaly, R. (1997). *Structural social work: Ideology, theory and practice.* Toronto:
McClelland & Stewart.

National Anti-Poverty Organization. (1998). *Poverty and the Canadian welfare state:
A report card.* Ottawa: Author.

National Council of Welfare. (1999). *Welfare incomes 1997 and 1998.* Ottawa: Author.

National Council of Welfare. (1998). *Profiles of welfare: Myths and realities.* Ottawa:
Author.

National Council of Welfare. (1997). *Another look at welfare reform.* Ottawa: Author.

Ontario Legislative Assembly. (1997). *Bill 142: An act to revise the law related to
social assistance by enacting the Ontario Works Act and the Ontario Disability
Support Program Act.* Toronto: Author.

Ontario Ministry of Community & Social Services. (1988). *Towards independence:
Highlights of the evaluation of the Employment Opportunities program.*
Toronto: Queen's Printer.

Ontario Ministry of Community & Social Services. (1996). *A summary of the Ontario
Works program.* Toronto: Queen's Printer for Ontario.

Ontario Ministry of Community & Social Services. (2001). *Ontario Works.* Online at
<www.gov.on.ca/CSS/page/services/ontworks.html>

Organisation for Economic Co-operation and Development (OECD). (1999a). *The
local dimension of welfare-to-work: An international survey.* Paris: Author.

Organisation for Economic Co-operation and Development (OECD). (1999b). *The
battle against exclusion: Social assistance in Canada and Switzerland.* Paris:
Author.

Peck, J. (2001), *Workfare states.* New York: Guilford Press.

Porter, E. (1991). *The long-term effects of three employment programs for social assistance recipients.* Toronto: Ontario, Ministry of Community & Social Services.

Primus, W., Rawlings, L., Larin, K., & Porter, K. (1999). *The initial impact of welfare
reform on the incomes of single mother families.* Washington, DC: Center for
Budget and Policy Priorities.

Pulkingham, J., & Ternowetsky, G. (1998). *A state of the art review of income security
reform in Canada.* Ottawa: International Development Research Council.

Regional Municipality of Waterloo. (1999). *Survey of recipients who left social assistance: Fall 1998.* Waterloo: Author.

Rein, M. (1974). The welfare crisis. In L. Rainwater (Ed.), *Social problems and public policy* (pp. 89-102). Chicago: Aldine.

Rose, N. (1995). *Workfare or fair work: Women, welfare, and government work programs.* New Brunswick, NJ: Rutgers University Press.

Rose, N. (2000). An analysis of welfare reform. *Journal of Economic Issues, 34*(1),
143-157.

Scott, K. (1998). *Women and the CHST: A profile of women receiving social assistance
in 1994.* Ottawa: Canadian Council on Social Development & Status of Women
Canada.

Scott, K., & Lochhead, C. (1997). *Are women catching up in the earnings race?*
Ottawa: Centre for International Statistics at the Canadian Council on Social
Development.

Snyder, L. (2000). Successes of single mothers on social assistance through a voluntary employment program. *Canadian Social Work Review, 17*(1), 49-68.

Social Research and Development Corporation. (2001). The Self-Sufficiency Project:
Welfare-to-work experiment producing impressive findings. Online at <www.
srdc.org/english/publications/volume_1number_1-en.pdf>.

Sorensen, E., Mincy, R., & Halpern, A. (2000). *Redirecting welfare policy toward building strong families.* Washington, DC: Urban Institute.

Straits, R. (1999). Issues raised by welfare reform in the United States. In Organisation for Economic Co-operation and Development (Ed.), *The local dimension of welfare-to-work: An international survey* (pp. 177-196). Paris: OECD.

Strong-Boag, V. (1979). Wages for housework: The beginnings of social security in Canada. *Journal of Canadian Studies, 14* (1), 24-34.

Struthers, J. (1996). *Can workfare work? Reflections from history.* Ottawa: The Caledon Institute of Social Policy.

Swift, J. (1997). From cars to casinos, from work to workfare: The brave new world of Canadian employment. In A. Duffy, D. Glenday, & N. Pupo (Eds.), *Good jobs, bad jobs, no jobs: The transformation of work in the 21st century* (pp. 35-52). Toronto: Harcourt Brace.

Torjman, S. (1996). *Workfare: A poor law.* Ottawa: Caledon Institute of Social Policy.

World Bank. (1995). *World development report 1995: Workers in an integrating world.* Oxford: Oxford University Press.

7

Heterosexism: Shaping Social Policy in Relation to Gay Men and Lesbians

Brian O'Neill

One of the most striking social changes in Canada and much of the world over the past three decades has been the increase in acceptance of gay and lesbian people, and the decrease in discrimination based on sexual orientation. This change, though contentious and hotly debated, represents a shift in Canadian values that is evident in social policies at various levels. Four developments have been pivotal: decriminalization of sexual acts between members of the same sex by changes to the Criminal Code in 1969; declassification of homosexuality as a mental disorder by the American Psychiatric Association in 1973; recognition of the rights of gay, lesbian, and bisexual people under the 1982 Canadian Charter of Rights and Freedoms and federal and provincial human rights codes that began in the late 1970s; and increased awareness of human service needs related to same-sex sexual orientation as a result of the HIV/AIDS epidemic since the 1980s. This chapter first discusses heterosexism, the ideology that underlies the oppression encountered by gay, lesbian and bisexual people. It then introduces concepts related to sexual orientation and highlights features of the gay and lesbian communities. The remainder of the chapter traces changes in the expression of heterosexism in public policies and identifies directions for future development.

Heterosexism

Historically, the response in Canada to same-sex sexual orientation has been shaped by heterosexism. Analogous to racism and sexism, heterosexism is "the ideological system that denies, denigrates, and stigmatizes any non-heterosexual form of behavior, identity, relationship, or community"(Herek, 1996, p. 101). Based on the premise that all people are, or should be, heterosexual (Friend, 1993), heterosexist discourses promulgate stereotypes of gay men and lesbians as dangerous sex offenders, threats to the family, and mentally ill (Kinsman, 1995; O'Brien & Goldberg, 2000). As with other oppressive ideologies, heterosexism is reproduced at the structural, cultural, and personal levels (Thompson, 1998), privileging those who conform to the dominant sexual orientation, heterosexuality, and disadvantaging those who are gay, lesbian, and bisexual (Kinsman, 1996). Because heterosexuality is presented as natural and universal, oppression related to sexual orientation has been widely supported at least tacitly, and, for the most part, gone unrecognized. However, the emergence of gay and lesbian communities, and challenges to heterosexism by members of these communities and their allies, have led to social changes that are reflected in legislation, organizational policies, and public attitudes.

Sexual orientation

The term "homophobia," coined by Weinberg in 1972 to identify the irrational fear of same-sex sexual orientation, is commonly used to refer to prejudice against gay men and lesbians. The term is not used in this chapter in that way because to do so obscures the systemic nature of oppression based on sexual orientation, creating the impression that discrimination against gay people is related solely to individuals' attitudes and psychological problems (Herek, 1996; Williamson, 2000). Rather, "homophobia" is employed here more narrowly to refer to the negative impact on people who are sexually attracted to members of their own sex, of internalizing heterosexism.

Sexual Orientation

Terms related to gender and sexuality are often confused despite their distinct meanings (Berger & Kelly, 1995). "Gender identity" is the sex individuals believe they are, usually male or female, based on their primary physical sex characteristics. Despite stereotypes to the contrary, most gay men think of themselves as male and most lesbians consider themselves to be female. It is transgendered people who have gender identities different than that ascribed to them based on their physical characteristics, for instance, people with male genitalia who consider themselves to be female. Policies regarding transgendered people are not addressed in this chapter because their oppression is related to their gender identity rather than their sexual orientation. "Gender roles" are behaviours deemed appropriate for each sex, and vary across cultures. They may be defined loosely or rigidly, and extend to all areas of life, including not only speech and behavioural mannerisms, but also choices of occupation, family roles, and sexual partners. Heterosexism shapes gender roles in our culture to exclude same-sex sexual behaviour.

The terms "sexual identity" and "sexual orientation" are often used interchangeably in referring to sexual attraction and behaviour. The common sense understanding of sexual orientation in the northern European traditions that have shaped the dominant cultures of Canada is that sexual orientation is defined by the gender of the people to whom one is predominantly sexually attracted (Murphy, 1997). Thus, heterosexuality refers to attraction between males and females, homosexuality to attraction between members of the same sex, and bisexuality to attraction to people of both sexes. Nevertheless, it is an oversimplification to assume that sexual orientation is a clear-cut and stable trait. Kinsey's pioneering investigations of sexuality suggested that 5-10% of males (Kinsey, Pomeroy, & Martin, 1948), and 3-5% of females

(Kinsey, Pomeroy, Martin, & Gebhard, 1955) participate in sex primarily with members of their own sex for a period of three or more years during their adult lives. However, these studies also revealed that in addition, at least as many people are bisexual, do not act on their same-sex attractions, or experience changes in the focus of their sexuality during their lives. Although more recent studies have found a lower incidence of same-sex sexual orientation (e.g., Harry, 1990), data from around the world (e.g., Binson et al., 1995; Diamond, 1993; Sell, Wells, & Wypij, 1995) continue to support the conclusion that a significant proportion of the population is sexually interested in members of their own sex for at least a period of their adult lives. There is a lack of Canadian data, but it is reasonable to assume that the occurrence of same-sex sexual orientation here is consistent with that in other Western countries.

Theories about the causes of variation in sexual orientation abound (Murphy, 1997). Some explanations focus on biological factors such as differences in brain structures, prenatal hormonal influences, and genetic heredity. There is some empirical support for these propositions, but it is not conclusive. A second set of theories points to social environmental influences. For instance, some interpretations of psychoanalytic theory hold that same-sex sexual orientation is an aberration in psychosexual development due to deficiencies in parent-child relationships. Other explanations propose that same-sex sexual orientation is a result of child sexual abuse. Again, there is a lack of evidence to support these hypotheses. Yet a third line of thinking holds that sexuality is socially constructed, and that all people have the potential to develop attraction to people of either sex, depending on the circumstances (Archer, 1999). The fact that some people who have previously been exclusively heterosexual participate in sexual behaviour with members of their own gender when in sex-segregated environments or when they meet a particular individual supports the argument that human sexuality is extremely flexible. Whatever the determinants of sexual attraction, it appears that the expression of human sexuality is shaped by biological, social, and individual factors, and that it may change over the course of individuals' lives (De Cecco & Elia, 1993). However, there is no evidence supporting claims that sexual orientation can be changed by means of behavioural, psychological, or other forms of therapy (Murphy, 1997).

Knowledge about Same-Sex Sexual Orientation

In the development and analysis of policy, information is needed about the population affected by the problem. Unfortunately, there is a lack of accurate knowledge about the lives of those most seriously affected by heterosexism, people who are attracted to their own sex. A multitude of characteristics have been thought to be associated with same-sex sexual orientation (Murphy, 1997). These include physical traits such as particular body shapes, behaviours such as gender atypical mannerisms and speech patterns, and aptitudes for certain artistic and athletic endeavours. Of more serious concern in relation to social policy are stereotypes that those who are oriented to their own sex are likely to be sexual predators, disturbed, and unable to form stable mature relationships (Schneider, 1997).

Despite concerted efforts by social scientists as well as the police and military, a valid and reliable method of detecting and categorizing people according to their sexual orientation has not been developed (Archer, 1999; Kinsman, 1996; Murphy, 1997). This imposes a limitation on conducting research in the area, as it is not feasible to draw representative samples of people who are oriented to their own sex. However, studies conducted over the past thirty years based on samples of gay, lesbian, and bisexual people drawn from non-clinical populations discredit earlier harmful beliefs about same-sex sexual orientation. Nevertheless, this body of knowledge does not provide information about the lives of those who have some degree of same-sex sexual orientation but do not identify as gay, lesbian, or bisexual or are unwilling to come out.

Social Construction of Identities Based on Sexual Orientation

Although there is evidence of same-sex eroticism occurring in most cultures throughout history (Churchill, 1967; Hinsch, 1990; Williams, 1993), having particular sexual interests, whatever their cause has usually not been the basis for ascribing identity. Rather, having sexual contact with another person of the same sex was considered simply to be a behaviour, though often censured. For instance, same-sex sexuality may have been disapproved of as immoral in much the same way that heterosexual adultery was. Until the Kinsey studies, it was thought that same-sex sexual orientation was relatively rare because its expression was largely covert due to its stigmatization. It was not until the late nineteenth century that the concept of homosexuality as a defining characteristic of identity appeared primarily within medical discourse, and people who were attracted to others of their own sex came to be known as homosexuals (Kinsman, 1996). In some cultures, sexual identity is ascribed on the basis of behaviour rather than the gender of the people involved (Irvine, 1995). For instance, in Latin cultures, the man who is penetrated during anal intercourse may be considered homosexual, while the man who penetrates may retain his identity as heterosexual.

In reaction to the creation of the "homosexual" as a stigmatized category of person, during the second half of the twentieth century people who were sexually attracted to members of their own sex began to define themselves as gay, lesbian, or bisexual, but gave these identities a positive connotation (Kinsman, 1996). Although the term "gay" may refer to both men and women, more recently it has been used to refer specifically to males who are sexually attracted to males. In contrast, although the term "lesbian" alludes to sexual and emotional attraction between women, it may be used without necessarily inferring a sexual element (Tully, 1995). The process of becoming aware

Social construction of identities based on sexual orientation of and disclosing one's gay, lesbian, or bisexual identity is referred to as "com-ing out." There are various models of coming out, with some differences in the pattern for men and women (Tully, 2000). The number of people who come out is smaller than those who experience same-sex sexual orientation in part because of fear of discrimination, but also because not all people who are attracted to or participate in sex with members of their own sex identify as gay, lesbian, or bisexual (McKirnan, Stokes, Doll, & Burzette, 1995). However, siz-able gay and lesbian communities have emerged around the world, exerting considerable influence on the development of social policies, particularly in Canada (Adam, Duyvendak, & Krouwel, 1999).

Gay and Lesbian Communities

There are well-developed, but largely unnoticed, social networks among peo-ple who are attracted to members of their own sex throughout rural Canada (Riorden, 1996). However, it is the communities that have developed in the centres of large Canadian cities, in part due to migration from rural and sub-urban areas, which have shaped public images of gay and lesbian people (Kinsman, 1996). These communities originated primarily around commer-cial establishments catering to gay men, such as bars, baths, and restaurants, but over time have come to include organizations focusing on the needs of both men and women. Gay and lesbian communities include businesses that provide various products and services, newspapers and magazines, cultural organizations, religious groups, sports and recreational clubs, political asso-ciations and social change movements, support groups for youth and seniors, as well as health care and counselling services. The advent of HIV in the 1980s stimulated the development of AIDS service organizations based largely in gay communities (Cain, 1997). In addition to their participation in commu-nities dominated by gay men, lesbians have also developed separate com-munities within the context of the women's movement (Stoller, 1998). No comparable bisexual communities have emerged (Schneider, 1997).

Media coverage has contributed to a distorted image of gay and lesbian populations (Kinsman, 1996). Gay men, and lesbians to a lesser extent, are portrayed as relatively wealthy, youthful, white, middle class, and able-bod-ied. Gay men in particular are presented as being unencumbered by family responsibilities and focusing mainly on achieving sexual and social satisfac-tion. In reality, there is diversity within the gay population with respect to race/ethnicity, age, social class, physical and intellectual ability, and religion (Greene, 1997; O'Neill, 1999) and many gay men and lesbians are caring for their children as well as supporting aging parents (O'Brien & Goldberg, 2000).

Current Attitudes

Individuals' opinions about sexual orientation have been found to be corre-lated with their social locations and belief systems (Herek, 1996). In general heterosexist attitudes are associated with being male, older, less educated, and living in rural areas. Negative beliefs are also stronger among those who hold conservative religious beliefs and support traditional gender roles. In contrast, attitudes are more positive among those who have had personal contact with gay men and lesbians. Since 1975, when only 28% of Canadians were accepting of same-sex sexual orientation (Bibby, 1995), attitudes have consistently become more positive. For instance, a 1994 national survey indicated that 61% of respondents had at least some degree of tolerance for same-sex sexuality (Widmer, Treas, & Newcomb, 1998). In part this change may be related to more gay and lesbian people coming out, as 50% of respondents in a 1998 poll indicated that they had friends, coworkers, and relatives who were gay or lesbian (Canadian Press, 2000). However, although attitudes have become more positive, a 1999 poll by the British Columbia Human Rights Commission (2001) found that gays and lesbians were the least tolerated minority group in the province.

Gay men and lesbians who are members of other minority groups may be simultaneously disempowered by several oppressive ideologies (O'Neill, 1999). For instance, they may be subjected to racism, ethnocentrism, sexism, ablism, and ageism in both the general community as well as the gay and lesbian communities. Furthermore, they may be marginalized by heterosexism within their particular minority groups. In the past, individuals who did not conform to conventional gender roles were accepted and honoured in some North American Aboriginal societies (Brotman, Ryan, Jalbert, & Rowe, 2002a). However, due in large part to colonialism, modern First Nations communities have incorporated many of the values that inform the dominant culture. Thus Aboriginal lesbians and gay men now must cope with heterosexism within their Native communities as well as the dominant culture. Similarly, many Canadian immigrants come from cultures that highly stigmatize same-sex sexuality, with the result that gay and lesbian newcomers may face exclusion within their ethnic communities and families (Tremble, Schneider, & Appathurai, 1989).

Canadian Social Policies

The expression of heterosexism in public policy has evolved from outright denunciation of same-sex sexual behaviour, to requirements for tolerance of differences of sexual orientation, to the currently emerging recognition of the equality rights of gay and lesbian people. This section of the chapter discusses key changes in legislation, professional guidelines, and organizational policies that have reduced the stigmatization of same-sex sexual orientation and increased the accessibility and responsiveness of human services.

Criminal and Immigration Law

Historically, the most direct and wide-reaching expression of heterosexism has been in criminal laws. As early as 1533 in England, sex between men was punishable by death, and remained an offence there until 1967 (Kinsman,

1996). Currently, although the criminalization of same-sex sexuality has decreased, sexual activity between people of the same sex is still an offence in over forty countries around the world, including the United States (International Lesbian and Gay Association [ILGA], 2001). The death penalty continues to be the punishment in nine countries. As Canada's Criminal Code was based on that of Britain, it included gross indecency and anal intercourse as sexual offences. Although there was no definition of gross indecency in the Code, until 1954 the offence could be laid only in relation to acts between males (Casswell, 1996). In practice these offences were prosecuted primarily against men who had consenting sex with men, and repeated conviction could lead to being declared a dangerous sexual offender and indefinite incarceration. In 1969, the Criminal Code was amended to allow these acts between married couples and consenting adults in private. Subsequently, in 1988, the offence of gross indecency was deleted from the Code and the age of consent for anal intercourse was lowered to eighteen.

Another significant expression of heterosexism in federal law is found in the Immigration Act. Until 1978, gay people were barred from entering Canada (Casswell, 1996). Currently, it is not specified that members of same-sex couples have the right to sponsor their partners as immigrants, whereas those in male-female couples are able to do so. Interestingly, individuals who have claimed that they were persecuted on the basis of their sexual orientation have been admitted as refugees under the act. This practice is consistent with the interpretation of the United Nations High Commissioner for Refugees, which recognizes gay men and lesbians as social groups that can suffer persecution (ILGA, 2001).

The heterosexist provisions of the Criminal Code and the Immigration Act continue to influence discourse about sexual orientation even though for the most part they have been repealed. The impression persists among many that same-sex sexuality is illicit and that gay men and lesbians are somewhat disreputable. This perception subtly shapes the administration of justice, so that gay men and lesbians are treated more harshly than heterosexuals (Casswell, 1996; MacDougall, 2000). Nevertheless, the most serious implication of the stigmatization of same-sex sexual orientation is that it provides a rationale for discrimination and violence perpetrated against those perceived to be gay or lesbian (Richardson & May, 1999). Studies have found that more than one-third of gay men and lesbians have experienced anti-gay attacks (Casswell, 1996, p. 8; Trussler et al., 2000). The positive evolution in public values, however, is evident in the addition to the Criminal Code in 1995 of stiffer sentences for crimes motivated by hatred against gay men and lesbians.

Psychiatric Classification

After its decriminalization, the declassification of homosexuality as a mental disorder was the next significant step in the evolution of policies regarding same-sex sexual orientation (Taylor, 1994). With the development of psychiatry in the late nineteenth century, homosexuality had come to be considered a mental illness (Murphy, 1997). This theory was buttressed by research conducted largely on samples drawn from mentally ill and incarcerated populations and informed by the assumption that same-sex sexual orientation was a problem in itself. However, studies conducted in the latter half of the twentieth century with appropriate research designs did not detect any differences in mental health or cognitive abilities related to sexual orientation (American Psychological Association [APA], 2001). Nevertheless, homosexuality remained classified as a disorder by the APA until 1973 (Murphy, 1997) and by the World Health Organization until 1991. These guidelines shaped the provision of mental health services in Canada, with serious repercussions for clients as well as care providers (Kinsman, 1996). Clients who revealed their same-sex sexual orientation were diagnosed as mentally ill and often subjected to abusive and ineffective interventions aimed at changing their sexuality. Furthermore, health and social service workers who were gay or lesbian were reluctant to reveal their sexual orientation, depriving clients of the benefits of their knowledge and experience.

> Canadian social policies

Although no longer endorsed by professional bodies, the psychiatric classification of homosexuality continues to shape the perception of same-sex sexual orientation as an illness. Influenced by the previous criminalization of same-sex sexual behaviour, and the more recent advent of HIV/AIDS, gay men and lesbians are frequently portrayed in popular culture as strange, dangerous, and contaminated. The declassification of homosexuality as a mental illness allowed for the possibility of the development of health and social services that could be supportive to gay and lesbian people (Taylor, 1994). However, there is evidence that health care and social service providers have continued to hold negative beliefs regarding same-sex sexual orientation (Brotman, Ryan, Jalbert, & Rowe, 2002b), contributing to the lack of accessibility and responsiveness of services.

Human Rights Legislation and the Charter

Following the achievement of changes in the Criminal Code, and supported by the depathologization of homosexuality, the focus of Canadian gay and lesbian activism turned to gaining protection from discrimination through the inclusion of sexual orientation in human rights codes. Human rights legislation identifies grounds on which discrimination is prohibited in areas such as housing, services, employment, and membership in organizations, and applies in both the public and private spheres (Casswell, 1996). In addition to harassment and violence, people perceived to be gay or lesbian have frequently encountered discrimination in areas addressed by human rights legislation (e.g., Coalition for Gay Rights in Ontario, 1986). An example is the 1991 termination of a gay teacher in Alberta, where sexual orientation was not included in the human rights code (Casswell, 1996). Since 1977, Canadian public opinion has consistently supported inclusion of sexual orientation in human rights legislation (EGALE, 2001). For instance, 84% of respondents in the above-noted 1998 national poll advocated protection of gays and lesbians from discrimination (Canadian Press, 2000). As a result of a concerted campaign of political action and court challenges, sexual orientation was added to the Quebec Charter of Human Rights and Freedoms in 1977 and has subsequently been incorporated into most of the other provincial and territorial human rights codes (EGALE, 1998). Furthermore, The Canadian Human Rights Act was amended in 1996 to include protection for gays and lesbians (Casswell, 1996). In contrast, sexual orientation discrimination is proscribed in only twenty-one other countries (ILGA, 2001) and is not addressed in the Universal Declaration of Human Rights. Although Canadians generally disapprove of overt discrimination, policy makers have been more reluctant to affirm same-sex sexual orientation by explicitly extending to gay and lesbian people the same rights enjoyed by heterosexuals (Carter, 1998).

With discrimination on the basis of sexual orientation prohibited by human rights laws, the achievement of full equality became the focus of attention. The Charter of Rights and Freedoms (the Charter), part of the 1982 Canadian constitution, addresses the right of Canadians to equal treatment by public services, regardless of ethnicity, gender, or other differences (Casswell, 1996). Subsequent to the introduction of the Charter, gay men and lesbians successfully mounted court challenges to policies that denied same-sex partners access to public services such as benefits under the Old Age Security Act. As a result, although it does not refer explicitly to sexual orientation, since 1996 the Charter has been interpreted by the Supreme Court as applying to sexual orientation. This change has had far-reaching implications for the legal recognition of same-sex couples and policies regarding employment benefits, pensions, taxes, inheritance, and family life. At the time of writing, the federal and some provincial governments are amending their laws so that they apply equally to both same-sex and heterosexual couples (EGALE, 2000). For instance, same-sex couples are now able to adopt children in British Columbia and Ontario (Arnup, 1999). These changes are widely supported by public opinion. A national poll taken in 2001 suggested that 75% of Canadians believe that gay and lesbian people should have the same rights as heterosexuals, and 65% of respondents supported same-sex marriage (McInnes, 2001). Laws restricting the right to marry to male-female couples have been challenged in the courts, and the federal government is now considering changing the way that relationships are recognized legally.

Despite these successes in the courts and legislatures, some gay men and lesbians have reservations about being included in policies that formerly have applied only to heterosexuals (Donovan, Heaphy, & Weeks, 1999; Smith, 1999). They fear that inclusion of gay and lesbian people in mainstream social institutions may reinforce the status quo rather than advance social changes in relation to sexuality and gender that have been goals of the gay liberation and feminist movements. For instance, the achievement of same-sex spousal benefits privileges only those involved in long-term relationships, particularly if they are in higher tax brackets. In addition, there are concerns about

same-sex couples being able to marry, given that this institution has histori- Canadian
cally been an unequal relationship, usually benefiting the male partner at social
the expense of the woman (Antoniuk, 1999). In any case, a significant impli- policies
cation of the recognition of the rights of gay and lesbian people to equal treatment is that human services are required to provide services that are
accessible and appropriate regardless of sexual orientation.

Impact of HIV/AIDS

A major impetus to addressing issues related to same-sex sexual orientation
in human service policies has been the HIV/AIDS epidemic. Although the
rate of infection among men who have sex with men declined during the
1990s, this group still accounts for 78% of Canadian AIDS cases (Health
Canada, 2001). Thus, health and social services have been called on to
respond to the needs of gay and bisexual men, and their families and friends.
The initial appearance of the illness in North America primarily among gay
men buttressed the stereotype of same-sex sexual orientation as a dangerous
pathology (Herringer, 1996). However, the response to the epidemic also had
positive impacts because it mobilized the gay and lesbian communities,
bringing them closer together (Stoller, 1998) and stimulated the development
of community-based AIDS service organizations (Cain, 1997). The need to
develop policies for the prevention of HIV infection and to address the complex medical and social needs of those already living with the disease (Cadwell, 1998) forced mainstream services to address issues related to same-sex
sexual orientation in more supportive ways (Adam, 1995). One of the barriers
to accessing services for people with HIV/AIDS is the stigma attached to the
disease because of its association with same-sex sexuality (Mykhalovskiy &
Smith, 1993), a stigma some agencies have attempted to avoid by downplay-
ing their connections to the gay community (Cain, 1997).

Policies of Social Services and Professional Education

In addition to having the same health and social service needs as heterosexuals, gay, lesbian, and bisexual people may have needs specifically related to
the pervasive social stigmatization attached to their sexual orientation. In
particular, they may need help in coping with discrimination and harassment (Connolly, 1996; Mancoske, 1997; McCreary Centre Society, 1999;
Richardson & May, 1999), integrating their sexuality into their lives and developing a positive identity (Gochros & Bidwell, 1996; Lipton, 1996; O'Neill, 1999;
Shernoff, 1998; Tully, 2000), and establishing and maintaining supportive
relationships (Appleby & Anastas, 1998; Frederiksen, 1999; Hart, 1995; McVinney, 1998; Mendez, 1996). Despite the progressive policy developments
described earlier in relation to same-sex sexual orientation, heterosexism
continues to present barriers to accessing services that respond adequately to
these needs.

A lingering effect of the history of criminalization and pathologization of
same-sex sexuality is that agencies are slow to respond to the rights of gay

people to equitable services. Although agency policies proscribe direct discrimination on the basis of sexual orientation, for the most part they do not provide for services that support the lives of gay and lesbian people (Carter, 1998). The intent of this omission may be to provide services equally to all (Brotman et al., 2002b); however, another purpose may be to avoid the controversy that officially addressing gay and lesbian issues could provoke (Reilly, 1996). Unfortunately, because of the pervasiveness of heterosexism, the effect is to silence discussion of sexual orientation, impeding the development of accessible and responsive programs, and leaving decisions regarding service delivery to individual workers. This approach may not only prevent clients from receiving adequate service, but also leave workers without guidance and support in their practice (Mallon, 2000; O'Brien, Travers & Bell, 1993).

When differences of sexual orientation are not comprehensively addressed throughout organizational policies, heterosexist assumptions subtly shape practices. Most health and social services do not gather information regarding the sexual orientation of clients (Harris & Licata, 2000). However, if they did, in the absence of official statements affirming respect for gay, lesbian, and bisexual people, clients may not feel safe enough to reveal their sexual orientation, withholding information that could be crucial in their care (Brotman et al., 2002b). The result is that agencies remain for the most part unaware of the presence of people who are oriented to their own sex in the populations they serve and do not recognize their unique needs (Daley, 1998). For example, child welfare services and schools may fail to protect youth who are questioning their sexual orientation from abuse and harassment, and may not support them in integrating their sexuality into their identities (Fontaine, 1997; Khayatt, 1995; Mallon, 1998; O'Brien, 1994). Similarly, geriatric services may overlook the needs of elderly gays and lesbians (Jacobs, Rasmussen, & Hohman, 1999) who may fear that they will have to conceal their sexual orientation when living in long-term care facilities, thus increasing their isolation (Koth, 2001). The presupposition that battering occurs only in male-female relationships may contribute to services being unresponsive to the needs of those abused by same-sex partners (Lutz, 1998; Merrill & Wolfe, 2000). Unawareness of the pervasiveness and impact of heterosexism may cause addiction services to disregard the stress of coping with anti-gay discrimination in their programs (Travers & Schneider, 1996). Finally, lack of acknowledgement of same-sex relationships by health care providers may result in exclusion of the partners of gay patients from involvement in their care (Mule, 1999).

In the absence of affirmative policies, agency personnel may also conceal their sexual orientation, contributing to the impression that all service providers are heterosexual, and denying colleagues and clients the benefit of their knowledge and experience (Hidalgo, 1995). Furthermore, the lack of attention to heterosexism leaves undisturbed the knowledge deficiencies and negative attitudes of many helping professionals (Brotman et al., 2002b; Mule, 1999). Although there is evidence that inclusion of issues of sexual orientation

in professional education has improved the quality of services to gay and les- Conclusion
bian clients (Liddle, 1999), there are still educational policy and curriculum
gaps in this area (O'Neill, 1995; Stainton & Swift, 1996). Similar to the policies References
of many service providers, while the Canadian Association of Schools of Social
Work (CASSW, 2000) prohibits discrimination on the basis of sexual orientation, it does not specify that content regarding heterosexism and same-sex
sexual orientation be included in curricula.

The first step in addressing the lack of attention to sexual orientation in
mainstream social services is to acknowledge that gay, lesbian and bisexual
people are among the clients of the agency (Taylor, 1994). Subsequently, gay
and lesbian people can be involved in the systematic review and development of policies to comprehensively address issues related to sexual orientation (Mule, 1999). A successful approach to the development of services is
collaboration between mainstream agencies and the plethora of social services that have developed within gay and lesbian communities (Poverny, 1999).
In particular, it would be useful for non-gay community organizations that
focus on countering discrimination to join with gay and lesbian organizations in addressing heterosexism.

Conclusion

This overview of social policy developments in Canada relevant to sexual orientation reveals a steady movement toward respect for gay and lesbian people and recognition of their rights to equitable access to social resources. This
trend is consistent with Canadian ideals regarding acceptance of diversity
and the achievement of social justice. It seems inevitable that the process
will continue and that gay and lesbian people will eventually achieve full participation in social institutions. With changes well underway at the legislative
level, the focus now shifts to challenging heterosexism at the program level.
Health and social services will need to systematically examine their policies
and practices to determine how they subtly silence, ignore, and disadvantage people who are oriented to members of their own sex. This process will
require openness, sensitivity, and courage, as addressing issues related to
sexuality touches on strongly held values that are integral to identity. At the
same time, it needs to be recognized that heterosexism is but one oppressive ideology. To successfully advance social justice, policies at each level
simultaneously need to address the expression of all forms of marginalization.

References

Adam, B.D. (1995). *The rise of a gay and lesbian movement* (rev. ed.). New York:
Twayne.
Adam, B.D., Duyvendak, J.W., & Krouwel, A. (Eds.). (1999). *The global emergence of
gay and lesbian politics: National imprints of a worldwide movement.* Philadelphia: Temple University Press.
American Psychological Association (APA). (2001). *Guidelines for psychotherapy
with lesbian, gay and bisexual clients.* Online at <www.apa.org>.

References   Antoniuk, T. (1999). Policy alternative for a diverse community: Lesbians and family law. *Journal of Gay & Lesbian Social Services, 10*(1), 46-70.

Appleby G.A., & Anastas, J.W. (1998). *Not just a passing phase: Social work with gay, lesbian, and bisexual people.* New York: Columbia University Press.

Archer, B. (1999). *The end of gay (and the death of heterosexuality).* Toronto: Doubleday Canada.

Arnup, K. (1999). Out in this world: The social and legal context of gay and lesbian families. *Journal of Gay & Lesbian Social Services, 10*(1), 1-25.

Berger, R.M. & Kelly, J.J. (1995). Gay men overview. In R.L. Edwards (Ed.),*Encyclopedia of social work* (19th ed.) (Vol. 1, pp. 1064-1075). Washington, DC: NASW.

Bibby, R. (1995). *The Bibby report: Social trends Canadian style.* Toronto: Stoddart.

Binson, D., Michaels, S., Stall, R., Coates, T.J., Gagnon, J.H., & Catania, J.A. (1995). Prevalence and social distribution of men who have sex with men: United States and its urban centers. *Journal of Sex Research, 32*(3), 245-254.

British Columbia Human Rights Commission. (2001). 1999 Public Opinion Survey. Online at <www.bchrc.gov.bc.ca>.

Brotman, S., Ryan, B, Jalbert, Y., & Rowe, B. (2002a). Reclaiming space-regaining health: The health care experiences of two-spirited people in Canada. *Journal of Gay & Lesbian Social Services, 14*(1), 67-87.

Brotman, S., Ryan, B., Jalbert, Y., & Rowe, B. (2002b). The impact of coming out on health and health care access: The experiences of gay, lesbian, bisexual and two-spirited people. *Journal of Health and Social Policy, 15*(1), 1-29.

Cadwell, S.A. (1998). Providing services to gay men. In D.M. Aronstein & B.J. Thompson (Eds.), *HIV and social work: A practitioner's guide* (pp. 411-429). New York: Harrington Park Press.

Cain, R. (1997). Environmental change and organizational evolution: Reconsidering the niche of community-based AIDS organizations. *AIDS Care, 9*(3), 331.

Canadian Association of Schools of Social Work (CASSW). (2000). Educational policy statements. Online at <www.cassw-acess.ca>.

Canadian Press. (2000, February 9). [Excerpts from 1998 Angus Reid poll on homosexual rights]. *Canadian Press Newswire.*

Carter, D.D. (1998). Employment benefits for same sex couples: The expanding entitlement. *Canadian Public Policy, 24*(1), 107-117.

Casswell, D.G. (1996). *Lesbians, gay men, and Canadian law.* Toronto: Emond Montgomery Publications.

Churchill, W. (1967). *Homosexual behavior among males: A cross-cultural and cross-species investigation.* New York: Hawthorn Books.

Coalition for Gay Rights in Ontario. (1986). *Discrimination against lesbians and gay men: The Ontario human rights omission.* Toronto: Author.

Connolly, L. (1996). Long-term care and hospice: The special needs of older GAY men and lesbians. *Journal of Gay & Lesbian Social Services, 5*(1), 77-91.

Daley, A. (1998). Lesbian invisibility in health care services: Heterosexual hegemony and strategies for change. *Canadian Social Work Review, 15*(1), 57-71.

De Cecco, J.P., & Elia, J.P. (1993). A critique and synthesis of biological essentialism and social constructionist views of sexuality and gender. In J.P. De Cecco & J.P. Elia (Eds.), *If you seduce a straight person, can you make them gay?* Binghampton, NY: Harrington Park Press.

Diamond, M. (1993). Homosexuality and bisexuality in different populations. *Archives of Sexual Behavior, 22*(4), 291-310.

Donovan, C., Heaphy, B., & Weeks, J. (1999). Citizenship and same sex relationships. *Journal of Social Policy, 28*(4), 689-709.

EGALE. (1998). State of the play: Gay and lesbian rights in Canada. Online at <www.egale.ca/features>.

EGALE. (2000, December 16). Federal omnibus legislation. Online at <www.egale. **References**
ca/politics/politics.htm>.

EGALE. (2001). Historical polls on sexual orientation. Online at <www.egale.ca/
features/polls1.htm>.

Fontaine, J.H. (1997). The sound of silence: Public school response to the needs of
gay and lesbian youth. *Journal of Gay & Lesbian Social Services, 7*(4), 101-109.

Frederiksen, K.I. (1999), Family caregiving responsibilities among lesbians and gay
men. *Social Work, 44*(2), 142-155.

Friend, R. (1993). Choices not closets: Heterosexism and homophobia in schools. In
L. Weis & M. Fine (Eds.), *Beyond silenced voices: Class, race, and gender in United
States schools.* Albany, NY: SUNY Press.

Gochros, H.L., & Bidwell, R. (1996). Lesbian and gay youth in a straight world: Implications for health care workers. *Journal of Gay & Lesbian Social Services, 5*(1),
1-17.

Greene, B. (Ed.) (1997). *Ethnic and cultural diversity among lesbians and gay men.*
Thousand Oaks, CA: Sage.

Harris, H.L., & Licata, F. (2000). From fragmentation to integration: Affirming the
identities of culturally diverse, mentally ill lesbians and gay men. *Journal of
Gay & Lesbian Social Services, 11*(4), 93-103.

Harry, J. (1990). A probability sample of gay males. *Journal of Homosexuality, 19*(1),
89-104.

Hart, J. (1995). Same sex couples and counselling: The development of a multicultural perspective. In G. Sullivan, L.W.-T. Leong (Eds.), *Gays and lesbians in Asia
and the Pacific: Social and human services* (pp. 89-108). New York: Harrington
Park Press.

Health Canada. (2001, October). EPI update, May 2001. Online at <www.hc-sc.
gc.ca>.

Herek, G.M. (1996). Heterosexism and homophobia. In R.P. Cabaj & T.S. Stein (Eds.),
Textbook of homosexuality and mental health (pp. 101-113). Washington, DC:
American Psychiatric Press.

Herringer, B. (1996). A clash of knowledges: Toward an analysis of the social ogani-
zation of AIDS "suicide." *Canadian Social Work Review, 13*(1), 39-52.

Hidalgo, H. (1995). The norms of conduct in social service agencies: A threat to the
mental health of Puerto Rican lesbians. *Journal of Gay & Lesbian Social Services, 3*(2), 23-41.

Hinsch, B. (1990). *Passions of the cut sleeve: The male homosexual tradition in
China.* Berkeley: University of California Press.

International Lesbian and Gay Association (ILGA). (2001, July 13). *ILGA World Legal
Survey.* Online at <www.ilga.org>.

Irvine, J.M. (1995). *Sexuality education across cultures: Working with differences.*
San Francisco: Jossey-Bass.

Jacobs, R.J., Rasmussen, L.A., & Hohman, M.M. (1999). The social support needs of
older lesbians, gay men, and bisexuals. *Journal of Gay & Lesbian Social Services, 9*(1), 1-30.

Khayatt, D. (1995). Compulsory heterosexuality: Schools and lesbian students. In
M. Campbell & A. Manicom (Eds.), *Knowledge, experience, and ruling relations:
Studies in the social organization of knowledge* (pp. 149-163). Toronto: Univer-
sity of Toronto Press.

Kinsey, A.C., Pomeroy, W.B., & Martin, C.E. (1948). *Sexual behavior in the human
male.* Philadelphia: W.B. Sanders.

Kinsey, A.C., Pomeroy, W.B., Martin, C.E., & Gebhard, P. (1955). *Sexual behavior in
the human female.* Philadelphia: W.B. Sanders.

Kinsman, G. (1995). The textual practices of sexual rule: Sexual policing and gay
men. In M. Campbell & A. Manicom (Eds.), *Knowledge, experience, and ruling*

References

relations: Studies in the social organization of knowledge (pp. 80-95). Toronto: University of Toronto Press.

Kinsman, G. (1996). *The regulation of desire: Homo and hetero sexualities* (2nd ed.). Montreal: Black Rose Books.

Koth, C. (2001). *Exploring the lives of elder gay men: A framework for social work practice.* Unpublished MSW thesis, UBC School of Social Work and Family Studies, Vancouver.

Liddle, B.J. (1999). Recent improvements in mental health services to lesbian and gay clients. *Journal of Homosexuality, 37*(4), 127-137.

Lipton, B. (1996). Opening doors: Responding to the mental health need of gay and bisexual college students. *Journal of Gay & Lesbian Social Services, 4*(2), 7-24.

Lutz, J. (1998). *Support services for lesbians experiencing relationship abuse: Barriers to healing.* Unpublished graduating essay, UBC School of Social Work, Vancouver.

MacDougall, B. (2000). *Queer judgments: Homosexuality, expression, and the courts in Canada.* Toronto: University of Toronto Press.

Mallon, G.P. (1998). *We don't exactly get the welcome wagon: The experiences of gay and lesbian adolescents in child welfare systems.* New York: Columbia University Press.

Mallon, G.P. (2000). Gay men and lesbians as adoptive parents. *Journal of Gay & Lesbian Social Services, 11*(4), 1-22.

Mancoske, R.J. (1997). Rural HIV/AIDS social services for gays and lesbians. *Journal of Gay & Lesbian Social Services, 7*(3), 37-52.

McCreary Centre Society. (1999). *Being out: Lesbian, gay, bisexual and trangendered youth in B.C.: An adolescent health survey.* Burnaby, BC: Author.

McInnes, C. (2001, July 17). B.C. quits same-sex challenge. *Vancouver Sun,* p. A3.

McKirnan, D.J., Stokes, J.P., Doll, L., & Burzette, R.G. (1995). Bisexually active men: Social characteristics and sexual behavior. *Journal of Sex Research, 32*(1), 65-76.

McVinney, L.D. (1998). Social work practice with gay male couples. In G.P. Mallon (Ed.), *Foundations of social work practice with lesbian and gay persons* (pp. 209-227). New York: Haworth Press.

Mendez, J.M. (1996). Serving gays and lesbians of color who are survivors of domestic violence. *Journal of Gay & Lesbian Social Services, 4,* 53-59.

Merrill, G.S., & Wolfe, V.A. (2000). Battered gay men: An exploration of abuse, help seeking, and why they stay. *Journal of Homosexuality, 39*(2), 1-30.

Mule, N. (1999). Social work and the provision of health care and social services to sexual minority populations. *Canadian Social Work, 1*(1), 39-55.

Murphy, T.F. (1997). *Gay science: The ethics of sexual orientation research.* New York: Columbia University Press.

Mykhalovskiy, E., & Smith, G.W. (1993). *Hooking up to social services: A report on the barriers people living with HIV/AIDS face accessing social services.* Toronto: Community AIDS Treatment Information Exchange and Ontario Institute for Studies in Education.

O'Brien, C.A. (1994). The social organization of the treatment of lesbian, gay and bisexual youth in group homes and youth shelters. *Canadian Review of Social Policy, 34,* 37-57

O'Brien, C.A., & Goldberg, A. (2000). Lesbians and gay men inside and outside families. In N. Mandell & A. Duffy (Eds.), *Canadian families: Diversity, conflict, and change* (2nd ed.) (pp. 115-145). Toronto: Harcourt Brace Canada.

O'Brien, C., Travers, R., & Bell, L. (1993). *No safe bed: Lesbian, gay and bisexual youth in residential services.* Toronto: Central Toronto Youth Services.

O'Neill, B.J. (1995). Canadian social work education and same-sex sexual orientation. *Canadian Social Work Review, 12*(2), 159-174.

O'Neill, B.J. (1999). Social work with gay, lesbian and bisexual members of racial and **References**
ethnic minority groups. In G. Lie & D. Este (Eds.), *Professional social service
delivery in a multicultural world* (pp. 75-91). Toronto: Canadian Scholars' Press.

Poverny, L. (1999). It's all a matter of attitude: Creating and maintaining receptive
services for sexual minority families. *Journal of Gay & Lesbian Social Services,*
10(1), 95-113.

Reilly, T. (1996). Gay and lesbian adoptions: A theoretical examination of policy-
making and organizational decision making. *Journal of Sociology and Social
Welfare, 23*(4), 99-115.

Richardson, D., & May, H. (1999). Deserving victims? Sexual status and the social
construction of violence. *Sociological Review, 47*(2), 308-332.

Riorden, M. (1996). *Out our way: Gay and lesbian life in the country.* Toronto:
Between the Lines.

Shernoff, M. (1998). Individual practice with gay men. In G.P. Mallon (Ed.), Foundations of social work practice with lesbian and gay persons (pp. 77-103). New
York: Haworth Press.

Schneider, M.S. (1997). Pride, prejudice and lesbian, gay and bisexual youth. In
M.S. Schneider (Ed.), *Pride and prejudice: Working with lesbian, gay and bisexual youth* (pp. 11-27). Toronto: Central Toronto Youth Services.

Sell, R.L., Wells, J.A., & Wypij, D. (1995). The prevalence of homosexual behavior
and attraction in the United States, the United Kingdom and France: Results of
national population-based samples. *Archives of Sexual Behavior, 24*(3), 235-
248.

Smith, M. (1999). *Lesbian and gay rights in Canada: Social movements and equality-
seeking, 1971-1995.* Toronto: University of Toronto Press.

Stainton, T., & Swift, K. (1996). "Difference" and social work curriculum. *Canadian
Social Work Review, 13*(1), 75-87.

Stoller, N.E. (1998). Lesbian involvement in the AIDS epidemic: Changing roles and
generational differences. In P.M. Nardi & B.E. Schneider (Eds.), *Social perspectives in lesbian and gay studies: A reader* (pp. 366-376). London: Routledge.

Taylor, N. (1994). Gay and lesbian youth: Challenging the policy of denial. *Journal
of Gay & Lesbian Social Services, 1*(3/4), 39-73.

Thompson, N. (1998). *Promoting equality: Challenging discrimination and oppression in the human services.* London: Macmillan.

Travers, R., & Schneider, M. (1996). Barriers to accessibility for lesbian and gay
youth needing addictions services. *Youth and Society, 27*(3), 356-378.

Tremble, B., Schneider, M., & Appathurai, C. (1989). Growing up gay or lesbian in a
multicultural context. *Journal of Homosexuality, 17*(3/4), 253-267.

Trussler, T., Barker, A., Buchner, C., Dolan, T., Granger, P., Jagosh, J., Marchand, R.,
Mo, E., Peralta, V., & Perchal, P. (2000). *Gay health in Vancouver: A quality of
life survey.* Vancouver: Community-Based Research Centre.

Tully C. T. (1995). Lesbians overview. In R.L. Edwards (Ed.), *Encyclopedia of social
work* (19th ed.) (Vol. 1, pp. 1591-1596). Washington, DC: NASW.

Tully, C.T. (2000). *Lesbians, gays, and the empowerment perspective.* New York:
Columbia University Press.

Weinberg, G.H. (1972). *Society and the healthy homosexual.* New York: St. Martin's
Press.

Widmer, E.D., Treas, J., & Newcomb, R. (1998). Attitudes toward nonmarital sex in 24
countries. *Canadian Journal of Human Sexuality, 7*(4), 349-59.

Williams, W.L. (1993). Being gay and doing research on homosexuality in non-west-
ern cultures. *Journal of Sex Research, 30*(2), 115-120.

Williamson, I.R. (2000). Internalized homophobia and health issues affecting lesbians and gay men. *Health Education Research: Theory and Practice, 15*(1), 97-
107.

References   **Additional Resources**

American Psychological Association. (2001). *Guidelines for psychotherapy with lesbian, gay and bisexual clients.* Online at <www.apa.org>.

Canadian Journal of Human Sexuality.

Coalition for Lesbian and Gay Rights in Ontario. Online at <www.web.ca/~clgro>.

EGALE. Online at <www.egale.ca/>.

International Lesbian & Gay Association. Online at <www.ilga.org>.

Journal of Gay & Lesbian Social Services.

Immigration and Refugee Policy in Canada: Past, Present, and Future

8

Usha George

C anada is one of the few countries in the world that has an active immigrant and refugee admission policy and program. Even before 1860, when figures on immigration became available, immigrants and refugees from different countries have made Canada their home. The 1990s can be described as the decade of immigration, as the average number of arrivals per annum exceeded 200,000, the highest in Canadian history (George & Fuller-Thompson, 1997). The numbers of newcomers and source countries have depended on the immigration policies and practices in effect at particular times. Immigration has become an enduring feature of Canada's policy milieu; however, this does not imply that immigration is an uncontested topic in Canada. As Freeman (1995, p. 882) points out, in liberal democracies such as Canada, the political economy model of policy making, with a constitution based on individual rights, competitive party systems, and periodic elections, influences the direction of immigration policy: "The politics of immigration in such systems can be analyzed at the level of individual voters, organized groups, and state actors."

The inevitable question is: Why immigration? The question can be answered at a general analytical or theoretical level, as well as by examining factors specific to Canada. At the analytical level, push-and-pull factors can explain immigration. Push factors operate when individuals decide to leave their country of origin because of worsening economic conditions, including high levels of unemployment. Pull factors operate when people are attracted to a country because of the opportunities it offers for economic betterment and social mobility. The distinction between push-and-pull factors is not always clear (Isajiw, 1999). Simmons (1998) argues that economic globalization leads to greater income inequality between developed and developing countries, and thus creates pressure for emigration in less developed countries. In the context of increased international competition, producers in wealthy nations get immigrant workers to work for low wages, resulting in conflicting views about immigration in those countries.

There are two explanations specific to the Canadian situation. First, Canada's natural population growth "has declined steadily in recent decades from 3 percent in the 1950s to less than 1 percent in the late 1990s" (Knowles,

2000, p. 4). Mackenzie King's 1947 statement in the House of Commons clearly indicated the population-enhancing goal of Canada's immigration policy: "The policy of the government is to foster the growth of the population of Canada by the encouragement of immigration. The government will seek by legislation, regulation, and vigorous administration, to ensure the careful selection and permanent settlement of such immigrants as can advantageously be absorbed in our national economy" (Knowles, 2000, p. 67).

The main reason for the decline in population growth is the drop in the fertility rate as a result of women entering the workforce as well as the general growing tendency for couples to have fewer or no children at all. The fertility rate declined from four children per woman in 1959 to less than two per woman by 1998. As Knowles (2000, p. 4) has observed, "should this low fertility rate continue—and all the indications are that it will—immigration will become essential for this country's healthy growth and even, perhaps, for its survival." Canada also has an aging population because people are living longer. The number of seniors has steadily increased over the last century. In 1991, 12% of the population was sixty-five years and older. Estimates are that by the year 2011, one-quarter of the population will be older than sixty-five years (Grant, 2000). Young immigrants thus offset the growing dependency ratio.

Second, there is the need for skilled labour. In fact, early immigration was spurred by the demand for labour to build railways and support industries such as mining, fishing, and lumber. As the supply of manual labour from the United States and Europe began to dwindle in the 1880s, over 1,500 labourers were recruited from China to lay the track for the Canadian Pacific Railway (Bolaria & Li, 1988; Henry, Tator, Mattis, & Rees, 2000). In more recent times, the need for skilled labour for Canada's expanding industrial and high-tech fields has been well recognized. Under current plans for the overhaul of Canada's immigration system, the temporary worker program will be redesigned to address the acute labour shortages in high-tech, building trades, and other areas identified by the private sector, in conjunction with the federal Human Resources Department (Thompson, 2001).

This article provides a brief overview of Canada's immigration and refugee policy and practice. Due to the extensive amount of scholarship on this topic, only a summary review is possible. The first section defines key terms such as immigrants, refugees, and newcomers. The next section provides a brief overview of the history of immigration in Canada, followed by an examination of the provisions in the new Immigration Act passed in the House of Commons on June 13, 2001.

In order to illustrate the workings of the Immigration Act, a summary of the annual plan for 2001 and 2002 follows. The final section offers an analysis of immigration and refugee policies in Canada. The term "immigrant" generally refers to anyone from another country who is legally admitted to live in a country. In Canada, these people are also called permanent residents or landed immigrants. Landed immigrants can apply to become Canadian citizens after three years. Canadian citizenship is granted to any landed immigrant, provided the person meets residency requirements, has no criminal record, and passes a simple citizenship test. A landed immigrant is entitled to all the privileges of a citizen, except the right to vote in provincial and federal elections; however, once a citizen, regardless of the country of origin, a person is entitled to all rights and privileges.

In practice, however, immigrants experience landed immigrant status and citizenship differently because of discrimination and prejudice in Canadian society. While each group of immigrants has its own experiences of discrimination and prejudice, people from visible minority backgrounds generally continue to be perceived as immigrants, regardless of their length of stay in Canada. A great deal of scholarship has developed around the notion of the "social construction of immigrants and refugees." Li (1997) calls this "bench marking," as the term "immigrant" is used as a folk, bureaucratic, and analytical concept.

As Isajiw (1999, p. 71) observes, " refugees are people who have to leave a country because they are denied a human existence and are accepted by another country on account of this country's humane or humanitarian concerns." These refugees are also called convention refugees, as per the United Nations' Convention on the Status of Refugees, 1951/1967, to which Canada is a signatory. Two distinct groups of refugees are recognized in Canadian policy and practice circles: sponsored refugees and asylum seekers or refugee claimants. Sponsored refugees can be either government or privately sponsored. Privately sponsored refugees are those sponsored by religious or other non-profit groups. Once in Canada, sponsored refugees receive landed immigrant status and all related entitlements. Asylum seekers or refugee claimants, on the other hand, are people who arrive in Canada as visitors and apply for refugee status for fear of persecution in their countries of origin. Asylum seekers must undergo a lengthy process of hearings and appeals with the Immigration and Refugee Board (IRB). Once accepted by the IRB, these people acquire the status of convention refugees, but they have to go through the immigration process to become landed immigrants. Canada's domestic law integrates its international obligation by stipulating that convention refugees legally in Canada cannot be deported unless they pose a threat to national security or commit serious crimes (Christensen, 1999).

Asylum seekers/refugee claimants as a separate refugee group are mostly invisible, mainly because they are excluded from receiving many of the entitlements awarded to landed immigrants and citizens. Most claims come from refugee-producing countries (Adelman, 1991; Richmond, 1994), yet because of its distance from refugee-producing regions, Canada receives fewer refugee claimants than, for example, European countries (Macklin, 2001). Currently an estimated 150 million people are on the move worldwide, fleeing civil strife, ethnic conflict, natural disasters, and economic and political upheaval (Citizenship and Immigration Canada, 2001a).

Immigration and refugee policy in Canada

In recent times, the term "newcomer," which does not distinguish people on the basis of their legal status, has been used by academic, bureaucratic, and social service communities because it is considered more inclusive. This term distinguishes individuals based on their length of time in Canada, and this distinction serves an instrumental purpose for the federal Department of Citizenship and Immigration settlement services, which are generally available to landed immigrants who have been in the country for less than five years. Service providers, however, contend that the term "newcomer" masks the ongoing problems faced by immigrants in general, regardless of the length of their stay in Canada. Discrimination in employment, stereotyping faced by visible minorities, and family and youth issues faced by second-generation immigrants are examples of such problems.

Another important term in Canadian immigration policy is "family class." Generally, family-class or family-related immigrants are those who migrate to another country to join immediate relatives. Family-class relatives may include lineal relatives such as spouses, parents, children, and grandparents, as well as lateral relatives such as brothers, sisters, and uncles (Isajiw, 1999). Although historically, Canadian immigration policy and practice have allowed a mix of lineal and lateral relatives, the current policy restricts family class to lineal relatives.

History of Canadian Immigration Policy and Practice

Canadian immigration policy and practice have attracted a great deal of scholarly attention. Bolaria and Li (1988) examine the experiences of different visible minority ethnic groups in Canadian society in terms of Canada's attempts at capital accumulation for the development of a capitalist state. Other scholars have divided the history of Canadian immigration into stages or phases, often according to major policy changes (Abu-Laban, 1998; Christensen, 1999; Green & Green 1996; Henry, Tator, Mattis, & Rees, 2000; Isajiw 1999; Knowles, 2000). Isajiw (1999) divides the history of settlement, colonization, and immigration in Canada into eight stages. For the purpose of providing a brief overview of Canadian immigration, we turn to Isajiw (1999), as he provides a chronologically comprehensive account of Canada's immigration history.

The original settlers of Canada were the ancestors of today's First Nations or Native peoples. When European settlers arrived, about 220,000 Indians and Inuit were living on the land. Isajiw describes the years 1600-1759 as the period of French immigration to Canada. The British defeat of the French in 1759 marked the next phase of colonization and immigration, when large numbers of English, Scottish, and German immigrants, along with many Loyalist refugees and exiles from the American Revolution, settled in Canada. In the latter half of the eighteenth century, the basic "pattern of continuous annual immigration was set." "Another pattern, however, was also being established, that of migrant subordination of other ethnic and racial groups who were beginning to immigrate to Canada. This pattern was enormously reinforced in the next period of Canadian history" (Isajiw, 1999; p. 80).

The beginning of the 1880s was unique: people from many parts of the world started coming to Canada because the country needed additional labour not only for its farms but also for the industries that were being built by the expanding railway system. Among workers recruited to Canada for the Canadian Pacific Railway were prominent groups of Chinese, Japanese, and East Indians. Between 1880 and 1914, many refugees and immigrants arrived in Canada: Jews, Hungarians, Mormons, Ukrainians, Sikhs, Japanese, and Italians, as well as people from Britain and America. While Canada had immigration laws since 1869, the first Immigration Act of 1906 established formal policies and gave power over national borders (Knowles, 2000).

The period between the two world wars was one of immigration restriction and reduction. The Canadian government took specific measures to prevent immigration from non-European countries and to limit the arrival of the families of the immigrants already here. Concern about the ethnic composition of the Canadian population was foremost in the minds of policy makers. The continuation of the Head Tax for the Chinese, the limitation of Japanese immigration to 400 per year, introduction of the Continuous Passage rule, and restriction of Black immigration are all examples of how policy makers handled such concerns. At the end of World War II there was large-scale immigrant and refugee movement to Canada; however, the restrictions on Asian immigration remained, as it was believed that large-scale immigration from the Orient would alter the "fundamental composition" of the Canadian population (Isajiw, 1999).

Government policy began to change during the first half of the 1960s, which signalled a movement toward the removal of restrictions on nationality-based immigration, although preference remained for Caucasian immigrants. For example, in 1961, British immigration was only 17% of the total immigration for the year; in 1966, it rose to 37% (Isajiw, 1999). The number of immigrants from other ethnic groups, including Asian and Black, also increased during this period.

The white paper on immigration, released in 1966, formed the basis for the new immigration regulations of 1967 (Isajiw, 1999). Through regulatory changes, racial discrimination was eliminated as the basis for selecting immigrants; in addition, the point system was introduced in an attempt to bring justice and fairness to the immigration process, as well as to meet the needs of the country. Under the new merit-point structure, applicants in the category of "independent immigrants" were to be assessed on the basis of a number of characteristics, each of which was assigned a range of merit points. The characteristics included education and training; personal qualities such as adaptability, motivation, and initiative; demand for the individual's occupation in Canada; occupational skill; arranged employment; knowledge of English or French; relatives in Canada; and employment opportunities in the area of destination (Isajiw, 1999). Beginning in 1968, the ethnic composition

History of Canadian immigration policy and practice

of immigrants changed as a result of this non-racist immigration policy. The period 1968-1976 "represented the reversal of the proportion of the white to non-white immigrants to Canada" (Isajiw, 1999; p. 85). Furthermore, Canada's endorsement of the United Nations' Convention on Refugees in 1970 led to refugees from Czechoslovakia, Tibet, Uganda, Chile, Vietnam, and Cambodia being admitted to Canada.

The volume of immigration became more of a concern in 1974, the year in which Canada had one of the largest influxes in the postwar period. A government study of immigration—the green paper on immigration—was tabled in the House of Commons and became the Immigration Act of 1976, which took effect in 1978. The changes introduced in the new legislation resulted from a number of factors: internal pressure for a multiculturalism policy that would recognize the racial and ethnic diversity in Canada; increasing politicization and mobilization of minority immigrant groups demanding a fair immigration policy; pressure by human rights activists; pressure from the international community to eliminate open racism; and, most importantly, economic need. Faced with dwindling European immigration, the shortage of highly educated and skilled workers was a major government concern (Henry et al., 2000).

The 1976 Act was a piece of framework legislation that included only the main provisions, leaving most of the details to regulations. The Immigration Act and Regulations were based on such fundamental principles as non-discrimination, family reunion, humanitarian concern for refugees, and the promotion of Canada's social, economic, demographic, and cultural goals (Citizenship and Immigration Canada, 2001a). Major features of the Act included linking immigration to economic conditions and demographic needs. It also required the minister of Immigration to announce annual immigration plans, which would estimate the number of immigrants Canada could absorb comfortably each year. These plans were to be presented to Parliament after mandatory consultations with both provincial and territorial governments, and private and voluntary sectors. The Act stipulated four basic categories of individuals eligible for landed immigrant status: 1) family class; 2) humanitarian class consisting of refugees defined in the 1951 United Nations' Convention relating to refugees and a designated class of displaced persons who do not qualify as refugees under the UN definition; 3) independent class, selected on the basis of the point system; and 4) assisted relatives who are distant relatives sponsored by a family member in Canada and who meet some of the selection criteria of the independent class (Knowles, 2000). It also established the Immigration and Refugee Board and required immigrants and visitors to obtain visas from abroad. The Act protected the civil rights of immigrants and visitors through a quasi-judicial inquiry and provided short-term alternatives to permanent deportation for cases involving violation of the Immigration Law (Citizenship and Immigration Canada, 2001a).

In the next twenty-eight years of its operation, the Act was changed through a number of regulations (Simmons, 1998). By the end of 1980s, there was new criticism of immigration because of an economic recession and an increased number of asylum seekers. In 1993, the Immigration Act was amended to link it to population and labour market needs. The 1993 amendments introduced three classes of immigrants: family class, refugees, and independent immigrants consisting of business immigrants, skilled workers, and assisted relatives. Since then, more of Canada's immigrants have been arriving from non-traditional source countries (Isajiw, 1999). For example, the top ten source countries during 2000 were China, India, Pakistan, Philippines, South Korea, Sri Lanka, United States, Iran, Yugoslavia, and Great Britain (Citizenship and Immigration Canada, 2001a).

Live-in caregiver program

Live-in Caregiver Program

The review of Canadian immigration policy and practice would not be complete without noting another significant initiative, the domestic worker program or Live-in Caregiver Program, as it is known today. Since its inception, this program has undergone a number of changes, and Cohen's (1994) account of the evolution of the domestic worker program is summarized below.

During the late nineteenth century, when settlement in the Canadian prairies was expanding, Canada recruited domestic workers from rural areas in England, Scotland, Ireland, and Wales to perform various household tasks. In the 1920s, under the Servant-Turn-Mistress Program, Northern European women were recruited for the Canadian Northwest. However, during the Depression and World War II, the modification of exclusionary immigration laws and shortage of domestic workers from Britain compelled Canada to recruit domestics from countries such as Germany, Italy, and Greece. Between 1950 and 1954, 15,000 Central European domestics arrived in Canada.

In 1955, in response to the great need for domestics, Canada and the United Kingdom signed an agreement called the West Indies Domestic Scheme. Consequently, between 1955 and 1967, 3,000 Black women were allowed to enter Canada. The point system introduced in 1967 applied to domestics as well, although the criteria were different. In 1973, a new policy called the Employment Authorization Program was introduced. Under this policy, domestic workers were not allowed to apply for landed status. As a result of the lobbying efforts by organizations supportive of domestic workers in Canada, the then minister of Immigration appointed a task force to review this policy, and the government introduced a new policy called the Foreign Domestic Movement in 1979. The main provision of the policy was that domestics could apply from within Canada to be permanent residents after two years of continuous service if they also demonstrated self-sufficiency or the potential to achieve self-sufficiency. The new policy detailed

Bill C-11:
The Immi-
gration and
Refugee
Protection
Act 2001 the salaries and benefits for workers, as well as employers' responsibilities. In 1988, the government introduced new guidelines to evaluate each applicant, and in 1992, the program was revised to become the Live-in Caregiver Program. Two sets of conditions apply to any candidate: one for admission to the program, and the other for eligibility for landed status. The program has attracted a great deal of criticism (e.g., Calliste, 1991; Cohen, 1994; Cunningham, 1995; INTERCEDE, 1992; Stasiulis & Bakan, 1997a, 1997b; Villasin & Phillips, 1994) for its sexist and classist regulations such as the "live-in" requirement.

Bill C11: The Immigration and Refugee Protection Act 2001

In 1994, the federal government held public consultations to decide future directions for immigration and refugee policy. A non-partisan advisory group set up by the federal government reviewed legislation, programs, and policies relating to immigrants and refugees, and in 1998 the group produced a report entitled *Not Just Numbers: A Canadian Framework for Future Immigration*. The report, with its 172 recommendations, was to form the basis for a new immigration law, replacing the 1978 Immigration Act. Originally proposed as Bill C-31, it was then revised and renamed Bill C-11 when it was presented to the House of Commons in February 2001. The House passed the Act Respecting Immigration to Canada and the Granting of Refugee Protection to Persons Who Are Displaced, Persecuted or in Danger on June 13, 2001.

The Act is framework legislation, similar to the 1978 Immigration Act; however, it incorporates some core principles previously intended to be included in the regulations. These include the principles of equality and freedom from discrimination; of detaining a minor child only as a last resort and in the "best interests of the child"; and of equality of status for both official languages. The Act specifies separate objectives for immigration and refugee admission (sections 3.1 and 3.2; Bill C-11). The Act and regulations consist of provisions regarding consultations with provinces, the volume and selection criteria of immigrants, definition and processing of refugees, sponsorship rights, fees, and appeals and deportation. Although it does not specify each covenant to which Canada has subscribed, the Act does refer to the Canadian Charter of Rights and Freedoms and states that immigration policy must fulfill Canada's international legal obligations. Such obligations include the Convention on the Rights of the Child, the Convention on the Status of Refugees, the Convention Against Torture, the Convention on the Reduction of Statelessness, and the Declaration of the Rights and the Duties of Man.

The Act recognizes three categories of foreign nationals for permanent resident status: family class; economic class, to be selected on the basis of each applicant's ability to become economically self-sufficient in Canada; and Convention refugees to be selected inside or outside Canada. Family class is established for the first time in the Act, and parents are now included in the definition of family class. Family class also includes common-law and same-sex partners. The Act also broadens the definition of dependent child from under age nineteen to under age twenty-two.

Government can now collect from a sponsor the amount of social assistance given to a sponsored family member. The length of sponsorship requirement has been reduced from ten to three years for spouses and common-law partners, both opposite and same-sex. The age at which Canadian citizens and permanent residents can sponsor has been reduced from nineteen to eighteen. The Act has also created an in-Canada landing class for sponsored spouses and partners of both immigrants and refugees, and it exempts sponsored spouses, partners, and dependent children from inadmissibility on the basis of excessive demand on health and social services (Citizenship and Immigration Canada, 2001c). Family reunification provisions are mostly left to regulations (Canadian Council for Refugees, 2001; p. 48). Sponsorship obligations have been strengthened for people who default on court-ordered child-support payments, and individuals who have been convicted of domestic abuse and not demonstrated rehabilitation do not have sponsorship privileges. People on social assistance, except in cases of disability, also do not have sponsorship privileges. Through legislative provisions, the Act strengthens the federal government's ability to recover the cost of social assistance in cases of sponsorship default.

The Act sets up criteria for permanent residents. Permanent residents have to meet the physical residency requirement of being present in Canada for a cumulative period of two years for every five working years. Exceptions are allowed for people who have to spend time outside Canada to accompany a Canadian citizen, to work for a Canadian company, or for humanitarian reasons. All permanent residents are to have fraud-resistant permanent resident cards. Loss-of-status cases can present an oral appeal to the Immigration and Refugee Board (Citizenship and Immigration Canada, 2001c).

In terms of selecting skilled workers in the economic class, perhaps one of the most unique features of the Act is its movement away from using an occupation-based model to using a model based on flexible and transferable skills. The proposed human capital model will replace the general occupation list and intended occupation concepts. Education and knowledge of an official language are given more weight; however, language is no bar to admission. An in-Canada landing class has been created for temporary workers, including recent graduates who have a permanent job offer and have been working in Canada. The temporary worker program will be expanded to meet the immediate needs of employers. The Act also proposes to establish objective criteria to assess the business experience of both investor and entrepreneur programs, and to establish a net worth for entrepreneurs (Citizenship and Immigration Canada, 2001c).

The Act defines two classes of refugees: Convention refugees and people in need of protection. The Act proposes to strengthen refugee protection and overseas resettlement by ensuring that people in need of urgent protection are brought to Canada within days, and by pursuing agreements with non-

Bill C-11:
The Immigration and Refugee Protection Act 2001

Bill C-11:
The Immi-
gration and
Refugee
Protection
Act 2001
governmental organizations to locate and prescreen refugee applications in areas where refugees are most in need of protection. It also proposes to amend the criteria for claimants' ability to establish themselves in Canada to include social as well as economic factors. To facilitate family reunification of refugees, overseas families (including extended family members) are to be processed as a unit whenever possible. Dependants of a refugee, whether living in Canada or abroad, will be processed as part of the same application within one year of the refugee's obtaining permanent status. Another feature of the Act is its provision for faster and fairer refugee processing inland. Referral to the Immigration and Refugee Board is to be made within three working days, with single interviewers supported by paper appeal being the norm. A single hearing is to examine all risk grounds, such as the Geneva Convention, the Convention Against Torture, and the risk of cruel and unusual punishment. The waiting period for landing in Canada for undocumented refugees, who are unable to obtain documents from their country of origin, has been reduced from five to three years. A security check is to be initiated when a person makes a refugee claim; merit will be determined by an independent adjudicator. Perhaps the most controversial provisions of the Act concern enforcement: the Act increases penalties for existing offences and creates a new offence for human trafficking. The penalty for migrant smuggling and trafficking is life in prison.

Many organizations, such as Amnesty International, the Canadian Bar Association, the Canadian Council for Refugees, the Maytree Foundation, and the United Nations High Commissioner for Refugees, along with provincial and citywide advocacy groups, have raised significant concerns about the new Act. Criticisms of the two documents leading to the new Immigration Act (Bill C-11) and its precursor (Bill C-31) can be grouped into three main areas: the framework legislation's lack of transparency, human rights, and class and gender concerns.

Lack of Transparency

Like previous legislations, the current Act is framework legislation, in that many important details are left to regulations. Consequently, Citizenship and Immigration Canada can implement immigration policy changes without having to face the House of Commons or public scrutiny. This latitude allows the government to say one thing but, in effect, do another (Green & Green, 1996). Although it is recognized that this structure allows the system to be more flexible and responsive, such wide powers of discretion are seen as problematic (Amnesty International, 2001; Canadian Council for Refugees, 2001; Maytree Foundation, 2001). For example, family unification provisions, the selection of independent immigrants, and the definitions of terms such as "international rights" and "terrorism" are all left to regulations; the articulation of these will have serious implications for many individuals and families.

Human Rights and Humanitarian Concerns

The potential for human rights abuse, evident from the tone and substance of the Act, is a major concern for many (Amnesty International, 2001; Canadian Bar Association, 2001; Canadian Council for Refugees, 2001; Maytree Foundation, 2001; United Nations High Commissioner for Refugees, 2001). The Act bestows expanded privileges on immigration officers and is more restrictive toward asylum seekers and permanent residents. Overall, the Act emphasizes economic objectives. Admissibility criteria—such as the ability to settle, find work, and become independent—are also applied to refugees (Hyndman, 1999). Similarly, the Act's emphasis on finding refugees resettlement close to their own country is more of a political strategy to reduce the numbers of refugees who are asylum seekers in Canada (UNHCR, 2001, cited in Hyndman, 1999).

Class and Gender Issues

The class and gender biases in the 1976 Immigration and Refugee Act have received much attention (Bolaria and Li, 1988; Boyd, 1995; Das Gupta, 1994). Similar observations have been made of the new Immigration Act and the consultations that preceded it. Since 1976, the Canadian government has held consultations with various stakeholders to determine immigration policy. However, despite the government's espousal of democratic ideals, the framing of questions and issues in immigration consultations reaffirms sexist and racist ideology (Thobani, 2000). The requirement for official language competence for independent immigrants is bound to have a gendered impact (Hyndman, 1999). The relative positioning of the family class and the independent immigrants in relation to the latter's potential for self-sufficiency is seen as "a new problematization of the immigrant family. More specifically, because immigrant women typically come under the family class, the plan also reflects a problematization of immigrant women" (Abu-Laban, 1998; p. 200). The Act will have differential negative consequences for women and racialized minorities (Canadian Council for Refugees, 2001).

Annual Immigration Plans 2000-2002

As previously mentioned, immigration policy since 1976 has required the minister of Immigration to announce annual plans for immigration. The year 2001 saw the beginning of multiyear planning, consisting of three major components: outcomes, analysis, and activities. The outcomes are related to the goals and results of the immigration program; analysis uses the tools of research and consultation to increase the efficiency of the program; and activities are based on the outcomes and analysis in order to set future priorities and directions that will, in turn, warrant a review of existing policies and programs. Multiyear planning is to focus on issues related to the processing and selection of immigrants, refugees, temporary workers and students, and the settlement of immigrants and refugees. Instead of presenting the annual plan for only one year, the 2001 plan proposes annual targets for a minimum of two years.

In the 2001 Annual Immigration Plan presented to Parliament, the stated objectives of the immigration program are "to ensure that the movement of people into Canada contributes to Canada's social and economic interests and that it meets Canada's humanitarian commitments" (Citizenship and Immigration Canada, 2001b, p. 3). The long-term plan is to "move toward immigration levels of approximately one percent of the population" (Citizenship and Immigration Canada, 2001b, p. 4). The plan states that the factors considered for planning immigration levels are constantly shifting domestic and global environments, operational capacities, the consequences of legislative and policy changes, and the capacity of provinces and territories to absorb and integrate new immigrants. It is also noted that targets for 2002 may change when the Annual Immigration Plan for 2002 is presented to Parliament next year. Thus, government has more flexibility to respond to changes in the global and domestic environments. The Annual Report is a snapshot of immigration in time, and it also provides targets for multiyear immigration levels.

The multiyear planning process takes into consideration international and domestic trends and challenges. The major international trends affecting Citizenship and Immigration Canada's (CIC) selection and integration programs are an increase in the non-government movement, global labour shortages in certain key economic sectors, competition in the global market, a shift in source countries, and growing numbers of people in transit. The major domestic trends are an aging population, a shrinking labour force, and ever increasing settlement in urban centres. The CIC document also lists international and domestic challenges arising from these trends. At the international level, challenges include managing processing demands, remaining competitive, and maintaining client service and program integrity. At the domestic front, the key challenges are ensuring that all parts of Canada share in the benefits of immigration, and removing barriers to successful settlement and integration. The 2001 Annual Immigration Plan lists the indicators of successful integration and acknowledges the difficulties faced by immigrants in gaining recognition of foreign credentials so as to obtain appropriate employment.

Table 8.1 provides the immigration plan for 2000 as well as the actual arrivals.

Table 8.2 provides details of the immigration plan for the years 2001 and 2002.

Review of Immigration and Refugee Policy Directions

Immigration policy is influenced by a number of considerations, such as national goals and the cost of achieving these goals (Simmons, 1998); market,

Table 8.1	Immigration Arrivals			Review of immigration and refugee policy directions

Immigrants	2000 Plan (as announced 1 Nov. 1999)	Actual
Skilled workers	100,500-113,300	118,307
Business	15,000-16,000	13,645
Provincial/territorial nominees	1,400	1,249
TOTAL economic	**116,900-130,700**	**133,201**
Spouses, fiancés, & children	42,000-45,000	42,702
Parent & grandparents	15,000-16,000	17,724
TOTAL family	**57,000-61,000**	**60,426**
Other*	**4,000**	**3,244**
TOTAL immigrants	**177,900-195,700**	**196,871**

Refugees	2000 Plan (as announced 1 Nov. 1999)	Actual
Government-assisted	7,300	7,367
Privately sponsored	2,800-4,000	2,905
Refugees landed in Canada	10,000-15,000	12,955
and dependants abroad	2,000-3,000	3,481
TOTAL refugees	**22,100-29,300**	**26,708**
Kosovo refugees	**—**	**3,258****
TOTAL immigrants & refugees	**200,000-225,000**	**226,837**

* Includes live-in caregivers and special categories.
** Kosovo refugees who arrived in 1999 as part of a special movement and who obtained permanent resident status in 2000.

Source: Citizenship and Immigration Canada. (2001a) Appendix B: Immigrant Arrivals, 2000.

non-market, and international considerations (Timmer & Williamson, 1998); and the politics of liberal democracies (Freeman, 1995). These factors do not operate in isolation: their influence at a particular time depends also on the immigration history of a country, as evidenced clearly in the evolution of Canadian immigration policy and practices. Green and Green (1996, p. 1) note that the defining feature of Canadian immigration policy is its flexibility, and that the goals of immigration policy in Canada are often difficult to determine as the policy is "a complex entity consisting of an interconnected set of guidelines, regulations and actual actions by government agents," mostly outside the realm of public scrutiny. Since the 1910 Immigration Act, Parliament has entrusted a great deal of power with the Cabinet, and thereafter with the minister of Immigration. Such flexibility has been a useful feature in times of emergency.

Canadian immigration policy until 1967 was highly discriminatory, with a strong preference for people from European backgrounds (Abu-Laban, 1998; Green & Green, 1996; Henry, et al., 2000; Isajiw, 1999). The same is true of Canada's refugee history (Adelman, 1991; Richmond, 1994). Historically, Cana-

Table 8.2   Immigration Plan, 2001 and 2002

Immigrants	2001 Range	2002 range
Skilled workers	100,500-113,300	105,800-118,500
Business	15,000-16,000	15,700-16,700
Provincial/territorial nominees	1,400	1,500
TOTAL economic	**116,900-130,700**	**123,000-136,700**
Spouses, fiancés & children	42,000-45,000	44,100-47,000
Parents & grandparents	15,000-16,000	15,700-16,700
TOTAL family	**57,000-61,000**	**59,800-63,700**
Other*	4,000	4,200
TOTAL immigrants	**177,900-195,700**	**187,000-204,600**

Refugees	2001 Range	2002 range
Government-assisted	7,300	7,500
Privately sponsored	2,800-4,000	2,900-4,200
Refugees landed in Canada	10,000-15,000	100,500-15,600
and dependants abroad	2,000-3,000	2,100-3,100
TOTAL refugees	**22,100-29,300**	**23,000-30,400**
TOTAL immigrants and refugees	**200,000-225,000**	**210,000-235,000**

* Includes live-in caregivers and special categories.

Source: Citizenship and Immigration Canada. (2001b). Appendix C: Immigration plan, 2001 and 2002. Ottawa: Minister of Public Words and Government Services Canada.

dian immigration policy was driven by short- and long-term economic objectives, absorptive capacity, family reunification, demographic needs, and cultural factors (Abu-Laban, 1998; Christensen, 1999; Green & Green, 1996). During the 1970s and 1980s, recession and high levels of unemployment led to economic factors dominating immigration policy. For example, as a result of the economic downturn in the 1980s, the independent worker category was reduced to only 14% of all immigration, the lowest level in postwar history. Major policy initiatives were launched for immigration policy to focus more on family class and the increasing number of refugees and asylum seekers (Simmons, 1998). During the 1970s and 1980s there was also immigration policy interest in issues of social, economic, and cultural incorporation. In the 1991 Canada-Quebec Accord, the two governments agreed to share the responsibilities for immigration to Quebec. While the government of Canada continues to be responsible for determining national standards and objectives for immigration, as well as for family class and refugees, the government of Quebec is responsible for the linguistic and cultural integration of permanent residents and has sole responsibility for selecting independent immigrants.

During the late 1980s and 1990s, policy changes arose when the government recognized how international immigration could improve Canada's productivity and lower the public cost from all categories of immigration (Abu-Laban, 1998; Simmons, 1998). The category of economic-class immigrants, consisting of independent workers, business immigrants, and entrepreneurs, was carefully revised and its allotted proportion increased alongside a reduction to the family class proportion. In 1994, economic class accounted for 43% of all immigration, and this figure increased to 53% in 2000. Family class was reduced from 51% in 1984 to 44% by 1997 (Simmons, 1998).

In order to contain the costs of immigration and reduce immigrants' and refugees' dependence on public funds, a landing fee was introduced in 1994. Refugee claimants were also allowed to work while their claims were being processed. Sponsoring relatives were given financial responsibility for their sponsored relatives for ten years. Bill c-44 was also introduced to respond to public concern over rising rates of crime involving immigrants and refugees (Simmons, 1998).

Canadian immigration policy has paid a great deal of attention to absorptive capacity. During the postwar period, immigration levels were reduced during periods of high unemployment. Selecting immigrants to fill specific occupations that are in high demand also illustrates this concern. However, recent evidence suggests that absorption is no longer a key issue in policy making (Green & Green, 1996).

During the 1990s there was also a clear and new preference for "integration" as a policy objective (Abu-Laban, 1998). The 1994 Immigration Working Group noted that it accepted the notion of integration as a policy objective in Canada. Distinct from assimilation and segregation, integration "ideally involves a two-way process of accommodation between newcomers and Canadians"(CIC Discussion Document, 1994 in Abu-Laban, 1998, p. 202). This shift addressed one of the criticisms of Canadian multiculturalism policy, which was that it undermined Canadian unity by promoting a multiplicity of cultures without a shared core of Canadian values. In fact in 1996, the revised multiculturalism program incorporated integration as the framework and emphasized the themes of identity, civic participation, and social justice (Abu-Laban, 1998). The trend toward encouraging integration is also evident in the Annual Immigration Plan, as well as the stated goals of the new Immigration Act.

Conclusion

Conclusion

As indicated earlier, Canada's Immigration Act is framework legislation, which leaves most of the details to regulations. The regulations for the new Immigration and Refugee Protection Act have been published in two phases. Consultations on the proposed regulations with all stakeholders have been ongoing since the publication of the first set of regulations in December 2001.

Conclusion
The first set of regulations addresses such areas as selection, enforcement, refugees, and the selection transition provisions. The second set of regulations published in March 2002 relate to fees, loans, debt collection, seizures, transportation companies, and transitional provisions. The House of Commons Standing Committee on Citizenship and Immigration was to present its final recommendations on these regulations. According to a CIC news release (March 8, 2002), the new Act and the accompanying regulations take a balanced approach in being tough on those who pose a threat to public safety while building on the important contributions of immigrants and refugees past, present, and future. In a more recent development, the CIC has launched the e-Client Application Status (e-CAS) Service, which is an on-line service to check the status of an immigration application.

In 2001, 250,386 immigrants were admitted to Canada (Citizenship and Immigration Canada, 2002). This exceeded the targets set for the year by 25,386. The success of the immigration and refugee program should not be judged only by how closely the numbers projected and the numbers admitted coincide. As the minister of Citizenship and Immigration observed, "Immigration is about the people who come to this country to contribute to our economy, to join their families or to start a new life free from persecution" (Citizenship and Immigration Canada, 2002, p. 1). Although there is no overall evaluation of the Canadian immigration policy, academic and practice communities have consistently raised critical issues for research and debate. Some of the academic debates centre on questions such as the annual number of immigrant and refugee admissions; the proportions of family, economic, and refugee classes; and immigration's role in economic growth (DeVoretz, 1995). Immigrant and refugee advocates have raised concerns about issues such as the landing fee, criminalization of racial minorities, processing delays, and lack of access to trades and professions for newcomers.

This chapter should have been titled "Social Policy in Relation to Newcomers to Canada" rather than "Immigration and Refugee Policy in Canada" because while the current immigration and refugee policy enables Canada to meet its overall goal of population growth, there is a major policy vacuum concerning the adaptation and integration of newcomers to Canada. As economic goals are high on the agenda for immigration, an important question is: Do immigrants to Canada, especially those in the economic class, have adequate opportunities to become contributing members of Canadian society? The systemic barriers associated with credential evaluation and licensing for trades and occupations are well documented (Basran & Zong, 1998; Brouwer, 1999; Calleja, 2000). Newcomers to Canada have higher levels of education on average than Canadian-born citizens, yet the newcomers find it more difficult to find jobs (Badets & Howatson-Leo, 1999; McDonald & Worswick, 1997). Earning differentials between visible minority newcomers and White Canadian-born citizens because of unrecognized credentials and direct discrimination toward the former (Harvey, Siu, & Reil, 1999; Ornstein, 2000) cost the Canadian economy about $55 billion a year (Reitz, in Siddiqui, 2001) and create a highly stratified society. Reitz (1998) argues that four institutions—immigration, labour market structure, educational institutions, and the welfare state—should work together to form an institutional approach to immigration and immigrant adjustment in Canada.

References

Abu-Laban, Y. (1998). Welcome/STAYOUT: The contradiction of Canadian integration and immigration policies at the millennium. *Canadian Ethnic Studies, 30*(3), 190-211.

Adelman, H. (1991). Canadian refugee policy in the postwar period: An analysis. In H. Adelman (Ed.). *Refugee policy: Canada and the United States* (pp. 173-223). Toronto: York Lanes Press.

Amnesty International. (2001). Brief on Bill C-11: An act respecting immigration to Canada and the granting of refugee protection to persons who are displaced, persecuted or in danger.

Badets, J., & Howatson-Leo, L. (1999). Recent immigrants in the workforce. *Canadian Social Trends, 52* (spring), 16-22.

Basran, G., & Zong, L. (1998). Devaluation of foreign credentials as perceived by visible minority professional immigrants. *Canadian Ethnic Studies, 30* (3), 6-23.

Bolaria, B.S. (2000). *Social issues and contradictions in Canadian society* (3rd ed.). Toronto: Harcourt Canada.

Bolaria, B.S., & Li, P.S. (1988). *Racial oppression in Canada* (2nd ed.). Toronto: Garamond Press.

Boyd, M. (1995). Immigrant women: Language and socio-economic inequalities and language issues. In S.S. Halli, F. Trovato, & L. Driedger (Eds.), *Ethnic demography: Canadian immigrant, racial and cultural variations* (pp. 275-296). Ottawa: Carleton University Press.

Brouwer, A. (1999). *Immigrants need not apply.* Ottawa: Caledon Institute of Social Policy.

Calleja, D. (2000). Right skills, wrong country: Why is Canada making it next to impossible for talented newcomers to practice in their fields of expertise? *Canadian Business, 73*(12), 34-39.

Calliste, A. (1991). Canada's immigration policy and domestics from the Caribbean: The second domestic scheme. In J. Vorst et al. (Eds.), *Race, class, gender: Bonds and barriers* (pp. 136-168) Toronto: Garamond Press.

Canada. Ministry of Citizenship and Immigration. (2001). Bill C-11.

Canadian Bar Association. (2001). New bill is "unfair" to immigrants says CBA's immigration section. Online at <www.cba.org/cba/news/2001>.

Canadian Council for Refugees. (2001). Bill C-11 brief.

Christensen, C.P. (1999). Immigrant minorities in Canada. In F. Turner (Ed.), *Social work practice: A Canadian perspective* (pp. 179-211). Scarborough: Prentice Hall.

Citizenship and Immigration Canada. (2001a). Appendix B: Immigrant arrivals, 2000. 2001 Annual Immigration Plan. Ottawa: Minister of Public Works and Government Services Canada.

Citizenship and Immigration Canada. (2001b). Appendix C: Immigration plan, 2001 and 2002. Ottawa: Minister of Public Works and Government Services Canada.

Citizenship and Immigration Canada. (2001c, February). Immigration and Refugee Protection Act Introduced. News release. Ottawa.

References   Cohen, R. (1994). A brief history of racism in immigration policies for recruiting domestics. *Canadian Woman Studies, 4*(2), 83-86.

Cunningham Armacost, N. (1995). Gender and immigration law: The recruitment of domestic workers to Canada, 1867-1940. *Indian Journal of Gender Studies, 2*(1), 25-43.

Das Gupta, T. (1994). Political economy of gender, race and class: Looking at South Asian women in Canada. *Canadian Ethnic Studies, 26,* 70-71.

DeVoretz, D.J. (1995). *Diminishing returns: The economics of Canada's recent immigration policy.* Ottawa: C.D. Howe Institute.

Freeman, G.P. (1995). Modes of immigration politics in liberal democratic states. *International Migration Review, 29*(4), 881-903.

George, U. & Fuller-Thompson, E. (1997). To stay or not to stay: Characteristics associated with newcomers planning to remain in Canada. *Canadian Journal of Regional Science, 1*(2), 181-193.

Grant, K. (2000). Health care in an aging society: Issues, controversies, and challenges for the future, In B. Singh Bolaria (Ed.), *Social issues and contradictions in Canadian society* (3rd ed.) (pp. 363-390). Toronto: Harcourt Canada.

Green, A., & Green, D. (1996). The economic goals of Canada's immigration policy, past and present. Research on immigration and integration in the Metropolis, Working Paper Series.

Harvey, E.B., Siu, B., & Reil, K.D.V. (1999). Ethnocultural groups, period of immigration and socioeconomic situation. *Canadian Ethnic Studies, 31*(3), 94-103.

Henry, F., Tator, C., Mattis, W., & Rees, T. (2000). *The colour of democracy: Racism in Canadian society* (2nd ed.) Toronto: Harcourt Canada.

Hyndman, J. (1999). Gender and Canadian immigration policy: A current snapshot. *Canadian Woman Studies, 19*(3), 6-10.

INTERCEDE. (1992). Response to the proposed reform of the Ontario Labour Relations Act.

Isajiw, W. W. (1999). *Understanding diversity: Ethnicity and race in the Canadian context.* Toronto: Thompson Educational Publishing.

Knowles, V. (2000). Forging our legacy: Canadian citizenship and immigration, 1900-1977. Public Works and Government Services Canada.

Li, P.S. (1997). Biases in benchmarking immigrants. In B. Abu-Laban & T.M. Derwing (Eds.), *Responding to diversity in the metropolis: Building an inclusive research agenda* (pp. 112-118). Proceedings of the First Metropolis National Conference on Immigration. Edmonton: Prairie Centre of Excellence for Research on Immigration and Integration.

Macklin, A. (2001). New directions for refugee policy: Of curtains, doors and locks. *Refuge, 19*(4), 1-4.

The Maytree Foundation. (2001). Brief to the Standing Committee on Citizenship and Immigration regarding Bill c-11, Immigration and Refugee Protection Act.

McDonald, J.T., & Worswick, C. (1997). Unemployment incidence of immigrant men in Canada. *Canadian Public Policy, 23*(4), 353-373.

Ornstein, M. (2000). Single and multi-dimensional disadvantage. Ethno-racial inequality in the City of Toronto: An analysis of the 1996 census. Prepared for the Access and Equity Unit, Strategic and Corporate Policy Division.

Reitz, J.G. (1998). Warmth of the welcome: The social causes of economic success of immigrants in different nations and cities. Boulder: Westview Press.

Richmond, A. (1994). Global apartheid: Refugees, racism and the new world order. Toronto: Oxford University Press.

Siddiqui, H. (2001, January 14). Immigrants subsidize us by $55 billion per year. *The Toronto Star*, A13.

Simmons, A.B. (1998). Economic globalization and immigration policy: Canada   **References**
and Europe. *Journal of Contemporary International Issues, 1*(1).

Stasiulis, D.K., & Bakan, A.B. (1997a). Regulation and resistance: Strategies of
migrant domestic workers in Canada and internationally. *Asian and Pacific
Migration Journal, 6*(1), 31-57.

Stasiulis, D.K., & Bakan, A.B. (1997b). Negotiating citizenship: The case of foreign
domestic workers in Canada. *Feminist Review, 57* (autumn), 112-139.

Thobani, S. (2000). Closing ranks: Racism and sexism in Canada's immigration
policy. *Race and Class, 42*(1), 35-55.

Thompson, A. (2001, June 27). Ottawa to open door for "temp" workers. *The Toronto
Star,* A1.

Timmer, A.S., & Williamson, J.G. (1998). Immigration policy prior to the 1930's:
Labor markets, policy interactions, and globalization backlash. *Population and
Development Review, 24*(4), 739.

United Nations High Commissioner for Refugees (UNHCR). (2001, March 5). Comments on Bill C-11 "An Act respecting immigration to Canada and the granting
of refugee protection to persons who are displaced, persecuted or in danger."
Submission to House of Commons Standing Committee on Citizenship and
Immigration.

Villasin, F.O., & Phillips, A.M. (1994). Falling through the cracks: Domestic workers
and progressive movements. *Canadian Women Studies, 14*(2), 87-90.

Additional Resources

Bolaria, B.S. & Li P.S. (1988). Racial oppression in Canada (2nd ed.) Toronto: Garamond Press.

Canadian Council for Refugees. Online at <www.web.net/~ccr>.

CERIS. Online at <www.ceris.metropolis.net>.

Citizenship and Immigration. Online at <www.cic.gc.ca>.

Driedger, L. (1996). Multi-ethnic Canada: Identities & inequalities. Toronto: Oxford
University Press.

Henry, F., et al. (2000). The colour of democracy: Racism in Canadian society.
Toronto: Harcourt Canada.

Isajiw, W.W. (1999) Understanding diversity: Ethnicity and race in the Canadian
context. Toronto: Thompson Educational Publishing.

Maytree Foundation. Online at <www.maytree.com>.

Ontario Ministry of Citizenship. Online at <www.gov.on.ca/MCZCR>.

9

Universal Health Care:
Current Challenges to Normative Legacies

Mike Burke and Susan Silver

anada's national health care system, known as medicare, is a source of immense collective achievement. Unlike other facets of Canadian social policy, it sets out a vision of distributive justice based on the principle of "equity." Equity as a distributive principle requires that "need," not ability to pay, be the sole determinant of access and distribution of health services. Equity based on need alone means that no one has a prior entitlement based on status, wealth, race, or other social differences (Churchill, 1987, p. 94). Medicare escaped the "residual trap" (Taylor, 1978) characteristic of other social policy measures by adopting a universal, one-tier, publicly financed model of insurance covering hospital services and physician services for all Canadians, rich and poor alike. Though aggressively contested, there is clear evidence that the founding principle of "equity of access" has endured as a normative legacy in relation to "medically necessary" hospital services and doctors' services. Medicare has remained an egalitarian institution in an otherwise inegalitarian society.[1]

While escaping this residual trap, we have not succeeded in quelling privatization pressures, which are inevitable in a nation that allows the private market, with its inherent inequities, to prevail as the dominant mechanism for allocating income and other scarce resources in Canadian society. These privatization pressures, while a mainstay of capitalist society, have been aggressively fuelled by the current neo-liberal political climate. Neo-liberalism, as a political ideology, calls for a profound reconfiguration of social welfare responsibilities among the public sector, the private sector, the family, and the non-profit sector (Burke, Mooers, & Shields, 2000). It seeks to minimize the social role of the state by recommodifying public services and, consequently, to expand the space available for the market provision of such services. It justifies this reconfiguration by an appeal to a narrow and distorted discourse of "efficiency" that equates efficiency with cutting public expenditures on social services.[2] In the case of health care, neo-liberalism identifies efficiency as the predominant if not sole criterion of health policy evaluation, asserts that publicly funded systems of health care are inefficient by definition, and concludes that the state's role in health care must be severely curtailed in

order to contain public costs. This definition of efficiency threatens to under-
mine the integrity of our medicare system, marginalizing the consideration of
equity and with it the *quality* of health care provision.

These issues are critical, and the stakes are high for Canadians in general and for various interest groups specifically. With total health care expenditures exceeding $95 billion in 2000 alone (Canadian Institute for Health Information, 2001), proponents of privatization stand to achieve huge financial rewards. As expressed by an American health care firm, medicare is "one of the largest unopened oysters in the Canadian economy" (quoted in Canadian Centre for Policy Alternatives, 2000, p. 4).

These are the fundamental choices facing policy makers. Do we reaffirm and strengthen the public system and thereby the equity principle, or further accelerate the neo-liberal program of privatization and the inevitable erosion of accessibility and quality? The health care debate is, however, not explicitly framed in terms of choices, but as a fiscal imperative obligating privatization.

This chapter begins with the assumption, borrowed from Richard Titmuss, that values are central to policy debates. Titmuss (1974, p. 132) contends that "policy is all about values," and he defines policy as the "principles that govern action directed towards given ends" (p. 23). Titmuss further argues that, the goal of policy analysis is to "expose more clearly the value choices confronting society" (p. 136). Using this framework for policy analysis, this chapter initially examines the normative foundations or dominant values that framed the original intentions of medicare. The chapter then briefly reviews the early successes and the political shift from a concern with equity to a concern with cost control. Recent federal and provincial commissions and initiatives such as the Social Union Framework Agreement are reviewed in relation to their contribution to the debate over the future of medicare. Three challenges to the normative foundations are then examined. These challenges, central to neo-liberal thought, are: 1) the retrenchment of the federal role in relation to national standards; 2) the privatization thrust, and with it the increasing commodification of health care services; and 3) the relegation of responsibility from the public sector to the family and the community. These challenges threaten the erosion of the normative foundations of medicare and have the capacity to fundamentally alter the manner in which Canadians meet their health care needs.

Medicare's accomplishments extend far beyond the field of health care. It is a beacon, a constant reminder of the possibilities of equality and inclusiveness within Canadian society. The ties that bind Canadians together are the shared and common experiences that result from a consistent interpretation of our fundamental national values. The chapter concludes with a rallying call to progressive social work activists to add their voices and values to the social policy debate, clearly articulating the normative possibilities of collective action.

Normative
policy
framework

Normative
foundations
of medicare

Normative Policy Framework

A normative analysis attempts to expose and clarify the values that influence policy debates and policy outcomes (Titmuss, 1974). Values are conceptions of the desirable within every individual and society and serve as standards or normative criteria to guide action, attitudes, and judgments. A primary objective of a normative analysis is to clarify and understand the values that represent a nation's policy choices (Silver, 1993). Public policies, thus, constitute choices among alternative normative intentions, among competing perceptions of the common good (Kronick, 1982). Normative choices are fundamentally distributive, defining what constitutes a "social" as opposed to a "private" good, and setting out the conditions of allocation.

Titmuss (1968) distinguished between residual/selective and institutional/universalist modes of distribution. Services delivered on a residual/selective basis almost always involve means tests that foster "both the sense of personal failure and the stigma of a public burden" (Titmuss, 1968, p. 134). With residually delivered services or programs, state responsibility begins only when the private realms of the family and the market fail. In contrast, universalist services are distributed as a social right, accessible to all citizens in a manner that does not involve any "humiliating loss of status, dignity or self respect" (Titmuss, 1968, p. 129). There is no assumption of personal blame or failure. The service or program in question is considered an appropriate institutional, and not residual, function of the state.

Esping-Andersen (1989) extends this analysis, maintaining that the essence of a welfare state is its capacity to grant "social rights," rights that are embedded in citizenship and distributed universally outside of the market. The concept of decommodification refers to the degree to which a service or basic good is detached from the market as the distributive mechanism. Social rights cease being commodities, emancipating individuals from their market dependence (Esping-Andersen, 1989, p. 21). *Commodification* in health care refers generally to an increasing reliance on the market for either the financing or delivery of health care services (Esping-Anderson 1989; Offe, 1984).

With this framework, we will now explore the normative foundations of medicare, specifically examining the set of social rights and allocative principles that were established.

Normative Foundations of Medicare

Medicare originated with two pieces of legislation: the Hospital Insurance and Diagnostic Services Act of 1957 (insuring hospital services) and the Medical Care Act of 1966 (insuring doctors' services). Four federal-provincial cost-sharing conditions were imposed:

1. Universal coverage: Every provincial resident must be covered under uniform terms and conditions.
2. Portability: Requires that all Canadians can receive health care services across Canada.

3. Comprehensiveness: All medically necessary hospital services and physician services are to be covered.

4. Public administration: Each provincial plan must be publicly administered on a non-profit basis without the involvement of the private sector.[3]

By the end of 1971, every province had taken advantage of the federal cost-sharing incentive and approximately 100% coverage was attained in Canada.[4] The national plan was achieved through interlocking ten provincial plans, all of which shared certain common features. Canadians are free to choose their own physicians and hospitals. There is no limit on the benefits payable as long as medical need is determined. There are no limits on the number of days of hospital care or the number of visits to physicians. With respect to the scope of coverage, benefits are intended to be virtually complete. There is no distinction between basic and non-basic services. Instead all medically necessary physician and hospital services are covered by all provincial plans.

From the onset, physician and acute-care hospital services have been the defining national aspects of our health care system. Specifically excluded from coverage were mental hospitals, tuberculosis sanatoria, and institutions providing custodial care, such as nursing homes. These categories were excluded on the grounds that care in such hospitals was already being provided by the provinces, virtually without cost to provincial residents (LeClair, 1975). Other services not covered under the cost-shared agreement were home care services, ambulance services, drugs administered outside hospitals, dentists, and any health care services not provided by physicians. These omissions have resulted in an overemphasis on doctors and hospitals, resulting in the lack of comparable national standards across these other health care services.[5]

With medicare, a right to "medically necessary" health care services was established. This right was entrenched in a set of program conditions requiring universal coverage on uniform terms and conditions to a comprehensive set of medically necessary services available to all Canadians regardless of their province of residence. These program conditions succeeded in decommodifying medically necessary services. Access to these services was determined solely on the basis of medical need and not on one's ability to pay. All Canadians were treated on uniform terms and conditions. The doctor's office and the acute care hospital ward became "public" spaces where all Canadians shared common experiences of citizenship. Consequently the principle of equal access became the normative foundation of medicare. The principle of equal access was further embedded by the stipulation that over 90% of residents must be covered by provincial plans, and that each provincial plan was to operate on a non-profit basis and be administered by a public agency. These two conditions essentially eliminated any incentives for private insurers and, with it, a private tier of coverage. Our one-tier system has successfully precluded an "exit option" for Canadians wishing to "jump the queue." The lack of an exit option requires that the system meet the expectations of all Canadians, a necessary prerequisite for high-quality public services.

Medicare further established a dynamic and often tense federal-provincial relationship that has remained a mainstay of future health policy debates. As spelled out in the British North America Act of 1867, the provision of health care services, along with education and other social services, is primarily a provincial responsibility. The constitution further generated a fiscal imbalance in which the primary responsibility for raising money resides with the federal government while the significant obligations to spend money reside with the provincial governments (Van Loon & Whittington, 1971). The provinces are generally not willing to acquiesce, to trade their jurisdictional powers for federal funds. Through the federal conditional grant and the cost-shared program, the federal government gained access to areas of health and social assistance. However, the degree of "shared" responsibility in medicare was unparalleled in Canadian social policy at the time.[6]

Much to the dismay of reluctant provincial governments and medical associations, the four program conditions for cost sharing resulted in a substantive set of national standards that were uniformly implemented across all provincial plans. The federal government's pivotal role as the guardian of national standards was indelibly etched in the foundations of medicare.

Early Success

By the end of 1971, every province had been in medicare for at least one full year, and 100% coverage was achieved in virtually every province. Canada experienced marked changes in many vital statistics. Prior to the introduction of the Hospital Insurance Program, Canada's infant mortality rate was approximately 40% higher than Australia's, 30% higher than that of England, and 5% higher than that of the United States. By the end of 1971, Canada's infant mortality rate was almost identical to Australia's and England's and 10% lower than that of the United States. Maternal mortality rates also dropped by a third toward the end of 1971, and studies indicated that pregnant women were seeking medical attention a few months earlier than they had been (LeClair, 1975, p. 43).

With respect to utilization rates, hospital admission rates increased from 143.4 per 1,000 in the mid-1950s to 165.9 per 1,000 in 1970 (Taylor, 1978, p. 417). By enacting the Hospital Insurance Program ten years before the Physicians' Services Insurance Program, Canadians became accustomed to using hospitals whenever possible. During the mid-1970s Canada had the highest hospital admission rate in the world and spent 60% of all health care expenditures on institutional care (Van Loon, 1978, p. 457).

Physician utilization patterns also reflected an initial spurt of about a 4% increase within the first year of medicare (LeClair, 1975, p. 47). By 1975 it was also recognized that adding a new physician to the system costs an additional $200,000 to $250,000 per year in health services utilization (Van Loon, 1978, p. 457).

By 1974, medicare had successfully replaced income-based access with needs-based access, with consumption patterns more closely aligned with health care risks (Manga, 1984). The association between income and health care utilization was inversed, with the lowest income groups consuming more than double the health care services of the higher groups (National Council of Welfare, 1982, p. 23). Total government spending on health services by 1976 accounted for 7.2% ($7.1 billion or $10.8 billion in current dollars as derived by CIHI) of the GNP in Canada. The United States was at 8.6%, while England was only at 5.4% (Van Loon, 1978, p. 456).

With these early successes, the politics of medicare quickly moved from a concern with equal access to issues of cost containment. More recently, a social rights analysis has been eclipsed by a preoccupation with controlling and significantly reducing the public role in the financing and delivery of health care to Canadians. We will now more closely examine the current debate and the related challenges to medicare's normative legacies.

Current Challenges

Canadians are reminded, on an almost daily basis, of the fragility of the health care system and warned of the pressure points that are destined to destroy it. Newspaper headlines are replete with stories of insured services being delisted; increasing numbers of private, for-profit clinics and hospitals; ever-growing waiting lists for surgery and medical treatment; overcrowded emergency departments; escalating conflicts between health care providers and governments; shortages of nurses and physicians; shorter hospital stays coupled with decreasing home care budgets; an increasing expectation that families and friends assume responsibility for care in the home; and the repeated posturing of federal and provincial governments, each accusing the other of funding shortfalls.

Recently, there has been an intensification of the debate on the future of health care in Canada, exemplified by the explosion of intergovernmental negotiations on health and the proliferation of federal and provincial health reports. This debate centres on the sustainability of the health care system and defines sustainability as a question of controlling public costs. For instance, while the report of Premier Ralph Klein's Advisory Council on Health, chaired by Don Mazankowski, notes that the concept of sustainability involves not just the financial resources to pay for health care but also the human resources to deliver the care, its major premise—that "the current health system is not sustainable"—is derived entirely from its (flawed) analysis of the public *costs* of health care.[7] And this premise determines all the report's conclusions and recommendations about the need for an infusion of private funds into the health care system. Ontario Finance Minister Jim Flaherty expresses the same kind of concern about the financial sustainability of the Ontario health care system, as does the Clair report on Quebec (Maioni, 2001; Ontario, 2001). Roy Romanow, in a statement releasing his interim report on "the future of health care in Canada," recognizes that the health debate is being driven by the imperative of cost control." He characterizes the debate by saying that the economic, not social, arguments for medicare are being questioned and that "this is especially so in regard to its long-term sustainability" (Commission on the Future of Health Care in Canada, 2002a). It may be premature to judge the Romanow report because it is an interim report that takes no final position on the questions it poses. But it is fair to say that in the interim report, the cost criterion of evaluation is all encompassing (Commission on the Future of Health Care in Canada, 2002b, chapters 3, 4, and 5).

This overriding concern with controlling public costs does not mean that the contemporary debate in health completely ignores other relevant issues. The various federal and provincial health reports also address such matters as primary care, the mix of health care professionals, home care, pharmacare, the social determinants of health, and health promotion and wellness. But, fundamentally, these reports evaluate the relative worth of proposed reforms according to their potential effect on the public costs of health care. This focus on costs is certainly apparent in the Mazankowski report on Alberta. It is also apparent in the statements of those who have not fully embraced the neo-liberal project in health. As might be expected, the Fyke report on Saskatchewan affords the quality of publicly funded care a much more prominent place than does the Mazankowski report (Canadian Union of Public Employees, 2002). But it too seems compelled to assess the value of reforms according to their implications for cost control, which stands as evidence of the widespread influence of the neo-liberal discourse of efficiency (Commission on Medicare, Saskatchewan 2001, chapter 6).

The report of the Senate Standing Committee on Social Affairs, Science, and Technology, chaired by Michael Kirby, gives one of the purest expressions of the degree to which "public" cost cutting is determining and restricting policy options. In dismissing the option of paying for health care by increasing government tax revenues, the report says: "While cuts to personal income tax are important to Canadians, reinvesting in health care is also rated as a very high priority. However, regardless of what public opinion polls say, this option runs counter to the tax reduction strategies undertaken at both provincial and federal government levels in recent years" (Senate 2001a, p. 61). In other words, public opinion is a useful guide to public policy only insofar as it unequivocally supports the tax-cutting and therefore cost-cutting projects of neo-liberal governments. The neo-liberal challenge to public health care is successful precisely to the extent that its fixation with costs "crowds out" or marginalizes other relevant criteria, like quality and equity, which might be employed to assess the worth of proposals for reform.

This debate is insistently fuelled by parallel forms of welfare state dismantling, three of which will be examined here: the decentralization of the federal system of government, the commodification of health care, and the relegation of health care. Taken together, these forms of dismantling constitute an unmistakable shift from collective to individual responsibility and from universal to residual modes of distribution as health care increasingly becomes a private commodity. **Current challenges**

The debate about the decentralization of the Canadian federation is intimately linked to the debate about national standards in social policy. Arguments for and against decentralization are often arguments about which level of government should take the primary fiscal and legislative responsibility for social policy. Although the provinces have clear constitutional jurisdiction for the general area of health care policy, the historical use of the federal spending power has given Ottawa a large role in determining the resources available for health and in setting the broad conditions of health care provision.

Subsequent to the establishment of medicare in the 1960s, the use of the federal spending power in relation to national standards reached a pinnacle with the Canada Health Act (CHA), passed in 1984. The purpose of the CHA was to consolidate the Hospital Insurance and Diagnostic Services Act of 1957 and the Medical Care Act of 1966 and to define more precisely the terms and conditions upon which federal payments would continue to be made. The Act reaffirmed the five program conditions that had been previously included in the Medical Care Act. The most controversial aspect of the Act pertained to Section 12(1) in which the conditions relating to the criterion of accessibility were specifically operationalized. The Act stated that provincial plans "must provide for insured health services on uniform terms and conditions and on a basis that does not impede or preclude, either directly or indirectly whether by charges made to insured persons or otherwise the reasonable access to those services by insured persons." For every dollar of extra billing or hospital user fees, the federal government will withhold one dollar from its cash contribution. With the CHA, "equity of access" was affirmed as a national standard, and with the elimination of user fees, the CHA did succeed in harnessing efforts at privatizing physician and hospital services.

A decade later, the trend toward decentralization of power or "provincialism" is unmistakable and supported by both Ottawa and the provinces. The passage of the Canada Health and Social Transfer (CHST) in 1996 clearly signalled this trend. The CHST consolidated funding into a single block transfer for health, postsecondary education, and welfare. According to Ottawa, one purpose of the fundamental restructuring of social policy arrangements embodied in the CHST was to decentralize power by providing provinces with "greater flexibility in determining priorities and in designing programs to meet local needs" (Canada, 1996, p. 10). Battle and Torjman regard the CHST as "a watershed in the history of Canadian social policy" that consolidates "a withdrawal of both federal *dollars* and federal *presence* from the provincially-run welfare, social services, postsecondary education and health programs that constitute a significant part of Canada's social security system" (Battle & Torjman, 1995, p. 1). They also point out that it represents a declining federal commitment to maintaining national standards in social policy.[8] Others have

**Current
challenges**

likewise suggested that strengthening the federal presence is the only way to prevent the erosion of national standards in health care and other areas of social policy (Barlow, 2002; Begin, 1999; Osberg, 1996; Silver, 1996).

The Social Union Framework Agreement (SUFA) of February 1999 between the federal government, all provincial governments except Quebec, and the territories is a prime example of the linkages between decentralized federalism and declining federal interest in maintaining national standards. In that agreement, Ottawa reconfirmed its policy not to introduce any new national initiatives in health care, postsecondary education, and social assistance without the agreement of a majority of provincial governments; recognized the provincial role in identifying the national priorities and objectives of such initiatives; and acknowledged the authority of the provinces and territories to determine the details of program design and mix (Canada, 1999).

SUFA evoked much negative comment from social policy advocates and other observers. Recalling the opposition to the CHST, critics noted that the social union discussions indicated a weakening of federal support for enforceable national standards in health care and social assistance. They also noted that the requirement of gaining majority provincial support for new initiatives would probably prove to be an insurmountable obstacle to the creation of new programs in pharmacare, home care, and child care (Council of Canadians, 1999; PovNet, 1999; Walkom, 1999).

As Boismenu and Jenson suggest, though, this debate goes beyond the question of decentralizing power from Ottawa to the provinces:

> despite often being presented in the language of "decentralizing federalism," and sometimes vaunted as a solution to the constitutional tangle of Quebec-Canada relations, the social union concept is more than that. The model of the social union involves decentralization to be sure. It is not a *shift within federalism* of decision-making power going from one level of government to the other, however. Rather, the power that is being decentralized is going from states to markets, and from public to private. The private sector, communities, families, and individuals are being exhorted to take more responsibility, as governments scale back their roles. At the same time…the nine provinces acting together assert themselves as co-managers of the social union, seeking to establish institutional guarantees that they will be consulted and involved in Ottawa's actions in their areas of constitutional jurisdiction. (Boismenu & Jenson, 1998, pp. 60-61)

This shift from states to markets and from public to private brings us to the second challenge to medicare, that of intensified commodification. In the process of commodification, health care service itself becomes a commodity, that is, it becomes a "unit of output" that is produced and packaged for sale in the sphere of capital accumulation (Leys, 2001, p. 84). The intricate and ever-changing mix of public and private principles in Canadian health insurance obscures some of the trends towards commodification (Deber, 2000; Deber et al. 1998; Naylor, 1986). But there are identifiable trends whose

recognition is made easier by explicit comparisons that policy makers draw
between the proper roles and responsibilities of the public and private
sectors.

First, the discourse of health care reform is becoming increasingly characterized by the language, meanings, values, and assumptions of the market. Deber et al. capture the generality of, and tensions between, the old and
new paradigms in health:

> In general, every industrialized country, with the exception of the United
> States, espouses the principle of universal health coverage for its people as
> a right of citizenship, rather than as a commodity to be bought and sold in
> the open market. Historically, principles of universality and equity of access
> have been the driving force behind decisions about financing health. These
> principles have recently been challenged as the general social and eco-
> nomic climate has turned to questions of efficiency and cost-effectiveness.
> (Deber et al. 1998, p. 504)

In the neo-liberal conception of efficiency, to increase efficiency and sustainability, public costs must be curtailed by expanding the role of the market
and diminishing the role of the state.

A principal recommendation of the Mazankowski report is that "it's time
to put 'customers' first" (Premier's Advisory Council on Health for Alberta,
2001, p. 43). This conversion of patients into customers reinforces the notion
that health care should properly be a commodity that is "bought and sold in
the open market" (Deber et al., 1998, p. 504; Friends of Medicare, 2002). It
also undermines the conventional relation between the patient-as-citizen,
who has common rights and entitlements, and the state, which has social
welfare obligations and responsibilities. And it replaces this relation with one
privileging the market exchange between individual customers and corporations (Pierre, 1995). Consistent with this frame of meaning, the Mazankowski report calls for a greater private role in health care and explicitly
ties the "customerization" of the health sector to the "individualization" of
responsibility for unhealthy lifestyles and health care utilization rates. The
Kirby report also illustrates how the extension of market values in the health
care debate weakens the case for a collective public role in the financing of
care. The report both dilutes the notion of citizenship rights in health by suggesting that such rights are based on the *perceptions* of patients (Senate,
2001a, p. 67), and expands the reach of market "rights" by referring to the
"right of individual Canadians to establish and use a private market alternative to the publicly funded system" (Senate, 2001b, p. 105).

Another example of commodification is the process of "privatization by
default," or "passive privatization," in which the private share of health care
funding has been slowly creeping up over time until very recently (Tholl,
1994, p. 61). In virtually each year from 1984 to 1997, private health spending
increased faster than did public expenditure. The discrepancy in public and
private annual growth rates was particularly wide from 1992 to 1996, years in

which governmental restraint measures held the average annual rate of
growth of public health spending to only 0.5%. As a result of these trends,
the private share of total health expenditures reached its maximum of 29.8%
in 1997. There has been a reversal of trends since 1998, with public spending
growing faster than private expenditure, reflecting particularly heavy governmental spending on capital projects and drugs. The private share of total
health expenditures is forecast to decline to 27.4% in 2001 (Canadian Institute
of Health Information, 2001).

The commodification of health care is, however, a much more vigorous,
explicit, and purposeful process than is suggested by the term "passive privatization." To be sure, the passive privatization of health care that characterized most of this period was partly the result of technological change:
increasingly health care was moving out of sectors dominated by public insurance, like hospital and medical services, and into sectors in which private
financing played a much larger role, like home care and drug therapy outside hospitals. But this kind of privatization was not simply passive. It was
also the result of proactive governmental decisions that constrained the
growth of public health expenditures, removed health services from coverage
under the public insurance plan, encouraged a kind of asymmetrical competition that marginalized not-for-profit health care providers and privileged
for-profit providers, and failed to reinvest in community care the resources
that were saved by closing and restructuring hospitals (Baranek, 2000;
Browne, 2000; Epps & Flood, 2001; Fuller, 1998; Tuohy, Flood, & Stabile, 2001).

Pat Armstrong uses the phrase "cascading privatization" to describe the
process in which decisions made by different health care players reinforce
the privatization of the heath care system: the federal government adopts
the neo-liberal project and slashes social spending; neo-liberal provincial
governments justify their own project of cutting costs, downloading services,
and closing hospitals by pointing to federal cutbacks; the community health
care sector, which remains seriously underresourced, is overwhelmed by the
spiraling demands for its services; these engineered problems in the publicly
funded system are used as evidence that medicare is not working and become
a rationale for further privatization; the principle of universality is eroded as
the wealthy pay for private health services; and the publicly funded system
becomes increasingly vulnerable to additional privatization (Browne, 2000;
Canadian Centre for Policy Alternatives, 2000).

Evans et al. provide an illustration of cascading privatization in their
examination of Premier Klein's proposal to allow for-profit facilities to offer
overnight health care:

> One of the principal justifications offered by the Alberta proposal is that of
> "meeting unmet needs," of expanding service capacity to deal with short-
> ages and waiting lists for care. But this argument seems at best seriously
> incomplete. Alberta cut provincial hospital spending by 30% between 1992
> and 1995. The 1999 level was still 15% below that of 1992. Over that seven

years, Alberta's per capita hospital expenditures fell from 6% above the

Overcoming
the challenges

Canadian average to 6% below. To reduce public hospital expenditures and then turn around and argue the need for private hospitals or equivalent facilities to meet shortages of capacity seems disingenuous at best...(Evans, Barer, Lewis, Rachlis, & Stoddart, 2000, p. 1)[11]

Relegating health care is a third challenge to medicare. Relegation refers to the direct or indirect transfer of responsibility for health care to the family and the non-profit sector.[12] It involves shifting the provision and costs of care to family and friends, volunteer labour, and organizations that rely disproportionately on volunteer labour or are otherwise in the non-profit sector.

There is an observable trend toward relegating health care, with more and more patients receiving informal care at home from friends and relatives or in the community from volunteers and voluntary organizations (Armstrong & Armstrong, 1996). Governments certainly see relegation as an attractive policy option. For some years, both the federal and provincial levels of government have been calling for increased voluntarism and developing initiatives to encourage donations and enhance the resources available to charitable organizations (Canada, 1997; Ontario, 1995).

Governments often use the progressive language of health promotion, community development, social empowerment, and mutual support to justify this shift in the responsibility for health care. But the predominant concerns of the neo-liberal agenda in health care demand that relegation be used to contain or externalize costs. This view of the economic rationale for relegating health care is consistent with the conclusion of a recent study of home care in Ontario: it is likely that the "real driving force of the shift to home care has been governments' desire to reduce costs" (Browne, 2000, p. 82). Generally, the transfer of funds to the family and community sector lags behind the transfer of responsibility. Governments are not willing to make a substantial financial commitment to home care. We know, for example, that not a single government has emerged to champion the 1997 recommendation of the National Forum on Health that home care be considered "an integral part of publicly funded health services" (National Forum on Health, 1997, p. 21).[14]

Overcoming the Challenges

Paradoxically, the pressure for privatization continues to grow in the face of overwhelming and incontrovertible evidence that undermines virtually all the assumptions and conclusions of privatized health care. Recent examinations of the Canadian health care system show that the sustainability of the system is not in question (Friends of Medicare, 2002; Murnighan, 2001) and that there is no fiscal crisis in health, although public opinion polls show that there is a popular perception of crisis (Deber et al., 1998; Evans et al., 2000; Rachlis, Evans, Lewis, & Barer, 2001). Increasing the role of the private sector in health will expand, not contain, costs and jeopardize equity of access, the quality of care, and the comprehensiveness of coverage (Deber et al., 1998;

Evans et al., 2000; Tuohy, Flood & Stabile, 2002). Downloading responsibilities and offloading costs to the family and non-profit sector will place a disproportionate burden on women because of their social role as primary caregivers. This will threaten the quality of care as informal caregivers are increasingly asked to provide sophisticated kinds of care requiring skills that they do not have. It will further increase total costs to the system in the form of increased stress on caregivers and inadequate care of patients, and lead to a debilitating transformation of the non-profit sector as it loses government support and competes with for-profit providers (Browne, 1996; Canadian Centre for Policy Alternatives, 2000; Hall & Reed, 1998).

Direct comparisons of the relative benefits of publicly and privately financed health care systems end with the endorsement of the public system. One such review suggests "the evidence generally points away from increased private financing as a means to achieve effective health care reform." And it concludes that: "In order to achieve the goals of a publicly funded health care sector (to allocate care on the basis of need and not ability to pay) requires that the *funding* of the system remain concentrated within the realm of the public and quasi-public (social insurance systems)" (Flood, Stabile, & Tuohy, 2001, p. 42).

The relative superiority of public over private finance in the health care sector has long been established in Canada and elsewhere. The analysis, conclusions, and recommendations of the National Forum on Health, which reported in 1997, said much the same thing as the research quoted immediately above. It emphasized that the Canada Health Act "is critical to preserving medicare, yet flexible enough to accommodate organizational reforms. It should not be opened." And it saw "maintaining—and expanding where appropriate—the role of public funding for health care as the key to successful restructuring" (National Forum on Health, 1997, pp. 13, 21).[15]

Despite the extensive literature documenting the superiority of public funding, the current debate has opened up the Canada Health Act and put the entire system of medicare at risk by affording enhanced legitimacy to proposals that privilege private over public funding. This marginalization of arguments supporting medicare occurs partly because the health care debate is, in its essentials, a political matter. Just as the so-called fiscal crisis in health is less an economic trend than a political construction, so the case for privatization is based more on political myth than reasoned argument.

Meeting these challenges to medicare requires that health care analysts and social work activists do things differently. They have done a credible job at undermining the conceptual, logical, and empirical case for privatization, but with negligible political effect. They need to do a better job at popular education by engaging and mobilizing social constituencies in support of progressive political change. The battle for medicare will not be won in academic journals, although it may be lost there. It will be won by constructing a political coalition to oppose the disproportionate and debilitating political influence wielded by neo-liberalism.

Notes

1 This conception of "equity" was formulated in Silver (1993).
2 This argument is based on the analysis in Burke (2000).
3 Reasonable access subsequently became the fifth independent program condition in the 1984 Canada Health Act.
4 When the program began on 1 July 1968, only Saskatchewan and British Columbia were operating schemes that were eligble for cost sharing.
5 The earlier proposals contained in the Heagerty report on health insurance in 1945 had included the full range of benefits such as dental, pharmaceuticals, and nursing services, but then omitted them, only to implement them in the next series of health care reforms, which, due to costs, never did materialize (Guest, 1985).
6 In contrast with the Canada Assistance Plan, also passed in 1966, the federal government neither specified the precise eligibility conditions nor the level of benefits. Consequently, very little in the way of national standards of assistance have emerged. The amount of provincial discretion permitted by the legislation has resulted in a social assistance system that is extremely complex, treats similar cases of need differently, relies on an intrusive and stigmatizing determination of need, and sets assistance rates well below the most conservative poverty lines (National Council of Welfare, 1982, p. 7).
7 The quotation is from the report of the Premier's Advisory Council on Health for Alberta (2001, p. 4; see also 26-31). See also the report's Context Paper, "Is Alberta's Health System Sustainable?"
8 In recent budgets, Ottawa has increased the cash component of the CHST, but the money restored to health does not equal the money taken from health.
9 As Leys (2001) notes, this conversion of a public service into a commodity fundamentally transforms not only the service itself but also the relations between those who provide the service (sellers) and those who use it (buyers).
10 Some of the trends mentioned in the text were derived from the health expenditure tables from the CIHI website at <www.secure.cihi.ca>.
11 The last phrase of the last sentence is "unless the argument is being made on efficiency grounds." The authors demonstrate that the argument for privatization cannot be made on efficiency grounds.
12 This definition is similar to but broader than what Brodie calls refamilialization: "the growing consensus among policy-makers that families (whatever their form) should look after their own and that it is up to the neo-liberal state to make sure that they do" (Brodie, 1996, pp. 22-23).
13 The quoted phrase is emphasized in the original.
14 As Health minister, Allan Rock showed a rhetorical commitment to home care and pharmacare, but did not transform the rhetoric into public policy (Canada, 1998).
15 See also the paper by Deber et al. (1998) commissioned by the National Forum on Health.

References

Armstrong, P., & Armstrong, H. (1996). *Wasting away: The undermining of Canadian health care.* Toronto: Oxford University Press.

Baranek, P.M. (2000). *Long term care reform in Ontario: The influence of ideas, institutions and interests on the public/private mix.* PhD dissertation, Department of Health Administration, Faculty of Medicine, University of Toronto.

Barlow, M. (2002, February). *Profit is not the cure.* Ottawa: Council of Canadians.

Battle, K., & Torjman, S. (1995, April). *How finance re-formed social policy.* Ottawa: Caledon Institute of Social Policy.

Begin, M. (1999, September). *The future of medicare: Recovering the Canada Health Act. Ottawa:* Canadian Centre for Policy Alternatives.

Boismenu, G., & Jenson, J. (1998). A social union or a federal state? Competing visions of intergovernmental relations in the new Liberal era. In L.A. Pal (Ed.),

References   *How Ottawa spends, 1998-99: Balancing act: The post-deficit mandate* (pp. 57-79). Toronto: Oxford University Press.

Brodie, J. (1996). Canadian women, changing state forms, and public policy. In J. Brodie (Ed.), *Women and Canadian public policy* (pp. 1-28). Toronto: Harcourt Brace, Canada.

Browne, P.L. (1996). *Love in a cold world? The voluntary sector in an age of cuts.* Ottawa: Canadian Centre for Policy Alternatives.

Browne, P.L. (2000). *Unsafe practices: Restructuring and privatization in Ontario health care.* Ottawa: Canadian Centre for Policy Alternatives.

Burke, M. (2000). Efficiency and the erosion of health care in Canada. In M. Burke, C. Mooers, & J. Shields (Eds.), *Restructuring and resistance: Canadian public policy in an age of global capitalism* (pp. 178-193). Halifax: Fernwood.

Burke, M., Mooers, C., & Shields, J. (2000). Critical perspectives on Canadian public policy. In M. Burke, C. Mooers & J. Shields, (Eds.), *Restructuring and resistance: Canadian public policy in an age of global capitalism* (pp. 11-23). Halifax: Fernwood.

Canada. (1996). *Renewing the Canadian federation: A progress report.* Background document for the First Ministers' meeting, 20-21 June 1996.

Canada. (1997). *Budget 1997: Budget plan.* Department of Finance. Ottawa: Public Works and Government Services Canada.

Canada. (1998, February 4). Minister marks first anniversary of National Forum on Health report. Health Canada news release. On-line at <www.hc-sc.gc.ca/english/media/releases/1998/98_07e.htm>.

Canada. (1999, February 4). *A framework to improve the social union for Canadians.* Canadian Centre for Policy Alternatives (CCPA). (November 2000). *Health care, limited: The privatization of medicare. Synthesis report prepared by the CCPA for the Council of Canadians.* With guidance from CCPA research associates P. Armstrong, H. Armstrong, and C. Fuller, and in collaboration with the Canadian Health Coalition.

Canadian Institute for Health Information (CIHI). (2001). *National health expenditure trends, 1975-2001: Report.* Executive Summary. On-line at <www.secure.cihi.ca>.

Canadian Union of Public Employees. (CUPE). (January 2002). An analysis of a *framework for reform: The report of the Premier's advisory council on health in Alberta.* CUPE Research.

Churchill, L.R. (1987). *Rationing health care in America: Perceptions and principles of justice.* Notre Dame: University of Notre Dame Press.

Commission on Medicare, Saskatchewan. (Fyke report). (April 2001). *Caring for medicare: Sustaining a quality system.*

Commission on the Future of Health Care in Canada. (6 February 2002a). Statement by Roy J. Romanow, Q.C., Commissioner, on the release of the interim report of the Commission on the Future of Health Care in Canada at the National Press Theatre, Ottawa.

Commission on the Future of Health Care in Canada. (Romanow report). (2002b, February 6). *Shape the future of health care.* Interim report.

Council of Canadians. (1999, January). Power game. Five problems with the current social union talks. On-line at <www.canadians.org>.

Deber, R. (2000). Getting what we pay for: Myths and realities about financing Canada's health care system. Background paper prepared for the Dialogue on health reform: *Sustaining confidence in Canada's health care system.*

Deber, R., Narine, L., Baranek, P., Sharpe, N., Duvalko, K.M., Zlotnik-Shaul, R., Coyte, P., Pink, G., & Williams, A.P. (1998). The public-private mix in health care.

In National Forum on Health (Ed.), Canada health action: Building on the legacy. Papers Commissioned by the National Forum on Health. Vol. 4 (pp. 423-545). Sainte-Foy: Editions MultiMondes.

Epps, T., & Flood, C. (2001). The implications of the NAFTA for Canada's health care system: Have we traded away the opportunity for innovative health care reform? Working draft.

Esping-Andersen, G. (1989). The three political economies of the welfare state. *Canadian Review of Sociology and Anthropology, 26*(1), 10-35.

Evans, R.G., Barer, M.L., Lewis, S., Rachlis, M., & Stoddart, G.L. (2000). *Private highway, one-way street: The deklein and fall of Canadian medicare?* Centre for Health Services and Policy Research, University of British Columbia. On-line at <www.chspr.ubc.ca>.

Flood, C., Stabile, M., & Tuohy, C.H. (2001, September). The borders of solidarity: How countries determine the public/private mix in spending and the impact on health care. *Health Matrix, 12*(2), 277-356.

Friends of Medicare. (2002, January 9). Real reform or road to ruin: Friends of medicare analysis of the Premier's health advisory council report.

Fuller, C. (1998). *Caring for profit: How corporations are taking over Canada's health care system.* Vancouver: New Star Books.

Guest, Dennis. (1985) *The emergence of social security in Canada.* Vancouver: University of British Columbia Press.

Hall, M.H., & Reed, P.B. (1998). Shifting the burden: How much can government download to the non-profit sector? *Canadian Public Administration, 41* (Spring), 1-20.

Kronick, J. (1982). Public interest group participation in congressional hearings on nuclear power development. *Journal of Voluntary Action Research, 11,* 45-59.

LeClair, M. (1975). The Canadian health care system. In Spyros Andreopoulos (Ed.), *National health insurance: Can we learn from Canada?* (pp. 11-88). Malabar: Krieger.

Leys, C. (2001). *Market-driven politics: Neo-liberal democracy and the public interest.* New York: Verso.

Maioni, A. (2001, January 26) Emerging solutions: Quebec's Clair Commission report and health care reform. *Canadian Policy Research Network* Backgrounder.

Manga, P. (1984). Preserving Medicare: The Canada Health Act. *Perception, 70,* 12-15.

Murnighan, B. (2001, April). Selling Ontario's health care: The real story on government spending and public relations. *Ontario Alternative Budget. Technical Paper No. 11.* A project of the Canadian Centre for Policy Alternatives.

National Council of Welfare. (1982). *Medicare: The public good and private practice.* Ottawa: Supply and Services Canada.

National Forum on Health. (1997). *Canada health action: Building on the legacy (Vol. 1: The final report of the National Forum on Health).* Ottawa: Minister of Public Works and Government Services.

Naylor, D.C. (1986). *Private practice, public payment: Canadian medicine and the politics of health insurance, 1911-1966.* Montreal: McGill-Queen's University Press.

Offe, C. (1984). *Contradictions of the welfare state.* Edited with an Introduction by John Keane. Cambridge: MIT Press.

Ontario. (1995). *1995 Fiscal and Economic Statement.* Toronto: Queen's Printer for Ontario.

Ontario. (2001, May 9). Budget delivers greater investment, greater accountability to health care. Ministry of Finance. News release.

References   Osberg, L. (1996, January). *The equity, efficiency and symbolism of national standards in an era of provincialism.* Ottawa: Caledon Institute of Social Policy.

Pierre, J. (1995). The marketization of the state: Citizens, consumers, and the emergence of the public market. In B.G. Petera and D.J. Savoie (Eds.), *Governance in a changing environment* (pp. 55-81). Kingston: Canadian Centre for Management Development and McGill-Queen's University Press.

PovNet. (1999, February 4). Social union framework heartless say social justice groups. PovNet social union press release and backgrounder. On-line at <www.povnet.web.net/socialunion.html>.

Premier's Advisory Council on Health for Alberta. (Mazankowski report). (December 2001). A framework for reform: Report of the Premier's council on health for Alberta. Edmonton: Government of Alberta.

Rachlis, M., Evans, R.G., Lewis, P., & Barer, M.L. (2001, January). *Revitalizing medicare: Shared problems, public solutions.* A study prepared for the Tommy Douglas Research Institute. On-line at <www.tommydouglas.ca>.

Senate. Standing Committee on Social Affairs, Science and Technology. (Kirby report). (2001a, September). *The health of Canadians: The federal role (Vol. 4: Issues and options).Ottawa: Government of Canada.*

Senate. Standing Committee on Social Affairs, Science and Technology. (Kirby report). (2001b, September). *The health of Canadians: The federal role (Vol. 1: The story so far).* Interim report on the state of the health care system in Canada.

Silver, S. (1993). *Universal health care: The Canadian definition.* PhD dissertation, Bryn Mawr College, Philadelphia.

Silver, S. (1996). The struggle for national standards: Lessons from the federal role in health care. In J. Pulkingham & G. Ternowetsky (Eds.), *Remaking Canadian social policy: Social security in the late 1990s.* Halifax: Fernwood.

Taylor, M. (1987). *Health insurance and Canadian public policy: The seven decisions that created the Canadian health insurance system.* Montreal: McGill-Queen's University Press.

Tholl, W.G. (1994). Health care spending in Canada: Skating faster on thinner ice. In J. Blomqvist & D.M. Brown (Eds.), *Limits to care: Reforming Canada's health system in an age of restraint* (pp. 53-89). Toronto: C.D. Howe Institute.

Titmuss, R. (1968). *Commitment to welfare.* London: George Allen and Unwin.

Titmuss, Richard. (1974). *Social policy.* London: George Allen and Unwin.

Tuohy, C.H., Flood, C.M., & Stabile, M. (2001, June). How does private finance affect public health care systems? Marshalling evidence from OECD nations. Working paper.

Van Loon, R.J. (1978). From shared cost to block funding and beyond: The politics of health insurance in Canada. *Journal of Health Politics, Policy and Law, 2* (Winter), 454-478.

Van Loon, R., & Wittington, M. (1971). *The Canadian political system.* Toronto: McGraw-Hill.

Walkom, T. (1999). Social union deal a step backward for Canadians. *Toronto Star.* February 9.

Additional Resources

Badgely, R. & Wolfe, S. (1967). *Doctor's Strike.* Toronto: Macmillan of Canada.

Begin, M. (1988). *Medicare: Canada's Right to Health.* Ottawa: Optimum.

Canadian Association for Community Care. Online at <www.cacc-acssc.com/page2.html>.

Canadian Centre for Policy Alternatives. Online at <www.policyalternatives.ca/>.

Canadian Council on Social Development. Online at <www.ccsd.ca/>.

Canadian Health Coalition. Online at <www.healthcoalition.ca/>.

Canadian Home Care Association. Online at <www.cdnhomecare.on.ca/e-index.htm>.

Canadian Institute for Health Information. Online at <secure.cihi.ca/cihiweb/disp-Page. jsp?cw_page=home_e>.

Canadian Public Health Association. Online at <www.cpha.ca/english/index.htm>.

Centre for the Study of Living Standards. Online at <www.csls.ca/>.

Commission on the Future of Health Care in Canada. (2002, November). Building on values: The future of health care in Canada. Final Report. Ottawa: Author.

Evans, R. & Stoddart, G. (Ed.). (1986). *Medicare at maturity*. Calgary: University of Calgary Press.

Hall, E.M. (1980). *Canada's national-provincial Health Insurance Program for the 1980's: A commitment for renewal*. Ottawa: Department of National Health and Welfare.

Health Action Lobby (HEAL). Online at <www.cna-nurses.ca/heal/healframe.htm.>

Health Canada. Online at <www.hc-sc.gc.ca/english/>.

Lalonde, M. (1974). A new perspective on the health of Canadians. Ottawa: Supplies and Services. National Council of Welfare: <www.ncwcnbes.net/>.

National Council of Welfare. (1990). Health, health care and medicare. Ottawa: Supply and Services.

Tommy Douglas Research Institute. Online at <www.tommydouglas.ca/>.

World Health Organization. Online at <www.who.int/home-page/>.

10

Caring and Aging:
Exposing the Policy Issues

Sheila Neysmith

As people age the quality of their lives is affected by a range of social policies. However, it is long-term care policy that the public generally associates with aging. In Canada and the United States finding ways of meeting the forecasted caring needs of old people has taken centre stage as the policy concern of an aging population. This problem arises from the fact that the Canadian population is aging, albeit still quite young when compared to European countries, and it is anticipated that this demographic phenomenon will make heavy demands on the health care system, necessitating a growth in services that will be costly. The history of research that discredits causal thinking linking aging to rising health costs is also a reminder that research alone does not bring about policy change. Research that puts the lie to this claim (for example, Evans, McGrail, Morgan, Barer, & Hertzman, 2001; Gilleard & Higgs 1998; Robertson, 1997) is routinely ignored as correlations between health care costs and utilization data are proclaimed as "obvious." The power of the demographic crisis discourse remains quite unabated and seems to reappear in a new guise as soon as one form is discredited. It obviously serves some purpose.

The focus on caring and aging in this chapter means engaging with a large and varied body of health care literature. The shape and contents of this literature reflects the presence of professions and organizations which are powerful players in, and thus definers of knowledge about, the health care services used by elderly people. This literature tends to position old women in particular, because of their higher morbidity and longevity rates, as a caring problem (Gibson, 1996), a problem that will get worse and will be costly to address. An aging population does present different policy challenges than that of a demographically young nation. Whether this translates into a "caring problem" depends on how the issue is taken up—how this demographic fact is incorporated into social policy.

Older people do have more chronic health conditions than younger people. The aging process within Canadian society frequently means that people need help with some of the activities of daily living. An important policy issue is how to ensure that the resources, types and amounts of service needed are

available and provided. The complexity of meeting this policy objective cannot be reduced to media sound bites which assert that Canada is committed
to universal health care or that seniors want to remain in their own homes.
Such statements gloss over important debates about where responsibility lies
for guaranteeing that needed services exist and are accessible. At present
families, not the health care system, do the lion's share of caring for relatives
who are in need of daily assistance. We know that this proves costly to many
women as they age. Yet our social policies and health care services seem
unable to ameliorate, let alone eliminate these costs. In many cases it seems
that existing policies actually perpetuate inequities.

As will become evident in this chapter, the "caring problem" tells us less
about old people than it does about the issues facing health care providers
and the types of distinctions that Canadian society makes between familial
and social responsibilities. In fact, most gerontological research is focussed on
issues related to current and foreseen costs of dependency. The fact that this
dependency is socially constructed does not lessen its impact on the quality
of life of old people and/or decisions about where and how human and capital resources are invested. This claim is substantiated in a November 2001
editorial of *Ageing and Society*—a journal from the United Kingdom founded
some twenty years ago to examine broad societal issues regarding population
aging. Bill Bytheway, the retiring editor, observes that the majority of articles
have been based on samples obtained through agencies of various types.
"Revealing and exciting though much of this research is, I felt it tended to
reinforce rather than challenge an underlying ageism....Almost inevitably,
questions about how 'we' cope with their 'dependency' is reflected in discussions of what we have learnt from 'our' samples" (Bytheway, 2001, p. 679).
I juxtapose this summary of research and its reflection in current policy in
countries like Canada to the "dependency problem" facing some Third World
countries. There the issue is not about caring for frail elders but the caring
responsibilities shouldered by the older generation as younger adults migrate
to urban areas for work and/or the middle generation of adults is decimated
by HIV/AIDS (United Nations, 2000).

The population of older Canadians, like younger age cohorts, is marked
by social disparities based on gender, class, ethno-racial differences, ability
and sexuality, to name but those most visible. These differences are as important as age in determining how social policies affect the quality of people's
lives as they age. For instance, housing and transportation are issues for many
people. The single family home, the housing paradigm in Canada, is designed
with the assumption that people are able-bodied adults who can climb stairs,
drive a car, and want to live on the outskirts of a city. This model does not
work for people with disabilities, children, extended family households or
those wishing to live in rural areas or urban centres. The same types of arguments can be made for transportation policies that centre the car as the desirable mode and thus alternatives never get serious policy examination—not to

mention funding to make them feasible. For example, the fact that the Toronto Transit System is expected to self-fund on passengers' fares leaves one shaking one's head in disbelief. The point in singling out these two policy areas is that current practices construct major barriers for old people. A less obvious effect is that other services such as home care need to accommodate inappropriate housing. Similarly, services become inaccessible because of transportation difficulties. Thus, community-based care is forced to become home-based care not by design but by necessity.

In the following pages I consider how several key concepts are used in defining the "caring problem." This will be followed by considering who some of the stakeholders are. The next section will step back to consider what it is that Canadians envision for the aging members of our society. The final part of the chapter points to directions that Canadian social policy could pursue to start realizing a future where groups of aging citizens are not excluded.

The Power of Concepts in Defining Reality

Language is important—it shapes our thoughts as well as communicates meaning. However, concepts and theories used in social policy are not neutral. They emphasize what is important to consider, and effectively what can be ignored. For instance, what is often called "long-term care" policy varies across provinces and policy statements are littered with ambiguous concepts. Long-term care policy is usually seen as part of health care policy. Although the concept of health seems to be used in a very broad sense in policy statements such as the preamble to the Canada Health Act (CHA), when operationalized in terms of services covered, it is narrowed to hospitals, physician fees, drugs and lab tests. This effectively means that most of the services needed by elderly people in the community are excluded. Policy concepts such as community care, managed care, the mixed economy of care etc., reverberate with service delivery implications. Yet most actual health care occurs in peoples' homes delivered informally by family members where the minimal formal services that are available are not covered by the CHA.

"Caring" is a word that carries positive overtones but it also is used ambiguously. One is never sure exactly what it covers, so its meaning needs to be investigated in each setting. The now considerable feminist literature on the topic of caring defines the concept as the physical, mental, and emotional activities involved in looking after, responding to and supporting others (Baines, Evans, & Neysmith, 1998). It includes both paid and unpaid work. Caring labour is done in both the private and the public spheres. Most caring labour is unpaid and provided by aging spouses or daughters whose parents require ongoing assistance. Some care is also provided by paid workers, both professional and paraprofessionals.

One of the biggest issues in the literature on caring labour is that, despite its prevalence, it tends to be socially invisible. In that sense the 1996 Canada census can be considered a milestone because there was a three-part question in the census that asked Canadians to estimate the hours they spent on unpaid housework, child care and elder care. Replies to these questions clearly revealed that family members were doing a lot of unpaid caring work. According to Statistics Canada, this information was collected to "provide a better understanding of how these unpaid activities contribute to the well-being of Canadians" (Statistics Canada, 1995, p. 4). Well, that may be a somewhat grandiose claim of what such questions can accomplish. The data can really only describe what replies people gave to these specific questions. The meaning of the words to respondents, how they understood caring work and the relationship between these answers and the "well-being" of Canadians is a moot point. For instance we know from other research that questions about caring are interpreted differently by male and female respondents (Hooyman & Gonyea, 1995; Miller, 1990). Spouses may report doing roughly equivalent work but women underestimate the amount because they seem to have higher thresholds for "normal" caring and thus do not categorize it as such. Questions such as those used in the census hide this dynamic. But the work hours were measured, so at least we now can publicly declare that it really does exist!

> **The power of concepts in defining reality**

Another much used, yet ephemeral, policy concept is that of community. The term will probably always be ambiguous, but the challenge is to determine how the idea is being employed today in long-term care policy. The concept of community-based care captures both a range of services that exist *and* expresses a policy goal for what we would like to exist. With such a mandate the concept needs to be robust indeed. "Community" is an intriguing idea. Nobody is against it but probably no two readers would agree on its exact meaning. Not surprisingly, once we start to operationalize it we discover some very contradictory ideas. The term seems to be part of a response to a perceived weakening of the social fabric in multicultural countries such as Canada. On the one hand, it counters an emphasis on individual rights with one of social responsibility. On the other hand, the concept invokes a nostalgia for what family and community were in some imagined past. Used in this way the concept is a thread in what might be termed a moral communitarian discourse.

There is, however, an alternative community discourse which stresses how to make communities inclusive rather than exclusive. The use of the plural here is important. The challenge is around how to build alliances across differing communities in pursuit of a desired goal; how to recognize in our policies and programs that Canadian civil society at any given historical moment is made up of individuals who belong to multiple communities; and that these memberships will change over our life course. A pressing question is "What ideas of community inform our current models of community-based care?" At present, at least in long-term care policy, community support seems to be limited to shoring up families and encouraging the use of volunteers as ways of meeting need (Hughes, 1998, pp. 98-99).

As programs based on universal entitlements shrink under the mixed economy of care, services get more and more targeted. Expert definitions of need (Fraser, 1989) are usually the basis for definitions that guide narrowing service categories. Enforcing these definitions is not administrative or professional malevolence or power tripping. Rather, it is one of the limited options available to local managers for staying within their budgets. This being said—all of us—in our respective roles as professionals, administrators, users, researchers, advocates, etc.—use language that can reinforce rather than challenge how caring labour is thought about. With this in mind I want to consider some of the assumptions behind the concept of "community" that is being enacted on the long-term care policy/program stage at this particular historical hour.

The drama is supposedly about providing services that can help people remain engaged in the life of their families and communities even as physical abilities decline. The plot line, however, is unclear. Indeed at points the players seem to be reading from different scripts. In the current production the character of "client" has disappeared. The "consumer/customer" has taken her place. Rather oddly, sometimes this role is played by an old person but just as often "Family" is cast in the role. Either way, these actors speak quietly. Indeed their microphone seems to have been usurped by service providers and industry reps who march around the stage loudly proclaiming "consumer choice" and "customer satisfaction." There are times when this chorus line is so loud one can hardly make out the dialogue, let alone follow the story. Hovering in the wings is a tattered character called "Citizen" who can be most charitably defined as having an identity crisis. When she or he occasionally says something, there is silence for an instant, and then the chatter continues as if Citizen had never spoken. It is worth stopping to consider what is going on here.

Community-based care policy is ambiguous because contradictory language and concepts are at play. The market language of consumer/customer is about choice and purchase power, not need and access, the language of citizen based claims. It is ironic that in the mixed economy of care models (Baldock, 1997; Evers, 1993) operating across countries today, if choice exists at any point it is where a designated access agency tenders contracts to provide services. An old woman, or family member, gets little choice—they receive service from a designated provider. Granted, for those with sufficient resources, there is the option to purchase from commercial firms, if these exist where one lives. Like all market transactions, however, it is a case of buyer beware.

Receiving services in one's own home does not mean that one is part of a community, or that the services are developed by or in a community, yet the use of the term carries both these overtones. Surely a community-based policy implies at least the opportunity for social participation? However, as programs based on universal entitlement shrink under the mixed economy of care, expert definitions of need become the basis for social allocation.

Programs get targeted to certain groups and thus are not available to those who do not meet categorical definitions. Historically this has always been a problem with targeting programs. To those who do qualify the cost is stigma. Today, home care services that are available are a limited and relatively expensive number of professional hours. The scope of home based support has been narrowed and only those who require personal care qualify. It is well known in home care circles that this professional discourse translates into practice guidelines that mean that anyone who does not require help to take a bath, does not get service (Brotman, 2000).

Who are the stakeholders in the "caring problem"?

Who Are the Stakeholders in the "Caring Problem"?

At one level the well-being of elderly persons is clearly at stake because they are experiencing the conditions that give rise to the service debate. At another level it can be argued that the problem is in fact a creation of the health care system. It is the former, however, who are seen as needy and resource users; the latter is positioned as a service provider with limited resources that are being inundated by ever-increasing demands. In this scenario the old person is depicted as a dependent rather than a senior citizen—with the latter's sense of entitlements. In fact, the image projected is that of a poor old woman. As I have argued elsewhere, aging is a gendered process, so women experience old age differently than do men. One of these differences is that old women inhabit an aging body in a culture which devalues both. To be old, non-White, disabled or female is not only to be different but also to be inferior (Neysmith & McAdam, 1999).

The implications of this for the well-being of women as they age has not received a lot of attention in gerontology. Certainly, there has been much written about the state of the aging female body. Unfortunately, much of it reflects a continuation of the tradition wherein the female body is a site for regulation and control (for feminist assessments of this literature see Jaggar & Bordo, 1989; Nicholson, 1990; Shildrick, 1997). Professional concerns connect the deteriorating condition of this body to service use implications. That is, the effects of physical frailty on an elderly person's ability to perform certain tasks are not taken up in policy discourse as problematic because they are a threat to a person's sense of identity, nor are they seen as an indicator that the health care system is failing to meet need. Rather, they are seen as warning signs of potential demands on service budgets. Ironically, research has consistently demonstrated that these are in fact poor predictors of service use; that it is the presence or absence of informal carers that is most critical.

The social construction of aging as a problem of physical deterioration allows certain conditions to be named and appropriated as treatable. These defined medical problems fall under the authority of the CHA, which covers hospital and physician costs. Most conditions, however, fall outside the acute care focus of these services. As such, once a medical treatment regime is completed, the case is handed to a social worker to do discharge planning. Plans

Who are the stakeholders in the "caring problem"? assume that there is a family who will be able to provide most of the care and manage what limited community services are available. In this current version of community-based services the old person and their family are considered as a service unit for assessment of services purposes. In other words, what an old person needs is conflated with what family can provide at the point of assessment. Front-line workers are aware of this dynamic but see few options except to factor in family caring potential as they ration the very limited services available. No matter how understandable, given front-line realities, such practices are built on dangerous assumptions. First, there is no evidence that family members can provide the type of care delivered by a qualified nursing assistant or home care worker. This off-loading onto families means that services are moved off the public stage and rendered invisible by relocating them in the private sphere of family responsibility. The item effectively is removed from public scrutiny, avoiding the debate that occurs when items are moved from one column in the health care ledger to another. Second, as well documented in the caring literature (Hooyman & Gonyea, 1995; Neysmith, 2000), the emotional, mental and physical costs to both parties are ignored. Third, little attention is paid to what is happening to home care staff, and how the discourse of scarcity pits professional and paraprofessional personnel (most of whom are women) against each other. In my own research I have documented the racial tensions that are sparked in a stratified labour force where women of colour hold the poorest jobs (Neysmith & Aronson, 1997). However, this is just the tip of the iceberg.

The mental health of women as they age has been largely neglected in health care research. However, it has been associated with the stress and financial implications of caring across the life cycle. Milne and Williams (2000), in a wide-ranging assessment of what literature is available, came to the conclusion that social inequality was a much neglected but powerful determiner of the mental health of aging women. The emphasis of health care research and aging literature needs to be watched to ensure that knowledge needed to develop equitable policies is not undercut by current health care priorities. Provider generated definitions of problems such as inappropriate service use, duplication of service or gaps in service do filter down, however, to the micro level of the health care practitioners, social workers, old people and informal carers—and have consequences! These images and categories may, at one level, be seen as social constructions but they have a reality in terms of their power to effect service funding, delivery, and older persons' sense of entitlement. It is all too easy to blame the victim if the analytic gaze focuses too strongly on individuals struggling to survive under very oppressive conditions. Thus, context, social conditions and an appreciation of the social location of the parties involved are recurring themes in this analysis.

What Approaches Have Been Tried to Address the "Caring Problem"?

The discussion in this section comes with a big caveat. Since kin provide most of the care to people as they age, working conditions and quality control of what happens in the home are considered to be outside the purview of public policy. Thus, the services discussed in the following paragraphs are only minor players in accomplishing the task of caring for people who need help with the activities of daily living, even though they seem to occupy centre stage. Each province has developed some form of community-based care legislation. Canada does not have a national home and community care program like, for example, what exists in Australia—a country with many similar state structures (Neysmith, 1995).[1] Consequently, there is not the same guarantee of funding as results from the funding formula for hospitals and physician fees covered by the Canada Health Act. Federal funding for the most part is in the form of block transfers, which impose few restrictions on provinces as to how the funds are to be allocated among competing health care priorities.

Home care has grown rapidly in the last decade, and will expand in the future, not because it is a preferred service approach (although most endorse it) but because hospital budgets and changes in the financing of acute care dictate early discharge. As a well-known Canadian home care policy analyst, Evelyn Shapiro, has wryly noted, if you want to understand what is happening in home care, start with looking at what is happening to hospital budgets. Unfortunately, when hospitals sneeze, home care gets pneumonia.

In most provinces public agencies are not the providers of services, rather regional bodies are mandated to oversee the contracting out of service provision to competing non-profit and for-profit home and public sector care providers. I will go no further on the problems of this model; there has been considerable ink spilled on it already (Aronson & Neysmith, 1997; Canadian Association of Retired Persons, 1999; Drache & Sullivan, 1999; Williams, Barnsley, Legatt, Deber, & Baranek, 1999). What is important is that this model of health care funding and delivery, and the discourse of scarce resources that accompanies it, is the context within which case managers are deciding how to ration their very tight budgets and suggest to families that they investigate getting more service through the rapidly developing for-profit market of home care services. This service crunch has encouraged researchers to undertake a closer examination of other approaches to providing care.

One alternative is the development of schemes for making money or vouchers available to elderly persons so that they can hire their own personal care workers—frequently referred to as consumer-directed care. One of the attractions of this approach is that it seems to avoid the problem of policies reinforcing socially created dependency, it promotes consumer empowerment, expands choice, and is consistent with a mixed market approach to care. This is popular with younger people with disabilities because it gives

What
approaches
have been
tried to
address
the "caring
problem"?

them control. However, implementation of similar programs for elderly persons needs to be considered in terms of the desires of elders, the varying economic circumstances of their families, and the conditions of the home care worker labour force. There have been many versions of this piloted in the United States. Sharon Keigher (1999) has compared different renditions of this model in Wisconsin. She concludes:

> Casual discussion about consumer-direction and control needs to be replaced with examination of the submerged power, dependency and interdependency inherent in the structure of these private two- and three-way relationships. The problem is that "giving" a disabled elder "decision-making authority," does not necessarily mean that he will have choices. To exercise choice consumers must know or be able to find carers who can do what is needed, when it is needed. (Keigher, 1999, p. 207)

Another response has been the development of respite services. Respite relieves the caregivers' burden by providing them with temporary relief through in-home or out-of-home care. Understanding what respite is and a commitment to providing it—because it is the one service consistently requested by users—does not mean that there is agreement on what is meant by the call for respite. We all use language that is available to us. This relief service has been named respite. The pressing question is why carers are experiencing burden to the point that they need respite. Respite may provide relief but perhaps prevention should be the focus of our enquiries. Thus, it is important to know under what conditions the cry for respite arises; what does respite mean for users, providers and policy makers. How important is respite compared to other services in the highly political health care priority list? These questions are not directly answered in the available research but such studies can throw light on how we might start to address them.

Much of this research is based on caring for aging persons with Alzheimer-types of cognitive impairment. The later stages of this disease frequently mean that carers are coping with cognitive and behavioural changes. Respite services come in various forms, the three most common being in-home, day care, and short-term stays in an institutional setting. These respite programs are seldom set up primarily to provide respite. Rather they are existent services with some spaces set aside for respite care. In other words, respite users look like other users of such services. Respite is what the caregiver experiences but the service is the regular package of services that make up home care. Respite users are either not regular home care clients or clients who need more service than they regularly get.

Providers voice concern that users express satisfaction with respite but its impact is uncertain (Burdz, Eaton, & Bond, 1988; Deimling, 1991/92; Kosloski & Montgomery, 1993; Lawton, Brody, & Saperstein, 1989; Montgomery, 1988; Scharlach & Frenzel, 1986). Impact has been defined in terms of how much respite enhances the carer's sense of well-being or lessens burden. A question arising from the research is why these particular dependent variables were chosen? Is it realistic to expect a crisis intervention like respite to have such an powerful impact?

Research suggests that carers with the help of a mediator, or an advocate, were more likely to use respite. Use of the service tends to be more common among adult children than spouses and users were more knowledgeable about formal services than non-users. In a study exploring these difference, Cotrell & Engel (1998) note that spouses often report that they would never have used respite if not encouraged to do so by children. Furthermore, they needed information that was tailored to their circumstances, help and encouragement with the instrumental activities of applying for the service, and emotional encouragement to do so. Also, in-home respite was more likely to be used if a professional recommended it. Such findings again suggest that most service users are not informed consumers. It also suggests some important roles to be played by social workers.

Finally, the field of health care respite is not high on the priority agenda. It is there but one is not inundated with references when looking up studies as one is when searching for studies of health care financing or even caregiver burden or the broader area of consumer-directed care. This is interesting given the focus these days on participatory approaches to research, empowerment of users, and consumer/customer satisfaction language. Whatever are the strengths and limitations of respite programs, it appears that this user-driven demand is not getting the response that market rhetoric claims is to be expected.

The existence of respite services is one of the few concrete indicators of recognition of who is doing most of the caring work. Respite is not being called for by those who are employed to do caring work, that is, formal care providers. No matter how large the disparities between the salaries and working conditions of doctors, nurses, social workers and home care workers, respite is built into the organization of their work through the institutional structures of a workday, benefits, vacation, etc. Not so for those who do most of the caring work, that is family members. Study after study shows that kin carers want some relief. Respite is one word used to describe services that might address this well-documented need. But, does the word challenge assumptions around kin-based care that make respite necessary? The current concept of respite puts it in the same type of service model as food banks and shelters. They are necessary to the survival of users but at the same time their use implies a certain weakness on the part of users and questions their ability to cope. Thus respite is a good temporary response, but in and of itself will not address the basic issue. If caring labour needs such services, then it is an indicator of a problem, not the answer—much as food banks and shelters are indicators of policy, not family failure. Now we can confine ourselves to the equivalent of building more shelters and developing more food banks or we can ask the policy question—how do we eliminate the need for respite?

A third approach to increasing the supply of caring labour is the development of caring allowances, which are available to relatives in a number of

What approaches have been tried to address the "caring problem"?

What
approaches
have been
tried to
address
the "caring
problem"?

countries. This policy option is not well developed in Canada—in fact only four provinces have some form of it in place (Guberman, 1999). This attempt to undergird the care provided by kin is fraught with dubious outcomes for many women. There continues to be debate about its merits in the international literature, so it seems prudent to post huge "Proceed with caution" signs along this policy road. The money available is usually more of a compensation (allowance) rather than payment for work done. Kin carers cannot negotiate pay scales or working conditions. Perhaps most worrisome are the types of differences between women who use such programs and those who do not. For instance, Janice Keefe in Nova Scotia has undertaken a series of studies that compare those who use carer allowances with those who use home care services (Keefe & Fancey, 1997). The former are non-urban, they live in areas where services are scarce and where unemployment is high. Thus, any choice that such programs might make available theoretically come up against the stark reality that women make decisions under conditions where few options in fact exist. In such circumstances programs can reinforce rather than decrease disparities in the larger society. In this case, home care becomes only an urban option because it is uneconomical to provide it beyond the city—a situation that will be exacerbated if the delivery of service is based on competitive bidding. Such considerations are important when examining what is happening to elderly people and their families in the mixed economy of care.

I do not want to leave this examination of efforts taken to address the "caring problem" without mentioning one other sector that is getting a lot of publicity in policy documents these days—the volunteer. A discourse on volunteering emerged in the 1990s that could not have been imagined during the decades that marked the reign of the Keynesian Welfare State. Then the word "volunteer" was avoided because it conjured up images of charity that were quite at odds with ideas of citizen entitlements and state obligations. Yet today volunteers have become players in a wide array of social programs. At least at the level of official policy, their presence is articulated as essential to the achievement of both program and organizational goals. For instance, in the ongoing long-term care debate in Ontario, volunteers are key players in a series of policy documents released over a ten-year period by three different political parties that were in power between 1985 and 1995 (Ontario Minister for Senior Citizens' Affairs, 1986; Ontario Ministry of Community and Social Services, 1990, Ontario Ministry of Community and Social Services, 1991; Ontario Ministry of Health and Ontario Ministry of Citizenship, 1991, 1993a, 1993b, 1993c). Volunteers may be positioned in policy documents as critical for ensuring that services reflect community concerns. Nevertheless, the work of volunteers is also becoming increasingly essential to the capacity of organizations' ability to carry out their mandates. Thus, we can add volunteers to profit and non-profit organizations, families, and public services that make up the mixed company of players who deliver community-based care. In policy documents the volunteer is assigned an array of responsibilities, but there is limited understanding of what the work means to those who are doing the volunteering. In fact, existent literature is mainly written from the perspective of organizations that use volunteers and funding bodies that seek to ensure the presence of community representatives in programs (Fischer, Mueller, & Cooper, 1991; Horch, 1995; Pearce, 1993).

In summary, we cannot avoid the paid/unpaid labour dilemma by reinventing the volunteer. The contributions that seniors make as volunteers are noted in many policy documents (Chappell & Prince, 1997; Fischer et al., 1991; National Advisory Council on Aging, 1999). They do indeed, but the question is "How is the discourse on volunteering developing in a rhetoric of scarce resources?" A pressing concern is the implications of this renewed emphasis on volunteerism in a hollowed-out welfare state (Aronson & Neysmith, 1997; Jessop, 1993; Reitsma-Street & Neysmith, 2000).

These sketches of what is happening to different sectors of the caring labour force together paint a picture that formal and informal carers have much to be concerned about. In the mixed economy of care that characterizes what we call community care policy today, the much discussed restructuring of health care is not resulting in the transfer of resources from institutional to home care—but the costs are. In addition, as they are jettisoned from the health care budget period, at home women pick up the responsibilities with no say as to the terms and conditions under which caring is done.

In 1999 I edited a special edition of the *Canadian Journal on Aging* based on the theme of community-based care. The articles do not suggest that community support is very supportive. Several pieces in that collection raise serious concerns about how the contracting process is being played out on the ground. One study found, for example, that

> compared to findings from the Canadian National Population Health Survey, employees of home care agencies are significantly more likely than working women of all ages to suffer from allergies, asthma, arthritis or rheumatism, back problems, high blood pressure, migraine headaches and work-related injuries in the past year. (Denton, Zeytinoglu, Webb, & Lian, 1999, p. 55)

I add these data to what we know of the physical, emotional, and mental strains experienced by kin carers.

Another article summarizes the managed care reform process in the province of Ontario based on interviews with senior government officials and provider organizations as well as public documents. The final paragraph is chilling:

> In conclusion we note that at this point Ontario's managed care reform has proceeded with relatively little public debate and discussion. Such debate has been limited by the complexity of the issues, by the regionalized nature of the reform, by limited access to information, by competition

amongst providers seeking to protect their own interests, and by fear of political retaliation. (Williams et al., 1999, p. 147)

In a bidding atmosphere collective action is impossible because strategies used have to be kept confidential so as not to undercut one's negotiating position. Claims of transparency or consumer right to information are very questionable in such circumstances.

Can Caring Be a Policy Goal Rather Than a Scapegoat?

One of the underlying causes of the "caring problem" is that family-based caring is not recognized as labour, and when it is provided by non-kin, a low value ascribed to it. Getting both of these into the policy making agenda has been, and continues to be, an uphill struggle.

Most caring work is done by women, but there is a disjuncture between the obligations that women carry and the paucity of citizenship entitlements that flow from assuming these responsibilities. One policy direction is to recognize the work involved, acknowledge that it is done disproportionately by women, and provide the same types of citizenship benefits to this work that is now given to those who are employed in the labour market.

One route is to recognize that caring work is done disproportionately by women in lower-income households and provide pay and benefits for it through mechanisms such as the consumer-directed care, care allowances, or voucher systems as discussed earlier. In Canada some minimal compensation comes in the form of a tax deduction, but those living in higher income households benefit more than low-income women. The Canadian National Advisory Council on Aging (NACA) has recently recommended that the work of caring be recognized in pension adjustments rather than pay per se (NACA, 1999). Whatever are the limitations of these schemes, not the least of which is the low monetary value attached to the work, they do give some resources in the hands of carers that they could use in ways that work for them. However, warnings have already been sounded that the seemingly empowering potential for users—both people requiring services and informal carers—can be illusionary.

The allowance approach has garnered support from quite a mixed bag of interests. Perhaps most worrisome about policies that are taking off in this direction is that they continue to reinforce the separation of the public and private lives of citizens noted earlier. Responsibility is off-loaded even more so onto the family, with some help possible when the load becomes unbearable. Shared responsibility, not shoring up families, is what is needed. Doing so is pivotal if women's citizenship claims are to be realized. This will happen only if caring for others is seen as central to the lives of all citizens, as central as holding down a paid job, participating in community affairs, paying taxes, and being a consumer (Feinberg & Whitlatch, 1998).

We talk about old people who need care as users or consumers (or sometimes even customers), on the one hand. On the other, we refer to family carers as service providers. The former takes, the latter gives. In this scenario the actors are positioned in ways that guarantee conflict, guilt, and resentment. The setting is disempowering for all. What are the possibilities if we change the script? Let me suggest that perhaps the problem is the image we have that normally people are not carers. Certainly many aspects of social life are organized without regard to the caring responsibilities that citizens carry. Employment practices do not build in caring as a normal and expected responsibility of adults, a responsibility that requires work schedules that accommodate the demands of caring. Most jobs are regulated by employment standards and minimum wage schedules; many also have pension benefits and supplementary health insurance. In the last few years some unions and progressive employers have even brought in family care benefits, but these are concessions from the "normality" of paid employment. They are defined as fringe benefits, suggesting that they are not central to paid employment, even though the demands made on the employee may be anything but fringe-like in their impact. Of course, for those who provide unpaid care, this is not even regarded as work. Thus, those family members who take up the responsibility of providing care suffer the economic consequences of doing so. Behind this is the continued existence of a framework that separates the public and the private lives of citizens. This assumption that family life and its responsibilities is a private matter is rooted in nineteenth-century industrial models yet continues to dominate policy thinking at the beginning of the twenty-first century.

> Can caring be a policy goal rather than a scapegoat?

It might help to shake up assumptions if we asked ourselves how long-term care programs would be described if we took out all references to family providing care. One approach to crossing the public/private sphere divide that is so costly to women is to ungender caring labour and institutionalize what Nancy Fraser (1997), an American political scientist, terms a universal caregiver model. Such a model would assume that all adults carry caring responsibilities; the ebb and flow of these may change over the life cycle of individuals but caring responsibilities are a social given. Under such a model employment policies and job descriptions would have caring-related rights and benefits that complement the health and pension benefits today. Promotion ladders that do not allow for caring responsibilities could be challenged as discriminatory. In addition, such an orientation would force us to recognize that quality control cannot be assured when care is assumed to be provided by family members, so we would have to figure out how to ensure that neither party is forced into provider or receiver roles against their wishes. At least such a stance would be reassuring to that 25% of the population with no spouse or children for whom kin-based care is a myth. I am not saying this would be easy. What I am saying is that we would be preoccupied with a different set of issues. Such a discussion is important because it will affect the hard choices all of us have to make regarding what to support, what to steer away from, and what coalitions we participate in.

Yes, this is visionary, but we need to keep protesting the discriminatory effects of policies. Responses that resources are scarce are not responses. Resources are always scarce; decisions around priorities need to be debated. If we are silent, the process of marginalizing those who provide informal care—those who do 80% of the work—will increase even more. It will not cease because we stop naming it.

Although feminist debates about how to conceptualize as well as promote citizenship have consistently highlighted the deleterious effects of the private/public spheres split, in the 1990s the issue took on a certain edge as neo-liberalism began to equate citizenship rights with ideas of choice, in particular choice in the market place (for a synopsis of some of the arguments, see Lister, 1997). The new citizen became the consumer of goods and services in one domain and the taxpayer in another. Such a rendition permeates professional as well as market and government programs and restricts our thinking about alternatives. Totally absent from this discourse is an awareness of how exclusionary such talk is. One needs time and money to be both consumer and taxpayer. If this is what it takes to be a citizen, then those who are carrying out caring responsibilities lack the coinage to be citizen-like. The exclusionary circle is now complete. Policies that emphasize the centrality of choice are a bad joke if your only option is sole responsibility (Gill, Hinrichsen, & DiGuiseppeet, 1998, p. 50).

The analysis I have presented is premised on the assumption that citizenship debates during these restructuring times are critical to the well-being of carers. However, it is not caring that is the problem; rather, it is that caring takes place in a society where inequities of gender, class, race, and ability—to name but those highlighted in this paper—play themselves out to the advantage of some and the oppression of others. Through the caring labour that they do, women make major contributions to their communities as surely as they do in the labour market and within their families. Any discourse can be picked up in ways that reinforce oppression rather than promote equity. Discussions of connecting caring labour to citizenship claims are as susceptible to this as any other policy discussion. This threat notwithstanding, avoidance would be costly. Not conceptualizing caring work in terms of contributions to the community, and ultimately to the nation, reinforces its invisibility while leaving intact gendered definitions of who are "contributing" members to their society, what qualifies as work and, ultimately, who is entitled to make claims as citizens. The result will be the reinforcement of social exclusion.

The work to be done is daunting. It entails ongoing contestation of definitions as well as coalition building with groups of people all of whom come with shifting alliances and unequal power. However, these are the daily ingredients of social change work. For those who wish to engage, I would argue that the caring labour done by women is as legitimate a basis for claiming social entitlements as that of individuals who currently are enshrined in images of the rights-bearing taxpayer or the sovereign consumer.

Note

References

Note

1 There have been numerous attempts to create such a mechanism in Canada, but to date they have failed to garner the polical support that undergirds the Canada Health Act. The most recent was the National Forum on Health in the mid-1990s (National Forum on Health, 1997). In 2002 the agenda of the Romanow Commission, and similar inquiries, seems to be completely highjacked by threats of a move to market-based approaches to services now covered by the CHA. In such a climate claims of those outside this circle have little chance of being heard.

References

Aronson, J., & Neysmith, S. (1997). The retreat of the state and long-term care provision: Implications for frail elderly people, unpaid family carers and paid home care workers. *Studies in Political Economy, 53,* 37-66.

Baines, C., Evans, P., & Neysmith, S. (1998). Women's caring: Work expanding, state contracting. In C. Baines, P. Evans, & S. Neysmith (Eds.), *Women's caring: Feminist perspectives on social welfare* (pp. 3-22). Toronto: Oxford University Press.

Baldock, J. (1997). Social care in old age: More than a funding problem. *Social Policy and Administration, 31*(1), 73-89.

Brotman, S. (2001). Accessing care through a trusted individual: Help seeking patterns of ethnic minority elderly women. *Vital Aging, 7*(1), 1-4.

Burdz, M., Eaton, W., & Bond, J. (1988). Effects of respite care on dementia and non-dementia patients and their caregivers. *Psychology of Aging, 3,* 38-42.

Bytheway, B. (2001). Editorial. *Ageing and Society, 21*(6), 679-680.

Canadian Association of Retired Persons. (1999). *Putting a face on home care.* Kingston: Queen's Health Policy Research Unit, Queen's University.

Chappell, N.L., & Prince, M. (1997). Reasons why Canadian seniors volunteer. *Canadian Journal on Aging La Revue canadienne du vieillissement, 16*(2), 336-353.

Cotrell, V., & Engel, R. (1998). The role of secondary supports in mediating formal services to dementia caregivers. *Journal of Gerontological Social Work, 30*(3/4), 117-132.

Deimling, G. (1991/92). Respite use and caregiver well-being in families caring for stable and declining AD patients. *Journal of Gerontological Social Work, 18,* 117-134.

Denton, M., Zeytinoglu, I.U., Webb, S., & Lian, J. (1999). Occupational health issues among employees of home care agencies. *Canadian Journal on Aging, 18*(2), 154-181.

Drache, D., & Sullivan, T. (Eds.). (1999). *Health reform: Public success, private failure.* London and New York: Routledge.

Evans, R., McGrail, K.M., Morgan, S., Barer, M., & Hertzman, C. (2001). APOCALYPSE NO: Population aging and the future of health care systems. *Canadian Journal on Aging, 20*(suppl. 1), 160-191.

Evers, A. (1993). The welfare mix approach: Understanding the pluralism of welfare systems. In A. Evers & I. Svetlik (Eds.). *Balancing pluralism: New welfare mixes in care for the Elderly* (pp. 3-31). Aldershot: Avebury.

Feinberg, L.F., & Whitlatch, C. (1998). Family caregivers and in-home respite options: The consumer-directed versus agency-based experience. *Journal of Gerontological Social Work, 30* (3/4), 9-28.

Fischer, L., Mueller, D., & Cooper, P. (1991). Older volunteers: A discussion of the Minnesota Senior Study. *The Gerontologist, 31*(2), 183-194.

References   Fraser, N. (1989). *Unruly practices: Power, discourse and gender in contemporary social theory.* Minneapolis: University of Minnesota Press.

Fraser, N. (1997). *Justice interruptus: Critical reflections on the "postsocialist" condition.* New York: Routledge.

Gibson, D. (1996). Broken down by age and gender: The "problem of old women" redefined. *Gender and Society, 10*(4), 433-448.

Gill, C., Hinrichsen, G., & DiGuiseppeet, R. (1998). Factors associated with formal service use by family members of patients with dementia. *Journal of Applied Gerontology, 17*(1), 38-52.

Gilleard, C., & Higgs, P. (1998). Old people as users and consumers of healthcare: A third age rhetoric for a fourth age reality? *Ageing and Society, 18*(2), 233-248.

Guberman, N. (1999). *Caregivers and caregiving: New trends and their implications for policy: Final report.* Ottawa: Health Canada.

Hooyman, N.R., & Gonyea, J. (1995). *Feminist perspectives on family care: Policies for gender justice.* Thousand Oaks, CA: Sage.

Horch, H.D. (1995). On the socio-economics of voluntary organizations. *Voluntas, 5*(2), 219-230.

Hughes, G. (Ed.). (1998). *Imagining welfare futures.* London: Routledge & Open University.

Jaggar, A., & Bordo, S. (Eds.). (1989). *Gender/body/knowledge: Feminist reconstructions of being and knowing.* New Brunswick, NJ: Rutgers University Press.

Jessop, R. (1993). Toward a Schumpeterian workfare state? Preliminary remarks on post-Fordist political economy. *Studies in Political Economy, 40*(spring), 1-39.

Keefe, J., & Fancey, P. (1997). Financial compensation or home help services: Examining differences among program recipients. *Canadian Journal on Aging, 16*(2), 254-278.

Keigher, S. (1999). The limits of consumer directed care as public policy in an aging society. *Canadian Journal on Aging, 18*(2), 182-210.

Kosloski, K., & Montgomery, R. (1993). The effects of respite on caregivers of Alzheimer's patients: One year evaluation of the Michigan model respite program. *Journal of Applied Gerontology, 12*, 4-17.

Lawton, M., Brody, E., & Saperstein, A. (1989). A controlled study of respite service for caregivers of Alzheimer's patients. *The Gerontologist, 29*, 8-16.

Lister, R. (1997). Citizenship: Towards a feminist synthesis. *Feminist Review, 57*, 28-48.

Miller, B. (1990). Gender differences in spouse management of the caregiver role. In E. Abel & M. Nelson (Eds.), *Circles of care: Work and identity in women's lives* (pp. 92-104). New York: State University of New York Press.

Milne, A., & Williams, J. (2000). Meeting the mental health needs of older women: Taking social inequity into account. *Ageing and Society, 20*(6), 699-723.

Montgomery, R. (1988). Respite care: Lessons from a controlled design study. *Health Care Financing Review*, Annual Supplement, 133-138.

National Advisory Council on Aging. (1999). *1999 and beyond: Challenges of an aging Canadian society.* Ottawa: Author.

National Forum on Health. (1997). *Canada health action: Building on the legacy. Final report of the National Forum on Health.* Ottawa: Health Canada.

Neysmith, S. (1995). Would a national information system promote the development of a Canadian home and community care policy? An examination of the Australian experience. *Canadian Public Policy, 31*(2), 159-173.

Neysmith, S. (Ed.). (2000). *Restructuring caring labour: Discourse, state practice and everyday life.* Toronto: Oxford University Press.

Neysmith, S., & Aronson, J. (1997). Working conditions in home care: Negotiating race and class boundaries in gendered work. *International Journal of Health Services, 27*(3), 479-499.

References

Neysmith, S., & McAdam, M. (1999). Controversial concepts. In S. Neysmith (Ed.). *Critical issues for future social work practice with aging persons* (pp. 1-26). New York: Columbia University Press.

Nicholson, L. (Ed.). (1990). *Feminism/Postmodernism.* New York: Routledge.

Ontario Minister for Senior Citizens' Affairs. (1986). *A new agenda: Health and social service strategies for Ontario's seniors.* Toronto: Author.

Ontario Ministry of Community and Social Services, Ontario Ministry of Health, & Ontario Ministry of Citizenship. (1990). *Strategies for change: Comprehensive reform of Ontario's long-term care services.* Toronto: Queen's Printer for Ontario.

Ontario Ministry of Community and Social Services, Ontario Ministry of Health, & Ontario Ministry of Citizenship. (1991). *Re-directions in long-term care and support services in Ontario: A public consultation paper.* Toronto: Queen's Printer of Ontario.

Ontario Ministry of Health, Ontario Ministry of Community and Social Services, & Ontario Ministry of Citizenship. (1993a). *Building partnerships in long-term care: A new way to plan, manage and deliver services and community support. A logical planning framework.* Toronto: Queen's Printer for Ontario.

Ontario Ministry of Health, Ontario Ministry of Community and Social Services, & Ontario Ministry of Citizenship. (1993b). *Building partnerships in long-term care: A new way to plan, manage and deliver services and community support. An implementation framework.* Toronto: Queen's Printer for Ontario.

Ontario Ministry of Health, Ontario Ministry of Community and Social Services, & Ontario Ministry of Citizenship. (1993c). *Building partnerships in long-term care: A new way to plan, manage and deliver services and community support. Guidelines for the establishment of multi-service agencies.* Toronto: Queen's Printer for Ontario.

Pearce, J.L. (1993). *Volunteers: The organizational behavior of unpaid workers.* New York: Routledge.

Reitsma-Street, M., & Neysmith, S. (2000). Restructuring and community work: The case of community resource centres for families in poor urban neighbourhoods. In S. Neysmith (Ed.), *Restructuring caring labour: Discourse, state practice, and everyday life* (pp. 142-163). Toronto: Oxford University Press.

Robertson, A. (1997). Beyond apocalyptic demography: Toward a moral economy of independence. *Ageing and Society, 17*(4), 425-446.

Scharlach, A., & Frenzel, C. (1986). An evaluation of institution-based respite care. *The Gerontologist, 26,* 77-82.

Shildrick, M. (1997). *Leaky bodies and boundaries: Feminism, postmoderism and (bio)ethics.* New York: Routledge.

Statistics Canada. (1995). *Household's unpaid work: Measurement and valuation.* Ottawa: Supply and Services Canada.

United Nations. (2000). Expert group meeting on sustainable social structures in a society for all ages. Addis Ababa, Ethiopia: Author.

Williams, P., Barnsley, J., Leggat, S., Deber, R., & Baranek, P. (1999). Long-term care goes to market: Managed competition and Ontario's reform of community-based services. *Canadian Journal on Aging, 18*(2), 125-153.

11

Canadians with Disabilities

Peter A. Dunn

The concept of disability can be considered socially constructed. People have different views of who is disabled or what conditions constitute a disability. These ideas may change over time and location (Oliver & Barnes, 1998). Policy makers determine who is disabled and who deserves financial and other benefits as a result of their disability. They often categorize people and limit services to individuals with certain types of conditions. Rather than responding to individual needs, eligibility rules are often restricted to reduce costs. This leaves many, including people with multiple disabilities, ineligible for services. Unresponsive social policies have resulted in gaps in services and regional differences in the types and number of services available in Canada. One of the challenges of social policy is to respond to the needs of Canadians with disabilities in a comprehensive, just, and effective manner (Dunn, 1999; Torjman, 1993, 2000).

Many Canadians confront multiple oppressions in the form of environmental, economic, social, and attitudinal barriers (Baker, 1992; Beachell, 2000; Enns, 1991; Neufeldt, 1993; Walters & Ternette, 1994). A survey of seniors with disabilities in Canada found that approximately 32% still required ramps to get in and out of their homes, 43% had problems obtaining accessible transportation, and 53% required more help with personal supports (Dunn, 1990). Aboriginal peoples with disabilities have very limited access to resources, especially on reserves. Barriers to entering the labour force and extremely low public assistance payments have left Canadians with disabilities economically marginalized. Oliver and Barnes (1998) explain that capitalism has forced many to the bottom of the labour market. Roughly 31% live under Statistics Canada's poverty line (Ross, Scott, & Smith, 2000). Statistics Canada (1995) found that approximately 14% were unemployed and another 44% had given up looking for jobs and, as a result, were classified by the federal government as "not in the labour force." Approximately 65% of working-age adults with disabilities did not complete any postsecondary education. Many individuals confront multiple problems being integrated into the educational system.

Many individuals face discrimination and attitudes that stress charity rather than equal rights and citizenship. The many forms of oppression they experience often overlap and reinforce each other. Visible minorities who are disabled, for example, confront a double disadvantage, experiencing both racism and demeaning stereotypes related to their abilities. Women with disabilities have extremely low incomes (Dunn, 1990) and many experience physical and sexual abuse (Driedger, Feika, & Giron Batres, 1996).

The nature and cause of the problems

Statistics Canada has undertaken several studies related to the number of people with disabilities in Canada and the barriers they confront. The Health Activities and Limitation Surveys (HALS) were conducted in 1983/84, 1986, 1991, and 2001. They included people with physical, developmental, and mental disabilities. These surveys illustrate the subjective nature of categorizing people. Statistics Canada (1995) defined people as disabled if they were limited in activities of daily living because of long-term physical conditions, mental conditions, or health problems, or if they were told by health professionals that they had learning or mental health disabilities. People who use technical aids such as eyeglasses or hearing aids to eliminate their limitations were not considered disabled.

The results of the Statistics Canada surveys indicate that approximately 4.2 million people in Canada—or 16% of the population—have some form of disability. This rate increases with age. Roughly 7% of the population under fifteen is disabled, 13% of those fifteen to sixty-four years old, and 46% of people aged sixty-five or older (Statistics Canada, 1995). As the population ages, the percentage of Canadians with disabilities grows. Social policies are essential in order to respond to these needs and trends.

The Nature and Cause of the Problems

How social problems are defined has an impact on the types of policy responses formed by government organizations (Wharf & McKenzie, 1998). As a result of the grass-roots efforts of the disability movement, there has been a transformation in our understanding of issues related to disability and their solutions. The paradigm has shifted from a medical and rehabilitation model to one based on consumer control, empowerment, and self-help (Hanes, 2001; Nagler, 1990).

The medical paradigm emphasizes that medical and rehabilitation practitioners are in charge. It views disability as a sickness and focuses on limitations of individuals, their inadequate performance of daily tasks, and their lack of compliance. People are considered patients or clients and often socialized to the role of a sick person. The paradigm focuses on policy principles of medicalization, categorizing people, and functional limitations. Social policies associated with the medical model emphasize institutional care, separate programs, isolation, dependency, and stigma (Dunn, 1999).

The disability movement has offered an alternative analysis of the issues related to disability and their solutions. This paradigm suggests that pathology can be found in the environment, in unprotected rights, in overdependency on relatives and professionals, and in a lack of responsive supports (DeJong, 1993). It focuses on how consumers are oppressed and emphasizes that people must live in the community and lead productive lives through risk taking, self-help, peer support, advocacy, and the removal of environmental, social, economic, and attitudinal barriers (Walters & Ternette, 1994). The disability movement has proposed social policies that emphasize consumer control and self-direction, choices and options, flexibility and freedom (Woodill & Willi, 1992).

Government policies appear to be in transition between these paradigms. As people with disabilities were deinstitutionalized, they found some of the same attitudes and approaches to service provision in the community as they had experienced in institutional settings. These included categorization, separation, isolation, dependency, and stigma. Often community programs are unresponsive, complex, and fragmented (Dunn, 1999; Torjman, 1993). Nevertheless, there is a growing emphasis on transforming how we think of the issues related to disability and creating more consumer-driven models of service delivery. Part of this transformation is taking place because of the consumer movement in Canada. Consumers have established their own initiatives and have developed partnerships with government organizations to create new approaches to service delivery (Dunn, 1999; Lord, 1997).

Historical Context

Throughout history there have been a number of trends in the way we have responded to the needs of people with disabilities. First Nations provided supports within their tribes or bands in a collective fashion. Early European settlers in Canada provided services in the community for people with disabilities who were considered deserving, although many ended up in poorhouses or jails. By the mid-nineteenth century, people were moved to newly built permanent institutions. Over time these institutions grew in size and specialization. This period of government intervention evolved in the 1960s and 1970s with the beginning of deinstitutionalization. People were moved into the community, but often with very limited supports. Although with time more services—including preventative programs—were developed, many programs retained a medical model with an emphasis on professional control (Armitage, 1996).

During the period of deinstitutionalization, the disability movement gained strength and had an impact on government policies. The broader disability movement was made up of several submovements. Although these initiatives had somewhat different roots, they had many commonalities and joined together to lobby for change. Many of these efforts arose from the increased consciousness of social injustices and violations of human rights brought about by the human rights movement in the 1950s and 1960s (Pedlar, Haworth, Hutchison, Taylor, & Dunn, 1999).

The independent living (IL) movement has had a major impact on social   **Historical**
policies and programs in Canada. This movement began in the United States   **context**
in the early 1970s with the development of three independent living centres.
Although many of the initial consumers had physical disabilities, the centres
increasingly emphasized a cross-disability approach that served people with
a wide range of conditions. They grew rapidly and, by the early 1990s, included
several hundred centres in the United States. These centres lobbied for
improved human rights, deinstitutionalization, and the full participation of
consumers in all aspects of society (Pheiffer, 1993). The IL movement began
later in Canada, but grew quickly from a few centres in the early 1980s. These
independent living resource centres followed four principles: consumer control, a cross-disability approach, community-based services, and the promotion of integration and full participation. Although each centre responds
to the unique needs of its particular community, they have four common
core programs: information and referral, peer support, independent liv-
ing/empowerment skills and development, and research and demonstration.
The centres are run by and for consumers (Hanes, 2001; Walters & Ternette,
1994). In 1986 the Canadian Association of Independent Living Centres
(CAILC) was formed to act as a national coordinating body for the IL movement and to provide training, support, networking with government and
non-governmental organizations, and information dissemination. The centres have promoted a new service delivery system in which citizens with disabilities have the responsibility for the development and management of
personal and community resources (Hutchison et al., 1997).

The community living movement in Canada had its roots in the 1960s as
parents of children with developmental disabilities began to fight for their
children's right to be included in publicly funded education and recreation, to
have adequate residential and vocational programs, and to live outside institutions in small residences and group homes. During this time, the normalization principle was introduced from Scandinavia. It emphasized
physical and social integration. Some advocated for a continuum of services
ranging from segregated services, such as group homes and sheltered workshops, to more integrated programs. The segregated services were increasingly criticized as institutionalizing people in the community. Alternatives
were developed, including supported independent living (housing) arrangements, integrated education, supported employment, and participation in
mainstream recreation. The focus turned in the 1990s to quality-of-life issues,
people's strengths and friendships, strong social networks, consumer empowerment, and individualized planning and funding. Rights, choices, and individual preferences were emphasized. People First, an advocacy organization
of people with developmental disabilities, played a critical role in lobbying for
social change. They called for an end to institutional care, group homes, and
sheltered workshops (Pedlar et al., 1999).

Denton (2000) has reviewed the significant developments of mental
health reforms in the last century. Humanitarian reform helped change the

focus of services in institutions from custody to treatment. The psycho-dynamic/holistic approach began to emphasize the need to understand and treat the social causes of mental health problems. It was followed by the community mental health movement, which focused on community-based services; the prevention of long-term hospitalization; and local, accessible, integrated, and coordinated services. Primary and secondary prevention programs were developed to provide early detection and intervention and the alleviation of adverse conditions, such as poverty, that contributed to mental health problems.

Lord (2000) discusses the recent growth of the psychiatric consumer/survivor movement in Canada since the 1980s. This movement developed as a reaction to people's experiences of alienation and oppression within the mental health system. The psychiatric consumer/survivor movement uses an empowerment-community integration paradigm that stresses self-help, mutual aid, peer support, and advocacy. The movement challenges approaches such as case management and clubhouses as expert-driven, segregated, and failing to respond to the social conditions they face. Psychiatric consumer/survivors propose a model that emphasizes stakeholder participation and empowerment, community support and integration, and social justice and access to valued resources. Organizations such as the National Network for Mental Health have played an active role in promoting policies based on these approaches (Everett, 2000; Ochocka, Nelson, & Lord, 1999).

Other consumer initiatives in Canada have dealt with issues related to women, Aboriginal peoples, students, and people with hearing and visual disabilities. Provincial and national organizations have helped to coordinate the efforts of some of these organizations. For example, the Council of Canadians with Disabilities (CCD) has advocated for the full and equal participation of its members. It argues that institutionalization, inaccessible public places, and negative attitudes have excluded people with disabilities from the mainstream of Canadian life. The CCD advocates for citizen rights, self-determination, consumer control, and equality. Along with the Canadian Disability Rights Council, the CCD has had a major impact on disability rights and service delivery systems across Canada (Beachell, 2000). However, consumer groups have not worked in isolation. They have worked with disability-specific service agencies, government organizations, and other non-profit groups (Lord, 2000). Despite the disability movement's relatively recent beginnings in Canada, it has increasingly transformed notions of disability issues, developed an alternative vision of services, and created innovative interventions operated by consumers.

Evolving Roles

The 1867 British North America Act delegated to the provinces responsibility for policy development related to housing, transportation, social supports, education, and other human services. Nevertheless, the federal government plays a significant role in the cost sharing of services, setting standards for programs, controlling some forms of accessible transportation, and providing direct services such as some income maintenance and employment programs. The provinces and territories have the major role in developing many areas of disability policy. They develop social policies related to personal supports, barrier-free housing, accessible transportation, education, social assistance, employment training, and other community resources such as recreation. Government agencies, non-profits, and increasingly for-profit organizations actually implement the programs.

Many of these services are being eroded by government funding reductions as a result of free trade agreements and globalization. Another influence on the service system has been the devolution of responsibilities from the federal government to the provinces and then to the municipalities (Dunn, 1999). The federal government established the Canada Assistance Plan (CAP) in 1966 to cost-share 50% of eligible provincial and municipal expenditures on community services and social assistance. Postsecondary education and health, including some personal support services, were covered by Established Program Financing (EPF), which included a cash payment and tax transfer from the federal to provincial governments. The federal government placed limits on CAP funding in 1990, then froze it in 1995-1996. It also froze the per capita EPF entitlements from 1991-1996. It eliminated both the CAP and EPF in 1996-1997 and introduced the Canada Health and Social Transfer (CHST).

CHST block funding, which consists of both cash and tax transfers, is intended to offer the provinces more flexibility while, at the same time, provide greater predictability and financial sustainability for the federal government. Many claim that the real purpose of CHST funding is to reduce transfer payments with the least political fallout by giving more discretion to the provinces. The movement to block funding and the reduction of national standards have resulted in increased disparities among the provinces (Dunn, 1999). As federal standards have diminished and provinces further fragment the service delivery system by downloading responsibilities and reducing supports, private for-profit disability agencies have emerged. Many of these agencies are concerned with profits rather than with the empowerment of consumers (Pedlar & Hutchison, 2000).

Disability Policies and Programs

This section will discuss developments in some of the major policy areas that enable Canadians with disabilities to live independently. Disability policies have moved from helping people just to function in the community to enabling consumers to participate fully in all aspects of community life and to take increased control over service delivery. To keep this section manageable, only those policies related to housing, transportation, personal supports, income, education, employment, and community supports will be

discussed. A brief history of recent developments at the federal level will provide an overall context for policy development in Canada.

The International Year of the Disabled Person in 1981 was a catalyst for
the federal government to work with Canada's disability community to identify and take action on outstanding issues. The Special Parliamentary Committee on the Disabled and Handicapped (1981) documented, in a report
entitled *Obstacles,* the major barriers confronting people with disabilities in
Canada. *Obstacles* listed 130 recommendations for actions on the part of specific federal government departments. A special follow-up report released in
December 1981 listed twelve further recommendations for action on issues
related to Aboriginal peoples.

In 1982 physical and mental disabilities were included under Section 15 of
the Canadian Charter of Rights and Freedoms, marking the first time any
national constitution referred specifically to individuals with disabilities. The
United Nations declared 1983-1992 the Decade of Disabled Persons. It was
not until 1985 that Prime Minister Brian Mulroney signed an agreement to
recognize the Decade in Canada. That same year, a Sub-Committee on Equality of Rights produced a report entitled *Equality for All,* which highlighted
the delays in implementing *Obstacles* and recommended the establishment
of a federal coordinating agency as a permanent parliamentary committee to
deal with disability issues. The federal government designated the Secretary
of State as the Minister Responsible for the Status of Disabled Persons and
established a Status of Disabled Persons Secretariat to plan and coordinate
federal actions concerning people with disabilities. It also expanded its Court
Challenges program to provide funding for litigation dealing with equality
rights under the new Charter. In 1987 the work of the Special Parliamentary
Committee culminated in the establishment of the Standing Committee on
Human Rights and the Status of Disabled Persons (Secretary of State, 1991).

The Standing Committee produced a report in 1990 entitled *A Consensus for Action: The Economic Integration of Disabled Persons.* It urged the federal government to make economic integration of Canadians with disabilities
a national priority; to ensure more responsible policy, legislation, and regulations; to pursue employment equity provisions; and to develop a federal-
provincial-municipal plan for consultation with consumers and follow-up
actions. It documented some of the major limitations of the federal government's efforts and the frustration of consumers at having to repeat well-
known and well-worn arguments for actions that they felt had been promised
ten years ago. In 1991 the federal government announced a $158 million
National Strategy for the Integration of Persons with Disabilities over a five-
year period (Secretary of State, 1991).

In 1992 the federal-provincial-territorial governments produced *Path-
ways to Integration,* better known as Mainstream 92, as a final report on their
collaborative review of services. The Standing Committee on Human Rights
and the Status of Disabled Persons continued to focus on employment issues;
produced *Completing the Circle,* a report (1993a) that outlined ongoing issues

related to Aboriginal peoples with disabilities; and wrote *The Grand Design*, a document (1993b) arguing for better programs and services. But when concrete actions failed to occur, consumers became increasingly bitter. They demanded that the federal government treat their concerns more seriously. These demands led to the creation of a Task Force on Disability Issues in 1996. Its report, *Equal Citizenship for Canadians with Disabilities: The Will to Act*, incorporated many of the recommendations made by the consumer movement over the past several years (Federal Task Force on Disability Issues, 1996). It proposed an approach to disability issues that would build disability considerations into mainstream policies and programs. In 1998 the federal, provincial, and territorial ministers responsible for social services produced a report, *In Unison: A Canadian Approach to Disability Issues*, that emphasized developing a collective approach to disability issues. Despite all these reports and efforts, Canadians with disabilities continue to confront discrimination and extensive barriers.

Disability policies and programs

Housing

Federal, provincial, and territorial government policies and programs have had a major impact on barrier-free housing and affordable housing arrangements. Barrier-free housing can help people with disabilities get in and out of their homes and enables independent use of facilities such as bathrooms, kitchens, and bedrooms. It also includes provisions for individuals with visual, hearing, and developmental disabilities such as audio signals in elevators, tactile and colour-contrasting cues, visual alarms for fires, and concise easy-to-read signs. Although housing is a provincial and territorial responsibility, the federal government's National Research Council develops national building codes approximately every five years. Since 1965 they have included some barrier-free standards. These standards act as advisory standards for provincial and territorial governments. A separate section for barrier-free standards (Section 3.7) was added to the Code in 1985, but does not include universal design standards that would ensure that all units could be unobtrusively and easily changed to accommodate individual needs. Such standards would require modifications such as adjustable counters and bathrooms large enough to accommodate wheelchair access.

The provinces and territories usually revise their building codes every five years and incorporate many of the federal provisions. Eight of the twelve provinces and territories have building codes with accessible regulations. These regulations apply primarily to new apartment buildings or those undergoing substantial renovations and do not include single-family homes or existing apartments. Although the provincial and territorial codes have become more progressive, most do not go as far as the United States' Fair Housing Act Amendment to include universal features in all apartments units. Instead, a specific percentage of units—often 5%—is usually required to be accessible.

The federal, provincial, and territorial governments have established housing adaptation programs to make existing housing more accessible. The federal government's role in housing is designated in the National Housing Act and is primarily carried out by the Canada Mortgage and Housing Corporation (CMHC). Its national Residential Rehabilitation Assistance Program (RRAP), which was started in 1973 as a home improvement program, was expanded in 1981 to include grants and loans to adapt existing housing. In 1986 the program was modified to include RRAP-D specifically for people with disabilities. The CMHC provided up to $10,000 in loans, including $5,000 in grants depending upon income, to modify people's homes. In 1992 the CMHC introduced Housing Assistance for Seniors' Independence to pay for minor modifications of seniors' home.

Seven of the provinces and territories developed their own housing adaptation programs and ten had home improvement programs, most of which included funding for home modifications. Most of the programs provided money directly to homeowners and, in some cases, landlords or tenants so they could hire contractors to undertake modifications. The most extensive programs were in Ontario and Quebec, but Ontario ended its program in 1993. Funding for many of the programs in other provinces was reduced in the 1990s. Of the programs still available, many provide limited funding and cover only a small number of home modifications. Since qualifying for these programs is often difficult, many people continue to face many barriers in their own homes (Dunn, 1999).

Canadians with disabilities confront other issues related to housing. Cmhc has reduced or eliminated programs intended to increase the affordability of housing. The CMHC Rent Supplement Program, cost-shared with the provinces, helped low-income people and families obtain suitable rental housing by subsidizing the rents in designated rental or co-operative housing. CMHC also cost-shared the Non-profit Housing Program to create more affordable housing units and provided support for the development of co-operative housing for moderate-income families who could not afford to own their own homes. Funds for all of these programs were reduced in the early 1990s. In 1996 CMHC indicated it would phase out its role in social housing. Many of the provinces and territories took over the administration of existing federal co-op and non-profit housing at that time. In 1997 the Ontario government decided to devolve social housing to municipal control. Not surprisingly, as governments are cutting social housing programs and budgets, many more people with disabilities are becoming homeless. Even recent federal government initiatives have not substantially changed the overall supply of affordable housing. In the meantime, many of the emergency hostels are inaccessible and unsafe. Individuals with disabilities face housing discrimination and a lack of adequate legal protection. Many who live in boarding homes or group homes are not covered by most landlord and tenant legislation and existing legislation was weakened in many jurisdictions in the 1990s (Carpenter, 2001; Torjman, 1990, 1993).

Transportation

Jurisdictional issues related to accessible transportation are complex. Generally, if a public carrier crosses borders between provinces or territories, it falls under the responsibility of the federal government. The federal government has jurisdiction over air travel, shipping, and interprovincial rail and buses. The provinces and territories have jurisdiction over ferries; local trains, including commuter trains and northern transport; commuter buses; buses crossing municipal boundaries; and traffic rules. The municipalities generally have responsibility for taxis, municipal buses, subways or light-rail transit, and specialized parallel transportation. Many of the municipal services receive provincial funding.

Nine of the provinces established funding for specialized parallel transportation in the late 1970s and early 1980s. The exception, Prince Edward Island, offered non-profit accessible bus services in its major communities, but does not have a formal provincial funding program. The northern territories have not provided specialized transportation because many northern communities are remote and not serviced by roads. Provincial government expenditures substantially increased for specialized transportation during the Decade of Disabled Persons, but by the 1990s eligibility was restricted and funding reduced.

During the Decade most provinces and territories initiated programs to help municipalities or taxi companies purchase and operate accessible taxis. The advantage of these programs for consumers is increased control over the timing of rides and the reduced stigma associated with taxis as compared to segregated transit. For funders, these programs often cost less to operate than other alternatives. Surprisingly few of the provinces offer funding to modify consumers' automobiles unless they qualify for specific vocational rehabilitation or workers' compensation. As a result of pressure from consumer groups, many provinces have introduced policies emphasizing a family of transportation services that give consumers more flexibility of choice. Accessible municipal and commuter buses, subways, light rail, and commuter trains began to receive funding by the end of the Decade. Some municipalities introduced low-floor community buses that are operated in specific neighbourhoods for seniors and for those who have difficulty getting on and off conventional buses.

Still, many municipal, commuter, and intercity trains and buses continue to be inaccessible. The older Toronto and Montreal subways offer poor accessibility and many trains have limited accessibility. Bus and train stations are often inaccessible too, both to people with mobility problems and to those with visual or hearing disabilities. As a result, many people cannot travel freely in Canada.

The Americans with Disabilities Act, passed by the US Congress in 1990, offered a different approach to regulating accessible transportation (Dunn, 1999). It required all new private and public buses, train and bus stations,

and rapid and light-rail trains to be accessible. All communities with conventional transportation were required to provide a specialized parallel system to serve eligible people, and bus and rail companies were required to
install telephone devices for individuals with hearing limitations.

Personal Supports

Social policies related to personal supports are very complex and confusing
in Canada. There are multiple levels of jurisdiction. People with different disabilities or ages may fall under different government departments or multiple ones. And these arrangements change constantly. There are no common
agreed-upon definitions of personal supports. They may include home health
care, homemaker services, attendant services, respite for care-givers, technical aids, or equipment. Individuals with developmental or mental health disabilities often make use of skills training, home support workers, and
community living skills coaches. Torjman (1993, 2000) raises some fundamental concerns about the overall system of personal supports, including
disparities in the availability of supports, high costs for some users, and complicated eligibility rules. Personal support services are rarely portable, making
it difficult for consumers to travel or to move to another location. Many services are based on a medical model. They fail to respond to individual needs
and they foster dependency.

While the provinces and territories have responsibility for personal supports, the federal government has had an indirect role through cost-sharing
arrangements and as part of its responsibility for Status Indians. Today it
funds many personal support services through the Canada Health and Social
Transfer. Provincial and territorial departments of health and community
services provide support services either directly or through purchased services, direct cash assistance or vouchers, and/or by offsetting expenses through
tax provisions. Municipalities often assist in delivering and paying for these
supports. Commercial agencies such as insurance organizations may also
play a role in funding personal supports. Generally, non-profit agencies actually provide the services (Torjman, 1993).

Many of the provinces developed home support policies and programs in
the early 1970s, primarily for seniors. During the Decade of Disabled Persons
these programs were adapted and expanded to other groups. New programs
were developed, including attendant services to assist individuals with long-
term disabilities; children's benefits to provide funding for parents to purchase services for their children with complex needs; and independent living
services for people with developmental and mental health disabilities. By the
end of the Decade, all provinces and territories offered some form of personal supports and, increasingly, they coordinated services through a single
entry point, provided cross-disability supports, and decentralized community
services. However, funding was reduced in the 1990s and did not keep pace
with the increasing demand as the population aged and more people were living independently in the community (Dunn, 1999).

Some of the provinces and territories have developed innovative programs. One model is supportive service living units, which combine housing
and personal supports. Consumers live in apartments dispersed throughout
large rental complexes. A service agency in the complex provides twenty-
four-hour support and on-duty attendants. Unfortunately, consumer control of these services is often limited. Community brokerage associations
were developed for people with developmental disabilities. These organizations offer help in finding appropriate services, developing circles of support, and advocating for individual needs. One of the major innovations has
been individualized funding. These programs provide money directly to consumers to obtain the supports they require. They enable consumers to hire,
fire, and direct their support workers. Often less expensive than alternative
models, individualized funding has been adopted in most provinces and territories. Consumer organizations, such as the independent living and
resource centres in Winnipeg and Toronto, have worked with government
departments to establish and administer individualized funding programs.
They have also been involved in teaching consumers how to obtain and control their own services. Micro-boards are a unique innovation developed in
British Columbia initially for individuals with developmental disabilities.
Micro-boards are non-profit organizations of five to eight unpaid members.
They are contracted by the government to provide circles of support and to
oversee individualized funding to purchase supports for one or two people.
Despite all of these innovations, many consumers have overwhelming prob-
lems simply obtaining basic personal supports in Canada (Dunn, 1999).

Income

Not only are many Canadians with disabilities poor, but they often face
extraordinary costs associated with having a disability. Many cannot find
paid employment because of a variety of work-related barriers, leaving them
dependent on Canada's disability income security system. This system is not
based on need. Rather, the amount of money a person receives depends on
how he or she became disabled. There is a hierarchy of programs—from private pensions down to welfare assistance—available to different groups of
people. This system has evolved in a haphazard, piecemeal fashion. It is not
integrated, coordinated, comprehensive, or fair (Council of Canadians with
Disabilities, 1998; Rioux, 1992).

Rioux (1992) describes three kinds of income programs for people with
disabilities including personal injury awards through the courts, insurance
programs, and non-insurance supports. People can sue for compensation
for personal injury by establishing negligence through civil litigation or torts.
Private and public insurance programs have been established to compensate for lost income or wages. Relatively generous private long-term disability insurance plans have been developed, usually for higher income earners,
to provide for illness-related disabilities. Private and public automobile insur-

ance plans cover road accidents. The two key public insurance programs are the provincially administered Workers' Compensation and the Canada/Quebec Pension Plan. Workers' Compensation is designed to protect workers and their families from wage loss due to occupational injury or disease. The Canada/Quebec Pension Plan was established in 1966 as a social insurance plan for people who are retired and for previously employed people who experience severe and permanent disabilities. This program picks up sickness benefits for those whose benefits have expired under Employment Insurance. These two public insurance programs are available only to those with an earnings record. People who have not worked cannot qualify and must rely on non-insurance forms of support such as welfare. Welfare provides assistance significantly below Statistics Canada's poverty line. It is stigmatizing and often has built-in disincentives to work. Other non-insurance supports include tax deductions and benefits in-kind.

A number of proposals have been made to reform the social insurance system. They focus on the need for a more comprehensive system that covers all people regardless of earning status or extent of disability. Such a system must provide adequate financial supports, recognize individual needs, and ensure labour market participation through effective rehabilitation. Many consumers have argued against a separate disability income program, instead favouring a comprehensive program for all Canadians in need (Council of Canadians with Disabilities, 1998; Rioux, 1992).

Education

From the creation of special segregated classes for a few people grew the concept of inclusive, integrated education for many. Initial steps toward deinstitutionalization in the 1950s and 1960s, along with parental pressure, led to the development of segregated special education for children with disabilities at the primary and secondary school levels. These parallel segregated services proliferated in the 1970s and 1980s. In the 1980s parents began to advocate for a shift toward integrated education for their children. They found their children were often labelled and isolated in segregated school systems, which acted as ghettos. In contrast, children in integrated schools developed new communication abilities, skills, and friendships. Non-disabled students learned how to accommodate and relate to their new peers. These changes in education occurred as the concepts of normalization and human rights gained momentum in Canada.

Although education is a provincial and territorial responsibility, a dramatic shift occurred when the Charter of Rights and Freedoms was entrenched in the Canadian constitution in 1982. When the equality rights section came into force in 1985, it provided an effective tool for parents' lobbying and litigation against segregated education (Porter & Richler, 1991). Nevertheless, the needs of many children with disabilities have not been accommodated, especially with recent cuts to education. There is considerable variation across Canada in terms of inclusive education at the primary and secondary levels.

Crawford and Porter (1992) point out that successful inclusive education depends on a number of factors. Schools must have effective mechanisms to include parents in decision making and problem solving related to the education of their children. Children need to be accepted as having a rightful place in the school. Supports, such as staff development and flexible planning time, must be offered to teachers. Students may need concrete supports such as accessible school facilities, computer-aided technologies and other assistive devices, tutorial and interpreter support, therapeutic services, and peer support. Classroom instruction needs to take into account different learning styles. Plus, teachers, families, and students must be committed to inclusion for it to be effective. Unfortunately, many students continue to face hardships within the educational system.

Inclusive postsecondary education is becoming an increasing priority in Canada, but there is little policy to support it. Funding for postsecondary education comes from both federal and provincial sources. Unfortunately, federal funding through the Canada Health and Social Transfer was reduced in the 1990s and many provinces have decreased funding to colleges and universities. As a result, many supports for students with disabilities have decreased while tuition has increased substantially. Although more colleges and universities have special needs staff, very few have policies related to inclusive educational practices. Postsecondary students who are disabled face multiple barriers. Many cannot obtain adequate funding for their education. Often they take longer to complete their education and have to cover these costs. Some who are funded by vocational rehabilitation services may be restricted in terms of their courses or career paths. Many colleges and universities are not physically accessible or may not have technology for individuals with hearing or visual disabilities. Frequently, there is inadequate funding for sign language interpreters in classrooms. Often faculty are not trained or sensitized to deal with the special needs of students. Without these supports, many students will not be able to complete their studies successfully or find meaningful employment (Crawford, 1996).

Employment

Approximately one million working-age Canadians with disabilities are unemployed or remain out of the labour force in Canada. Women, Aboriginals, and other minorities who are disabled are more likely to be unemployed. It has been estimated that the resulting cost of lost productivity ranges from $35 to $38 billion annually (Crawford & Martin, 2000). Consumers have argued for inclusion in meaningful, decent-paying jobs in the regular labour force, rather than being unemployed or segregated in demeaning sheltered workshops (Council of Canadians with Disabilities, 1998).

Disability policies and programs

Canadians with disabilities are excluded from the labour market because of discrimination, inadequate public policies, and other barriers (Crawford, 1992). Human rights legislation has not been very effective in addressing discrimination in employment. Public policies have often segregated people into sheltered workshops and failed to achieve any meaningful employment equity. Consumers have difficulty obtaining a variety of necessary employment-related supports such as aids and devices, home supports, rehabilitation services, transportation, and adaptations to the workplace. They often do not have equal access to training and education. The current system of funding and service delivery is not well coordinated; rather, it is highly complex, fragmented, and piecemeal. Those people who become employed have problems obtaining additional income to meet their disability-related costs.

A series of policy initiatives have been developed to address some of these issues. The Canadian Human Rights Act and all provincial/territorial human rights acts prohibit discrimination in employment on the basis of disability. Some human rights legislation includes "duty to accommodate" which requires employers to make a range of modifications to a given job or workplace to promote the employment of Canadians with disabilities. The federal government and some of the provinces have employment equity legislation that requires them to report the numbers of people with disabilities and to remove workplace barriers. In 1997 the federal government replaced a program called Vocational Rehabilitation of Disabled Persons, which was over thirty-five years old, with Employability Assistance for People with Disabilities (EAPD). The name reflects a stronger emphasis on employability. The EAPD is a partnership between the federal and provincial/territorial governments. The federal government contributes 50% of the costs of eligible provincial/territorial programs and services up to a maximum total cost. The provinces and territories administer the services and have greater flexibility to tailor programs to local needs. Services include employment counselling and assessment, employment planning, pre-employment training, postsecondary education, skills training, assistive devices, wage subsidies or earning supplements, and workplace supports. There are a variety of other initiatives including the federal government's Opportunity Fund, which supports a broad array of employment activities for Canadians with disabilities who are not eligible for employment benefits under the Employment Insurance Act.

Despite all of these policy initiatives, the unemployment and underemployment rate of Canadians with disabilities is extremely high. A number of policies are required to support people to obtain and retain meaningful employment. Social security programs must eliminate disincentives. People require adequate income supports, education, training, accessible housing and transportation, personal supports, and aids and devices. As part of this effort, some people require supported employment in the form of job coaches and special supports and training (Neufeldt, Sandys, Fuchs, & Logan, 1999).

However, many people continue to confront barriers that do not permit them to be part of the economic mainstream of Canadian society.

Other Community Resources

Other community resources enable Canadians with disabilities to live independently. Social policies related to health care are central to this aim. Fortunately, Canada has a universal health care policy. However, in the 1990s the federal and provincial governments began to reduce funding for health care, including preventative services and drug and prescription programs. This led to the erosion of the system of personal supports, which was partially funded by health care dollars. Although funding from the health system has been used to establish many innovative services, it often perpetuates a traditional medical model that disempowers consumers. Many consumers feel oppressed by government institutions, hospitals, and rehabilitation services. The plight of psychiatric consumer/survivors in these institutions has been well documented. People are often stripped of their identity and lose control over their lives. Self-help services have provided an alternative to this model (Capponi, 1997; Lord, 2000; Ochocka, Nelson, & Lord, 1999; Torjman, 2000).

Consumers continue to confront many barriers getting to and from school, work, or pursuing daily activities. Building codes are required to ensure that community facilities as well as housing are accessible. Other aspects of community life, such as leisure activities, have tended to be segregated. There is a movement toward more integrated recreational activities (Hutchison & McGill, 1998). Policies are evolving related to arts and culture. For example, libraries are becoming more accessible to people with visual disabilities through large-text formats and braille. Movies and theatres are becoming more responsive through new technology for those with hearing disabilities. Nevertheless, consumers continue to confront extensive barriers in the community.

Conclusions and Future Directions

Many social policies and programs were developed for Canadians with disabilities during the Decade of Disabled Persons. The budgets of some of these programs benefited from substantial increases in the 1980s, but by the early 1990s many of these gains were eroded by funding reductions. A major recession in North America, coupled with free trade deals between Canada and the United States and then Mexico, led to pressures in Canada to cut corporate taxes, reduce government expenditures, and harmonize human services with those of trading partners. The federal government diluted national standards and downloaded more of its services to the provinces and territories—and in turn to the municipalities—creating a patchwork of services across Canada. Even as the economy improved and government surpluses increased at the turn of the century, many programs continued to be cut or were not reinstated. As a result, some regions in Canada have few services and others have none.

Many programs are based on a medical model that categorizes and stigmatizes program users and leaves them with little control over services. Despite these barriers, a new concept of services is emerging in Canada— one based on consumer control, flexibility, and choice of services. Consumers have lobbied for a fundamental paradigm shift in policy development. They have advocated for universal adaptable housing features that are flexible to meet everyone's needs. Transportation policies are slowly moving from an emphasis on specialized separate transit systems to a family of accessible transportation in that consumers have more choice and flexibility. Direct individualized funding programs have been established that give consumers more control, choice, and flexibility over personal supports. There is increasing emphasis on integrated education and community resources. One challenge is to move these programs from small-scale initiatives to large-scale options.

As part of its British tradition, Canada has inherited a model of social policy that provides for a comprehensive social welfare safety net. However, this approach is crumbling under the influence of government funding reductions. In contrast, the United States has focussed on developing civil rights legislation such as the Fair Housing Act Amendment and the Americans with Disability Act. This represents a promising approach for Canada, despite government jurisdictional dilemmas.

The federal government's report *The Will to Act* combines these two approaches. The Council of Canadians with Disabilities (1996) endorsed many of its proposals. This report proposes a comprehensive pan-Canadian approach that builds provisions for individuals with disabilities into mainstream policies and programs. The consumer movement has advocated for a joint federal-provincial-territorial effort to create comprehensive disability standards across Canada. *The Will to Act* recommends establishing a Canadians with Disability Act and that the federal government use a disability policy lens to develop future laws, policies, programs, and human rights regulations. It highlights the need for the federal government to fulfil its commitment to Aboriginal Canadians with disabilities by ensuring access to the supports and services they require. The report argues for labour market integration, in which mainstream employment programs explicitly include employment strategies for Canadians with disabilities. It suggests consumer organizations be funded to provide some of these supports. It recommends a renewal of vocational rehabilitation services, with a focus on broader needs. It advocates for replacement of the patchwork of existing income programs with a coherent, comprehensive, and sustainable approach to providing income to all Canadians. Finally, it proposes a comprehensive disability personal support program throughout the country.

Consumer groups have also advocated for more comprehensive disability policies at the provincial and territorial level. One proposal is to develop a Canadians with Disabilities Act within the provinces and territories. Such legislation would deal with issues such as public transportation, education, provincial and municipal services and facilities, and other goods and services. It would require government bodies to identify existing barriers, design plans to deal with them within set time frames, and prevent new barriers from being created.

Future policies must be directed at all levels of government and must guarantee national standards and citizenship rights. These policies must be comprehensive and respond to individual needs. Essential to this approach is consistent enforcement of legislation. Policies must stress integrated programs that ensure consumer control, choice, and flexibility. It is only though this multipronged approach that Canada can create an environment in which all citizens can live independently in the community.

References

Armitage, A. (1996). *Social welfare in Canada revisited.* Toronto: Oxford University Press.

Baker, D. (1992). Could it happen in Ontario? *Arch-Type,* 10(4a), 15-16.

Beachell, L. (2000). CCD *annual report 1999-2000.* Winnipeg: Council of Canadians with Disabilities.

Capponi, P. (1997). *Dispatches from the poverty line.* Toronto: Penguin.

Carpenter, S. (2001). Housing blues from institutions to community. *CAILC New Bulletin,* 6(1), 10-13.

Council of Canadians with Disabilities. (1996). CCD's *final presentation to the Task Force on Disability.* Winnipeg: Author.

Council of Canadians with Disabilities. (1998). *Disability income supports and service project: Consultation report.* Winnipeg: Author.

Crawford, C. (1992). *On target: Canada's employment-related programs for persons with disabilities.* Toronto: Roeher Institute.

Crawford, C. (1996). *Building bridges: Inclusive post-secondary education for people with intellectual disabilities.* Toronto: Roeher Institute.

Crawford, C., & Martin, T. (2000). *Job accommodation and* other employment measures in Canada. Toronto: Roeher Institute.

Crawford C., & Porter, G. (1992). *How it happens: A look at inclusive educational practice in Canada for children and youth with disabilities.* Toronto: Roeher Institute.

DeJong, G. (1993). Three trends to look for in the American independent living movement in the 1990's. In A. Neufeldt (Ed.), *Independent living: An agenda for the 1990's* (pp. 109-120). Ottawa: Canadian Association of Independent Living Centres.

Denton, L. (2000). From human care to prevention. *Canadian Journal of Community Mental Health,* 19(2), 127-134.

Driedger, D., Feika, I., & Giron Batres, E. (Eds.). (1996). *Across border: Women with disabilities working together.* Charlottetown: Gynergy Books.

Dunn, P. (1990). *Barriers confronting seniors with disabilities in Canada.* Ottawa, ON: Statistics Canada.

References Dunn, P. (1999). *The development of government independent living policies and programs for Canadians with disabilities.* Waterloo: Faculty of Social Work, Wilfrid Laurier University.

Enns, H. (1991). Introduction to Independent Living. *Compass 2* (9), 1-8.

Everett, B. (2000). *A fragile revolution: Consumers and psychiatric survivors confronting the power of the mental health system.* Waterloo: Wilfrid Laurier University Press.

Federal Task Force on Disability Issues. (1996). *Equal citizenship of Canadians with disabilities: The will to act.* Ottawa: Minister of Public Works and Government Services Canada.

Hanes, R. (2001). Social work with persons with disabilities. In S. Hick (Ed.). *Social work in Canada: An introduction.* Toronto: Thompson Educational Publishing.

Hutchison, P., & McGill, J. (1998). *Leisure, integration, and community* (2nd ed.). Toronto: Leisurability Publications.

Hutchison, P., Pedlar, A., Lord, J., Dunn, P., McGeown, M., Taylor, A., & Vanditelli, C. (1997). The impact of Independent Living Resource Centres in Canada on people with disabilities. *Canadian Journal of Rehabilitation, 10* (2), 99-112.

Lord, J. (1997, September 25-26). Empowerment process and community: Reflections and paradoxes. Presentation to Empowerment Practice in Social Work Conference. Toronto: University of Toronto.

Lord, J. (2000). Is that all there is? Searching for citizenship in the midst of services. *Canadian Journal of Community Mental Health, 19* (2), 165-169.

McKnight, J. (1995). *Careless society.* New York: Basic Books.

Nagler, M. (Ed.), (1990). *Perspectives on disability: Text and readings on disability.* Palo Alto: Health Markets Research.

Neufeldt, A. (1993). Signs of the times and their implications for independent living. In A. Neufeldt (Ed.), *Independent living: An agenda for the '90s* (pp. 83-98). Ottawa: Canadian Association of Independent Living Centres.

Neufeldt, A., Sandys, J., Fuchs, D., & Logan, M. (1999). Supported and self-directed employment support initiatives in Canada: An overview of issues. *International Journal of Practical Approaches to Disability, 23* (3), 24-36.

Ochocka, J., Nelson, G., & Lord, J. (1999). Organizational change towards the empowerment-community integration paradigm in community mental health. *Canadian Journal of Community Mental Health, 18* (2), 59-72.

Oliver, M., & Barnes, C. (1998). *Disabled people and social policy from exclusion to inclusion.* New York: Addison Wesley Longman.

Pedlar, A., Haworth, L., Hutchison, P., Taylor, A., & Dunn, P. (1999). *A textured life: Empowerment and adults with developmental disabilities.* Waterloo: Wilfrid Laurier University Press.

Pedlar, A., & Hutchison, P. (2000). Restructuring human services in Canada: Commodification of disability. *Disability & Society, 15* (4), 637-651.

Pheiffer, D. (1993). Overview of the disability movement: History, legislative record and political implications. *Policy Studies Journal, 21* (4), 724-734.

Porter, G., & Richler, D. (1991). *Changing Canadian schools.* Toronto: Roeher Institute.

Rioux, M. (1992). *Comprehensive disability income security reform.* Toronto: Roeher Institute.

Ross, D., Scott, K., & Smith, P. (2000). *The Canadian fact book on poverty.* Ottawa: Canadian Council on Social Development.

Secretary of State. (1991). *The national strategy for the integration of persons with disabilities.* Ottawa: Supply and Services Canada.

Special Parliamentary Committee on the Disabled and the Handicapped. (1981). **References**
  Obstacles. Ottawa: Minister of Supply and Services Canada.
Standing Committee on Human Rights and the Status of Disabled Persons. (1990).
  A consensus for action: The economic integration of disabled persons. Ottawa:
  Minister of Supply and Services Canada.
Standing Committee on Human Rights and the Status of Disabled Persons. (1993a).
  Completing the circle. Ottawa: Minister of Supply and Services Canada.
Standing Committee on Human Rights and the Status of Disabled Persons. (1993b).
  The grand design. Ottawa: Minister of Supply and Services Canada.
Statistics Canada. (1995). *A portrait of persons with disabilities*. Ottawa: Ministry of
  Industry, Science and Technology.
Torjman, S. (1990). *Poor places: Disability-related residential and support services*.
  North York: Roeher Institute.
Torjman, S. (1993). *Nothing personal*. North York: Roeher Institute.
Torjman, S. (2000). *Proposal for a national personal supports fund*. Ottawa: Caledon
  Institute.
Walters, T., & Ternette, E. (1994). Discover independent living. *Abilities Magazine*
  (Spring Issue), 1-3.
Wharf, B., & McKenzie, B. (1998). *Connecting policy to practice in human services*.
  Toronto: Oxford University Press.
Woodill, G., & Willi, V. (1992). *Independent living and participation in research:
  A critical analysis*. Toronto: The Centre for Independent Living Toronto.

Additional Resources

Canadian Association of Community Living (CACL). Online at <www.cacl.ca>.
Canadian Association of the Deaf (CAD). Online at <www.cad.ca>.
Canadian Association of Independent Living Centres (CAILC). Online at <www.
  cailc.ca>.
Canadian Centre on Disability Studies (CCDS). Online at <www.disabilitystudies.
  ca>.
Canadian Council of the Blind (CCB). Online at <www.ccbnational.net>.
Canadian Mental Health Association (CMHA). Online at <www.cmha.ca>.
Council of Canadians with Disabilities (CCD). Online at <www.pcs.mb.ca/~ccd>.
DisAbled Women's Network of Canada (DAWN). Online at <www.dawncanada. net>.
National Aboriginal Network on Disability (NAND). Online at <www.schoolnet.ca/
  aboriginal/health-e.html>.
National Education Association of Disabled Students (NEADS). Online at <www.
  neads.ca>.
National Network for Mental Health (NNMH). Online at <www.nnmh.ca>.
Office for Disability Issues (ODI) in HRDC. Online at <www.hrdc.gc.ca>.
Roeher Institute. Online at <www.roeher.ca>.

Introduction to Part III

Policy-Making Processes

Part III of the book contains six articles on the policy-making process at the international, federal, provincial, and program levels.

In chapter 12, Tim Wichert gives us a fascinating look at the complexities of attempts to influence international policy from the standpoint of a staff member in a non-governmental organization (NGO). Using refugee policy as an example, he first describes the policy-making process within the United Nations. We learn that it is perhaps even more replete with diverse perspectives than policy making within a national or provincial context because of the enormous variation in cultural and economic background of the countries involved in decision making. He describes for us the partnership that has evolved between the NGO sector and the United Nations High Commissioner for Refugees in shaping refugee policy over the years and describes the satisfaction of shaping policy at a level that will have a worldwide impact.

John English and Bill Young then provide us with an intriguing insight into the policy-making process at the federal level in chapter 13, based upon their experience as elected official and parliamentary policy analyst. Using a historical perspective, they set out in careful detail the struggles of the 1990s with debt and deficit, which led to the introduction of the Canada Health and Social Transfer, the National Child Benefit, and the Social Union Framework Agreement. They conclude that the period can best be characterized by the continued struggle to clarify the responsibilities of federal and provincial government with respect to the funding of social programs and to define the conditions under which new programs can be introduced by the federal government.

Carol Kenny-Scherber leads off chapter 14 with a challenge to social workers to draw on their knowledge of service user needs and how the human service system works to actively participate in the public decision-making process that determines the provincial government's response to social issues. She provides an insider's perspective on how policy is made at the political, pre-legislative, and legislative phases. The chapter concludes with a wealth of suggestions on how social workers can participate in the policy-making

process through involvement with political parties, as advocates, and as professional social workers.

Mac Saulis makes an insightful analysis of the policy and program development processes within the mainstream, and from a holistic, Aboriginal
perspective in chapter 15. He explains the meaning of The Circle, and how
this world view could be applied to policy development. It differs most dramatically from the mainstream perspective in its emphasis on four aspects of
humans—not only the emotional and the mental, or what the mainstream
might call cognitive, but on the physical and the spiritual as well. He also
explains the importance of inclusiveness for Aboriginal peoples in the policy-
making process, and how this could be accomplished if we were to work from
this cultural perspective. He notes the parallels between postmodern
approaches to planning and the traditional Aboriginal perspective.

Chapter 16, by Joan Wharf Higgins, John Cossom, and Brian Wharf, reinforces the previous two chapters when it argues that there is insufficient citizen input into the policy-making process. They use Dahl's concept of
"affected interests" to make the case that everybody impacted by a policy
decision should have a right to participate in making that decision, and to
offer some guidance on how one would define the players and the relative
influence of each. They offer practical suggestions on how a more inclusive
process can be fostered, whether one is dealing with "ordinary issues" like
promoting healthier communities or "grand issues" like the influence of the
World Trade Organization in shaping the economy of nation-states.

The final chapter in this section, chapter 17, discusses an essential but
sometimes overlooked aspect of the policy-making process—evaluation of
social policy and programs. Anne Westhues argues that the shift from a positivist (modern) to a more humanist (postmodern) way of thinking over the
past twenty-five years has had an impact on the role of the evaluator, the
kinds of questions asked in evaluation, and the way we design research, collect data, and report our results. Most significant in this shift is the valuing of
the subjective experiences of people affected by policies and programs. While
we now see political leaders promoting a return to an emphasis on traditional measurable outcomes, she suggests that social workers engaged in
evaluation can ensure that we do not lose our focus on these subjective experiences by consciously committing to work from a critical perspective.

12

Pursuing Social Policy Ideals at the International Level: An NGO Perspective

Tim Wichert

The international stage has become an important place to engage in social policy debate. Various agencies of the United Nations (UN) were created in the twentieth century to deal with social issues, including the World Health Organization, the United Nations High Commissioner for Refugees, the UN Children's Fund (UNICEF), and the UN Commission on Human Rights. The Charter, which created the United Nations at its founding conference in San Francisco on June 26, 1945, sought to "reaffirm faith in fundamental human rights, in the dignity and worth of the human person, in the equal rights of men and women," and to "promote social progress and better standards of life" (United Nations, 1945).

A positive approach to social policy development at the international level requires an understanding of the process and choosing how best to be involved. The international policy process involves a complex set of interactions involving individual states, regional groups of states, international agencies within the UN system, and private actors like non-governmental organizations (NGOs). Implementation of international standards ultimately requires governments to incorporate them into national legislation. But political and cultural differences between states and regions result in different levels of understanding and commitment. Even if there is general agreement that certain social policy issues may be universal, how they are implemented at a national or local level varies considerably.

Non-governmental organizations have played an important role in developing international social policy because of their understanding of these local dynamics. Those NGOs that are most effectively engaged in international social policy tend to be those with programs in various parts of the world focused on human health, safety, and well-being. NGOs therefore play an important role in both representing civil society at the international level and interpreting international social policy for everyday use.

My perspectives on international social policy making result from having ten years of experience in the NGO sector with the Mennonite Central Committee (MCC), which included a three-year secondment with the Quaker United Nations Office in Geneva, Switzerland. While MCC is an agency of Mennonite Churches in North America, its mandate is to work among people suffering from poverty, conflict, oppression, and natural disaster, and to work for peace, justice, and the dignity of all people (Mennonite Central Committee, 2000). Much of my work has focused on refugees and policies related to the human rights of refugees. This chapter will focus on developing international policy related to these issues.

Understanding International Policy Process

Policies for human rights related to refugees and asylum seekers have been developed through a vast array of instruments at the international, regional, and national level.

At the international level, these policies have developed throughout the United Nations system. The Universal Declaration of Human Rights gives everyone the right to seek and enjoy asylum (Article 14). As long as people cannot have their basic human rights protected in their own country, asylum remains their most effective means of protection. In the aftermath of World War II, governments were concerned about the refugee crisis in Europe and wanted to create a policy framework for dealing with the crisis.

The UN High Commissioner for Refugees (UNHCR) was created in 1951 by a resolution of the UN General Assembly.[1] A statute set out general provisions and functions of the high commissioner. The UNHCR was to provide protection to refugees falling within the scope of the UN statute. It was also authorized to seek permanent solutions for the "problem of refugees."[2]

In July 1951 a conference in Geneva completed the drafting and signing of the Convention Relating to the Status of Refugees. Together with the UNHCR statute, this refugee convention provided the legislative framework for the vision outlined in the original resolution of the UN General Assembly.

The refugee convention remains the most comprehensive codification of the rights of refugees at the international level, though it was augmented by a protocol in 1967 to include those who became refugees after January 1951. The convention sets out the popular definition of a refugee that is still used today, namely a person who has a well-founded fear of being persecuted for reasons of race, religion, nationality, membership of a particular social group or political opinion, and is outside their country of nationality or habitual residence.[3] It also sets out specific provisions regarding housing, public education, social security, and travel documents for refugees. For example, governments that have signed the convention "shall accord to refugees the same treatment as is accorded to nationals with respect to elementary education."[4] However, Article 42 of the convention allows states to make reservations to some of these provisions when signing, thereby limiting their obligations.

At the original conference, twenty-six governments were represented by delegates and two others by observers. Only eight were from outside Europe and North America: Brazil, Colombia, Cuba, Egypt, Iran, Iraq, Israel, and

Turkey. Today, there are 140 countries that have ratified the refugee convention or protocol. The refugee convention has evolved over time through both policy and practice. For example, the Organization of African Unity (OAU), comprising countries within Africa, has articulated a definition of refugees that includes those fleeing more generalized violence and civil war. And countries like Canada and the United States have specifically included violence and persecution aimed at women as a ground for refugee status in national policy.

International policy is continually developed by the Executive Committee of the UNHCR, known as Excom. Excom is made up of states that have a "demonstrated interest in and devotion to the solution of the refugee problem."[5] These have tended to be important asylum countries or major donors to UNHCR programs. There are approximately fifty states that are members of Excom. They meet annually in Geneva to agree upon decisions and conclusions for ultimate adoption by the UN General Assembly.

In addition to the refugee convention and the Universal Declaration of Human Rights, a number of other key international treaties provide important rights for refugees and asylum seekers (Gorlick, 2000). These include the International Covenant on Civil and Political Rights, and the International Covenant on Economic Social and Cultural Rights (both adopted in 1966), the Convention on the Elimination of Racial Discrimination (1965), the Convention on the Elimination of Discrimination against Women (1979), the Convention against Torture (1984), and the Convention on the Rights of the Child (1989). Each of these treaties have established supervisory mechanisms, usually committees of international experts. They provide authoritative interpretation of treaty provisions, assess compliance of the standards by state parties that must report to the committees, and receive and adjudicate on interstate and individual complaints.

This array of human rights is available to all people within the territory or under the jurisdiction of a state that is subject to the treaty. Refugees who have been forced to flee their country of nationality because of persecution have had these international human rights violated. After they flee to another country, they are still entitled to these rights, not because they are refugees but because these rights should be applicable to everyone.

Implementation of human rights obligations will vary from country to country. Individual states will often choose to comply with their international obligations on the basis of national policy priorities. They must choose whether to formalize international obligations by enacting national legislation, whether to establish national mechanisms for dealing with human rights complaints, and whether to interpret constitutional rights in a narrow or restrictive manner. Goodwin-Gill (1996) suggests that while implementation may vary, obligations should at the very least be implemented in good faith.

Governments can be pressured into complying with international obligations through these human rights mechanisms or through political pressure from other states. The UN Commission on Human Rights, which meets each spring in Geneva, is an intergovernmental body made up of fifty-three government members elected on a regional basis. Most other states send observers to participate. The political nature of the process offers mixed results for policy making. It allows pressure to be brought to bear on offending states for their human rights violations, especially through the use of rapporteurs who report on specific country or thematic issues. And it has arguably been an important factor in achieving progress in recent decades in places like Chile, Argentina, and South Africa. But it also allows states to avoid censure through political manipulation and negotiation.

Understanding international policy process

Non-governmental organizations play an important role in raising awareness of the obligations and issues at a national level. Canadian NGOs were instrumental in raising refugee-related concerns at the Canadian government's first appearance before the UN Committee on the Rights of the Child (CRC) in 1995. The Inter-Church Committee for Refugees of Toronto prepared a detailed brief outlining a number of concerns, including the issue of family reunification for refugee children. The CRC, in its report, recommended that the Canadian authorities take all feasible measures to facilitate and speed up family reunification, and that solutions should be sought to avoid deportations causing separation of families (Gorlick, 2000). The latter is an issue when children have been born in Canada during the asylum process. Since they are Canadian citizens, the CRC suggested that their "best interests" should be considered in determining whether their parent or parents should ultimately be deported from Canada if their refugee claim is rejected.

Canadian policy was further clarified on this issue by the Supreme Court of Canada in the 1999 case of Mavis Baker, following legal interventions by NGOS, which raised the CRC decision and Canada's international legal obligations. And the Canadian government's new immigration and refugee legislation of 2001 will specify the convention concept of the "best interests of the child." This new legislation will also provide some protection against deportation from Canada when there is a real risk of torture, as articulated by the UN Committee against Torture. NGOs in Canada have been instrumental in getting these provisions included in the new law.

The Committee on the Rights of the Child acknowledged that Canada basically sets a good example in terms of its policies and programs toward children. Indeed, on the international spectrum, children in Canada are better off than they are in almost all other countries in the world. As a result, the committee's conclusions and observations are one of the few ways in which international pressure can be brought to encourage better protection of children's rights in Canada. While offering its encouragement and expressing its concerns, the committee is very much dependent on other actors within Canada to take these concerns forward.

It is also important to note the array of regional human rights mechanisms that have been established in Europe, Africa, and the Americas (Buer-

gental, 1995). Canadian NGOs have used the mechanisms of the Organization of American States to promote social policy. In 2000, the Inter-American
Commission on Human Rights issued a detailed report on the situation of
human rights of asylum seekers within the Canadian refugee determination
system following a visit to Canada by a six-person commission delegation
(Inter-American Commission on Human Rights, 2000). The commission held
discussions with numerous high-level political, administrative, legislative,
and judicial authorities, as well as representatives of NGOs and other sectors
of civil society. NGOs subsequently used the commission's report when advocating for changes to proposed Canadian legislation on citizenship and immigration and refugees.

But international policy development is not simply about encouraging
states to implement their obligations. On occasion, the Canadian government and other states have played a significant role in the policy process at
the international level. The Canadian government in recent years has focused
its foreign policy on issues related to human security (Government of Canada,
2000). Part of this strategy was to play a leading role in the completion of the
UN Convention on Land Mines in Ottawa in December 1997. And the Canadian government continues to promote recognition at the international level
of the right to seek refugee asylum on the basis of gender-based persecution.

International policy making therefore involves a complex set of processes.
Effectively working within this system requires an understanding of where
to focus attention.

Developing a Thematic Focus

International refugee policy is enhanced by having an institutional base
within the office of the UN High Commissioner for Refugees. The UNHCR provides a programmatic framework for designing and delivering programs for
refugees. It has over 5,000 staff in 120 countries, with an annual budget of
US$1 billion (UN High Commissioner for Refugees, 2000). The Executive
Committee of the UNHCR approves and supervises the material assistance
program of UNHCR, for which various governments provide financing. It also
advises the high commissioner on the exercise of his or her functions. In
practice, the work of Excom is largely influenced and guided by the UNHCR
itself, especially through its policy papers and speeches given by the high
commissioner. Policies are continually developed through guidelines and
policy papers generated within UNHCR.

Excom is helped and hindered equally by its guiding principle to build
consensus. Public debate is dominated by government responses to the issues
raised by UNHCR, and by burning issues arising from specific refugee contexts. The final "conclusions" are the product of closed meetings between
UNHCR and governments. Achieving consensus on decisions and conclusions is a difficult task, and important matters are often in danger of being
excluded in the interests of agreement. However, once agreed, they arguably
take on added significance.

Apart from programming, UNHCR is also instrumental in urging states to support and implement the policy standards they have set. The refugee convention does not have a monitoring mechanism like the expert committees of other human rights conventions.

The dilemma for UNHCR, which is perhaps typical in international policy-making, is that while they are striving to uphold the rights and interests of refugees, and must criticize states when necessary, they are also almost entirely dependent on those states for their funding and ongoing mandate. As a result, the role of the NGO sector, which is much more independent from governments, has become fundamental to policy development.

There is an increasing awareness and understanding among NGOs of the opportunities for effective participation in the UNHCR process. This learning process has involved a number of things, including the recognition that coalitions and alliances are important: with policy advisers within the Canadian government, with NGOs from Canada and other countries, with officials within the UN system, and also with policy advisers from other national governments. International policy development is not simply about creating utopian policies and highlighting the violations of acceptable behaviour. It is also working together with those governments and international agencies that are seriously attempting to implement and demonstrate acceptable behaviour and urging others to do the same. Through such alliances, important strides have been made in the past decade on international refugee policy for women and children.

Women share the same protection needs as other refugees. They need protection against forced return to their countries of origin; security against armed attacks; legal status that grants adequate social and legal rights; and access to basic necessities like food, shelter, and medical care. But in addition, refugee women and girls have special protection needs. They are vulnerable to sexual and physical abuse, exploitation, and discrimination in the delivery of goods and services (UN High Commissioner for Refugees, 1999). In particular, they may endure physical and sexual attacks during conflict in their home countries, during flight to asylum, and even during asylum (Human Rights Watch, 1995; UN High Commissioner for Refugees, 1995b). National policies in countries of asylum may not provide for legal recognition or proper documentation.

Although gender is not specifically articulated in the refugee definition of the refugee convention, there have been important steps in recent years to include it in practice. In 1985, the European Parliament called on states to grant refugee status "to women who suffer cruel and inhuman treatment because they have violated the moral or ethical rules of their society" (UN High Commissioner for Refugees 1997, p. 196). That same year, Excom conclusion no. 39 recognized that states were free to adopt the interpretation that women asylum seekers could, in certain situations, be considered a "particular social group" within the convention definition. In 1995, Excom took this further with a conclusion calling on states to develop guidelines on persecution aimed at women, suggesting that these guidelines should recognize as refugees those women whose persecution consists of sexual violence or is otherwise gender-related. Canada continues to promote this issue, having pioneered such guidelines in 1993 when the chairperson of the Immigration and Refugee Board issued gender guidelines for use in refugee determination hearings.[6]

In 1996 UNHCR hosted a symposium on gender-based persecution. Later that year, an Excom conclusion called on states to adopt an approach that is "sensitive to gender-related concerns," and which "ensures" that persecution through sexual violence or which is otherwise gender-related is indeed persecution under the refugee convention.

But international protection for vulnerable groups goes beyond legal principles. Protection of refugee women requires practical programs and priorities that ensure their safety and well-being. In 1991, UNHCR produced *Guidelines for Protection and Care of Refugee Women*, and in 1995 they produced *Sexual Violence against Refugees: Guidelines on the Prevention and Response*.

These guidelines have been prepared to help the staff of UNHCR and its implementing partners to identify the specific protection issues, problems, and risks facing refugee women. In doing so, they cover traditional protection concerns such as the determination of refugee status and the provision of physical security. But the guidelines also provide suggestions on actions that can be taken, particularly within traditional assistance sectors, to prevent or deter protection problems from arising. These encourage practical interventions such as the early assessment of protection issues (e.g., ensuring that services and facilities are easily accessible with good lighting), involving women in decision-making structures (e.g., the design of health programs), monitoring the nutritional status of women and children to identify problems in food distribution, and using female staff when trying to elicit information from female refugees (UN High Commissioner for Refugees, 1999).

In 1994, UNHCR also developed a training module called People-Oriented Planning (POP). Although it was developed by the senior coordinator on refugee women within UNHCR, it provided a broader focus to include women, men, and children. The premise for the tool was that for staff to do the best job possible in providing protection and assistance to refugees in any particular situation, they must know specific things about who the refugees are in that particular setting. The POP programming tool helps UNHCR staff and partners identify the important facts about any group of refugees, and then organize that information to make programming decisions and to implement effective programs (Anderson, 1994).

NGOs were instrumental in initiating and encouraging discussions on the importance of addressing the needs of refugee women. They encouraged the development of the guidelines and the creation of a focal point within UNHCR to address these needs. The Canadian government funded the first senior coordinator for refugee women within UNHCR in 1994.

While much progress has been made, NGOS and others continue to express concern about the implementation of the UNHCR guidelines relating to refugee women. There was also concerted action by NGOS in 1997 when UNHCR suggested ending the mandate of the senior coordinator for refugee women because of the belief that the issues had been adequately "mainstreamed" within the overall work of UNHCR. But NGOS and various states didn't agree, and because of the pressure placed on UNHCR from both NGOS and states (which were prepared to continue funding the position), the position was retained. It is clear that even within the institutional framework of UNHCR, there are issues related to the adequate implementation of social policies that have been developed.

There has also been progress on policy related to refugee children. In 1987 Excom requested a set of guidelines for refugee children,[7] which UNHCR published the following year. Following an evaluation in 1991, UNHCR prepared a policy on refugee children in 1993, which was adopted by UNHCR Excom in October 1993, and a revised version of the guidelines in 1994 (UN High Commissioner for Refugees, 1994). At the same time, UNHCR established the position of senior coordinator for refugee children, with financial assistance from the government of Sweden, to encourage the implementation of the guidelines and policy.

The policy arose because of the recognition that refugee children have special dependence, vulnerability, and developmental needs. When resources are scarce, they are often the first to die. And refugee girls are even more vulnerable than boys to neglect, abuse, and exploitation. Girls' participation in education programs is often prematurely curtailed (UN High Commissioner for Refugees, 1994).

The policy also originated around the same time that the UN was completing the Convention on the Rights of the Child in 1989. This widely ratified convention set the normative international standards in which UNHCR could develop a framework of practical implementation. This in turn led to the directives of UNHCR Excom, which ultimately adopted a policy specific to refugee children.

The Canadian government has also taken steps to ensure some of these issues are incorporated into national policy. In particular, the chairperson of the Immigration and Refugee Board issued guidelines on child refugee claimants in September 1996. Among other things, these guidelines focus on appropriate procedures for assessing the refugee claims of children who are not accompanied by their parents. The guidelines stress the need to consider the best interests of the child, and make specific references to both the Convention on the Rights of the Child and the UNHCR guidelines on refugee children. As such, they are another example of how various policies developed at the international level make their way into national legislation where they have an ongoing practical application.

Understanding international policy process

Effecting Change

The role of non-governmental organizations in effecting the policies discussed cannot be underestimated. There were twenty-nine NGOs represented at the conference that created the refugee convention in 1951, including the World Council of Churches, Friends World Committee for Consultation (Quakers), World Jewish Congress, and YWCA. NGOs were allowed to submit written or oral statements to the conference.

Now over 150 NGOs are registered for the annual meetings of the UNHCR Executive Committee. Through a program called Partnership in Action, NGOs and UNHCR have increased their dialogue and co-operation through the use of NGO focal points from other regions of the world. Issues raised by NGOs include refugee children, urban refugees, detention of asylum seekers in the West, internally displaced people, women, and peacemaking. While many NGOs that go to Geneva for Excom emphasize their contacts with UNHCR and other NGOs, there is increasing attention to government delegates.

NGOs generally, and in particular those engaged in policy development at the international level, tend to have a commitment to social change. Many of them focus on and advocate for those who are vulnerable and voiceless. The most effective NGO advocates are those whose advocacy is rooted in actual programs, where expertise has been developed and best practices identified, along with gaps in social policy that need to be changed. There is also an increasing awareness and understanding among NGOs of the opportunities for effective participation in social change at the international level. I would like to highlight a number of specific interventions I was recently involved with.

The UNHCR policy process, as outlined above, revolves around the Executive Committee of the UNHCR. Although UNHCR officials may prepare policy papers and guidelines, these must ultimately by approved by the Executive Committee of government representatives. In 1995, Excom adopted new working methods that delegated authority for much of its decision making to a new Standing Committee that met quarterly throughout the year. It was given greater decision-making authority than the two subcommittees it replaced.

This had a number of implications. Firstly, the standing committee became the essential forum for directing international refugee policy. Secondly, participation in the standing committee became an important issue, in particular for NGOs and government observers that wanted to participate in this policy-making process. At the time, governments that were not Excom members were still allowed to participate in the standing committee, but NGOs were not. A number of Geneva-based NGOs informally created a working group to lobby for a role for NGOs in the new structure. The outgoing chair of the Executive Committee had signalled his interest in having NGOs participate. The incoming chair for 1996, when the decision was to be taken by the new standing committee on working methods, was supportive as well. We prepared a discussion paper that articulated why NGOs should be involved

(Quaker United Nations Office, 1996a). For example, we argued that NGOs are primary agents of protection and assistance for refugees, often as UNHCR implementing partners. They have important expertise and first-hand knowledge, are a source of current information, offer important analysis and ideas, and can engage in constructive and critical dialogue.

The NGOs that worked together on this initiative did not always agree on the nature of the participation requested. Some wanted full participation for any interested NGOs, with the ability to make oral or written presentations, while others were content to gain admission to the meetings even without the right to speak. Some suggested that since NGOs are allowed only one oral intervention at the annual meeting of the Executive Committee, we could not expect greater involvement at the standing committee. Other issues raised included the de-restriction of documents, so that NGOs could access UNHCR policy papers before they were presented to the standing committee for decisions. Gaining access to these papers would allow NGOs to provide useful inputs and commentary beforehand.

As a result of these efforts, the Executive Committee decided to "initiate consultations" among Excom members on this issue of NGO participation. After further consultations, which included the NGO working group, the standing committee decided in June 1997 to allow NGO participation in future meetings.[8] NGOs were given access to standing committee meetings upon written request, documents would be made available through established networks, NGOs would be permitted to make written contributions, and one oral NGO statement would be allowed on each standing committee agenda item (with NGOs making the selection based on expertise or direct knowledge of the issue).

Securing NGO access to this critical decision-making process ensured that NGOs would be able to participate more effectively in the policy process. It was successful for a number of reasons. There was a clear issue to work on, namely whether NGOs should be allowed to participate in the new committee process. The duration of the process was also quite clear, and NGOs knew that a decision was to be made within a year. Although NGOs did not always agree on the specific details of the request for greater NGO involvement, they nonetheless agreed that NGOs should have greater involvement. Speaking with one voice made a significant impact. Important political connections were fostered with government representatives that were based in Geneva and supportive of the NGO position. Others that were critical to the decision-making process, but were still uncertain about NGO participation, were also targeted through processes like informal lunch meetings. The senior bureaucrat within UNHCR was also involved in the critical discussions to ensure that the process was transparent and that NGOs were aware of the correct administrative details.

Many of the informal meetings through this process took place at the Quaker United Nations Office (QUNO). Quakers have had an official presence in Geneva since 1926 when they set up a liaison office for the League of

Nations and other international agencies. Over the years they became known for their independence and impartiality, and informal luncheons became a trademark for off-the-record dialogue on important policy issues (Bailey, 1993; Yarrow, 1978). Because of this history, NGOs, UN staff, and government delegates in Geneva were usually interested in participating in these discussions when invited. The role played by staff at QUNO was both advocate and broker. On issues like NGO participation in the Executive Committee process, we obviously had a position we wanted to convey. At other times, the purpose was to provide an opportunity for dialogue that might not otherwise happen.

For example, just prior to the Executive Committee meeting in October 1997 we organized an informal meeting for about twenty diplomats and NGO representatives. The purpose of the meeting was to provide an opportunity for dialogue on a variety of issues on the upcoming Excom agenda. There are numerous opportunities for informal meetings through the Excom process between government delegates and UNHCR staff, and also between NGOs and UNHCR staff. But informal meetings between NGOs and a group of government representatives rarely occur. We also wanted to provide a forum for informal cross-regional dialogue, and ensured that we had governments represented from all regions of the world. At another level, we wanted an opportunity to raise specific issues and demonstrate that we had an articulated interest. We had prepared a draft NGO statement, which we presented for discussion.

The meeting was successful in many respects. Participants expressed appreciation for the opportunity to get together in an informal way, and some diplomats said they heard positions from their colleagues that hadn't arisen in other informal discussions. The good turnout implied that diplomats were interested in this kind of forum and this kind of discussion, both with NGOs and with each other. Some expressed disappointment that we had not discussed the draft conclusions for the upcoming session of Excom, and were surprised to learn that NGOs were not allowed prior access to these. They were willing to encourage NGO inputs and feedback. Other issues raised included the relative importance of Excom conclusions, why some members of the Executive Committee have refused to sign the Refugee Convention, and whether there needs to be a stronger reporting mechanism under the refugee convention. The meeting highlighted the importance of informal channels for discussion. We can try to create new channels for formal dialogue, but the more interesting and useful discussions will continue to be done informally.

Another feature of our policy making in Geneva was to draw on our particular expertise and knowledge of given situations. We would facilitate informal meetings for people working in countries like Uganda and Burundi to offer current perspectives to UN staff and diplomats in Geneva concerned with the human rights and humanitarian agenda. We would also highlight particular concerns related to peacemaking efforts and reconciliation work in situations of conflict.

Understanding international policy process

At the Executive Committee in 1996, we decided to highlight the important role of refugees in national reconciliation. In particular, we wanted to urge the UNHCR and member states of the UNHCR Executive Committee to put the necessary resources into a program for peace education and training in conflict management and conflict resolution. QUNO prepared a written brief that highlighted the reasons why reconciliation and peace-building were important to achieving durable solutions, and why refugees were important participants in this process.

In 1995, the Executive Committee had recognized the role that refugee community education can play in national reconciliation. It specifically encouraged UNHCR to strengthen its support for education, and in particular to introduce elements of education for peace and human rights.[9] UNHCR also includes peace education in its *Refugee Children: Guidelines on Protection and Care*. Specifically, they indicate that "peace education, including teaching different methods of conflict resolution, may be relevant to children who are victims of conflict" (UN High Commissioner for Refugees, 1994, p. 113). The QUNO statement also highlighted documents that UNICEF had prepared for teaching and training children about conflict resolution and peace. Finally, it urged UNHCR to facilitate the efforts of NGOs and other UN agencies with experience and expertise in working at peace education, reconciliation, and conflict management; to develop a training process that specifically incorporates elements of conflict management into the planning process for refugee programs, especially within education and social services programming; and to allocate the necessary resources, both human and financial, to such a program and seek out donors to provide funding for initiatives in this area (Quaker United Nations Office, 1996b).

We discussed our proposals beforehand with UNHCR senior staff in the education and social services departments. They had been trying to implement programming related to peace education and training, but were glad for NGO support for putting the appropriate policy framework in place and soliciting political will and resources to implement it. We also shared the briefing paper with a number of key government representatives. One of them was particularly interested. He pursued the issue during the closed negotiations for the final conclusions (which involve only government representatives and UNHCR staff), and was successful in including language on the importance of reconciliation and education for peace and human rights.

This initiative was successful for a number of reasons. Although we had not obtained widespread NGO support, we had clearly articulated reasons for promoting reconciliation, which arose out of our own experience and that of other agencies. We also focused on key contacts within UNHCR and government. These were contacts that had been fostered before this particular issue arose, so that they were already familiar with the work of the Quaker office.

Other issues for which NGOs have been instrumental in effecting policy change through the UNHCR Executive Committee include refugee women and children, mentioned earlier, as well as detention of asylum seekers, family reunification, and the importance of resettlement in third countries like Canada.

It is also worth highlighting some of the specific work that has been done by NGOs at the UN Commissioner on Human Rights, which also meets in Geneva. The commission provides an opportunity for formally linking human rights with refugees and internally displaced people (IDPS). It focuses on the abuse of human rights as a cause of forced displacement, and on the human rights of refugees and IDPS themselves.

Internally displaced people are those who are forcibly displaced for similar reasons as refugees, namely armed conflict and violations of human rights. There are an estimated 20 to 22 million IDPS throughout the world (Global IDP Survey & Norwegian Refugee Council, 1998). Unlike refugees, they do not cross international borders, and so must rely primarily on their own governments to uphold their rights and provide assistance, even though those governments may be implicated in causing displacement. They cannot rely on the international protection of the refugee convention.

But at the urging of NGOs in Geneva, in particular the Quaker UN Office, the World Council of Churches, and Caritas Internationalis, the Commissioner on Human Rights requested the UN's secretary-general to appoint a representative for IDPS in 1992. Through NGO networking, and careful advocacy with key government representatives prior to the commission, they were able to draft a resolution that garnered sufficient support among members of the commission, articulated the relevant human rights concerns related to IDPS, and created a mechanism for examining the issue.

As a result of the work since then by the representative, Dr. Francis Deng, international awareness of the existence of IDPS has increased substantially. He has visited more than twelve countries with acute IDP problems, including Sri Lanka, Burundi, and Colombia, to look at internal displacement. He has issued reports for the commission and follow-up recommendations.[10]

In 1996, Deng prepared a significant compilation and analysis of international legal norms relating to IDPS. Then in 1998, the commission endorsed a set of guiding principles for IDPS, based on the earlier compilation. These thirty guiding principles have now been published in a compact and useable handbook by the UN Office for the Coordination of Humanitarian Affairs (1998). They set out key rights and obligations for IDPS as articulated in international humanitarian and human rights law. While they restate existing law, they make its application more specific to the needs of IDPS. For example, while existing law says that all people must have recognition before the law, the guiding principles specify that IDPS should be given documents that they need.

NGOs have continued to raise the problems related to IDPS, and increasingly both NGOs and UN agencies have been addressing the needs of IDPS.

For example, the International Committee for the Red Cross, the UNHCR, and the World Food Program now provide substantial assistance for IDPs. Indeed, over 20% of the people assisted by UNHCR are actually IDPs, even though UNHCR was set up to provide protection and seek solutions for refugees under the refugee convention. UNHCR has creatively justified this involvement by stressing that these IDPs are in "refugee-like" situations (UN High Commissioner for Refugees, 1997).

Closing comments

The process of getting internally displaced people officially on the international agenda is one of the most significant contributions that NGOs have made. Current efforts are now underway to have refugee rights more clearly articulated as well through the Commission on Human Rights. The commission's resolution on mass exoduses, first introduced by Canada in 1980, has consistently called upon all states to promote human rights and fundamental freedoms, and to refrain from denying these for reasons such as race and ethnicity. As a result of informal NGO interventions in 1996, gender was also included in this list.

For the past few years, Canadian NGOs have encouraged the Canadian government to refocus this resolution on the rights of refugees. In 2001, the Canadian Council of Churches (CCC) prepared a statement for the Commissioner on Human Rights that specifically requested such a resolution. I attended the commission on behalf of the CCC in order to raise awareness of the issues and generate support. While the link between refugees and human rights is increasingly being made within UN bodies, there needs to be a clearer articulation of the human rights of refugees in the context of asylum. Placing refugees more clearly on the agenda of the Commissioner on Human Rights through a specific resolution would ensure that refugees and human rights are clearly linked. There is increasing support among NGOs for such a resolution, and a number of government representatives are tentatively prepared to consider it, but this is an issue that will likely require sustained advocacy for the next few years.

Closing Comments

Important social policy development has taken place at the international level. While international bodies like the United Nations may seem ponderous at times, there are numerous benchmarks that have been set in the area of social policy. They offer us all in the global community something to strive for.

While the process may seem complex from afar, there is a way of working through the system to achieve desired results. Understanding the complexities and determining where to focus attention is the first step. Experience shows that alliances can be built with numerous stakeholders, including non-governmental organizations, United Nations staff, and government officials, including those from the Canadian government.

Notes

References

Perhaps the most satisfying aspect of social policy development at the international level is the possibility of setting high standards with universal applicability. Human rights have no borders. Public authorities can arguably pursue an ideal vision of society without requiring the same level of public support required at the national level. The general public is much less aware of international social policy than they are of the policies at a local or national level, which have a more recognizable or understandable impact.

Yet without this widespread public support, governments are less inclined to feel the need to implement international obligations. In this context, the role of non-governmental organizations takes on added significance. Because of their expertise and experience, they provide valuable inputs into the international policy-making process. They have the unique ability to serve as both advocates and brokers within the complexities of this system. And they serve an important function by raising awareness of international standards at the national level.

Creative ways must continually be found to ensure that we help those we are obliged to help, while also expanding our concepts of those in need. Ultimately, how we help those in need reflects our commitment to social policy.

Notes

1 GA Resolution 428 (v) of December 14, 1950.
2 Statute of the Office of the United Nations High Commissioner for Refugees, chap. 1.
3 Convention Relating to the Status of Refugees, Article 1.
4 Convention Relating to the Status of Refugees, Article 22.
5 Statute of the Office of the UNHCR, chap. 1.
6 Pursuant to Section 65 (3) of the Immigration Act.
7 Conclusion no. 47.
8 UN Doc. EC/47/SC/CRP.39, dated May 30, 1997.
9 UN Doc. A/AC.96/860, General Conclusion on International Protection, s. 19 (n).
10 See, for example, his main report for the 2001 Commission: E/CN.4/2001/5.

References

Amnesty International and International Service for Human Rights. (1997). *The UN and refugees' human rights: A manual on how UN human rights mechanisms can protect the rights of refugees.* Geneva: International Service for Human Rights.

Anderson, M. (1994). *People-oriented planning at work: Using POP to improve UNHCR programming.* Geneva: UNHCR.

Bailey, S. (1993). *Peace is a process.* London: Quaker Home Service.

Buergental, T. (1995). *International human rights.* (2nd ed.). St. Paul: West Publishing.

Global IDP Survey and Norwegian Refugee Council. (1998). Internally displaced-people: Global survey. London: Earthscan.

Goodwin-Gill, G. (1996). *The refugee in international law.* (2nd ed.). Oxford: Clarendon Press.

Gorlick, B. (2000). Human rights and refugees: Enhancing protection through international human rights law. *Nordic Journal of International Law, 69* (4). On-line at <www.unhcr.ch>.

Government of Canada. (2000). *Freedom from fear: Canada's foreign policy for*   **References**
  human security. Ottawa: Department of Foreign Affairs and International Trade.
Human Rights Watch. (1995, August). *The Human Rights Watch Global Report on
  Women's Human Rights.* New York: Human Rights Watch Women's Project.
Human Rights Watch. (2001). *World Report.* New York: Author.
Inter-American Commission on Human Rights. (2000, February 28). *Report on the
  situation of human rights of asylum seekers within the Canadian refugee deter-
  mination system.* OEA/Ser.L/V/II.106.
Mennonite Central Committee. (2000). *Mission Statement.* Winnipeg: Author.
Office for the Coordination of Humanitarian Affairs. (1998). *Guiding principles on
  internal displacement.* New York: Author.
Quaker United Nations Office. (1996a, July). *NGO participation in the UNHCR Exec-
  utive Committee: NGO Working Group Discussion Paper.* Geneva: Author.
Quaker United Nations Office. (1996b, October). *Refugees and reconciliation: A role
  for UNHCR* Briefing Paper for the 47th Session of the Executive Committee of the
  United Nations High Commissioner for Refugees Programme. Geneva: Author.
United Nations. (1945). *Charter of the United Nations.* New York: Author.
UN High Commissioner for Refugees. (1991). *Guidelines for protection and care of
  refugee women.* Geneva: Author.
UN High Commissioner for Refugees. (1994). *Refugee children: Guidelines on pro-
  tection and care.* Geneva: Author.
UN High Commissioner for Refugees. (1995a, June 8). *Women victims of violence
  project in Kenya: An evaluation summary,* EC/1995/SC.2/CRP.22. Geneva: Author.
UN High Commissioner for Refugees. (1995b). *Sexual violence against refugees:
  Guidelines on prevention and response.* Geneva: Author.
UN High Commissioner for Refugees. (1997). *The state of the world's refugees:
  A humanitarian agenda.* Oxford: Oxford University Press.
UN High Commissioner for Refugees. (1999). *Protecting refugees: A field guide for
  NGOs.* Geneva: Author.
UN High Commissioner for Refugees. (2000). Refugees by numbers. Geneva:
  Author.
Yarrow, C.H. (1978). *Quaker experiences in international conciliation.* New Haven:
  Yale University Press.

Additional Resources

Alston, P., & Crawford, J. (2000). *The future of human rights treaty monitoring.*
  Cambridge: Cambridge University Press.
Canadian Council for Refugees. Online at <www.web.net/~ccr>.
Charlesworth, H., & Chinkin, C. (2000). *The boundaries of international law: A
  feminist analysis.* Manchester: Manchester University Press.
Ife, J. (2001). *Human rights and social work: Toward a rights-based practice.* Cam-
  bridge: Cambridge University Press.
Inter-Church Committee for Refugees. Online at <www.web.net/~iccr>.
Mennonite Central Committee. Online at <www.mcc.org>.
Quaker United Nations Office, Geneva. Online at <hostings.diplomacy.edu/
  quaker>.
UN High Commissioner for Refugees (UNHCR). Refworld, CD Rom.
UN High Commissioner for Refugees (UNHCR). Online at <www.unhcr.ch>.
United Nations High Commissioner for Human Rights, includes Commission on
  Human Rights. Online at <www.unhchr.ch>.
UN Office for the Coordination of Humanitarian Affairs. Online at <www.reliefweb.
  int>.

13

The Federal Government and Social Policy in the 1990s: Reflections on Change and Continuity

John English and William R. Young

The 1990s began with the cold war's end, the collapse of the Soviet Union, extraordinary hopes, and new or reinvigorated structures in global politics. Despite the optimism and excitement on the international scene, Canadians watched the beginning of the decade with much nervousness when it came to the future of their own country. The well-known poll published in the New Year's issue of *Maclean's* in 1990 described an "uncertain Canada" despite a period of economic growth. It is true that Canadians in 1989 were more optimistic than in 1985 about their personal economic prospects. Yet Canadians also told the Decima pollsters in late 1989 that they were deeply divided, especially on the issues of national unity and the relationship between Quebec and Canada. There had been "a souring" of attitudes toward government since 1985 and a growing respect for "business." In 1984 when asked whether government, business, or unions "best look after your economic interests," the response was 49% government, 32% business, and 10% unions. In 1989 responses to the same question were 25% government, 50% business, and 15% unions.[1] These two issues—the constitution and the efficacy of government—were to dominate Canadian politics and deeply influence Canadian social policy in the 1990s.[2]

One critical element of this shift in reliance upon government and questioning the role of government—particularly the federal government—related to Canadians' concern about national unity and about federal/provincial relationships generally. By 1990, the Meech Lake Accord, which promised a fundamental reordering of responsibilities between federal and provincial governments and which had the support of all major parties and provincial premiers, was facing growing opposition. Serious implications for social policy in the accord came from limitations on the federal "spending power" and putting into the constitution the ability of any province to opt out of new shared-cost programs without a fiscal penalty.[3]

The concept of the "spending power" bedeviled federal/provincial relations in constitutional and non-constitutional discussions throughout the 1990s. This concept refers to the federal government's provision of program funds, either unilaterally or in co-operation with the provinces, for a variety

of programs in the areas of health, education, welfare, and social develop- **The federal**
ment. Use of the spending power allowed the federal government to shape **government**
issues and programs that fall essentially within provincial jurisdiction. His- **and social**
torically, provinces oppose this federal use of tax dollars and argue that **policy in**
the 1990s
because they run these programs that alter their spending and taxing priorities, the federal government should get their consent first. They also com-
plain that citizens of provinces that opt out of the programs paid taxes
without receiving any benefit. On its side of the argument, the federal government believes that the spending power remains vital in maintaining equal
opportunity for individual Canadians, in ensuring comparable provincial
services, and in putting in place programs of national importance.

At the intergovernmental level, doubts about the Meech Lake Accord
appeared first in New Brunswick where the Liberal Premier Frank McKenna
asked for revisions in the historic agreement. The election of another Liberal, Clyde Wells, in Newfoundland made things even more difficult. Wells,
Maclean's reported, was "less fearful of losing Quebec." Many Canadians,
notably the supporters of Pierre Trudeau and some provincial Liberals, had
serious doubts about, or opposed, the accord outright. In terms of its implications for the federal role in social welfare, various groups as well as smaller
provinces voiced concerns that Meech Lake might threaten national shared-
cost programs. Citizens told provincial committees studying the accord that
it could threaten any future programs such as child care, weaken the federal
government's ability to provide national health and welfare programs, and
increase regional disparities in social services.[4] These concerns had an impact
on the reaction to Meech Lake in both Manitoba and Newfoundland.

In terms of national unity, when asked about the effect of the failure of
Meech Lake in late 1989, 60% of Quebeckers thought that the failure to ratify
Meech Lake would make Quebec more likely to choose separation. The rest of
Canada disagreed. The majority in every province, except British Columbia,
which was evenly split at 49/49, thought the collapse of Meech would make no
difference. The Prairies, where a new Reform Party was attracting attention,
were most decisive in their opinion (38% yes, 58% no). In the Prairies and
British Columbia almost one-quarter of the population (23%) thought Quebec should separate from Canada, only 10% less than in Quebec itself
(*Maclean's*, 1990).

These views were put to the test after June 1990 when Meech Lake died as
Elijah Harper, an Aboriginal member of the New Democratic Party and the
Manitoba Legislature, used procedural tactics to deny approval by his
province. That same month, the Liberal Party chose Jean Chrétien as its
national leader after a bitter contest with runner-up Paul Martin. Martin had
supported Meech; Chrétien had been ambiguous. Later that year in the
province of Ontario, Premier David Peterson, who had vigorously supported
Meech, unexpectedly lost the premiership to Bob Rae of the New Democratic Party (NDP). Federally, the New Democrats moved ahead of the Liberals in

national polls, and the Liberal Party's future seemed difficult as it faced a
strong challenge from the left. In Quebec, the provincial Liberals under Robert
Bourassa were openly disdainful of their federal counterparts, and the NDP
took office in Saskatchewan and British Columbia in 1991. With democratic
socialists successfully reinventing their approach in Western Europe, Canadian socialists seem poised to replace a Liberal Party seeking to define a future
role for government.

The 1990s did not unfold as its beginning promised. Canadians were
wrong to be optimistic about their economic prospects at New Year 1990;
their personal incomes in real terms fell throughout the decade. Moreover,
their dollar lost one-third of its value when buying American goods or taking
Florida vacations. Some of the European postwar immigrants looked to the
lands whence they came and noticed that Canada's per capita GDP in 2000
(US$19,170) was lower than that of the Netherlands (US$24,780) Germany
(US$26,570) and even the United Kingdom (US$21,410).[5] Apart from Canadians who travelled outside of Canada, the groups that were affected the worst
in the 1990s were government employees—teachers, provincial and federal
public servants, and military personnel—whose salaries were, in many cases,
frozen for years and who faced strong pressure to accept early retirement
offers. Others, such as the employees of Canadian National Railways, became
a part of the private sector.

While Canadians were wrong about their economic prospects in 1990,
their other responses forecast the principal themes of social and economic
policy in the decade that followed. The shift to the left with the election of
New Democrats in Ontario, Saskatchewan, and British Columbia weakened
the national party, as the provincial governments became increasingly unpopular when they wrestled with their traditional union and activist supporters
over difficult policy choices. The memoir by Bob Rae describes the uneasiness
of the coalition among unions, feminists, social activists, and career politicians that ultimately caused the New Democrats to self-destruct in both
Ontario and British Columbia (Rae, 1997).

Things went better for other political parties and groups. The Liberals,
who chose the apparently left-leaning Jean Chrétien over the business
favourite Paul Martin, took advantage of the three years between their leadership convention and the federal election to reshape their party as a "middle
of the road" grouping that would focus on the possibilities of the "new economy." Chrétien shrewdly used Martin's reputation with the business community to place him in charge of developing a party platform. The central
event was a policy conference at Aylmer, Quebec, in November 1991 where the
keynote speakers were carefully chosen to stress that the Liberals had moved
away from their economic nationalism of the 1988 free trade election and
were embracing market-oriented programs, government reform, and fiscal
responsibility. Nevertheless, Chrétien and his party promised to adhere to
"Liberal tradition," which since the 1960s had meant medicare, pension plans,
and social programs.

The Liberals, however, were cautious about constitutional reform, a central consideration in the shaping of Canadian social programs, and the Mulroney government made one final attempt to redress the collapse of Meech in 1990. The Charlottetown Accord was a momentous agreement. In terms of its potential impact on social programs, Charlottetown contained the same opting out provisions as Meech Lake, but also committed the federal and provincial governments to establishing a framework for federal expenditures in areas of provincial jurisdiction that would contribute to the pursuit of national objectives, reduce overlap and duplication, respect and not distort provincial priorities, and ensure equality of treatment of the provinces while respecting their differing needs and circumstances.

Once again, the major parties agreed on a package for major constitutional change, but this time it was not a single member of the Manitoba Legislature who cast a deciding vote but rather the Canadian public. On August 28, 1992, Canadians voted against the ratification of the accord in a remarkable repudiation of the political elites of the country. This rejection reflected the growing distrust of government and politicians that was apparent in the 1990 poll and also (for some) a suspicion of handing too much control over social programs to the provinces. Opposition to the accord came from the new Reform Party, organized by Albertan Preston Manning, a party that quickly eroded the Progressive Conservative Party's support in Western Canada and parts of Ontario. The most significant opponent, however, was former prime minister Pierre Trudeau.

The Liberal Party Red Book, its election platform, which bore Martin's ideas about innovation, government reform, and deficit reduction, became a shield to protect the Liberals against their own past and the party's own internal differences. It was remarkably effective, not least because of its careful balance between the economic fears of the time and the remembrance of such previous Liberal policies as the Canada Health Act. Its title, *Creating Opportunity*, stressed employment and the economy, and it began with the statement that "A strong economy is the essence of a strong society." It promised "a balanced approach" that would deal with "the five major, interrelated problems facing the Canadian economy today: lack of growth, high unemployment, high long-term real interest rates, too high levels of foreign indebtedness, and excessive government debt and deficits."

What is striking about the Red Book is the place given to social programs. Part Two of the Red Book on "The Fabric of Canadian Life" promised no new programs, except in certain "niches," to use a term very popular at the time. There would be, for example, a Canada Prenatal Nutrition Program and an Aboriginal Head Start Program, but the financial promises were relatively small. There is a commitment to the preservation of universal medicare and a promise of a national forum on health. Still, the details are few, actual commitments rare, and the number of pages dealing with Canadian social policy significantly less than those devoted to the economy. Nevertheless, social

policy did better than constitutional reform, the topic that had preoccupied
Canadians for over a decade. It received no mention.

Although the Red Book reflected its principal authors (Martin and Chaviva
Hosek, a former minister in the Ontario Liberal government) and, in its constitutional approach, Liberal Leader Jean Chrétien, it was also the product
of profound intellectual shifts in North America and Western Europe. There
was, as we have seen in the 1990 poll, dissatisfaction with the efficiency of
the state, its employees, and its programs. For liberals in Canada and elsewhere, this dissatisfaction led to a program for "reinventing" government,
and the successful American campaign of Clinton and Gore used the slogan.
The Canadian political scientist Donald Savoie, who had extensive government experience, summarized the legacy of the 1980s in his 1994 study,
Thatcher, Reagan, Mulroney: In Search of a New Bureaucracy. Savoie (1994,
p. 319) pointed out that the three conservative Anglo-American leaders
wanted government managers to emulate the private sector and that all three
"shared the conviction that most of the perceived inefficiencies in government operations were simply a function of poor management." In redressing
the problem, privatization, deregulation, and reduction of the activities of
government were fundamental. Savoie thought that Canada under Mulroney
had been less imaginative, less effective, and more willing to retain bureaucratic tradition than Reagan, and especially, Thatcher had been. Savoie had
edited an earlier book, *Taking Power: Managing Government Transitions.* In it,
he noted the importance of the tendency to "blame the bureaucracy," not
only by the Mulroney ministers, but also by the media and large parts of the
public (Savoie, 1993, p. 217).

Attempts to "reinvent" and reduce government during the early 1990s as
government deficits soared were generally perceived to be failures. At the
same time, these efforts served as models for more successful measures that
came later in the decade. Some commentators blamed the failure on the subtle shift of the policy function in government to ministers' offices. During the
Mulroney years, the politicians' distrust of the bureaucracy showed up in the
increasing size and strength of ministerial staff who took an active role, not
just in providing overall direction, but in initiating and managing the policy
functions of government. For whatever reason, Erik Neilson's task force, which
reviewed and recommended cuts across the whole scope of federal spending,
was deemed ineffective. Mulroney had also failed in his plan to reduce transfers to individuals. When he tried to limit increases in Old Age Security payments to individuals, he ran smack dab into a protest by seniors on
Parliament Hill. It made for great television. When his government backed
down on this issue, he damaged beyond recovery his credibility as a cost
cutter. Government spending soared in areas such as the Canada Pension
Plan (disability) as eligibility criteria were loosened and premium increases
did not keep pace. His government also suffered, in business eyes at least,
for putting in place "boutique spending programs," such as the National
Strategy on the Integration of Disabled Persons, which were portrayed as

succumbing to the wishes of so-called special interest groups. Thus, the federal budget of February 1992 announced its intention of eliminating, merging, or privatizing forty-six government boards or commissions. But critics on the right continued their complaints, and the federal deficit for 1992-1993 stood at $36.7 billion, up from $33.5 billion in 1991-1992.

Another effort at dealing with the growing cost of universal social programs and entitlements came in 1989. That was the year when federal income tax forms contained a formula to calculate a clawback of part or all of the federal government's Old Age Pensions or Family Allowances for everyone with a net income over $50,000. Apart from criticizing its inequity, social activists argued that the clawback unilaterally eliminated what they saw as a social contract between the federal government and families or seniors. It eliminated universality and effectively made pensions and family allowances income-tested. They believed that it changed the rules without the consent of seniors and reduced or eliminated income that they had counted on in planning for their old age (Battle, 1990).

Using the tax system as the instrument of choice for dealing with a social issue was hardly new. Over the years, it had become not just a means of managing the economy but also a way of treating social benefits. By its very nature, the tax system is a blunt instrument for delivering or cutting social programs, particularly because of the time lag between earning income, filing a tax return, and receiving benefits. For the federal government, the major advantage of the tax system lay in its bypassing the provinces and providing federal benefits directly to Canadians. This was the case of refundable benefits, like those provided through the Goods and Services Tax (GST), where a cheque could go directly to Canadians. Federal tax credits (refundable and non-refundable) can contribute to putting in place national standards for income support and, given the relationship between federal and provincial tax system, can trigger provincial benefits to individuals. From the perspective of the provinces, because the benefits go to individuals and not to governments, the tax system could deal with the demand side, but could not address the supply side (or the amount of services available). In addition, the provinces can always nullify any federal tax reductions by cutting their benefits or services to individuals.

In its 1992 budget, the Conservative government continued an ongoing trend of using the tax system to address social issues—in this case reducing benefits to Canadians. The 1992 measure introduced the Child Tax Benefit (CTB). The Conservatives justified this as a rationalization and simplification since the CTB replaced Family Allowances (introduced first in 1944) and other refundable and non-refundable tax credits for children, and eliminated the clawback on Family Allowances. Many commentators saw it as a means of dealing with a benefits system for children that had become irrational, unfair, complex, and inadequate (Battle, 1993). The CTB, however, was designed to contain costs since it was income-tested and varied according to the number of children in a family.[6] It was complemented by a supplement for children under seven and a working income supplement for working poor families. The CTB was, however, to be only partly indexed to inflation so that its actual value would decline from year to year. Since 1985, the federal government had used de-indexation of the tax system as a tool for hiding increased taxes.

Another effort at cost cutting led the Tory government right to the courts. While the federal government wanted to maintain its right to use the spending power, it also wanted to be able to control the amount that it transferred to the provinces. In his 1990 budget, Finance Minister Michael Wilson announced measures to restrict federal transfers to the provinces by announcing an expenditure control plan that limited federal block grants to the provinces in the areas of education and health.[7] He capped payments to the three richest provinces (Alberta, British Columbia, and Ontario) for social welfare made under the Canada Assistance Plan. These federal payments had increased at an average annual rate of 6.6% in part because the largest number of poor Canadians lived in these three provinces (plus Quebec). This cap on CAP aimed to control this rate of increase and to introduce an element of stability and predictability into federal transfers to the provinces. Until the cap on CAP, the federal costs had climbed because spending was determined beyond the control of the programs themselves and certainly beyond the control of the federal government. Only the provinces had the ability to contain costs—or not. As a result of increasing unemployment, the provinces' social assistance caseloads had inexorably mounted. "Needs are increasing which by law must be covered," explained the Nielsen task force.[8] British Columbia challenged the constitutionality of the changes, but the Supreme Court of Canada accepted the federal government's argument that Ottawa must retain the right to control the federal purse strings. The Supreme Court's decision paved the way for further efforts by the federal government to contain costs and to eliminate the unpredictability and upward spiral of its fiscal transfers to the provinces. Critics, however, warned that the consequences of an expansion of the federal cost-containment exercise would jeopardize all health and social programs as well as potentially eliminate the opportunity to maintain national standards.

After Mulroney left office, his successor, Kim Campbell, linked the streamlining of government with a similar approach to income security in a speech on August 22, 1993. In that speech, she criticized existing skills training programs, the existence of welfare that stops single mothers from taking work and, when plants close, the preference for "handouts" rather than training programs. "What we must do," she continued, "is reward, not penalize, effort and initiative. Any serious attempt to reform our new income security system must be a national endeavour" (Campbell, 1993). After she took power on June 25, 1993, Campbell moved dramatically and reduced the number of government departments and ministers significantly. In doing so, she combined all or part of five various departments concerned with human security issues to create a new Department of Human Resources.[9] Assessing this change, which still remains in place, the Standing Committee on Human Resources

Development pointed out in 2000 that the "positive synergies" anticipated in Campbell's initiative had failed to materialize. The amalgamation meant that the policies and debates among five departments and ministers no longer existed; the level of political scrutiny of departmental activities had been reduced. Matters that had formerly been discussed and decided at the political level were now treated as internal bureaucratic matters. Assistant deputy ministers took on a large part of what had previously been ministerial responsibilities. The committee's MPs believed that the change had also diluted the accountability of the department to Parliament. They also found that the department lacked a unity of purpose and that employment-related policies and programs subsumed and controlled the social policy elements in the department's corporate culture. Social programs were treated as unwanted and subsidiary duties that got in the way of the jobs agenda (Human Resources Development Canada, 2000).

The federal government and social policy in the 1990s

Campbell did not see the results of her handiwork from within government. Mulroney was unpopular, his party fragmenting, and Campbell, his successor, took over too late. Campbell gave up her office to Jean Chrétien after her election loss on October 25, 1993. Canada's founding political party won two seats as Quebec separatists and western Canadian Reformers carved up the carcass of the Progressive Conservative Party. The New Democrats lost supporters among trade unionists and westerners to the Reform Party, and others who feared the shift to the right in North American politics voted Liberal despite ideological doubts. The New Democrats, who had led national polls in 1990, won only nine seats, and this weakness was most significant because that opposition from the left was to be muted in the new Parliament. The disastrous electoral defeat also brought the Bloc Québécois to the Official Opposition benches and made the conservative Reform Party the third party in the House of Commons. The Bloc's focus upon Quebec and the constitution made it ineffective in the national debate on social policy except on the issue of constitutional authority where it frequently expressed its view that the activities of the federal government in most social policy areas were infringements on provincial rights. Employment programs and labour market training was a particular target for them.

No one has done a better job of summing up the impact of the Conservative government on social policy and programs than the Caledon Institute of Social Policy. In a keynote address to the Seventh Social Welfare Policy Conference in Vancouver, the institute's Sherri Torjman pointed out that from the election in 1984 until its election loss, the Conservative government's actions undermined the policy rationale and operation of Canada's social welfare system, among them: the proposed limits on the federal spending power in the Meech and Charlottetown agreements, the cap on CAP, the clawbacks, the partial indexation of social programs, other changes in the transfers to the provinces, and the use of the income tax system and its non-refundable tax credits. She pointed out that:

Ken Battle [of the Caledon Institute] coined the term "social policy by
stealth" to describe these arcane, technical measures. And while many of
the hidden cuts in transfers to individuals and provinces are neither recognized nor acknowledged, their devastating impact *is still being felt* [sic].
New cuts are over and above a declining base.

Torjman (1995) concluded that when the Liberals took power in 1993,
social policy "reform" was already well underway.

From the Red Book, the Liberals brought the promise to reduce the federal
deficit to 3% of GDP, a few commitments to new social programs (especially
for children's and Aboriginal health), and a promise to continue the late Conservative moves to "streamline" or reinvent government. Campbell's Department of Human Resources was retained, and Lloyd Axworthy, widely regarded
as Chrétien's most leftist minister, became minister of Human Resources
Development. He inherited a department with enormous responsibilities
and the largest amount of federal government spending.[10] Since 1988-1989,
spending in some key areas had soared as in the case of Old Age Security and
Unemployment Insurance which had risen, respectively, from $15.2 and $10.9
billion in 1988-1989 to $19.5 and $18.9 billion in 1992-1993 (Statistics Canada,
1994). Education had remained stable (postsecondary spending by the federal
government had actually decreased from $2.71 to $2.64 billion, and Health
had also fallen from $7.69 to $7.60 billion). Despite the measures taken by
the previous government, federal expenditures on social welfare had risen
from $5.30 to $6.87 billion, again in this same period (Statistics Canada, 1994).
Throughout the 1990s, conservative think tanks like the Fraser Institute continued to point out the nature of the growth in spending on social programs
and to argue strongly in favour of "big-time cuts in subsidy spending and a
shift to old-fashioned investment-grade spending" by 15-25% (Riggs & Velk,
1995).

An activist by inclination, an intellectual by training, and an experienced
politician with a strong tradition of using government to achieve social and
economic ends, Axworthy grasped his opportunity quickly and in a speech in
the House of Commons on January 31, 1994, announced a national consultation that would culminate in a thorough revision of Canada's existing social
policy.[11] His options, when presented, were breathtaking in scope in that he
promised to alter the fundamentals of Canadian federal social policy. Several aspects were obvious. Axworthy wanted to emphasize the federal role in
social policy by making direct grants to individuals and thereby circumvent
questions of provincial responsibility and an outcry from the provinces over
unwarranted use of the spending power. He also wanted to assure that funds
went to those who needed them most, and in this respect he hoped to satisfy
the fiscal regimen thought essential by his Cabinet colleagues, notably the
minister of Finance and the prime minister.

The discussion paper that the HRD department prepared for Axworthy's
Social Security Review proceeded from the assumption that "the status quo is

not an option." Foreshadowing what was to come, it linked spending on social programs to the mounting debt and deficit and noted that "if the next generation of Canadians is to obtain reasonable government services for the tax dollar, we must change our approach" (Human Resources Development Canada, 1994, p. 8). It portrayed social programs for the future as equally driven by a desire to create economic growth as they were by a wish to share the wealth and protect the disadvantaged. Finally, it mirrored the employment focus of the amalgamated HRDC and talked about social programs in the context of creating jobs as the main objective. While the Social Security Review was touted as comprehensive, it was not because tax expenditures, increasingly a tool used by the federal government to deal with social issues, were excluded. Following the release of the discussion paper, a series of supplementary papers provided more information on the possible reforms, but again these echoed the overarching themes. These were all carefully vetted by officials from the Department of Finance.

The elements of Axworthy's review were a complicated affair: there would be a task force of "experts" supported by the bureaucrats in HRDC, as well as a national consultation by the House of Commons Standing Committee on Human Resources Development.[12] The committee received over 1,200 submissions and heard 637 witnesses before it approved its report on January 31,1995. Over 200 members of Parliament consulted relevant groups in their constituencies: social workers, universities and their professors and students, activist groups, and health professionals. Over 25,000 Canadians completed and sent in a workbook, *Have Your Say*, to the Department of Human Resources Development. During the two years following the election of the Liberal government, social policy issues assumed a prominence that was unprecedented since the Green Book proposals of the Mackenzie King government in 1945. Given the complexity and the attention the Social Security Review was receiving, it was no small wonder that the review quickly fell behind schedule.

The Liberal members of Parliament were deeply involved in the review. Most held so-called town hall meetings where the many groups interested in the substance of the review expressed their opinions. Those same groups appeared in constituency offices and, occasionally, picketed outside them. In university areas, student associations were generally opposed to the income contingent approach, fearing that it would mean higher tuition even though many on the left supported it as a fairer way to approach the question of tuition. Business groups were puzzled by the review, and such associations as the local chambers of commerce did not present coherent critiques of the review. On the one hand, they supported an overhaul of Unemployment Insurance; on the other hand, they were suspicious of Liberal designs, particularly when the artist was Lloyd Axworthy. Nevertheless, the reinventing and reduction of government were popular elements that Liberal MPs concentrated on in their speeches to business audiences.

The federal government and social policy in the 1990s

What MPs soon realized during the course of the review was how many business interests employed social programs for their own needs. School bus lines relied on unemployment insurance to retain employees over the summer months. Various private educational firms used student loans to finance their work, and the scrutiny brought to the subject by the review was embarrassing to them: by far the highest rates of default came from students at these private schools. Sometimes labour and management came together to argue for retention of the current system around which they had constructed their employment practices, and the construction trades were especially active in this respect. The construction trade unions, unlike the industrial unions, were not affiliated with the New Democratic Party, and many had close ties with the Liberal Party or individual Liberal MPs. Social housing was also an area that united social activists with construction and architectural firms that had benefited greatly from past federal programs. The decision to transfer responsibilities to the province aroused much anger among MPs, especially in the province of Ontario after its voters elected the Progressive Conservatives in 1995.

In the case of grants through Human Resources Development (HRDC), members of Parliament signed an approval form, a practice that even most Reform Party members came to sign without dissent. Later, when such grants became controversial, those signatures became politically useful to the embattled Liberals as they defended the grants in the House of Commons. These grants were the sole example of MP involvement in the delivery of programs, at least in the province of Ontario. As a result, the contacts between the MP and the HRDC bureaucracy were many. When HRDC turned down an applicant, that applicant went to the MP's office, and when an MP needed information about a group, he or she contacted HRDC. This relationship, therefore, was affected when HRDC reduced significantly the number of employees, centralized administration, and sought to replace workers by technology.

In fact, one of the major tenets of the "reinventing government" movement was the importance of reducing "red tape" through technology, and HRDC, the largest deliverer of government services, was the department most affected. HRDC services were delivered primarily by clerical employees who were among the lowest-paid government workers and mostly female. With the freeze in government salaries in the 1990s, the technological challenge, and the uncertainty of employment, these employees had low morale. MPs often heard their complaints; they also heard complaints from clients of HRDC about poor service. Technology did help as kiosks with interactive screens listing jobs appeared in malls and elsewhere, but the department in the 1990s was drowning in its details.[13]

What happened in the constituencies reflected vividly the changing dynamics in Ottawa. This situation is described in detail in *Double Vision: The Inside Story of the Liberals in Power* by journalists Edward Greenspon and Anthony Wilson-Smith. The book describes how Axworthy's ambitions crumbled as fiscal restraint and the politics of national unity gained pre-eminence:

> At the start of the government, Axworthy had been seen as the standard-bearer for the social Liberals in cabinet. But their vision—indeed the Trudeau vision—had trouble getting airborne in this Liberal government. A competing vision, more fiscally grounded and provincially oriented, appeared to be gaining ascendancy, a vision most forcefully propounded by the intergovernmental affairs minister, Marcel Massé, and supported by his partner, the most powerful minister in the Chrétien government, Finance Minister Paul Martin. (Greenspon & Wilson-Smith, 1996, p. 152)

This interpretation is accurate in many respects, and there is little doubt that HRDC's plan for income-contingent student loans, a more imaginative approach to training through the Unemployment Insurance system, and a more focused approach to need had collapsed in the aftermath of the Quebec referendum of November 1995. The remnants of the Axworthy plan (by the time he moved to Foreign Affairs in January 1996) were much less than the review's driving forces had hoped. Unemployment Insurance had become Employment Insurance, but the impact of the referendum in Quebec brought federal assurance that labour training would be carried out by the provinces, with few federally imposed conditions. Moreover, the income-contingent loan scheme, despite its support from elements of the political left and right, did not survive strident opposition from student groups, opposition that included noisy protest in front of the private home of Denise and Lloyd Axworthy. In the end, the complex web of federal social policy created in the postwar era became a more simplified and considerably less restrictive Canada Health and Social Transfer, which some thought clarified federal and provincial roles, while others maintained that it permitted the federal government to gain credit for those funds it spent on social programs. In fact, the funds were less, and the province of Quebec, the major concern, did not thank the federal government for the less restrictive transfer program. Nevertheless, the 1995 budget, with its major cuts in federal government spending, the consolidation of federal transfers for health, welfare, and education in the Canada Health and Social Transfer, and the end of the ambitious Axworthy plan, marked a watershed in Canadian social policy whose impact remains in the twenty-first century.

Why? The reasons illuminate the dark area where process and substance intersect. To begin with, there were the questions of who was doing what, to whom and when. To a large extent, the Liberals inherited a set of senior public servants who subscribed to the view of the primacy of the three "Ds"— dollar, deficit, and debt.[14] And on the advice of his unpaid adviser, Mitchell Sharp, Prime Minister Jean Chrétien made it perfectly clear to his ministers that these public servants were their primary advisers. The Prime Minister's

The federal government and social policy in the 1990s

Office would deal with troublesome issues and provide direction. As a result, the ability of many departments to anticipate problems and consider options "atrophied" (Savoie, 1999). At the same time, the centre was, and is, limited in its resources and can be slow in making decisions. Ottawa observers noted that instead of managing issues, policy resources were diverted into crisis management. This was certainly the case in Human Resources Development during the Social Security Review, particularly when Finance dropped the bomb in its proposal for the CHST. Gone were the large budgets and senior ministerial staffs of the Conservatives with their policy expertise and control. Instead, the Liberal ministers, including Axworthy, were restricted in the number of staff in their offices with the result that these mostly junior, inexperienced people were easily overwhelmed by their departments. To some extent, at least in the economic areas, government relations firms—lobbyists—thought of themselves as the successors to the Conservatives' ministerial advisers and the counterweight to the bureaucrats. There was, however, one key difference: their advice was self-interested, paid for by clients to advance their cause. Axworthy realized this and brought in senior advisers from outside, notably journalist Giles Gherson and former activist Patrick Johnston. But this was too late in the game.

The cutbacks in the public service, moreover, meant that corporate memory was diminished and policy expertise downplayed or lost. When a government's major concern is downsizing and cutting costs, imaginative policy solutions are deemed to be a distracting nuisance at best. As a result, much of the policy thinking regarding social security reform took place outside government in think tanks and universities. Axworthy used the outside think tanks, notably the Caledon Institute, but their input was always vetted through the public servants. The question then—and one that still remains—is about the capacity within government to deal with the advice tendered from outside in assimilating the information and converting it into public policy in a timely fashion.[15]

Finally, Axworthy's review achieved much less than anticipated because it ran into the united front of the minister of Finance, his bureaucrats, and their cost-cutting agenda. In effect, the Department of Finance took over the review in midstream with the announcement of the Canada Health and Social Transfer. With this, Finance also determined social policy. Axworthy's review had always been constrained by the fiscal framework, no more clearly than in the 1994 budget that had kept on with the fiscal agenda: additional cuts to federal transfers for social, health, and education and huge cuts to unemployment insurance. As Axworthy's review fell behind schedule and the ink was barely dry on the HRDC Standing Committee's report, the 1995 budget completed Finance's takeover of social policy. It announced the CHST and raised questions debated for the rest of the 1990s about the nature both of the federal role in social programs (Is there one?) and any national standards in their operation. Axworthy's successor in the HRDC portfolio, Douglas Young, was not shy about disavowing a federal role in both of these. For the time being, however, the 1995 budget stated that the job of the minister of Human Resources Development was to negotiate with the provinces any principles or objectives that would be attached to the transfer (Battle & Torjman, 1995). The minister of Finance kept for himself the job of determining the amount to be handed over.

The elements of the CHST are relatively straightforward. It combined the money from the Established Programs Financing Act (EPF) for health and education and the Canada Assistance Plan into a single block transfer with few conditions. In effect, it eliminated the legislative basis that had underpinned federal spending in the social area. It cut federal cash transfers to the provinces by $2.5 billion for 1996-1997 and by an additional $2 billion for 1997-1998. It eliminated the rules that had governed cost-shared programs under CAP and gave the provinces more or less full scope to spend federal transfer dollars as they wished (including on programs unrelated to assisting people in need). It did, however, retain the principles set out in the Canada Health Act and continued the prohibition on provincial residency requirements for applicants for social assistance.

Implications for the federal role were immense, particularly as the cash transfer to the provinces dropped annually as a proportion of the transfer as a whole.[16] If he who pays the piper gets to call the tune, the federal government was getting increasingly hoarse. Even before the CHST, there were predictions that the EPF transfer would become cashless by the end of the 1990s and the federal government would have virtually no say over how this money was spent. Analysts did not need a crystal ball to see that removing the protection that CAP gave to the provincial services would mean that the impact of the cuts would be felt by people across the country as provincial governments trimmed in turn (Social Planning Council of Metropolitan Toronto, 1995). In addition, the loose conditions attached to the transfer meant that the federal government and Canadian taxpayers had no way to measure how or where the money was being spent—in effect, the provinces were not accountable for the federal money they received. Commentators believed that the money would go to the provincial sectors with the squeakiest wheels and not necessarily to those who needed it most. They also questioned how the government would be able to achieve its other priorities such as eliminating child poverty (Clark & Carter, 1995).

The 1995 budget also signalled forthcoming changes to Canada's Unemployment Insurance program, and set out the parameters that Axworthy would use to bring in the legislation scheduled to take effect no later than July 1996. The aim of the changes was to help control the deficit and move money from areas that the budget saw as "creating dependence" to "investments in people to make them employable." As predicted, the newly renamed Employment Insurance (EI) tightened up the qualifying period, reduced the duration and level of benefits, and restricted expenditures for employment training to those who qualified for EI. Despite the doubts of some members of the federal Cabinet, devolution of labour market training to the provinces

The federal government and social policy in the 1990s

was pushed by ministers who wanted to show good faith to Quebec and to satisfy other provincial leaders who wanted more power. Theoretically, the argument in favour of moving responsibility to the provinces was to eliminate some duplication of programming between levels of government and allow training and other employment services to be integrated with provincial education programs.[17]

Although immigration remained an area of major federal involvement in the constituencies (although not in Quebec), the sense that the federal government was retreating from direct links with Canadians troubled many. The need to reduce the enormous deficit was almost universally accepted within the Liberal Party, and program review had almost no opponents. Yet the Red Book's promise of concentrating on where need was greatest led socially active MPS to create a social policy caucus. That caucus focused particularly on children's and disability issues. In the case of the former, there was much evidence that modern society's major victims were its children (Ross, Scott, & Smith, 2000; Torjman, 1995). With family dissolution increasingly common, single mothers and their children often slid into poverty and disadvantage.[18] The percentage of poor children in single-parent families reached 64.3% in 1993. Here, it seemed, was an area where the federal government could focus its more limited funds effectively. "Think tanks," such as the Caledon Institute, had developed a series of proposals that were actively considered by the federal government and were readily available for committee meetings and private consultations. For the right-wing members of the Liberal government, however, there was little enthusiasm for new programs. Although poverty, particularly child poverty, is universally acknowledged as a serious problem, the effort to define poverty, poverty lines, poverty level incomes, or minimum standards of living fuels debates among policy makers inside and outside governments in Canada. In addition, both the deficit and the opposition of the provinces restricted the federal government's freedom of action. The result was the use of the tax system to deal with social policy, notably in the area of disability and children.

In the latter part of the 1990s, the federal government undertook several measures to deal with poverty—child poverty in particular. Estimates of the number of children living in poverty reached 1.4 million. The National Children's Agenda, developed between 1997 and 1999, has a common vision for children that acted as a catalyst for national discussions on policy issues between various levels of government and the community. One of its important components is its recognition that income support and integrated child and family services must be pursued simultaneously. It attempts to address the fact that many low-income parents on social assistance would lose benefits for their children if they found work. In this situation, known as the "welfare wall," some parents find themselves financially worse off in low-paid jobs than they are when on welfare because without eligibility for welfare, they lose drug, dental, and additional health coverage for their children.

Although the federal/provincial Canada Child Tax Benefit had improved the income levels of families living and working in difficult circumstances, the government decided to reinforce its child poverty initiatives by introducing the National Child Benefit and providing $850 million for it starting in July 1998. Subsequently, the federal government added significant other resources. The 2000 budget also used the tax system to promote this and other social objectives by restoring full indexation of tax benefits to inflation.[19] In essence, the Canada Child Tax Benefit (CCTB) goes to working poor families, while families receiving social assistance may have this reduced by the provinces and territories by an equal amount to the CCTB increase. The provinces committed themselves to reinvesting the money saved on social assistance into improving benefits and services for low-income families. The provinces agreed, provided the federal investment was significant, incremental, and permanent and they had the freedom to determine where to invest their savings from social assistance.

The federal government and social policy in the 1990s

This program—the first new national program in two decades—would, therefore, help prevent and reduce child poverty and support parents in their transition to employment. The NCB was aimed at restructuring the system of income support for low-income families by replacing child benefits delivered through the welfare system with a national platform of income-tested child benefits delivered outside social assistance. Supposedly by providing child benefits to all low-income families with children, regardless of their source of income, the NCB is levelling the playing field for families on social assistance and the working poor.

The decade of the 1990s ended, as it began, with a federal/provincial agreement to deal co-operatively with social programs. Unlike Meech Lake, there was no attempt to use the constitution to achieve this goal in The Framework Agreement to Improve the Social Union for Canadians, (SUFA) which was signed on February 4, 1999.[20] The current jargon at the end of the 1990s used the term "social union" to describe discussions and agreements among the federal, provincial, and territorial governments regarding social programs and social policy issues. The provinces began the social union discussions (without the federal government present) in 1995 to find ways of dealing with the CHST and the cuts to federal transfers. Initially, these talks were to encompass health, social assistance, and education, with children, people with disabilities, and youth as particular groups targeted. In 1996, when the federal government was invited into the tent, the discussions revolved around whether the outcome should be a broad federal-provincial-territorial framework agreement to guide social policy renewal or a limited framework agreement on the use of the federal spending power or a step-by-step approach to conclude "sectoral" agreements in targeted areas with no overarching agreement.

However important it may be, the Social Union exercise has attracted little public interest; it is also a "yawner" for those who know about it and is very difficult to understand. The major reasons for this are the fact that so much of the discussions dealt with process and occurred behind closed doors.

The nub of the discussions, however, continued to be the tug-of-war over social programs that began the decade of the 1990s—questions about the role of government and, from the Ottawa perspective, the federal government. Should there be restrictions on the use of the federal spending power or not? Should there be enforceable national standards or none? Officials, ministers, and first ministers held an interminable series of meetings to find a middle way for almost three years. In negotiating positions reminiscent of the Meech Lake period, the provinces intensified their efforts at controlling the federal spending power after the 1998 budget when it became obvious that the federal government had a surplus. Their bottom line remained the demand for restoration of cuts to federal transfers (approximately $6 billion). They emphasized their health care needs—a cynic might think they were capitalizing on strong public support to maintain Canada's health system. For its part, the federal government wanted a flexible agreement that would preserve its discretion to spend as it wished as well as recognize national principles, standards and objectives. These aims, however, were recast in the language of "access," "mobility," "portability," and "common outcomes." Both sides agreed on the need for better accountability, including measuring outcomes of spending and publicly reporting on results.

The discussion of accountability regimes and outcomes, dull as it may appear, has the potential to affect social programs offered by all levels of government and the voluntary sector. For members of Parliament and officials, the SUFA highlighted the ongoing challenge to ensure accountability and transparency of spending on programs, particularly social programs, that affect groups whose interests cross over governmental and departmental boundaries. As a result, there is a stronger emphasis on the need to gather and make available information about the various programs in order to set national objectives or benchmarks. Outcome data provide an important foundation for discussions between the government and the community about what needs to be done—which goals have been met and which may need to be adjusted. In the area of social programs, positive outcomes need to be understood "horizontally." For example, employment for people with disabilities entails dealing with programs such as housing, transportation, supports and services, education and training, as well as programs that provide access to goods and services. In the current jargon, outcome measures provide feedback into the policy process and help to focus the government on its vision.

Given the linkage throughout the decade between cash and federal-provincial co-operation (or lack thereof), it is not surprising that the Social Union negotiations concluded just before the federal budget in 1999. The SUFA set the parameters for changing existing social programs and putting new ones in place. All the provinces except Quebec signed the agreement to recognize the need to ensure adequate, predictable, and sustainable funding for social programs; to modernize these programs to meet current needs; to restore the public's confidence by putting in place measures of citizen involvement, transparency, and accountability; and finally to better manage interdependence and encourage collaboration.

Who won? Overall, the federal government managed to retain a high level of flexibility, particularly in its unfettered ability to make transfers to individuals and organizations, to create the conditions required for access to national programs and mobility for Canadians, and to set up an accountability/reporting system. For their part, the provinces managed to get some limits on the federal spending power since new initiatives would require consultation and approval of most provinces. In addition, the provinces retained the right to decide on program design and to secure agreement that the total federal transfer for a program does not necessarily have to be devoted to a given objective and to require advance federal notice of changes to funding.

While the SUFA represents a considerable step forward in achieving the consensus that was denied at the beginning of the decade, it remains incomplete. What is required is to put meat on the bones in terms of real program and policy initiatives. Will it be respected? Will reports from the provinces be complete? What is the nature of a dispute resolution mechanism? Unfortunately, it is likely that ongoing attempts to clarify some of the language in the agreement will lead to ongoing preoccupation with processes which means that actual program needs and design will take a back seat. The decade ended much as it began with a struggle to understand the role of the federal government, and to find an agreement that would be acceptable to the various levels of government and to the Canadian people. "When I use a word," Humpty Dumpty said, in a rather scornful tone, "It means just what I choose it to mean—neither more nor less." "The question is," said Alice, "Whether you can make words mean so many different things." "The question is," said Humpty Dumpty, "Which is to be Master, that's all."

Notes

1 *Maclean's*, January 1, 1990, p. 24. The poll on business and government is found on p. 26. The following years brought a sharp recession to Canada. Some forecasters warned of the possibility of recession in the *Maclean's* issue.

2 This debate over the place of government and the nature of social security was taking place in most western countries. See Niels Ploug, "The Welfare State in Liquidation?" *International Social Security Review*, 48(2), (1995), 61.

3 Section 106A of the Meech Lake Accord stated that "The Government of Canada shall provide reasonable compensation to the government of a province that chooses not to participate in a national shared-cost program that is established by the Government of Canada after the coming into force of this section in an area of exclusive provincial jurisdiction, if the province carries on a program or initiative that is compatible with the national objectives."

4 For a summary of some of the presentations and arguments, see "Meech Lake," *Perception*, 12(1), (Winter 1988), 16ff.

Notes   5 *The Economist, World in Figures 2001* (London: Profile Books, 2001). In per capita GDP
Canada had fallen from its post-war second place to twenty-second, but in terms of
purchasing power it stood fourteenth, ahead of the United Kingdom, but considerably
behind some European countries, notably Norway, Denmark, and Belgium.

6 The maximum basic benefit was payable to all families with annual incomes less than
$25,961 and was reduced at a rate of 5% of family net income above this amount.

7 The Established Programs Financing Act (EPF) was put in place in 1977 and replaced
50/50 conditional grants for hospital insurance and medicare with a combination of a
single block grant (equal to 50%) of federal cash contributions indexed to GNP and
provincial population. It also transferred to the provinces 13.5% personal income tax
and 1% corporate tax points and finally supplementary elements to compensate
provinces to cover extended health care services. For the purposes of EPF, the provinces
were not obliged to spend to get federal money, although the federal government kept its
ability to withhold its contribution if a province failed to meet the criteria set out in hospital insurance and medicare legislation (later the Canada Health Act, of 1984). The EPF
mechanism was criticized because it was alleged that a number of provinces took advantage of federal money and diverted it from health and education.

8 Ronald Melchers, "The cap on CAP," *Perception*, 14 (4), (Autumn 1990), 19ff. The Canada
Assistance Plan put in place in 1966 had the objectives of alleviating poverty and preventing and removing the causes of poverty and dependence on public assistance. The
CAP Act required provinces to enter into agreements with the federal government under
which they agree to comply with some general conditions on the administration and
delivery of provincial social assistance and social services. In return, the federal government agreed to contribute 50% of eligible expenditures. CAP was comprised of two
elements: cost sharing of social assistance to people in need, which took two-thirds of the
funding as well as social services for those in need or likely to become in need, which
took the remaining one-third. In 1990, the Canada Assistance Plan was the largest single
source of funding for social services in Canada, accounting for an average of 38.5% of
provincial spending in this area.

9 The new department consisted of the employment part of the former Department of
Employment and Immigration, the welfare elements of the former Department of
National Health and Welfare, the former Department of Labour, as well as parts of the
former Department of Secretary of State and Multiculturalism and Citizenship. It was
later renamed the Department of Human Resources Development.

10 This is still the case. By the end of the decade, in fiscal year 2000-2001 HRDC had responsibility for approximately $60 billion or approximately 45% of federal spending. Com-
pared to other departments, HRDC spent five and a half times more than National
Defence, twenty-six times more than Agriculture and Agri-Food, and thirty times more
than Health Canada.

11 Chretien announced a four-part review of federal government finances and programs on
September 18, 1994, which formed the *Agenda: Jobs and Growth*. Axworthy's review was
one part of this as was Paul Martin's framework for economic growth, *A New Framework for Economic Policy*, released on October 17, 1994. This was followed by *Creating a
Healthy Fiscal Climate*, which provided an update on the state of the economy and federal finances. The minister of Intergovernmental Affairs and minister responsible for
Public Service Renewal (Marcel Massé) studied ways of streamlining programs and government operations to reduce expenditures. In late November 1994, the minister of
Industry released *Building a More Innovative Economy*, which set out focused actions
and strategies to foster economic growth.

12 The standing committee ultimately tabled a report in the House of Commons, *Security,
Opportunities and Fairness: Canadians Renewing their Social Programs* (Ottawa: House
of Commons, 1995).

13 Many of these problems surfaced during the investigation of the administration of
HRDC's grants and contributions programs that was carried out by Parliament. See Standing Committee on Human Resources Development and the Status of Persons with Disabilities, *Seeking a Balance: Final Report on Human Resources Development Canada
Grants and Contributions* (Ottawa: House of Commons, June 2000).

14 See the commentaries prepared by the Caledon Institute throughout this period.

15 *Inside Ottawa,* 7(9), (October 4, 1999). For another view, see Eva Kmiecic, "Canada's Policy Research Capacity: Observations from the Public Policy Forum," *Canadian Journal of Regional Science, 20,* 287-291.

16 Federal transfers dropped to $26.9 billion in 1996-1997 and then to $25.1 billion, which continued to be made up both of cash and tax points, but the cash component continued to drop as a percentage of the transfer.

17 For an evaluation of the changes to the income tax system, see Standing Committee on Human Resources Development and the Status of Persons with Disabilities, *Beyond Bill C-2: A Review of other Proposals to Reform Employment Insurance* (Ottawa: House of Commons, 2001).

18 The child poverty rate rose from 15.4% in 1980 to 20.6% as a result of the recession, then declined during the economic recovery to 14.8% then increased again to 21.3% in 1993.

19 Following the initial $850 million, the federal government added $425 million in July 1999 and an additional $425 million in July 2000. Taking into account the restoration of indexation and the additional commitment in the February 2000 budget, federal spending will increase to $2.5 billion by 2004. For details on how the NCB would work, see: National Child Benefit Progress Report: 2001 <www.nationalchildbenefit.ca/ncb/NCB-2002/toceng.html>.

20 For the text of the agreement see <www.sufa-review.ca>.

References

Battle, K. (1993). Missing a chance for a solid punch at poverty. *Caledon commentary.* Ottawa: Caledon Institute of Social Policy.

Battle, K. (1990). Clawing back. *Perception, 14*(3), 34.

Battle, K., & Torjman, S. (1995). *How Finance re-formed social policy.* Ottawa: Caledon Institute of Social Policy.

Campbell, K. (1993). Notes for an Address. Progressive Conservative Brunch, Montreal, August 22, 1993. On-line at <collections.ic.gc.ca/discourspm/anglais/kc/2208993e.html>.

Clark, C., & Carter, S. (1995). Budget realities: Unravelling the social safety net. *Perception, 18*(Spring), 27-28.

The Economist. (2001). *World in figures, 2001.* London: Profile Books.

Greenspon, E., & Wilson-Smith, A. (1996). *Double vision: The inside story of the Liberals in power.* Toronto: Doubleday.

Human Resources Development Canada. (1994). *Improving social security in Canada: A discussion paper.* Ottawa: Author.

Human Resources Development Canada. (2000). Standing Committee on Human Resources Development and the Status of Persons with Disabilities. *Seeking balance: A final report on Human Resources Development Canada grants and contributions.* Ottawa: House of Commons.

Inside Ottawa. (1999, October 4). 7(9).

Kmiecic, E. (2000). Canada's policy research capacity: Observations from the public policy forum. *Canadian Journal of Regional Science, 20,* 287-291.

Maclean's. (1990, January 1), 14-18.

Meech Lake. (1988). *Perception, 12*(1), 16.

Melchers, R. (1990). The cap on CAP. *Perception, 14*(4), 19.

National Child Benefit progress report. (2001). On-line at <www.nationalchildbenefit.ca/ncb/NCB-2002/toceng.html>.

Ploug, N. (1995). The welfare state in liquidation? *International Social Security Review, 48*(2), 61.

Rae, B. (1997). *From protest to power.* Toronto: Penguin.

References Riggs, A., & Velk, T. (1995). Social programs: Where they come from, where they are going. *Fraser Forum, 18.* On-line at <www.oldfraser.lexi.net/publications/forum/1995/june/june95/html#social>.

Ross, D.P., Scott, K., & Smith, P.J. (2000). *Canadian fact book on poverty.* Ottawa: Canadian Council on Social Development.

Savoie, D. (Ed.). (1993). Taking power: Managing government transitions. Toronto: Institute of Public Administration.

Savoie, D. (1994). *Thatcher, Reagan, Mulroney: In search of a new bureaucracy. Toronto: University of Toronto Press.*

Savoie, D. (1999). *Governing from the centre.* Toronto: University of Toronto Press.

Social Planning Council of Metropolitan Toronto. (1995). Budget 1995: Open intentions, hidden costs. *Social Infopac, 13*(4).

Standing Committee on Human Resources Development. (1995). *Security, opportunities and fairness: Canadians renewing their social programs.* Ottawa: House of Commons.

Standing Committee on Human Resources Development & the Status of Persons with Disabilities. (2000). *Seeking a balance: Final report on Human Resources and Development Canada grants and contributions.* Ottawa: House of Commons.

Standing Committee on Human Resources Development & the Status of Persons with Disabilities. (2001). *Beyond Bill C-2: A review of other proposals to reform employment insurance.* Ottawa: House of Commons.

Statistics Canada. (1994). *Canada Yearbook, 1994.* Ottawa: Author.

Summary of Provincial/Territorial/First Nations initiatives under the National Child Benefit 1999-2000. On-line at <www.nationalchildbenefit.ca/ncb/NCBprogress 2000/summary.html>.

Torjman, S. (1995). *Milestone or millstone.* Ottawa: Caledon Institute of Social Policy.

Active Citizenship, Social Workers, and Social Policy

14

Carol Kenny-Scherber

The renewed interest among political theorists in citizenship—particularly concepts of active citizenship—offers a framework for social workers to engage in the social policy arena. Active citizenship is founded on the concepts that: political activity is a particular and meaningful manner of living together (Arendt, 1958/1998), inclusion within the civil and political collectives is foundational (Baralet, 1988), and claims making for self and others breaks the culture of silence (Drover & Kerans, 1993). To think as an active citizen is "to switch from a generally passive outlook [to one] generated by the adoption of a political identity as a significant part of one's mode of life" (Clarke, 1996, p. 5). Citizenship affords the opportunity to combine, in rather unusual ways, the "public" and "social" with the "individual" aspects of political life (Held, 1991). In an era of social and economic restructuring, the well-being of many individuals depends on social workers actively promoting the public good and holding political authorities accountable. As Habermas (1992, p. 7) notes, "the institutions of constitutional freedom are only worth as much as a population makes of them." This classical view of citizenship seeks a vision of society as a community where deliberations on the public good transcend private interests and market individualism (Ignatieff, 1991).

I challenge social workers, regardless of their practice field, to actively participate in the public decision making that determines the government's response to social issues. I arrived at this view through being employed by the Ontario provincial government as a senior policy adviser for ten years and, for twelve years prior, as a social worker assisting people experiencing chronic unemployment. A social work perspective informs the best advice that I bring to labour force development policy, regardless of the ideology brought by the governing party. The view that it is necessary to involve the public in political decision-making is hardly disputed in the literature (Rosener, 1978). However, there is controversy over the public's role and authority in the decision making process (Barber, 1984). The postmodern view of policy analysis holds out the prospect that social workers' involvement in the political implications of identity construction can contribute to public policies (Schram, 1993). In writing this chapter, my objective is not to critique the policy process but to highlight opportunities that are present in the system. For social workers to be active citizens, we require an understanding of the provincial government's policy process, knowledge of participation opportunities, and intervention skills that can be put to use. Social workers bring something unique to the policy process: an understanding of clients' life circumstances and the social world, knowledge of how means and ends can work together, and a commitment for social change based on inclusion.

The View from Inside the Policy System

A multitude of definitions have been put forward since the 1920s when Charles Merriam initially identified the policy sciences as a "cross fertilization of politics with science,...or more strictly with modern methods of inquiry and investigation" (Merriam, 1921, p. 181). Since Harold Lasswell (1951) identified the basic characteristics, others have described public policy as the binding course of action (Pal, 1987) that results from government making the most important choices (Lasswell, 1951) about what to do or not to do (Dye, 1972) in setting public goals and selecting the means to achieve the identified outcomes (Jenkins, 1978). In day-to-day practice, policy development is affected by the new public management models (Charih & Rouillard, 1997); the degree to which the necessary decisions are imbedded (Jenkins, 1978); and the numbers of ministries, other governments, and non-governmental organizations involved (Anderson, 1984). Public policy is critically important to social workers and their clients because it is through policy that:

• society's responsibilities to its citizens are defined;
• the group or individual entitlement to society's resources are identified;
• the allocation and distribution of society's resources are determined; and
• the group(s) or sector(s) that make these decisions is given the authority.

Key decisions will continue to be made by government, but there is still the question of whether and by what means social workers will have input as the decisions are being formulated. Significant systemic barriers certainly exist within our governance system; however, through my own work I recognize that there are opportunities social workers could use to influence the system that are not currently being used to their advantage.

Although policy development proceeds through a number of steps, the logical linear models (Anderson, 1984; Brewer, 1974; Jones, 1984) do not do justice to the realities. The linear models also do not account for globalization, international policy convergence, society's institutional values, ideologies of the decision makers, and the lessons drawn from past experiences. I have experienced policy as a complicated and time-consuming strategy process defying the logic of planning models. In this neo-conservative period, policy is about trying to solve very complex issues in an environment characterized by powerful transnational companies, high public expectations, confrontational politics, competing and vocal stakeholders, intense media scrutiny, The view from inside the policy system and a distrustful citizenry. On any issue the objectives being pursued are broad, with numerous considerations that must be taken into account, few reliable reference points, and a diverse range of stakeholders' interests. The "wicked" problems of contemporary policy demand continuous examination to understand the pressures and tensions acting on them and the potential solutions. Edelman argues:

> Problems come into discourse and therefore into existence as reinforcements of ideologies, not just simply because they are there or because they are important for well-being. They signify who are virtuous and useful and who are dangerous and inadequate, which actions will be rewarded and which penalized. They constitute people as subjects with particular kinds of aspirations, self-concepts, and fears, and they create beliefs about the relative importance of events and objects. They are critical in determining who exercises authority and who accepts it. They construct areas of immunity from concern because those areas are not seen as problems. Like leaders and enemies, they define the contours of the social world, not in the same way for everyone, but in the light of the diverse situations from which people respond to the political spectacle. (Edelman, 1988, p. 12-13)

Governments and their networks maintain an ongoing discourse, articulating, interpreting, and creating public dialogue to discern the public problem. Public policies are simply the political agreements reached in the practical world where values and facts are inextricably interwoven (Fisher, 1980). Through legislation, regulation, rules, protocols, and access to media, governments not only define access to public resources, they also attempt to gain acceptance and support for their ideological framing of problems and solutions. What constitutes legitimate need, who has authority to define the need, what government's obligations are, and what program design tools the bureaucracy will use to respond to the need are continuously being examined.

Kingdon (1984) best describes policy-making as it is practised in the working lives of governments. In his model, three "families" of simultaneous processes operate, pursuing courses largely independent of each other until critical points in time when their intersecting paths create policy windows. First, the *stream of problems* gains the attention of government policy makers through a media crisis, government question period, formal inquiries, and stakeholder pressure. Second, the community of *policy specialists*, including bureaucrats and their external expert contacts, is continuously contributing to the mix of the policy "stew" as they refine their understanding of the problems and available responses. *Policy entrepreneurs* connect and participate informally by joining the process before it formally begins. Third, the value systems of Cabinet members, proximity of an election period, party policy conventions, interest groups with access to government members, and public opinion as constructed by the media encompass the *political stream* (Wharf & McKenzie, 1998). Kingdon argues:

> Windows are opened either by the appearance of compelling problems or by happenings in the political stream.... Policy entrepreneurs, people who are willing to invest their resources in pushing their pet proposals or problems, are responsible not only for prompting important people to pay attention, but also for coupling solutions to problems and for coupling both problems and solutions to politics. (Kingdon, cited in Wharf & McKenzie, 1998)

At some critical juncture problems, policies, and politics converge; solutions are joined to problems and both of them are joined to political forces (Kingdon, 1984). The three streams provide a first view of the opportunities for influencing the definition of the problem, contributing to technical understanding of the problems and their solutions, building linkages with policy specialists, and seeking opportunities to influence political party visions. Each is an avenue for social workers to contribute their professional understanding of their clients' life experiences, leadership and planning techniques, and community building skills.

Policy windows may be triggered by regularly scheduled items such as throne speeches, budget speeches, estimates process, or unplanned external events initiated by a media crisis, pressure groups, release of inquest findings, or a difficult question during question period. Developing policy within the available window is increasingly complex as governments make efforts to develop solutions that cut across policy fields, government ministries, and other levels of government. One recent effort in Ontario is the creation of policy clusters that group ministries with common policy interests, enabling staff-level advisers to better work together.

Regardless of their own personal views on the issues, policy advisers are expected to serve the elected government with neutrality, anonymity, and loyalty (Kernaghan & Langford, 1990). Working in a mode of non-partisanship requires that civil servants not publicly criticize government policies or "not at any time speak in public or express views in writing for distribution to the public on any matter that forms part of the platform of a provincial or federal political party" (Kernaghan & Langford, 1990, p. 80). The traditional public service model requires that public discussion of policy be restricted to ministers; public servants are to avoid discussing "advice or recommendations tendered to Ministers" and speculating "about policy deliberations or future policy decisions" (p. 81). Gordon Robertson, a former secretary to the federal Cabinet, argued:

> anonymity... involves a substantial act of self-denial. It means an unwillingness to hint at influential association with policies or decisions; refusal to give the private briefing to a journalist; avoidance of photographs with key individuals; and eschewing the physical trappings of status that are demonstrations to the beholders of unspoken power and importance. (Robertson, 1983, p. 13).

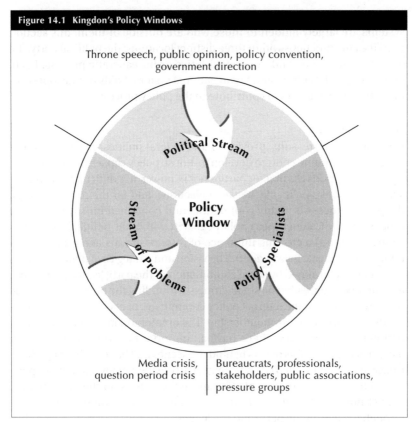

Figure 14.1 Kingdon's Policy Windows

From an idea to government policy

Throne speech, public opinion, policy convention, government direction

Political Stream

Policy Window

Stream of Problems

Policy Specialists

Media crisis, question period crisis

Bureaucrats, professionals, stakeholders, public associations, pressure groups

An increased emphasis on public participation in government decision making by bringing public servants into public forums has somewhat blurred these lines.

With the growth of policy networks, the monopoly position of career civil servants in the provision of advice to ministers is a thing of the past. At the same time, the need for quality advice founded on knowledge, research, and evaluation, tempered by informed practical experience, is even more critical given the proliferation of external sources of advice, public policy commentary, and special interest pleading by advocacy groups. The political debate that arises from claims on the public system is a struggle to give meaning to the world by defining legitimate participants, issues, and alliances. To be effective, social workers need to understand the policy system and its processes.

From an Idea to Government Policy

In a very practical way, the opportunities for social workers to be active citizens and influence public policy is largely determined by the policy infrastructure within governments and their bureaucracies. Recognizing that the systems are largely hidden to those who are outside of them, this section describes the functions within three distinct locations: the political party, the legislative structure, and the prelegislative or bureaucratic process. Each, depending on its culture and organizational system, holds unique opportunities for social workers to contribute to the policy process.

The Political Phase

For a number of reasons, provincial and federal political parties have not made much genuine effort to develop in-house policy capacity. The two most significant reasons are that for parties not in power, it is difficult to keep their supporters active politically between elections; and for the party in power, the policy process is highly confidential and contained mostly within the caucus and the Cabinet. Weak policy capacity within the political parties has contributed to the growing influence of interest groups and independent think tanks (Baier & Bakvis, 2001). The vision and strategies of political parties are usually determined by some combination of the party leaders, executive, and members: either by the small group surrounding the party leader, or the party executive and the internal policy committees, or at conventions including the grass-roots of the membership. The opinions of individual members, particularly Cabinet members, have an important bearing in formulating party positions, but this occurs behind the scenes and has little bearing on the House and its committees (White, 1997). Party leaders enjoy a dominant position and in most cases are able to impose their views on the party. In fact, almost nothing that occurs in the Legislature can be understood except through the lens of the party and the leader.

According to Robert Young (1991, p. 77) Canada's political parties "desperately need a stronger capacity to formulate policy.... In a self-reinforcing cycle, people with genuine policy concerns seek out interest groups to advance their causes, and the parties degenerate further into domination by leaders and their personal entourages, who play the politics of image and strategic vagueness." In fact, this is very descriptive of the manner in which the 1994 Ontario Conservative Party's "Common Sense Revolution" was crafted by a small group of the party executive, senior staff, and youth wing leaders (Jeffery, 1999). Some parties, as a means of building grassroots support, seek more inclusive methods. The Ontario Liberal Party has modelled itself after the federal party, endorsing a grass-roots system of policy committees at the riding level that then contributes resolutions at policy conventions (Ontario Liberal Party, 1993). The Ontario Liberal Party policy convention in March 2001 provided opportunity for riding association representatives, party executive, and members of Parliament, to hear and meet with international policy experts. Solidarity and dialogue underlie the policy resolution process of the Ontario New Democrats. The resolutions adopted at the convention held in June 2000 form the basis of party policy and direct the activities of the executive and the caucus (Ontario New Democrats, 2000). Regardless of the process and degree of inclusiveness, once elected, this policy vision forms the government's direction for the next four to five years of government activity.

From an idea to government policy

The Legislative Phase

The most visible location of policy making is the provincial Legislature. Westminister[1] government, as found in Canada and its provinces, is centred on ministers who are individually and collectively responsible to the House of Commons for the policies and programs of government. In the traditional Westminister model, ministers lead departments that are staffed with career civil servants. Each minister is also supported by political staff, whose job it is to advise the minister of his or her party's politics, as well as its policy preferences. On the Westminister system White (1989, pp. 73-74) writes: "these are in the nature of zero-order beliefs—so primal as to be accepted without justification and scarcely susceptible to rational challenge. They include the concept of responsible government, the notion of a loyal opposition, party discipline, and ministerial responsibility."

In debating the issues of the day, the Legislature brings new problems to public attention, educates the public about those problems and possible solutions to them, and enables the voters to assess the positions of the political parties. The Legislature legitimizes support for government policy by providing legal authorization for laws and government spending, and encourages people to accept measures that they dislike because of the perception that decisions made by their elected representatives reflect public opinion and public involvement as central elements (White, 1997). A brief description of the activities of the House follows.

Formal executive authority is vested in the Crown's representative, the lieutenant-governor, but exercised by the premier and the ministers of the Executive Council or the Cabinet. Ministers are accountable to the House of Commons for their exercise of executive authority, initiating legislation and administering public affairs. The throne speech, read by the lieutenant-governor at the opening of the session, details the government's plan for its agenda and policies. The subsequent budget is the financial estimate for the new and ongoing policy initiatives and identifies the funding source.

Legislation is introduced into the House in the form of public bills (government bills are introduced by a Cabinet minister) and private bills (introduced by any other member of provincial Legislature). Government bills are the end-product of processes of consensus building within Cabinet, between Cabinet and caucus, and between senior administrators and political advisers. Once a government bill is introduced to the Legislature, it is expected to pass with the full support of the caucus, barring opposition stalling, shifting government priorities, being held up in committee, or dying on the order paper when the House dissolves. Party discipline and the tendency of the electoral system to produce majority governments, combined with the considerable resources of the governing party, create a solid and predictable block of support for government initiatives.

At the introduction of new legislation, the speaker of the House moves that "leave be given to introduce the bill entitled (bill named) and the same to be read for the first time" (White, 1989). The member's brief statement explaining the bill's principles is followed by a vote on whether to accept the bill for future debate. If accepted, it is assigned a number, printed, and scheduled for second reading debate several days later. This allows MPPs time to study the proposed bill and the opposition parties to caucus on it. The second reading debate is the opportunity for the MPPs to make statements on the principles of the bill. Following the debate a unanimous vote of all members present in the House will enable a bill to bypass the committee stage and be ordered for third reading. Other bills receiving a majority vote are referred to committee.

The decision of whether to send a bill to the committee of the whole or a standing committee, is made by the minister introducing the bill, usually in consultation with the House leaders. In addition to reviewing and amending proposed legislation, standing committees, with their all-party representation, also conduct special inquiries into proposed policy changes that are not associated with a particular bill. Tradition expects that standing committees will hold public hearings, call for expert witnesses, hear directly from ministry staff, and accept submissions and oral presentations from private citizens and stakeholder groups (White, 1989). The committee also has the option of calling for public hearings before its clause-by-clause treatment or holding public hearings on specific clauses. Since meetings are less formal than House sittings and MPPs engage in real discussions among themselves and with witnesses, committees offer much greater scope for influencing policy. This is influenced by the extent to which the government members are open to advice and the degree to which committee members set aside partisan differences rather than scoring political points. Committee attention to an issue often raises public concern, which may force the government to modify a policy (White, 1997). Amendments may also arise independent of the committee process from the bureaucracy's interpretation of the public's concerns about the bill. Once the work of the standing committee is completed, the amended bill is returned to the House. Making a presentation to a standing committee and networking with government staff assigned to support the process is an opportunity for social workers to use their expertise to reframe the problems and present concrete solutions for changes. Individual and professional credibility can and does affect the recommendations developed by the standing committee. Making formal presentations is one venue for social workers to inject social knowledge into the process.

At third reading the bill is voted on by the members without debate or may be returned to the standing committee with instructions to make specific amendments. Following third reading, the bill receives royal assent from the lieutenant-governor; the lieutenant-governor has the constitutional authority to withhold royal assent, but in practice this does not occur. Royal assent and proclamation dates are set by the Cabinet. The most common reason for delaying implementation is to allow the bureaucracy to put the administrative machinery in place.

From an idea to government policy

Almost all government bills contain a crucial provision authorizing the government to issue legally binding "regulations" that set out details of the policy without requiring any approval from the Legislature. The consequence is that vast areas of policy-making do not come under the scrutiny of elected members (White, 1997). This is a serious weakness in the Legislature's ability to hold the government accountable.

The Pre-legislative Phase

In Westminister-style Parliaments, many critical decisions are made out of the public eye during the prelegislative phase by the Cabinet and the bureaucracy. Although a great number of policy issues arise, many initiatives are rejected, significantly revised, or ascribed such a low priority that they fall off the policy agenda. Policy advisers work in an environment fraught with dynamic tensions: political versus administrative responsibility for policy development, values versus technically driven policy, centralized versus coordinated models of development, and, finally, closed versus participative design models.

Internal policy units, producing analysis and advice to ministers and senior public servants, are located in the central agencies and throughout the line ministries. The central agencies oversee the functions of government policy approval and coordination, fiscal planning, fiscal approval, and government human resources planning. In Ontario these include Cabinet Office, Management Board, Ministry of Finance and SuperBuild.[2] As information-seeking and processing groups, they are concerned with policy development, program planning and design, liaison, quantitative and qualitative research, and, occasionally, evaluation. The relative emphasis placed on individual functions varies among ministries and can vary within the same policy unit over time. There has been very little variation in the primary policy functions since their inception (Prince, 1979):

- *problem definition:* clarifying, articulating, and interpreting problem "inputs"
- *policy development:* defining objectives or policies, conducting priority reviews
- *program design:* designing concrete courses of action to achieve policy
- *policy evaluation:* examining policies to determine if they have or will achieve their objectives
- *socio-economic research and forecasting:* research projects, long-term scanning, scenario writing, and extrapolations

- *policy firefighting:* short-term work under pressure, "quick and dirty" studies on "hot" issues
- *coordination and liaison:* coordinating operational and long-term plans of a number of branches, providing liaison within the ministry, with other ministries, the federal government, and interest groups

In addition, policy groups act as gatekeepers to the system by screening and reducing the demands made on ministries and their deputies. In some groups "firefighting," whether intended or not, dominates and may even prevent the development of planning and evaluation roles. Other constraints and considerations include insufficient resources (time, staff, position classifications, and facilities), difficulties in recruiting and retaining qualified personnel, the inexperience of some advisers, the absence of relevant data, and technical problems in the use of analytic methods. Lacking support and access to the deputy minister, some groups have remained outside the mainstream of the ministry policy processes. In a reorganization, a change in the title or location of a group often signifies changes in relations to clients, status in the ministry, intended policy roles, or an effort to reduce past bureaucratic antagonisms (Meltsner, 1976). The policy strategy is determined through an interactive process between the policy groups and their clients (clients are the minister, senior management, and members of the immediate policy network).

Understanding the dynamic tensions within the bureaucracy's role begins with the policy-administration dichotomy (Doern & Phidd, 1988). The crux of the tension is the bureaucracy's role in being sensitive to the political objectives and constraints, while initiating policy ideas and "massaging" policy proposals. During the drafting of Cabinet documents and memoranda, staff-level advisers attempt to bring the right nuance of meaning, provide the best supporting data, and the most cost-effective analysis while maintaining the integrity of the minister's policy vision. Advisers engage in constant discussions "up the tube" to the minister through the deputy and across ministerial lines and central agency officials. Frequently, there is also contact with outside interests and with other levels of government. Ideally, the end product of this iterative process is a polished Cabinet document, a mixture of verbal and written exchange of views, scientific and technical rationality, bounded by a values framework. It should not come as a surprise that some ministers hold the view that their excellent ideas were sabotaged by the bureaucracy, while the bureaucracy holds the opinion that citizens may have been saved from some hare-brained schemes.

Fisher (1980) points out that the major difficulties encountered by policy makers in policy development are inherently linked to the treatment of values. From the outset policy advisers pay attention to the political dimensions of policy values, recruitment of political support, and accommodating contradictory goals. Dror (1968, p. 35) argued against the exclusion of the political as the technical side of the policy sciences was gaining predominance: "The

need for evaluation of the probability that a policy will be sufficiently accept- From an idea to government policy
able to the various secondary political decision makers, executors, interest
groups and publics whose participation or acquiescence is needed for it to be
translated into political action."

There are two problem-solving sequences that tend to operate parallel
to each other in any policy formulation process: What is the mix required
between a political or a technical response? Bureaucracy staff intent upon
ascertaining the political acceptability or feasibility of a policy must evaluate
whether it generates support for the particular political party that will propose
it. The key question becomes: In the current environment, how are we most
likely to attain the policy goals? The technical skills that analysts bring to the
process are set into this framework and define the methodologies, selection
of data, analysis tools, and evaluation criteria, and selection of options for
determining the choice of directions are determined by it. As Faludi and
Voogd (1986) note, one can accept as a given that political and moral factors
will be part of the policy and planning process, but that does not rule out
using rationality as a decision-making rule. Rationality is the pragmatic way
for policy advisers to negotiate the recognition of diverse political values,
recruitment of political support, and accommodation of contradictory goals
and objectives. Analysts become adept at the language of rationality and its
application in well-prepared arguments to position problems, goals, and
potential solutions within the ideology of the party forming the government
(Fisher, 1980).

The current effort to achieve greater policy coordination is driven by pressure to reduce government expenditure, eliminate perceived duplication,
ensure internal coherence, and establish consistent policy priorities. The
challenging task is to find ways of making the activities of policy groups compatible with those that have similar responsibilities, while at the same time
complying with the legal rules of confidentiality in very narrow time frames.
Some bureaucrats argue that timely policy development is burdened by the
current state-of-the-art system of stewarding policy advice through a galaxy
of approval structures-central agency committees, cross-ministry deputies
committees, assistant deputy minister cross-ministry committees, staff-level
interministerial working groups, and third-party working groups. The problems of working across divisions and ministries are compounded when the
issues of coordination across levels of government is added (Toonen, 1985),
especially in federal regimes such as Canada.

From a policy perspective, the results of rights talk and cultural pluralism is that stakeholders expect to be consulted on public decisions. Putting
this expectation into practice raises issues of managing public expectation of
what will become of their advice. For the policy analyst, consultations are
another source of information and advice contributing to the policy "stew";
however, those who are consulted want to see their contributions reflected.
Considering the range of stakeholder views, this is not possible. In practice,

policy advisers seek a balance between competing interests while keeping the government's vision central. Pal maintains that consultation should:

> focus on the operational and programmatic level, as opposed to broad values or directions for policy development....This distinguishes consultation as a policy management activity from broader forms of political representation, such as parliamentary committee hearings on a piece of legislation....The objective is ongoing development and management of the policy or program in question, not the establishment of parameters for political discussion and debate. (Pal, 1987, p. 218)

From the political perspective, consultations also have their inherent dangers. Civil servants who are put in the public spotlight bleed power away from the elected ministers; in the public mind they become the figures who seem to "really" decide (Mitchell & Sutherland, 1997). Placing middle-level policy staff in direct contact with both politicians and the stakeholders also contributes to blurring their respective roles in the minds of the public.

Social Workers as Active Citizens

This section covers the wide range of opportunities social workers can involve themselves in to influence government, particularly during the between-elections period. The key in social workers being active citizens is to connect the macropractice of policy to our micropractices within social work. The most important avenues of influence are the accumulation of small opportunities that arise through building networks within the broader world of our practice lives. In referring to Milbrath's work, Verba, Nie, and Kim wrote in early 1971 (p. 10) that "there are not only gladiators and non-gladiators, but different types of gladiators with different goals using different political techniques." Participation is multidimensional. Social workers can choose where to engage and also the degree of their involvement. What we bring to the policy network is our social knowledge of the everyday world, knowledge accumulated through our day-to-day work with our clients. Our first-hand experience of the impacts when conflicting and overlapping policies are operationalized and the knowledge of practical program delivery is invaluable. As we think through our commitment to participation, we must consider three decisions: whether to act or not; in which direction the act should be focused; and what should be the intensity, the duration, and the degree.

Once we decide to act, the first step for us as social workers is to develop an avid interest in the policy decisions being made that directly affect our work with our clients. I prefer the analogy of following a social policy field as though it is a sport. Know the issues, the players, their positions, and their playing history. Know the rules of the game and how it is being played. Understanding how decisions are reached identifies new possibilities of methods and timing of interventions. To plan strategy, social workers should begin by seeking answers to these questions:

- How "hot" is the problem?
- How has the problem evolved?
- Have there been earlier attempts at solutions?
- Is more research needed?
- Who has a vested interest in particular solutions?
- Are there limitations on possible solutions?
- Who are potential allies on all sides of the issue?

It is not enough to know what was said and done; social workers must also grasp the motives behind those actions in order to anticipate future moves. Action in policy development must be understood as part of the complex patterns of interaction with other members of the policy community (Blumer, 1969). From the outset it is necessary to analyze the many stakeholders both as groups and as individual players. Each has a different view of the problem and its preferred solutions and, in turn, each is attempting to use networks to see their preferred solution implemented.

Opportunities for Participation

In planning an action strategy individual social workers should also consider in which arena their interests lie: family violence, child welfare, human rights, health care, homelessness, etc. Although there are similarities in the intervention required within the different environments, the actual influences on policy may be quite different. Patterns of activity meant to influence policy decision making also have an additive characteristic. This is true in two senses: activities that couple within one environment relate to activities in the other environment, and there is a hierarchy of involvement in that participants at one level also tend to perform many of the same actions, including those performed at lower levels of involvement. For instance, efforts to influence government policy about child welfare may well affect decision making in the area of family violence. People who are likely to make a presentation to a standing committee are also likely to engage in lower-level activities like writing letters to their MPP, or signing petitions. Participation's cumulative characteristics arise from the fact that social workers who engage in the topmost behaviours are very likely to perform those lower in the rank also.

The opportunities I propose build on the work of Milbrath (1965), Verba, Nie, and Kim (1971), and Langton (1978). The activities provide a great deal of flexibility for social workers to use their broad range of skills in a wide variety of contexts. While the listing is helpful, it is meant only as a starting point for us as social workers to examine our skills and our interests. In addition to our interpersonal skills, as social workers we bring certain skills from our practice fields: alliance building, conflict resolution, written communications, public speaking, best practices knowledge, and understanding of our clients' lives.

Table 14.1   Opportunities for Participation

Environment	Interventions	Influence on Policy
Political		
• Election campaign	• Voting, pamphlet distribution, public contact on issues, discussion with candidate	• Extremely minimal, influence dependent on election outcome
• Ridings association executive member	• Networking, volunteer on riding and regional policy committees, informal discussion with party members and MPPs, representation at policy conventions	• Collective outcome, encourage MPP to carry messages to caucus, coalition building, lobbying MPPs, and executive
• Executive position	• Strategy planning, local candidate selection, contact Cabinet members at conventions/meetings	• Highest influence, access to backroom, lobbying caucus, only big issues discussed at Cabinet
Advocacy/Advisory		
• Citizen initiated	• Contact with politician/ bureaucrat on single issue, individual problems	• Extremely minimal, usually self-interest
• Issue orientation	• Local nature, requires ongoing lobbying, media publicity, goal is to have politician take up the cause	• Can achieve or avert specific decisions, little influence on policy
• Pressure group	• Membership in larger organization, staffed through donations, internal specialized policy expertise, confrontation, and/or lobbying	• Degree of influence determined by prestige, power, contacts, multiple accesses to system
• Advisory group	• Invited expertise, subgovernment, interface with bureaucracy	• Continuous discrete influence, change in government may be detrimental
Professional		
• Individual worker	• Contact with politician/ opposition/bureaucrat on single policy impact, letter writing, lobbying on change status, advocates for service user	• Contribution to policy stew, builds foundation for ongoing contacts with politicians, opposition, and bureaucrats, contributes from practice field
• Agency representative	• Agency identifies client and organization issues, approach fits organization's decision models, coordinated through agency, letter writing, media, meetings, lobbying	• Build linkages to advisory group status, perceived as advocate for agency, networks with similar agencies
• Association	• Builds coalitions across practice fields, educates membership, meetings and lobbying, position papers, presentations, briefings	• Facilitates policy discussion across practice fields and agencies, adds credibility to expert input, ongoing input to policy process

Social Workers as Policy Entrepreneurs

To be policy entrepreneurs, either inside or outside of government as Kingdon (1984) describes, social workers must be ready to advocate for selected problems and solutions to be given a high priority in the policy arena, prompting policy makers to pay attention. I expect that social workers, moving in the direction of policy entrepreneurship, are motivated by a combination of several factors:

- Straightforward concern about certain problems that they witness on an ongoing basis
- Pursuit of benefits for their clients, profession, and/or workplaces
- The promotion of social work values within an identified policy field
- The satisfaction of participating and influencing the policy process on behalf of their clients and profession

Our claim to be heard as social workers has three sources: professional expertise, understanding of our clients, and knowledge gained from front-line service delivery. When combined with network building, negotiating skills, and political connections, the combination could be more influential than each quality taken separately. When we advocate for use of our definitions of the problems and the solutions, social work values and social knowledge gained from practice will affect the shape of social policy. To be successful policy advocates, we must be persistent and spend a great deal of time giving talks, writing papers, sending letters, attending meetings, and power lunching, all with the aim of pushing our ideas in whatever way and forum might further client-centred solutions.

The key to being successful policy entrepreneurs lies in our continuous preparatory work and then waiting for the policy window to open (Kingdon, 1984). Our ideas, policy expertise, and proposals must be developed well in advance of the policy window opening. Early preparation and planning is critical; waiting until the policy window opens to develop our proposals is waiting too long. By continuously monitoring the policy context, we will become sensitive to subtle shifts in the environment, we will read the timing of the policy windows extremely well, and we will be in a position to move at the right moment. An important outcome of reading a changing environment is that we will be alert to the nuances and will be able to position ourselves in relation to other stakeholders.

Even though casting a single vote in an election has an extremely low influence on policy, social workers should exercise their franchise and encourage their clients to do so as well. Deciding which party to support prompts us to ask questions, discuss future policy direction, and analyze what it may mean for our work. Most parties acknowledge that their policy capacity is weak, hence social workers bringing knowledge, researched ideas, and professional best practices are likely to be well received. Advanced volunteer work within a party brings social workers in closer contact with the centre of the political system. At a minimum, social workers should be attending public meetings and using this opportunity to discuss issues and share visions with other citizens, politicians, and administrators. When politicians and/or bureaucrats engage in discussion, particularly following the initial meeting, make a concerted effort to follow up in writing, thanking them for the opportunity to speak with them and inquiring about some specific aspect that in your opinion requires change. Town hall meetings are a prime opportunity to develop a network of like-minded people who will support social workers' proposed solutions. Moving a solution to the forefront is about building opportunities and support across individuals and groups. Although it may take a number of years to build networks and move ideas ahead, fresh solutions brought forward when the timing is right can have great impact. Political party participation provides many opportunities to become involved locally, regionally, and nationally in the system.

The first year of a new government is clearly the prime time for preoccupation with the subject of policy change. During a change of government, people throughout the policy communities watch to identify the political climate of the new government and anticipate the opening of policy windows. During the election campaign and throughout the transition period, policy entrepreneurs will sense the mood and seize opportunities to promote or restructure some of the items on their policy agendas. Where two or more levels of government have jurisdiction over a policy field, policy entrepreneurs may actually enhance their opportunities to move a solution ahead as the various players vie with one another for the credit and claim to jurisdiction.

As policy entrepreneurs, we must seek out opportunities to build linkages into policy networks and create support for our framing of the problems and solutions. As we build networks, we also build public profile for the problems we are concerned about. We can speak publicly, secure press coverage, and meet regularly with people who may be able to influence the policy makers. Informal networking builds deeper linkages into our communities and governments. It requires only a minimal amount of ingenuity to create linkages into the bureaucracy by using government Web sites to locate middle-level bureaucrats with policy responsibility for our fields of interest. Making contacts in a collegial manner, and then sharing our concept of the problem, research and best practices, and our thoughts on a potential solution takes our social knowledge into the policy fields. Invite policy staff for an informal visit to your agency, ask them to speak at a staff meeting, or perhaps provide an opportunity for them to hear from your clients. Staff enjoy and learn from opportunities to see and experience what they have been reading and writing about. As information packages are prepared for the deputy or the minister, the good ideas acquired from on-site visits or submitted in writing have a chance of being included. Policy analysts often network informally across ministries and will share well-researched information with their colleagues. Kingdon (1984) refers to the process as the "primeval soup" of policy. Through networking, policy analysts and social workers can become working partners. Both groups have similar objectives—to build a better system—except that policy analysts must also work within the vision of their political masters.

Social workers as policy entrepreneurs

Social workers can further make use of networking opportunities to take ideas and float them as trial balloons, solicit reactions, revise proposals in the light of reactions, and float the ideas again. As good strategists we can look at situations and see elements that have been there all along but were not noticed before. Making the most of an opportunity for a private meeting with the minister or senior bureaucrat responsible for the issue, perhaps at a conference, can focus the issues and contribute to moving the problem higher on the policy agenda. Often a private meeting can be formally requested through the minister's office staff after the commitment has been made for the minister to attend. Through contact with the policy makers, social workers will become more sensitive to the nuances of problem definition and be able to seize opportunities to present their solution as the preferable option. These meetings may prompt an ongoing policy dialogue about current governmental/program performance through letters, complaints, and visits to officials.

Making contact with the Official Opposition and all the parties in opposition can be very fruitful. The members of the shadow cabinet are constantly looking for any weaknesses in the policies and administration of the party in power. In opposing the governing party, they express their own views, the views of their supporters, and the views of interest groups that may hold the balance of voter power in the next election. Briefing the opposition parties can be critical; in fact, they often welcome input in their preparation for question period and for their policies, particularly when the next election is approaching. Some opposition party members may even ask stakeholder representatives for assistance on certain legislative initiatives that they hope to move forward upon forming the new government (Sarpkaya, 1988).

Lastly, there is a vital role for social workers in softening the views of the mass public, specialized interest groups, and the policy community itself. According to Kingdon (1984), policy entrepreneurs play two different roles— advocates and brokers—both of which are very familiar to social workers. As social workers, not only should we advocate for our ideas and solutions and soften up the process but we should also act as brokers, negotiating among the policy actors, making critical connections, and capitalizing on opportunities as they present themselves. From our practices with individuals and communities, social workers understand that change is not achieved through a single intervention effort, and likewise significant policy change will require substantial involvement.

Briefings, Meetings, and Presentations

Most formal transfer of information between social workers and politicians and bureaucrats concerning significant problems and proposed solutions will take place in prearranged briefing sessions, meetings, and formal presentations. No matter how well planned, meetings with policy makers can take a sudden turn from one subject to another, or the ebb and flow of discussion can quickly alter the intended dynamics and the tone of a meeting. Members of the public who are participating in briefings and making presentations do not always maximize face-to-face contact. Social workers attending briefings as expert witnesses are not always expert communicators. Hurried politicians and bureaucrats compound the tension by pressing for crisp information. Capitalizing on opportunities is about grasping procedural opportunities and delivering clear messages. This section sets the foundation for planning and managing presentations.

Getting on the policy agenda at the earliest stage is crucial to advancing an issue, and considering the tight schedules of policy makers, pre-meetings and briefings must be very focused. Briefing materials should be prepared and submitted in advance so there is time for the policy makers to review and consult with staff prior to the briefing. In a short covering letter, be very clear about the issue to be addressed and what recommendations and what decisions, if any, will be sought (Fraatz, 1982). Before you actually present your information, it is important to know that there are two questions foremost in the mind of every minister or politician: Are we doing the right thing? Will this help or hurt our re-election chances? Pre-meetings may allow policy makers to flag controversial issues, build mutual understanding on issues, and possibly make future discussions more productive.

Constaninou (1995) suggests a number of points, which in my view are extremely helpful to social workers when preparing for a briefing session. First, understand the minister's perspective and background, and what is important to him or her about the issue. Knowing about his or her background helps to identify loyalties, values, favourite causes, and approaches to problem solving. Through talking with other people, scan the big picture related to your proposed solution so that it can be positioned with the preferred spin. Since policy makers are often victims of information overload, consider what you think the minister needs to know to make an informed decision, including differentiation between advice and facts. Always anticipate questions and be prepared with answers. A positive approach that reveals an interest in finding answers is always more successful than a presentation that purports to have all the answers or does not consider alternative approaches. It is imperative that when seeking decisions time be allowed for consideration of what has been presented. Building effective working relations with the minister's staff can cultivate important allies and add legitimacy to your efforts in getting the minister's support. Lastly, consider whether the proposal will be well received by stakeholders, agencies, and the general public. This will weigh heavily with a minister making important choices.

We can also take advantage of the opportunities in the policy process when input on an issue or piece of legislation is invited from the public. These are royal commissions, legislative committees, task forces, appeal boards, advisory councils, public consultations, and responses to discussion papers. Although many members of the public feel that they are not listened to during the formal process, it is my experience that a creative and viable solution—well presented—will often find its way into the policy "stew," and if not used immediately, may be resurrected at a later time. Bureaucrats often provide administrative support to many public hearing procedures, so that a strong idea not picked up by the political side may surface again through bureaucratic input (White, 1997). Oral presentations and written briefs should be framed by:

Social workers as policy entrepreneurs

- clearly articulating the problem
- specifying what is not working now and why
- presenting the data or best practice examples on what could be a solution, and
- proposing well thought out amendments or viable alternative solutions

In presenting briefs to committees, commissions, and task forces, the challenge is to be comfortable with the players, the process, and the rules of engagement—and using this knowledge to deliver your message in such a way as to influence decisions. As McInnes (1999, p. 2) writes, "Your 15 minutes have to stand out." The most important task in making a presentation is to make a positive impact with your remarks and your submission. No matter how well prepared you may be, appearing before a parliamentary committee can be unpredictable. There is a long list of decisions to make before actually sitting down at the committee table, such as deciding who will go, who will represent your group, the length of the brief, etc. The most important decisions involve crafting the key messages.

Regular checks of the standing committee Web site will keep social workers informed about work assigned to committees, the dates, and the locations.[3] Social workers who wish to make presentations to standing committees should contact the clerk assigned to the committee about appearing, explaining why they should be heard, and if possible, contacting a member of the committee to advocate for them. If you are refused an invitation, look for allies in professional associations, networks of service deliverers, or local governments to form a coalition and carry your message. At a minimum, submit a written brief to the committee, the committee researchers, and the bureaucracy; they may be interested in your fresh perspective on an old problem.

Since the work of committees is to look at the big policy issues, presenters often think they have to come and address the big picture. What committee members need to hear are people's experiences and what worked in their lives—social knowledge. Hearing about individual experiences helps committee members to understand how the big picture affects "life on the ground." Most important, know your material well enough so that you will not have to read it. Remember that committee members have been sitting through many hours of presentations and you want to hold their attention.

In preparing for the presentation, the advantage goes to the individual or group who:

- *Communicates well:* Select the spokesperson on the basis of his or her communication skills;
- *Distinctly opens the presentation:* Briefly introduces himself or herself and the organization;
- *Understands the problem:* Distinctly defines the issue and builds a supporting case;
- *Makes the issue understandable:* Uses facts and anecdotes to help members understand the problem;
- *Understands the needed changes:* Clearly articulates the required changes and why they will work;
- *Selects a few key points:* Reinforces the message throughout the presentation in the written submission; and
- *Has respect for the process:* Speaks respectfully about the work of the committee if approached by the media. (McInnes, 1999)

In a written submission, write for quality, not for quantity. Your material should be succinct and inviting to the reader as often politicians and their staff do not have time to read all briefs submitted to the committee. An executive summary is essential to highlight your key points. When drafting the committee's final report, staff will cull through the hearing transcripts and the submissions to find "quotable quotes," representative statements that sum up a group's position. Other items such as key statistics or the projected cost of any proposal should leap from the page. Good written presentations help readers grasp your key points. Imagine reading dozens of lengthy briefs trying to determine what each group stands for on many multifaceted issues.

Moves over the number of years to decentralize the policy process have created a number of points of access and social workers should take advantage of this, particularly in view of the competition that pervades legislative debates (Fraatz, 1982). Although working with and managing coalitions of organizations making presentations can be especially challenging, the impact of cohesive groups embracing a common objective can be significant. Coalitions require additional planning as group representatives have to get positions endorsed from their respective organizations at each step along the way, all of which takes negotiation and time. If coalitions jell, a benefit is that they also demonstrate lobbying acumen to the group's broader membership. Partners in coalitions may also be called upon in the future for support in other initiatives.

It is important for social workers to be honest and straightforward in all dealings with people in government. Once an individual, agency, or organization loses credibility, and hence their ability to persuade people, they will have great difficulty in presenting their vision as viable. If a minister or senior bureaucrat is made to appear wrong, ignorant, or uninformed in front of his or her colleagues or constituents because of an error or omission on the part of a representative, the organization's credibility will always be called into question in the future. Such stories have a way of continuing to live on in the folklore of the civil service.

Closing comments

For governments, the questions of who to consult, how and when, about what and for what purpose are highly sensitive questions. Discussion and consultation are equally part of a citizen's right to know about decisions being made by government and to participate in the process of government (Anderson, 1996). Social workers embody two very important contributions to the "policy stew": expert knowledge and grass-roots input. Politicians like to reach for grassroots input by speaking to "ordinary citizens." As one committee member on a federal government panel said, "We must be careful to not let ourselves be influenced solely by very structured official lobby groups. They have their place, they are present and that is to be expected, but we must speak with ordinary Canadians" (Paul Crete, quoted in McInnes, 1999, p. 109).

Social workers must look for ways to get in the game early. The issues move up and down on organizational agendas, sometimes unpredictably. Moreover, organizations, committees, and their staffs tend to base their recommendations and decisions on the first available data and early discussions with players in the policy community. The suggestions in this section are intended merely as points of departure, largely because each policy debate is different. Not all issues call for the same kind of analysis, and not all analysis is appropriate for all audiences. Still, social workers and policy makers can engage in more fruitful partnerships—provided, of course, that social workers take the steps to become active citizens.

Closing Comments

The responsibility to be active citizens calls social workers from our places of practice to participate in influencing public discussion and shaping the decision making of governments. As social workers, I argue that we have an even greater responsibility because by being social workers we have accepted the responsibility of making claims on behalf of others and expanding the public domain so that more voices are heard. By bringing our professional social knowledge to the policy arena, we are focusing on securing the necessary resources for developing human capacities. Welfare is the development of human capacities and the primary concern of social workers. Policy-making is a value-laden political struggle centred on the interpretation and response to people whose voices are not present in the public arena: the poor, the homeless, and the vulnerable.

In this chapter I endeavoured to open the black box and share with my fellow professionals what I have learned over the last fifteen years of my practice. Although systemic barriers do exist in the Westminister model of governance, there are avenues of influence that social workers have left largely unused. We need to shoulder the responsibility for our own inaction and use it to push

Notes

References

ourselves into the future. While other professions and stakeholder groups have been using the system as it exists and using it to their own ends, our voices have been largely quiet. In this neo-conservative era of decision making we cannot continue to be silent, but must learn to use the system as it is, with all of its inherent problems, because it is the system we have. Politicians are influenced to make decisions that their stakeholders lead them to believe will increase their public support and secure their re-election. Bureaucrats struggle to balance perceptions of the public interest and respond to the vision of their political leaders. Vocal and powerful stakeholder groups bring their resources to bear on securing decisions that benefit their interests. If we don't embark on the journey to make public claims, the powerless will continue to be subordinate and unseen.

As social workers, we take our professional identity from being advocates, networkers, advisers, counsellors, communicators, and facilitators. When combined with our social knowledge, we have something much greater than only the necessary skills to be influential actors in the policy arena; we bring the knowledge and skills of responsible citizenship. Now is the time to be heard and to act.

Notes

1 Provincial parliamentary practice is a blend of written rules, British conventions, and adaptations of the British model. Underlying are the concept of responsible government, the loyal opposition, party discipline, and ministerial responsibility (White, 1989). The Westminster model allows elected politicians to bring local interests into the parliamentary arena and the Cabinet to be held publicly accountable for decisions (Whittington & Williams, 2000).

2 The Ontario SuperBuild Corporation will evaluate provincial businesses and services to determine where partnerships with the private sector can deliver higher quality services at a lower cost to taxpayers.

3 Alberta. Online at < www.assembly.ab.ca/ >.
British Columbia. Online at < www.legis.gov.bc.ca/ >.
Manitoba. Online at < www.gov.mb.ca/leg-asmb/ >.
New Brunswick. Online at < www.gov.nb.ca/legis/index.htm >.
Newfoundland and Labrador. Online at < www.gov.nf.ca/hoa/ >.
Northwest Territories. Online at < www.assembly.gov.nt.ca >.
Nova Scotia. Online at < www.gov.ns.ca./legislature/ >.
Nunavut. Online at < www.assembly.nu.ca/english/index.html >.
Ontario. Online at < www.ontla.on.ca/ >.
Prince Edward Island. Online at < www.gov.pe.ca/leg/index.php3 >.
Quebec. Online at < www.assnat.qc.ca/eng/indexne3.html >.
Saskatchewan. Online at < www.legassembly.sk.ca/ >.
Yukon. Online at < www.gov.yk.ca/leg-assembly/ >.
Canada. Online at < www.parl.gc.ca/common/index.asp?Language=E&Parl=37&Ses=1 >.

References

Anderson, G. (1996). The new focus on the policy capacity of the federal government. *Canadian Public Administration/Administration Publique du Canada*, *39*(4), 469-488.

References

Anderson, J. (1984). *Public policy making: An introduction* (3rd ed.). Boston: Houghton Mifflin.

Arendt, H. (1998). *The human condition.* Chicago: University of Chicago Press. (Original work published 1958.)

Baier, G., & Bakvis, H. (2001). Think tanks and political parties: Competitors or collaborators? *Canadian Journal of Policy Research, 2*(1), 107-113.

Baralet, J.M. (1988). *Citizenship: Rights, struggle and class inequality.* Minneapolis: University of Minnesota Press.

Barber, B. (1984). *Strong democracy: Participatory politics for a new age.* Berkeley: University of California Press.

Blumer, H. (1969). *Symbolic interactionism.* Englewood Cliffs, NJ: Prentice Hall.

Brewer, G.D. (1974). Dealing with complex social problems: The potential of the "Decision Seminar." In G.D. Brewer & R.D. Brunner (Eds.), *Political development and change: A policy approach* (pp. 439-461). New York: Free Press.

Charih, M., & Rouillard, L. (1997). The new public management. In M. Charih & A. Daniels (Eds.), *New public management and public administration in Canada.* (pp. 27-45).Toronto: The Institute of Public Management.

Clarke, P.B. (1996). *Deep citizenship.* Chicago: Pluto Press.

Constaninou, P.P. (1995). On briefing ministers. *Policy Options, 3*(May), 45-47.

Doern, G.B., & Phidd, R. (1988). *Canadian Public Policy: Ideas, Structure, and Process.* Scarborough: Nelson.

Dror, Y. (1968). *Public policy-making re-examined.* San Francisco: Chandler Publishing.

Drover, G., & Kerans, P. (1993). *New approaches to welfare theory.* Aldershot: Edward Elgar.

Dye, T. (1972). *Understanding public policy.* Englewood Cliffs, NJ: Prentice Hall.

Edelman, M.J. (1988). *Constructing the political spectacle.* Chicago: University of Chicago Press.

Faludi, A., & Voogd, H. (1986). *Evaluation of complex policy problems.* Delft, Netherlands: Delftsche Uitgevers Maatschappij.

Fisher, F. (1980). *Politics, values, and public policy.* Boulder, CO: Westview Press.

Fraatz, J.M.B. (1982). Policy analysts as advocates. *Journal of Policy Analysis and Management, 1*(2), 273-276.

Habermas, J. (1992). Citizenship and national identity: Some reflections on the future of Europe. *Praxis International, 12:* 1-19.

Held, D. (1991). Between state and civil society: Citizenship. In G. Andrews (Ed.), *Citizenship* (pp. 19-25). London: Lawrence & Wishart.

Ignatieff, M. (1991). Citizenship and moral narcissism. In G. Andrews (Ed.), *Citizenship* (pp. 26-36). London: Lawrence & Wishart.

Jeffery, B. (1999). *Hard right turn: The new face of neo-conservatism in Canada.* Toronto: HarperCollins.

Jenkins, W.I. (1978). *Policy analysis: A political and organizational perspective.* London: Martin Robertson.

Jones, C. (1984). *An introduction to the study of public policy.* Monterey: Brooks/Cole.

Kernaghan, K., & Langford, J.W. (1990). *The responsible public servant.* Toronto: The Institute for Research on Public Policy.

Kingdon, J.W. (1984). *Agendas, alternatives and public policies.* Toronto: Little, Brown.

Langton, S. (1978). *Citizen participation in America.* Toronto: Lexington Books.

Lasswell, H.D. (1951). The policy orientation. In D. Lerner & H.D. Lasswell (Eds.), *The policy sciences: Recent developments in scope and method.* Stanford: Stanford University Press.

References

McInnes, D. (1999). *Taking it to the hill: The complete guide to appearing before (and surviving) parliamentary committees.* Ottawa: University of Ottawa Press.

Meltsner, A. (1976). *Policy analysts in the bureaucracy.* London: University of California Press.

Merriam, C. (1921). The present state of the study of politics. *American Political Science Review, 15* (May), 173-185.

Milbrath, L.W. (1965). *Political participation: How and why do people get involved in politics.* Chicago: Rand McNally.

Mitchell, J.R., & Sutherland, S.L. (1997). Relations between politicians and public servants. In M. Charih & A. Daniels (Eds.), *New public management and public administration in Canada* (pp. 181-197). Toronto: The Institute of Public Administration in Canada.

Ontario Liberal Party. (1993). *A guide to policy development process.* Unpublished document.

Ontario New Democrats. (2000). *2000 Resolution book.*

Pal, L. (1987). *Public policy analysis: An introduction.* Toronto: Methuen.

Prince, M. (1979). Policy advisory groups in government departments. In G.B. Doern & P. Aucoin (Eds.), *Public policy in Canada: Organization, process and management* (pp. 275-300). Toronto: Macmillan.

Robertson, G. (1983). The deputy's anonymous duty. *Policy Options, 4* (July), 11-13.

Rosener, J.R. (1978). Matching methods to purpose: The challenges of planning citizen participation activities. In S. Langton (Ed.), *Citizens' participation in America* (pp. 109-112). Lexington: Lexington Books.

Sarpkaya, S. (1988). *Lobbying in Canada—Ways and means.* Don Mills: CCH Canadian.

Schram, S. (1993). Postmodern policy analysis: Discourse and identity in welfare politics. *Policy Sciences, 26* (3), 249-270.

Sutherland, S. (1993). The public service and policy development. In M.M. Atkinson (Ed.), *Governing Canada.* Toronto: Harcourt Brace.

Toonen, T.A.J. (1985). Implementation research and institutional design: The quest for structure. In K. Hanf & T.A.J. Toonen (Eds.), *Policy implementation in federal and unitary systems* (pp. 335-354). Dordrecht: Marinus Nijhoff.

Verba, S., Nie, N., & Kim, J. (1971). *The modes of democratic participation: A cross-national comparison.* Beverly Hills: Sage.

Wharf, B., & McKenzie, B. (1998). *Connecting policy to practice in the human services.* Don Mills, ON: Oxford University Press.

White, G. (1989). *The Ontario legislature: A political analysis.* Toronto: University of Toronto Press.

White, G. (1997). The legislature: Central symbol of Ontario democracy. In G. White (Ed.), *The government and politics of Ontario* (5th ed.) (pp. 71-92). Toronto: University of Toronto Press.

Whittington, M., & Williams, G. (2000). *Canadian Politics in the 21st Century.* Toronto: Nelson.

Young, R. (1991). Effecting change: Do we have the political system to get us where we want to go? In B. Doern & B. Purchase (Eds.), *Canada at risk? Canadian public policy in the 1990s* (pp. 59-81). Toronto: C.D. Howe Institute.

Malcolm Saulis

> Indian cultures have ways of thought, learning, teaching, and communi-
> cating that are different than but of equal validity to those of White cul-
> tures. These throughways stand at the beginning of Indian time and are
> the foundations of our children's lives. Their full flower is in what it means
> to be one of the people. (Hampton, cited in *Battiste & Barman*, 1995, p. 78)

The autonomous social welfare history of Aboriginal peoples in this country is very recent. By "autonomous," I mean that Aboriginal communities are involved in the management and provision of social welfare programs such as welfare payments (1960s), child welfare programs and agencies (1970s), addictions treatment and programs (1970s), community-based health programs and centres (1980s), and early childhood education programs and services (1990s). However, these programs and services are not autonomous in the following aspects:

- the design of these programs;
- the setting of standards or modes of delivery of these programs;
- the permanency of these programs, which largely remain funded year to year in a project context, with no funding agreements designating them as permanent institutional elements of the community; and
- the policies governing the programs, agencies, or services.

With regard to operational policies, the federal funders' views of Aboriginal programming, especially in the social program arena, mirror the provincial government standard, except where caseloads are concerned. There is no clear standard for caseloads specific to Aboriginal programs. In provinces other than Ontario, which has an agreement with the federal government for social programs for First Nations, caseload standards are not applied. Furthermore, program policies are outside the purview of decision making and, for the most part, are outside the purview of influence with regard to culture or contextualization of programs.

Even though Aboriginal communities have evolved in their comprehension and capacity to deliver and implement social welfare programs, they

Program
and policy
development
from a
holistic
Aboriginal
perspective
have not been provided with autonomy to do programming in a way that fully takes into account the culture of their people. In most cases where Aboriginal communities have taken a great deal of time to conceptualize more *culturally appropriate* models of program or policy delivery, the bureaucrats they work with in various government departments have not engaged in such rigorous conceptual thinking. Rather, governance issues preoccupy the discussions between Aboriginal groups and governments. In discussions of the approach to programs, practice modalities, program standards, protocol agreements, and prevention versus intervention as a strategy, the bureaucrats seem to think that there is an effective means of addressing such issues in society already. So why change when dealing with Aboriginal populations? However, Aboriginal communities would like to implement in their own way the programs that flow from the policies established by Aboriginal leaders. This would include program development (standards, protocols, and case management; program staffing and training; accountability and spending priorities). Most policy directions articulated by governments hint at the possibility of meeting the cultural needs of Aboriginal populations, but in practice, the bureaucratic mindset prevails. This has been a frustrating experience for Aboriginal peoples.

Traditions and cultures are inherited elements of social groups. They come to us from our ancestors with the requirement that we work to protect the essential elements of the culture so that it has a sense of permanence. The essential elements are these:

- the nature of relationships among the people;
- the ceremonies;
- the dances, songs, drums, and gatherings; and
- the medicines, which are both physical and spiritual.

As humans, we share the responsibility to nurture our culture, and we all have cultures to draw upon, if one goes back far enough in time. My sense is that prior to the Industrial Revolution, the essential natures of all people connected to a greater reality was strong.

It is important that the traditional cultures of Aboriginal peoples be expressed in the social welfare programs that we evolve for ourselves. The government of the present era has acknowledged this principle of Aboriginal programming. Examples are evident in programs such as those emerging in health transfer, child welfare, restorative justice and correctional initiatives, and in community-based education movements. Each of these examples represent movements in the right direction, although each is at a different stage of indigenization.

What has been difficult is undoing the institutional mindset of the "keepers of the Western tradition," who find it hard to grasp the scope of the change required in Aboriginal social welfare programming to make this happen. Aboriginal groups are indicating that they want to fully express their holistic world view in these programs. These programs need to have policies, standards, and modes of practice that truly reflect the reality of Aboriginal social welfare programming. This chapter will attempt to conceptualize an Aboriginal approach to program and policy development and describe how it would work.

This chapter is about understanding. It is about reframing an existing understanding within the Canadian mindset about Aboriginal peoples and the nature of social policy development regarding these Canadian citizens. Canadian Aboriginal peoples reside in Canada as a home territory. They do not reside here as an immigrant population, and therefore their relationship to this territory is rooted in a historical relationship, a cultural relationship, and an intimate relationship. They have, however, been the recipients of a foreign policy put into place hundreds of years ago, a policy that has not essentially changed.

An important concept for this chapter is the type of relationship that needs to emerge between Aboriginal peoples and the newcomers and to enable meaningful policy and program development. I would characterize this relationship as a *dialectic relationship*. One would expect that such a relationship would have already developed between them after so many generations, but this is not the case. In social work theory, we read about the importance of establishing a dialectic relationship with the people with whom we work. This relationship is characterized as follows:

1. It is egalitarian; the helper and the helped are equal in their *worth*, in their *importance* to the relationship.
2. It permits a range of views that are not *judged* by either member of the relationship, but which add to the *knowledge* of each person in better understanding where the other person *comes from* and what his/her experience has been.
3. It is based on the *trust* required to achieve the outcome. It has to be seen at many *levels* and experienced over a period of *time*. That is, it is not transitory. The statements "I mean what I say" or "I walk my talk" need to be real.
4. It operates not only on a linear or logical level but also allows and encourages the exploration of intuition, feeling, and values.

In the past, I would have concluded that it is in the hands of the newcomers to enable the development of this dialectic relationship, yet Freire takes a different view. He challenges the oppressed to be proactive on the matter:

> This then, is the great humanistic and historical task of the oppressed: to liberate themselves and their oppressors as well. The oppressors, who oppress, exploit, and rape by virtue of their power, cannot find in this power the strength to liberate either the oppressed or themselves. Only power that springs from the weakness of the oppressed will be sufficiently strong to free both. (Freire, 1970, p. 28)

Program and policy development from a holistic Aboriginal perspective

Program
and policy
development
from a
holistic
Aboriginal
perspective

I used to get very angry when I read this statement because it makes it the responsibility of the oppressed to find enough love and kindness to liberate themselves and others. But as with an Elder's teaching, the truth behind the thought cannot be escaped. I therefore strove to find the means of securing knowledge to underpin the action I needed to facilitate the journey to mutual freedom. This freedom would provide the basis to a good life for all concerned.

I will therefore provide insight into the knowledge base of the Aboriginal world view to help us all create a social policy process that supports a healthy dialectic relationship and a discourse that sustains the process. As a Malecite Indian (I use this term deliberately) who grew up on the Tobique Indian reserve in New Brunswick, and who worked in the social service field for ten years of direct practice in setting up reserve-based agencies in the late 1970s, I have been on the front line of the development of Aboriginal services. I have influenced policy development for community-based agencies and researched Aboriginal processes and systems that are responsive to community needs. I have taught social work for over twenty years to both Aboriginal and non-Aboriginal students in a mainstream school of social work. I have come to realize that we all need to work together, all people of all races, because we all share the responsibility of keeping The Circle strong. I cherish the moment an Elder took time to teach me this knowledge and to find a place for it in my own outlook in life. Bellefeuille supports this outcome when he and his colleagues look at child welfare evolution among First Nations: "Shared vision involves developing a shared vision of the future with guiding principles and practices to realize that vision. A shared vision is one that involves the skills of unearthing shared pictures of the future that foster commitment versus compliance" (Bellefeuille, Garrioch, & Ricks, 1997, p. 24).

Paradigm shift may be an appropriate way to describe the work that has to be done in order to achieve the dialectic result. This view is expressed in the report of the Special Parliamentary Committee on Indian Self-Government:

> The committee is strongly convinced that a major change in the orientation of federal policy must occur. There is little benefit to be gained by tinkering with the Indian Act or by adjusting the present policy of devolution (transfer of funds and authority to First Nations communities by means of funding arrangements that are not rooted in legal standing or policy authority). (Ponting 1986, p. 339)

Native writers agree that there needs to be a paradigm shift. In an Awasis Agency publication, *Mee-noo-stah-tan Mi-ni-si-win*, the point is made by Senge:

> Paradigms are the broader mental sets or world views which influence the kinds of models we develop and/or adopt. Paradigms are pictures of reality, or particular ways of constructing social realities which are shaped by our own needs and assumptions. And Thomas Kuhn...suggested that

paradigm shifts occur over time, as more and more dysfunction develops with a certain model or paradigm. Attempts to rescue the paradigm through reforms and adjustments eventually break down as the dysfunction becomes too great. (Awasis Agency of Northern Manitoba, 1997, p. 7)

Mainstream
social policy
and social
welfare
programming

It has been my experience that Canada has become aware that things have not worked for Aboriginal populations when it comes to health policies, justice policies, governance policies, social welfare and educational policies. The dysfunction of applying a mainstream paradigm of "social well-being" and its resulting programming to Aboriginal populations has become more and more evident. The oppressive nature of the existing relationship does not lead to functioning Aboriginal populations. It has not resulted in a dialectic relationship that enriches both parties.

Governments of all political parties have not been able to achieve their policy goals regarding Aboriginal populations. The implication of the constitutional entrenchment of Aboriginal rights and the creation of equal citizenship for Aboriginal peoples was that there would be an acknowledgment of the totality of Aboriginal reality. This means that there could be an expression of the Aboriginal world view within the confines of their own community. It also means that the attendant elements of the Aboriginal world view—including governance, cultural and traditional practices, and social organization—could be expressed.

However, a major obstacle in implementing the new paradigm has been the scarcity of resources. The entrenchment of Aboriginal rights in Section 35 of the Canadian constitution actually limits the resources available to all Aboriginal populations. Now fiscal allocations have to be distributed among all Aboriginal populations, and not just among the Status Indians, as indicated by the Indian Act. All governments of all parties now need to operationalize their strategies toward all Aboriginal populations within this Act. The groups entitled to be recognized under the rubric "Aboriginal" now include the following: Status Indians, as defined by the Indian Act; Métis populations, as defined in relationship to definitions worked out with provincial and federal governments; Inuit populations, which in the past were cared for exclusively by territorial governments; and Non-status Indians, who for reasons of marriage or enfranchisement can now reassert their Aboriginal entitlement. Thus, the available pool of resources, which was originally intended to be spent only on Status Indians living on reserves, must now be extended to cover entitlements to Indians off-reserve as well as other Aboriginal populations. Limiting such entitlements is becoming a full-time operation for governments, especially in this era of burgeoning Aboriginal populations.

Mainstream Social Policy and Social Welfare Programming

Every citizen of Canada is a social welfare recipient. Each one of us is a direct beneficiary of one or more provincial or federal programs that are part of the complex structures of Canadian social services.

In the Canadian constitution, the federal government has exclusive responsibility for social welfare matters dealing with Indians and their land and inherent rights; naturalization (immigration); criminal law; establishment, maintenance, and management of penitentiaries. The provinces have primary jurisdiction of social welfare issues that are not included in this specific list of federal powers.

Social policy can be defined as "action or inaction taken by public authorities to address problems which deal with human health, safety or well-being" (Westhues, 1999). Three major groups are crucially involved in determining the outcomes of a policy process: politicians, bureaucrats, and pressure groups. The influence of each of these groups differs at various times, depending on the composition of each group and on the information and insights available to those studying the process (Wharf & McKenzie, 1998). The Cabinet is the core institution for determining priorities, however. This means that while no one part of the political system has a monopoly over the determination of priorities where new policies are concerned, the Cabinet is by far the most important institution involved (Van Loon & Whittington, 1987, p. 337).

I would like to demonstrate the distinctions in the social policy process between the Aboriginal process and the mainstream process. It is important to underscore that social policy decision making in the Aboriginal process is rooted in the perceptions of the people of the communities, and that they play an active role in interpreting, priority setting, and evaluating the directions of policy. It is not a process isolated from people and located in the bureaucracy, as we see in the mainstream process.

Table 15.1 illustrates the potentially differing perspectives of Aboriginal peoples and mainstream contexts regarding the social welfare policy process. I have drawn on the thinking of George and Wilding (1985) and Douglass and Friedmann (1998) in making this analysis.

As one can see, the fundamental differences between the Aboriginal and mainstream approaches rest in the motivations for both the policy process and in the planning that flows from the policy process. The people within the context are differentially considered by the two processes, with a consequent loss of citizenship and democracy in the mainstream process. The two systems are fundamentally at odds with each other. However, that does not necessarily mean that the two processes are so different that they do not make sense to each other or that the fundamental differences make it impossible to communicate with each other. The two-row wampum example given in this text alerts us that work needs to be done to make the fundamental differences actionable to achieve good results.

Table 15.1 Aboriginal and Mainstream Policy-Making Processes Compared	
Aboriginal Social Policy and Social Welfare Planning	**Mainstream Social Policy and Social Welfare Planning**
1. Ideology/World View	**1. Ideology/World View**
• Collectivist (collective responsibility for well-being of all); leadership is for service to the people	• Individualistic (individual and family are primarily responsible for their own well-being, with help for the "deserving"); leadership represents the interests of elites
• All people are equal	• Inequality acceptable
• Freedom—being able to count on collective support and solidarity	• Freedom—limited government intervention
2. Justice and Humanism	**2. Justice and Humanism**
• Justice rests in the well-being of the collective and is contained within the consciousness of the collective; it is a relationship	• Justice rests in the responsibilities of a system of justice; it is about the harm done to the state, not the harm done to the relationship with other people
• The circle of humanity includes all people of the community, and the weakest need to be supported for the benefit of all	• All humans are as equal as is possible within a system of institutions and services, and within the confines of an economy
3. Theory of Planning/Policy-making	**3. Theory of Planning/Policy-making**
• Inclusive, not expert driven; concerned with the equity of policies for all people, and people have a voice in what is good for them	• Rational and comprehensive and takes into account the views of experts in the field; may reflect the views of a representative sample of the people affected by the policy/program
• "Circular," not linear; multidimensional and holistic, interrelated and inclusive	• Positivist and linear; not as sensitive to interconnection with a broad range of policy systems
• Intuitive as well as meaningful to the people who are concerned or affected by the outcome of the process, based on their own experience	• Logical, non-intuitive, legislated; not based on experience of people affected by the outcome of the process
• Strength based	• Deficit/medical model

Social Policy Process

The important observation in social policy is that the mainstream approach is a closed system of relationships between the key power holders of the political party system, their set of interests, the need to develop initiatives that enhance the chances of being re-elected, and those that a majority of voters can support through popular opinion. The players in this process need to be able to trust each other, and to solicit the best views and opinions of outsiders who can be trusted. The element of trust within the system makes it operate so that the following takes place:

1. The perceptions of mainstream Canadians are reflected in the proposed legislation, making it acceptable to them to spend tax money on these policy initiatives.
2. It fits the agenda of the ruling party.
3. The information generated is vetted by people who are trusted or at least trustworthy, and the views of these people will not generate too much opposition from unknown sources.
4. The measures proposed would pass through Cabinet.

The parties involved in policy development and the progressively higher levels of the administrative process need to be able to trust each other. Therefore, they examine each other with regard to their sympatico of identity; that is, they seem pretty much like each other. The higher the level of authority and influence, the more like each other they become. This is not necessarily a negative thing, but a reality that those of us who want to influence such people and processes need to know. This reality is one of the difficult elements in introducing what seem like radically different processes, such as those rooted in a holistic Aboriginal world view. It is difficult to affect people in positions of power because "getting to them" is a very difficult process of proving that such perspectives and processes make sense or are workable. Yet I suggest that the perspective influencing the Canadian policy view, such as that contained in the "population health" perspective, provides us with hope. This population health perspective includes the socio-economic health of Canadians, which allows us to look at factors such as poverty in health outcomes.

The governing party that holds power via elections needs to be able to determine that its elective goal is supported by the policies set and the antecedent processes of program design and implementation. The influence of marginalized people with radically different world views is severely minimized in this scenario. It is therefore the job of marginalized people to make themselves understood and to make room for their paradigms in this policy scenario. It would be naive to think otherwise. It is the task of this chapter to enable that understanding. I have observed that Canada has made room in recent years for such an undertaking. The notions of "restorative," "healing," or "holistic" paradigms have gained acceptance. There has also been an effort not only to root these notions in the experience and knowledge of the mainstream, but also to apply them to settings other than the medical/health settings. I have seen departments of Justice, Health, Correctional Services, Indian Affairs, and Social Services grasp the notion in a logical and linear way. It is now important to set them in a holistic way into the change processes of Aboriginal Peoples.

This mainstream paradigm of social policy development and the nature of institutional reality with regard to society are expressed in the following diagram, which I constructed as a useful tool for myself. This diagram illustrates the independent nature of the institutions, and shows that government operates as an institution unto itself. It may have a directive function with regard to the other institutions, but the accountability of the other institutions to government is not evident. The autonomy of the institutional structures is an important element of their existence, since they need to have autonomy to fulfill the tasks expected of them without undue interference from other agencies.

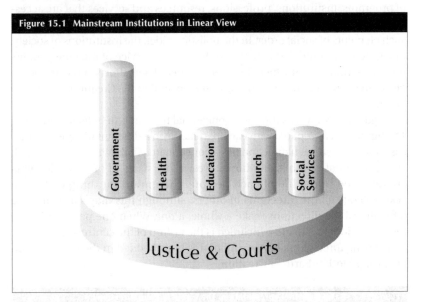

Figure 15.1 Mainstream Institutions in Linear View

This figure demonstrates the individualistic nature of the institutions of society. They exist for their own sake; that is, their primary goal becomes that of ensuring their existence rather than fulfilling the mission for which they were created. They compete with each other for funding, influence, importance, position, but not for service to their clientele. In fact, clientele must configure themselves to the culture of the institution.

An interesting dimension of this diagram is the place and responsibility of the institution of justice. Its place as the foundation or fabric upon which society is built, reminding society of its civilized nature, is more an illustration than a reality. The justice institution should be a reminder to society of its responsibility to its citizens. The outcomes of the dialectic relationship would inform the notion of a civil society as construed within the definition of civil law.

Aboriginal Social Welfare Understandings

Social welfare can be defined, within a capitalist paradigm and with a liberal perspective, as a complex network of legislation, policies, programs, institutions, professions, resources, and services that ensures for individuals access to a range of goods and services necessary to achieve their full potential in a manner acceptable to them and with due regard to the rights of others.

Aboriginal
social
welfare
under-
standings

Aboriginal populations with a holistic world view would add to this definition in the following manner: Ensuring the well-being of all people is the inherent responsibility of all people for one another, without consideration of class, gender, ability, sexual preference, or cultural orientation. In simple fact, we are all one in Creation. We fulfill our responsibility through the provision of programs, institutions, professions, resources and services that are accessible and responsive to the needs of people—not to the political viability of such elements of social order. In the holistic model, the institutions of society, in Figure 15.1, would dedicate themselves to the service of meeting people's needs, the purpose for which they were created. Their efforts and work would be an investment in the well-being of society and in the Creation that we are all a part of.

Figure 15.2 shows us the basic conceptual teachings of holistic traditions. The figure is in four parts, with each part facing in a different direction: north, east, south, west. Each direction has a concept attached to it; north is mental, east is spiritual, south is emotional, west is physical. All of these elements are reflected in the life of each person. The important thing is that we acknowledge all the directions in others, although this may sometimes be difficult. All the directions make a whole, a *one*. When one part is missing, there is no longer a totality. Included is the notion of the centre as the source and driving force of the system. All of this is embedded in the notion of the nurturing Mother Earth or Creation.

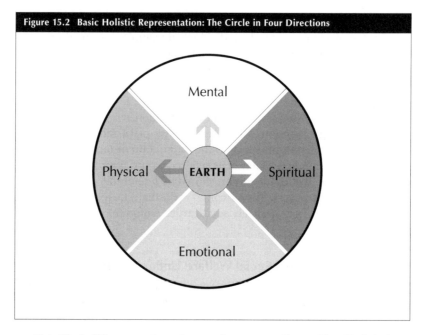

Figure 15.2 Basic Holistic Representation: The Circle in Four Directions

This Circle (Figure 15.2) teaches us that we are all one. The Circle is fragile because whatever happens affects all the other components of the *whole.*

No one is unaffected by the plight and experience of others. The centre contains our human spirit, which is the spark of the Creator from which we get our nature as people. We are provided with insight, anticipation, and understanding. Our job throughout our lives is to nurture this insight and to make the spark glow. The bond among us as elements of Creation (the whole) is our relationships and the behaviours that emerge from these relationships. The directions are all equal; no one direction is more prominent or important than another.

The notion of deserving or undeserving does not exist in this holistic scenario, as all that is provided to humans by Creation—whether it be wealth or space or time—is for the benefit of all people. The exploitation of any people by another group of people hurts everyone. Creation and reality are made up of both tangible (empirical) and non-tangible (spiritual, for lack of a better word) aspects. Our viability as humans depends on preserving both the tangible and the non-tangible. It is through the spirit in which we carry out our work to meet the social welfare needs of others that the world remains viable and valuable. If we do not carry out our work in a good spirit, the spirit and viability of those we affect is diminished.

Aboriginal social welfare understandings

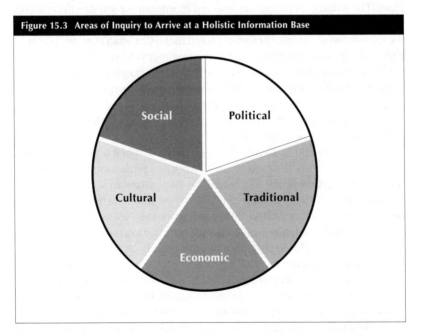

Figure 15.3 Areas of Inquiry to Arrive at a Holistic Information Base

Social

Political

Cultural

Traditional

Economic

Figure 15.3 provides us with a useful holistic way of analyzing the consequences of our behaviour. It also provides us with an analytical tool with which to anticipate the outcomes of behaviours before we engage in them. It provides us with a way of understanding and constructing the welfare measures we hope to put into place. At the same time, it demonstrates the ripple effect of a measure applied in one component of the whole affecting the other parts of the whole. For example, if we were to consider the implementation or creation of a child welfare agency for a community, we could not simply engage in determining the organizational and staffing structure, or the fiscal requirements of the agency. The agency must be structured in ways that meet the needs of the community as defined in the holistic world view. We also could not formulate the policies and protocols under which the agency would operate without considering the implications for the social and cultural structures of a given community or context. If we were to place this agency in a perspective of holistic healing, as is required by our culture as Aboriginal peoples, then we must consider how all the elements of the agency enable that process. This would include staffing, budgeting, planning of buildings, activities within the agency, the words and intent of documents created, and the place of traditional practices within the whole development.

Aboriginal teachings remind us that we must be contemplative about our efforts. We must be able to comprehend the impacts of our efforts not just on the tangible reality of humans but also on the non-tangible elements of Creation. A teaching that is powerful in this context is that all elements of Creation are related, and our whole reality is affected by any measures we put in place. The cultures of people are affected by measures rooted in the cultures of other people. For example, First Nations and their cultures are affected by the imposition of spiritual practices rooted in the Christian religion. The Aboriginal traditional practices honour the members of the animal and plant world as relatives, and without these relatives, our viability as humans is not possible. However, this view is judged unacceptable by the Christian traditions, even though there are similar beliefs in some Christian cultures.

In a more tangible case related to social work practice, the use of holistic healing practices could be challenged as not being rooted in the rigour of other empirically and academically based traditional practices of social work as a profession. Thus, their use in social work as a profession could be questioned. Child welfare is one area where this issue arises. In fact, though, most mainstream social work practice is not based on empirical findings at all, but on somebody's theory of how things will work best. What the mainstream social work profession has avoided considering, for the most part, is the spiritual aspect of life. This avoidance may have been in an effort to smooth over divisions among diverse cultural groups that were grounded in religious beliefs, thus creating greater "social order" or "social cohesion." The holistic perspective allows us to acknowledge spirituality once again, as spirituality is a resource that many people draw on in dealing with their troubles.

Child welfare practice is an area heavily influenced by the values, world views, and expectations of a certain class of people in mainstream society. The conclusion of policy makers is that most middle-class Canadians favour a certain kind of child welfare practice. The aim of protecting children from imminent danger means defining imminent danger. This definition includes not just physical harm but harm arising out of a lack of parental control and children being placed in harmful situations. These situations include the conditions arising from poverty, such as unsafe housing, unsanitary conditions, or unfamiliar parenting techniques. The primary consideration of the practice of child welfare is the safety of the child. However, the social worker's perception of safety and harm is determined by the culture in which the worker has been brought up and educated. These standards and norms also determine how the worker perceives the safety of an environment. When the investigative dimension of this practice unfolds, so do the values and world views of the workers and policy makers. Thus the elements of Figure 15.3 that are emphasized are the social and cultural elements, which are within a certain system of values.

The holistic policy process

The element of tradition in child welfare practice is historic practice, and mainstream child welfare practice is rooted in the use of authority and judgment. Here, the immediate and the imminent take precedence over the potential of the future, and the cultural reality of the context is not considered. The practitioner as an individual with his or her own set of cultural assumptions has decision-making authority and responsibility. In contrast, in a holistic approach, which considers Aboriginal reality and the Circle analysis, the practitioner would partner with people from the context. Decision making would be communal, and the determination of the next step would be consultative and not rooted only in the immediate and the imminent. The values of the community's culture would be respected and preserved, and the whole community would be involved in resolving the problem with the child and the family. Politics, economics, tradition, social relationship, and cultural values would all be preserved.

The Holistic Policy Process

Figure 15.4 allows us to view the relationship of the same institutions represented in Figure 15.1, but within the holistic world view of Aboriginal peoples. It shows an interdependence, an interrelationship, an interconnection, that strengthen society for all people. The institutions are geared to work for a social order's healthy existence. The Aboriginal approach would attempt to be more egalitarian, more of a partnership. This perspective also looks beyond the nuclear family and even beyond the extended family to the community to determine how the child can best be cared for. The Aboriginal model is based on values and cultural practices that could be useful in mainstream contexts as well.

Within this image of institutions people are at the centre. The people are the basis for all institutions and their functions, and have come forth from Creation, which is usually symbolized by the colour green. This Creation is embodied in our Mother Earth. The Earth provides us with all we need to live, and we have a great responsibility to respect all that Mother Earth provides. Through this respectful world view and our respectful behaviour, we

Figure 15.4   First Nations Traditional Directions with Mainstream Institutions in Circle Format

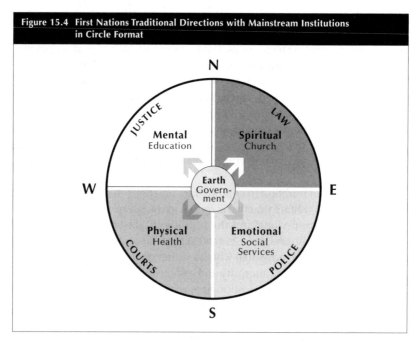

sustain the Earth and it will always sustain us. Without it, we will all perish. If people are the expression and the embodiment of this Creation, then we need to be reflective people, respectful people. We need to prepare ourselves for this responsibility in various ways, but in the end, we need to understand our responsibility.

In preparing ourselves for this responsibility, we must first understand and articulate what respect is and how we might embody it. We must place ourselves in humility so that we will be open to hearing the meaning of the knowledge people give in their stories of life. We need to be reflective in the context of others who are preparing themselves so that a collective consensus will emerge that provides wise insight and mutual understanding. We must engage in ceremony and work at being loving people who are strong enough to leave behind authority and power in favour of being one of, not one above. We need to present our thoughts and considerations to the people of the community and to learn from their insights. We need to adopt a language that allows us to communicate with them and use them in our processes, so that their words have meaning and impact. We must be willing to leave the process and allow others to emerge as leaders with their skills and gifts.

Social welfare and social policy are human processes wherein humans interrelate to achieve an outcome, which is policy statements and actions. We who do this work must therefore be special human beings. We must get ourselves ready and, finally, prove ourselves worthy to be participants in the process, to carry the truth of other humans, and we must be clear thinking and thoughtful as we engage in the process with other humans. It cannot be a process rooted in anger or resentment, or prejudice and racism. It must essentially be a human process.

Conclusion

We must put together all the Circles that we see above: the four directions teaching, the holistic analysis, and the holistic institutional visioning. We must pray for good direction and wisdom. We must ultimately be good leaders.

I have been told that leadership is a lonely journey, and that leaders are recognized by people because of the spirit they carry, a spirit that is seen before their physical presence arrives. They are able to have the Eagle's vision, which sees the interconnections and the interrelationship as if from a great height. They understand responsibility and the nature of the responsibility of their vision. But these are understandings that imply an active and lifelong process to achieve. They are qualities that are not transferable. Leadership is also contextual: different people possess leadership in different ways and in different places. Therefore, ego cannot be a major element of leaders because ego will blind them to the leadership insights of other people.

We need to perceive ourselves as leaders and to behave as leaders for all of our people, regardless of whether we are Aboriginal or not. Social welfare processes are about transformations and reaffirmations of citizens and of a civilized society, as Douglas and Friedmann point out:

> I see ... planners passionately engaged in a transformative politics for inclusion, opportunity for self-development and social justice. It is a politics driven by the energies of a civil society that is beginning to reassert itself in all of its diversity. Its vision is for a social formation where no one is excluded from the rights and duties of full citizenship. (Douglas & Friedmann, 1998, p. 34)

Freire (1970) reminded us that "Only the power that springs from the weakness of the oppressed will be sufficiently strong to free both (the oppressor and the oppressed)." One of my teaching Elders, Dr. Danny Musqua, reminded me that the fundamental purpose of life is for us to fan the spark of the Creator, which resides in all of us at our birth. If we do not fan this spark, it is destined to remain always just a spark. In order to have it burn in our lives, the spark needs constant attention and nurturing.

By engaging in the creation of social policy processes and outcomes for the benefit of all people, we are fanning the spark. We also learn that the essential purpose of life is not how great we can make ourselves individually but how great we can be in the context of all other people. We need to help create great human beings.

References

Awasis Agency of Northern Manitoba. (1997). *First Nations family justice: Mee-noo-stah-tan Mi-ni-si-win.* Victoria: Morriss Printing.

Bellefeuille, G., Garrioch, S., & Ricks, F. (1997). *Breaking the rules: Transforming governance in social services.* Victoria: Morriss Printing.

Freire, P. (1970). *Pedagogy of the oppressed.* New York: Seabury Press.

Douglass, M., & Friedmann, J. (1998). *Cities for citizens.* Toronto: John Wiley.

George, V., & Wilding, P. (1985). *Ideology and social welfare.* London: Routledge & Kegan Paul.

Ponting, R.J. (1986). *Arduous journey: Canadian Indians and decolonization.* Toronto: McClelland and Stewart.

Van Loon, R.J., & Whittington, M.S. (1987). *The Canadian political system.* Toronto: McGraw Hill.

Westhues, A. (1999). Social policy practice. In F. Turner (Ed.), *Social work practice: A Canadian perspective* (pp. 237-251). Scarborough: Prentice Hall Allyn and Bacon.

Wharf, B., & McKenzie, B. (1998). *Connecting policy to practice in the human services.* Toronto: Oxford University Press.

Additional Resources

Battiste, M., & Barman, J. (1995). *First Nations education in Canada: The Circle unfolds.* Vancouver: University of British Columbia Press.

Denis, C. (1997). *We are not you. First Nations and Canadian modernity.* Peterborough, ON: Broadview Press.

Joan Wharf Higgins, John Cossom, and Brian Wharf

T he objectives of this chapter are to address who participates in the development and implementation of social policy and to consider whether the extent of participation that presently prevails is sufficient. We use the terms "address" and "consider" rather than "answer" since, as will become abundantly clear as the discussion proceeds, the resolution of these issues depends to a large extent on the values and perspectives of those addressing them.

The chapter is organized in the following fashion. First, we provide a brief outline of our values, our interpretation of social policy, and of the levels or domains of social policy. Second, we review the various understandings of who participates in policy development, ranging from human service agencies to the federal government and to the international scene. In the chapter's concluding section we consider the extent of participation and indicate our dissatisfaction with the current state of affairs.

Values and Social Policy

Values are initially shaped by childhood experiences and more closely defined in adulthood. Our values have been sharply influenced by our experiences as practitioners and academics in the human services. We share a political view that espouses and cherishes social democracy. Such a philosophy holds that the state has an obligation to act for the well-being of its citizens. In turn, citizens have a responsibility to be actively involved in and contribute to the affairs of the state. This reciprocal, beneficial arrangement exists only as long as both the state and individuals make and are able to sustain a commitment to their respective responsibilities. As we note in the section on who participates, the state's commitment has waned in recent years with the consequence that many citizens see themselves as second-class members of an uncaring nation.

What Is Social Policy?

In chapter 1 Westhues notes that "there has been a long-standing debate within the literature as to what is meant by the term "social policy." The cen-

**What is
social policy?** tral issue that frames this discussion is how inclusive is the reach of social
policy" (p. 6). Some appreciation of the extent and complexity of the debate
can be gained from the discussion in a recent text where the attempts of eight
scholars to define the term are presented (Graham, Swift, & Delaney, 2000).
Westhues opts for a straightforward yet inclusive definition and claims that
social policy represents "action or inaction taken by public authorities to
address problems which deal with human health, safety, or well-being" (p. 8).

While appealing in brevity and elegance, short definitions inevitably
preclude full consideration of the issue at hand. One important aspect of
social policy is that of choice. Policies represent a decision to select one set
of approaches from among a number available. And the choice depends in
large measure on the values and the ideologies of those in policy positions.
Policy-making is "inevitably guided by a general conception of the role of the
state" (Banting, 1987, p. 147). A second important aspect of policy is the difficulty encountered in making choices. We have always been impressed by the
discussion on social problems by Rittel and Webber, captured by the following quotation:

> As distinguished from problems in the natural sciences which are definable
> and separable and may have solutions that are findable, the problems of
> government planning and especially those of social or policy planning, are
> ill defined and they rely on elusive political judgment for resolution. Not
> "solution." Social problems are never solved. At best they are only resolved
> over and over again. (Rittel & Webber, 1973, p. 180)

One only has to think of health care and how best to provide health services, of poverty and the various measures that have been proposed to eliminate or reduce this enduring social issue, and what to do about the puzzling
dilemma of child neglect and abuse, to gain an appreciation of the slipperi-
ness and complexity of social issues and the fragility of policies to resolve
them.

Hence we suggest an addition to the definition proposed by Westhues.

> Social policy is a course of action or inaction chosen by public authorities
> to address problems that deal with human health, safety, or well-being.
> This course of action represents the choices made by policy makers, which
> are largely determined by their values and ideologies.

Even this addition leaves out important matters such as the availability of
resources, timing, and the influence brought to bear on policy makers by
interest groups.

The Domains of Policy

Westhues identifies five levels or domains of policy: the agency; the municipal, provincial, and federal governments; and the international scene. However, for the purposes of brevity, we have limited our discussion to the

domains identified by Lindblom (1979) as the grand and ordinary issues of social policy. Lindblom describes grand issues as "pertaining to the fundamental structure of politico-economic life. They include the distribution of income and wealth and the distribution of political power and corporate prerogatives" (Lindblom, 1979, p. 523). We view health care and income security as of sufficient importance to qualify as grand issues. Until recently, and with the important exception of long-standing international organizations like the World Bank, national governments assumed responsibility for the grand issues. However, the locus of power for grand issues has shifted dramatically with the emergence of globalization and institutions like the World Trade Organization. Increasingly transnational corporations seek to establish policies that allow them to move capital and workplaces without interference by national governments.

What do we mean by citizens and citizen participation?

Ordinary issues are described by others (Graham, Swift, & Delaney, 2000) as the domain of social welfare policy and include the personal social services like child welfare, daycare, and recreation. These are dealt with mostly by provincial and municipal governments in Canada, and the precise division of responsibility varies from province to province. In addition, some provinces rely heavily on quasi-public agencies such as Children's Aid Societies and regional health organizations to actually provide services. Obviously the two levels are closely connected, and policies established at the grand level have a decided impact on ordinary issues.

What Do We Mean by Citizens and Citizen Participation?

As concepts, citizenship and citizen participation elude precision and consensus. Citizenship not only concerns membership, but also the rights and obligations that citizens should possess. Citizenship is an idea both of being and of doing (Prior, Stewart, & Walsh, 1995). The notion of "citizen" that emerged from Marshall's *Class, Citizenship and Social Development* (1977) implied equality of status and respect as a member of society and being accorded the same rights as every other citizen. Although Marshall's work represents the beginning of recent attention to citizenship, his view assumes that all citizens are the same, stripped of any group identification or differences. "Equal citizenship is extended to people despite all their differences of birth, education, occupation, gender or race. It is a slippery slope from saying that these differences should not count, to saying that they don't even matter" (Phillips, 1993, p. 77).

Citizenship has both formal and substantive effects (Prior, Stewart, & Walsh, 1995). The distinction is between the status that provides people with the possession of formal rights and entitlements (the civil, political, and social rights as conceptualized by Marshall), and the status that enables them to have the opportunity to realize those rights and entitlements. All citizens formally possess civil, political, and social rights, but not all possess the means of realizing—and hence enjoying—the substantive benefits of citizenship.

There are certainly no simple answers about what is meant by democratic participation. Canada is a democracy, but what kind of democracy? What are the expectations and opportunities for non-elected people to share in the decisions that affect them? Political philosophers have found the issues of citizen roles in the government of a democratic state and its institutions vexing ones. Indeed, the disagreements that exist today in Canada reflect the same conflicts between political philosophies that have been around for centuries.

Citizenship can be viewed on a continuum from representative to participatory democracy (Hemingway, 1999). Representative democracy, or passive citizenship, rests on the assumption that citizens themselves are not able (or perhaps willing) to become involved in the policy arena, and select representatives to look after their interests. Citizen involvement is limited to a passive role of responding to the political choices and delegating representation on issues to elected officials. The rights of citizens are emphasized at this end of the continuum, where entitlements overshadow obligations (Drover, 2000).

At the other end of the continuum, participatory democracy or active citizenship assumes that citizens can and do want to participate in the discussion and decision making concerning social policy. Their active engagement in ongoing dialogue with fellow citizens enhances their knowledge of social issues and capacity to participate. More recently, Drover (2000) and Kingwell (2000) suggest that in a global era, citizenship must take an active form, include an ethic of care, transcend national boundaries, and embrace diversity.

The Principle of Affected Interests

One ambitious attempt to answer the question "Rule by what people?" has been made by Robert Dahl (1970, p. 64), who begins with the Principle of Affected Interests: "Everyone who is affected by the decisions of a government should have a right to participate in that government." He concedes that this proposition raises many thorny issues, but concludes that it is nevertheless worth pursuit. One of the problems is that different sets of people are affected by different decisions, and "the logic of the Principle of Affected Interests is that for every different set of persons affected there will be a different association or decision making unit" (Dahl, 1970, p. 64). Dahl identifies three important criteria that can be used to unravel the complications of affected interests: personal choice, competence, and economy.

Personal choice is a criterion that assesses the degree to which the decision fits one's own preference. Since it is unlikely that people will agree, the "decisions must be made in such a way as to give equal weight to the personal choices of everyone" (Dahl, 1970, p. 12). In democratic systems this is usually resolved by majority decision making that grants individuals political equality. Of course, this criterion, by itself, leaves democratic organizations facing complicated issues, since majority rule cannot satisfy everyone's personal choice. For example, how are the special needs of minorities protected? Too often democracy has assumed a system of commonly held values and perspectives. Yet, a society like Canada is marked by sharp differences in culture, language, religion, and values. A moral consensus has become increasingly elusive and personal choice takes on greater significance in a society like ours.

The criterion of *competence* suggests that some decisions can be accepted because they are made by people who are particularly qualified by knowledge or skill to make them. We rely on a pilot to fly the plane. Passengers do not file a flight plan by majority decision! Most of us accept higher competence as a criterion for decision making in many areas that affect us. Some situations require a choice between personal choice and competence resulting in decisions based on a combination of these two factors.

The criterion of *economy* raises the issues that have headlined the last decade—efficiency, rationality, and the preservation of scarce resources. Organizations cannot avoid addressing these variables, because time, money, and effort are certainly not unlimited when it comes to citizen input. Individuals also address the costs and benefits of participation. How much satisfaction do they get from it? How significant are the decisions they make? Will their participation make a difference? Another important economic factor is that the costs of participation in decision making are higher for some groups and individuals than others (Warren & Weschler, 1975). For the poor the costs of citizenship may be very high.

Each of these three criteria is important and valid. But they cannot be translated into a simple equation to produce ideal types of participation. Every situation has to be weighed on the basis of its individual needs and merits. While majority rule may be preferred in one organization, reflecting an emphasis on personal choice, competency, and economy may be much more significant in another. We return to these criteria later in the chapter.

Assumptions and Impacts of Citizen Participation

Citizen participation relies on three assumptions. Citizens have the right to and want to participate; citizen participation leads to better decision making; and citizen participation is a good in and for itself. These assumptions argue that policy making is best done by those who will be the recipients of, or will be affected by, the resulting programs or services (Bregha, 1973). In addition, participation is thought to benefit the individual participant, the voluntary organization, and community by:

- empowering participants on an individual basis by increasing knowledge and skill levels, their feelings of greater control and competence to make a difference, and their sense of self-worth and dignity (Berry, Kent, & Thompson, 1993; Chrislip, 1995; Schulz, Israel, Zimmerman, & Checkoway, 1995);
- nurturing local planning skills and abilities (Arai & Pedlar, 1997);

Assumptions and impacts of citizen participation

- engendering a greater awareness of health and social issues among citizens (Tewdwrjones & Thomas, 1998);
- building community capacity to tackle future social policy issues (Smith, Baugh Littlejohns, & Thompson, 2001); and
- fostering the overall health of the community by strengthening citizens' trust in each other and their connectedness to the community (Putnam, 2000).

In Canada there is little opportunity for citizens to participate directly in the policy-making process, and there has been limited use of referenda, despite repeated calls by the Canadian Alliance Party to install referenda as an integral part of the policy-making process. At first glance, referenda appear to be an attractive method of including people. However, complex matters are best addressed after much thought and discussion. At the present time, the opportunity to engage in reflections and discussions is limited mostly to politicians and senior civil servants. An excellent example of inappropriate use of referenda is the recent case in BC where a set of poorly framed questions sought to elicit the opinions of BC residents on the issues of Aboriginal rights to land.

Participation in the Ordinary Issues of Social Policy

Ordinary issues appear to present more opportunities for citizens to participate because such issues immediately affect and are more relevant to people at the local level. Thus, while citizenship is often defined in terms of nationalistic and geographic terms and ties, its practice is most often played out in the contexts in which citizens live out their day-to-day existence (Kingwell, 2000). As Putnam (2000) points out, volunteering and participating in the life of the community are part of good citizenship, not an alternative to it. Specifically, Pateman (1970) makes the point that institutions such as education, health and social agencies, trade unions, churches, workplaces, and political parties are appropriate for citizen involvement. It is in these contexts that most citizens with an inclination toward involvement cut their participatory teeth. The voluntary social agency board or the recreation commission is a good training ground that can educate citizens and prepare them to participate in larger and more complex concerns of social policy. Many important decisions affecting the lives of citizens are made outside the representative political system. The Healthy Communities/Cities projects are examples of citizens actively engaging at the local level to improve the health and quality of life of their communities (Wharf Higgins, 1992).

Typically, participants are characterized by their advanced education, income, occupation, age (Jewkes & Murcott, 1998; Lomas & Veenstra, 1995), sense of empowerment (Smith, 1995), and involvement in community life (Putnam, 2000), compared to those who do not participate. Citizens who participate enjoy the formal and substantive benefits of citizenship (Wharf Higgins, 1999). The analysis of the National Survey of Volunteering, Giving, and Participating found a similar pattern among the four-fifths of Canadian adults who participate in community-oriented activities classified as "intensive community commitments" (e.g., service club, political, neighbourhood, school, or voluntary organization) (Jones, 2000).

For a number of reasons, professionals like physicians have blocked or narrowed the opportunities for citizens to participate. First, participation is often narrowly defined as asking community members about their health, education, or social welfare needs or opinions on prepackaged programs, and delegating the actual planning, implementation, and evaluation to practitioners. While needs assessments and pretesting programs are crucial components of planning, participation goes beyond responding to surveys or opinion polls.

As O'Neill (1992) has documented with respect to the Quebec experience with health care boards, community participation in health reform does not guarantee community empowerment. This certainly was the case during health reform in BC during the mid-1990s when local groups of citizens were assigned the task of developing community health plans and envisioning the future of health care delivery in their region. During the two years that participants worked to implement "New Directions for a Healthy BC," subtle and seemingly inconspicuous actions by the provincial government began to add up to what participants felt was a conspiracy against their work. In the end, the government dismissed the recommendations of the participants who perceived the government as disavowing two years of their work and with it their committed beliefs.

> It is difficult for ordinary citizens to know in any objective sense who won who lost in most public policy matters. However, their perception of who won and who lost affects their sense of whether government is fair and open to all.... Moreover, such perceptions affect individuals' calculus as to whether or not it is worth their while to become involved. (Berry, Kent, & Thompson, 1993, p. 102).

Thus, as Wharf Higgins (1999) has documented, participants individually emerged from the health reform experience feeling empowered at the personal level, yet collectively their ability to influence the implementation of health reform decisions was negligible. This left them calculating the price of their involvement and questioning their willingness to continue. Similarly, an evaluation of citizen participation in a United Way planning process found that relatively high socio-economic status participants believed their influence had been insignificant in deciding how funds should be allocated to meet local needs (Julian, Reischl, Carrick, & Katrenich, 1997).

Second, engaging participants who reflect the diversity of the community is difficult and rarely successful. It is often assumed that because everyone has the right to participate in the decision-making process, the opportunity to do so is identical for all. However, the participation process itself can discriminate against those in the community who are not well-

Participation in the ordinary issues of social policy

educated, well-spoken, or well off (Freedman, 1998; Wharf Higgins, 1999). While better-educated people tend to participate more, this does not necessarily imply a lower degree of interest among others in the community. The design flaws inherent in traditional participatory structures—committee meetings and public forums—often make them inconvenient, inaccessible, and intimidating to all but a few who possess the requisite professional experience, educational, and discretionary resources to attend (Chrislip, 1995; Henderson, 1990; Syme & Nancarrow, 1992).

For over twenty years, Rosener (1978, p. 114) has argued that participation techniques are often inconsistent with the interests and capabilities of the citizen they are intended to reach: "So while public officials claim apathy, citizens claim inequity." The circumstances that people face living in disadvantaged environments pose barriers to attending meetings or committing oneself to participating in the first place (Hunt, 1990). Innovative participatory opportunities, such as citizen panels (Kathlene & Martin, 1991), visual and practical planning experiences in malls (Anderson, Meaton, & Potter, 1994), and in neighbourhood associations and churches (Crawshaw, 1994; Wandersman, Florin, Friedmann, & Meier, 1987) have been much more successful in bringing together diverse members of the community.

The power hierarchy that often exists between professionals and citizens, particularly in health and social arenas, has also hindered diverse participation (Church & Barker, 1998). Professionals are often perceived as the more knowledgeable and expert decision makers (Scanlan, Zyzanski, Flocke, Stange, & Gravagubins, 1996), whereas involving citizens in the decisions concerning social services may compromise care (Brownlea, 1997). Here, Dahl's (1970) competence criterion becomes highly influential. Tensions emerge as competing pressures between a bottom-up, community-driven process versus a more centralized, professionally driven approach collide (Foley & Martin, 2000).

Third, and much more systemic than the previous challenges, lies in the perception that many community members hold regarding their status as citizens. The marginalized in Canadian society—lone parents, street youth, the disabled, minorities, and the unemployed—are those who depend on the state for survival. The irony is that receiving services from the very institutions established to help these citizens—which they have the legitimate civil and political right to access—has unintended effects (Rappaport, 1985), which include dehumanization, oppression (Merzel, 1991), humiliation (Sen, 1991), a loss of independent living skills, erosion of personal dignity and self-esteem, and disempowerment (Gorham, 1995; Younis, 1995). Taking decision making away from citizens and putting it in the hands of professionals who tend to slot people into client categories "robs citizens of their democratic standing in relation to the bureaucrat and the state" (Brown, 1994, p. 890). Hence, while in theory, all citizens are created equal, some are more equal than others (Brown, 1989), generating two classes of citizenship (Gorham, 1995).

Minimizing the economic and psychological costs of participation for historically underrepresented citizens demands a shift away from traditional participation structures. In addition to being convenient and welcoming, citizens must be able to see some reflection of themselves in the participatory endeavour in order to trust the process and become involved. In the absence of broad-based participation, particularly when economy of time and problems of scale restrict participation by all, experiential participation may be a step toward achieving better representation of diverse perspectives (Prior, Stewart, & Walsh, 1995). Here, the "meeting mindset" is abandoned and the context for participation takes place in schools, worksites, churches, street corners, and coffee houses, engaging citizens in a planning process that reflects their life experiences. It also demands acknowledging and respecting the diverse and non-traditional contributions of citizens to planning. In contrast to the technical and expert knowledge of professionals, citizens are recognized as having more immediate knowledge of local needs and resources (Richardson & Waddington, 1996). Meaningful participation may constitute sharing experiences as service recipients, providing input about the delivery and quality of health programs, as well as chairing meetings, interpreting statistics, and penning community plans and policies.

Participation
in the grand
issues of
social policy

Participation in the Grand Issues of Social Policy

We devote attention first to the grand issues at the national level, leaving the international scene to a later section of the chapter. We suggest that citizen participation in the grand issues such as taxation, the distribution of income, and the development of national frameworks for income security and health care has never been extensive. In the 1950s and 1960s the federal government attempted to secure some involvement through the establishment of advisory councils and commissions of inquiry. One review established two criteria to judge whether advisory councils had been effective. "The council is consulted by the government while policy and legislation is in the planning stage and it has to its credit at least a couple of occasions when the government altered some decision because of its intervention" (Shackleton, 1977, p. 100). On the basis of these criteria Shackleton concluded that all of the councils had been dismal failures. We disagree with Shackleton with respect to the National Council of Welfare, which has consistently and severely criticized the social policies and programs of the federal government. While it may not have succeeded in changing government policy, it has been a much-needed voice for reform and, unlike many councils, has from its inception included low-income citizens in its governing body.

Whether the federal government reached a similar conclusion to Shackleton or acted simply to save money is unknown, but most councils, including the Economic Council of Canada, have been eliminated. Ironically the National Council of Welfare, the most critical and radical of all, persists to this day.

Another and again very limited form of participation at the federal level occurred in earlier times when continuing relationships existed between senior staff of the federal government, academics, and the executive directors of major social welfare organizations.

Thinkers such as Leonard Marsh, Harry Cassidy, Charlotte Whitton, C.A. Curtis, and J.J. Heagerty wrote important reports or chaired important committees, while federal civil servants such as Joseph Willard, George Davidson, and Robert Bryce helped to put these recommendations in place (Rice & Prince, 2000, p. 54).

This loose policy community was composed of like-minded professionals dedicated to the task of building a comprehensive social security and health care system. At the present time, however, this socially conscious policy group has been replaced by a fiscally conservative policy cluster that includes the Business Council on National Interests (BCNI), the Canadian Tax Foundation, and right-wing think-tanks like the Fraser Institute and the C.D. Howe Institute. The resources and contacts of these organizations have enabled them to exert enormous influence on the actions of the federal government in both national and international arenas. Thomas D'Aquino, the president and chief executive officer of the Business Council on National Interests, is quoted in a recent best-selling book in the following terms:

> If you ask yourself in which period since 1900 has Canada's business community had the most influence on public policy say I would say it was in the last twenty years. Look at what we stand for and look at what all the governments, all the major parties including Reform have done, and what they want to do . They have adopted the agenda we've been fighting for in the past two decades. (Newman, 1999, p. 159)

Social policies have been a particular target of BCNI and the Fraser Institute and the C.D. Howe Institute. Together, and with the considerable help of the media (controlled by like-minded individuals), they have taken the leadership in a campaign to radically alter the social policy scene in Canada.

> What was once a viable, publicly funded, largely universal system of social security has been subjected to a process of fiscal strangulation. Corporate Canada has managed to pull off this underfunding strategy by draining public revenues through a series of measures, including tax write-offs that allow over 80,000 profitable corporations to avoid paying taxes every year, deferred tax schemes that result in corporations owing over $40 billion to the federal government alone, plus the $11 billion that Ottawa pays out to businesses each year in the form of subsidies. (Clarke, 1997, p. 150)

Some specific changes made by the federal government in recent years include the elimination of the universal programs of Family Allowances and Old Age Security, cancellation of the Canada Assistance Act, which in return for federal contributions to the provinces insisted on a set of national standards for income assistance, and other programs and drastic reductions in the benefits available to the unemployed.

In short, the BCNI has advocated for and has been effective in sharply limiting the role of government in social policy. This council has adopted an agenda that suits high income earners who can pay for health care, send their children to private schools and summer camps, and employ nannies to look after their infant children, and who can depend on private arrangements for their recreational and cultural pursuits. They have little or no need for publicly funded schools, recreation centres, and health care. Hence their agenda is blatantly self-serving in insisting that the state limit spending on these social utilities.

Citizen participation on the global scene

Both provincial and federal governments have invited citizens to contribute to the work of royal commissions and other forms of state-sponsored inquiries. However, commission members have most frequently been professionals and other upper-middle class individuals. Consumers of service and other marginalized citizens are not at the table when the agenda and work plans of the commission are set. Typically their contributions are requested as a response to plans already established. And, as noted in an earlier section of the chapter, the "meeting mindset" acts as a further barrier to these citizens.

To conclude, the participation of citizens in federal social policy matters is limited to a relatively few individuals who have been and are exceedingly powerful. Newman's summary is distressingly appropriate:

> The Canadian Establishment is thus no longer merely a social group or a high octane debating society. Operating through Tom D'Aquino and the Business Council on National Issues, its members have become a coherent instrument of unprecedented political power. A silent, seemingly bloodless war has delivered Canada's government into the hands of its former enemies—the market worshiping Titans of the new economy. (Newman, 1999, p. 162)

Citizen Participation on the Global Scene

Writing in *The Gutenberg Galaxy*, Marshall McLuhan (1962) proclaimed that "The new electronic interdependence recreates the world in the image of a global village." Surely, even this prophet of globalization could not have had the vision of the "global village" we are experiencing at the beginning of the twenty-first century. We are in a dramatically different global age from the one to which McLuhan opened our eyes not so long ago.

Globalization—with its various meanings—has become a key word in defining our contemporary way of life. The pace and degree of supranational change is phenomenal. Many would say that more important activities now occur across national boundaries than within them. And we speak not just of economic transactions where international capital moves at lightning speed, manipulated by supranational corporations and organizations that operate without reference to national borders. Social, demographic, political, cultural, and environmental dimensions of globalization are in evidence everywhere (Midgely, 2000).

By no means are citizen global activities new. After all, people have long been concerned about social issues that surpass national boundaries, and have participated in a multitude of ways to tackle global problems like peace, world hunger, poverty, health, the environment, and Third World development. Citizen action has long spurred the development of a myriad of both government and non-governmental organizations that attempt to ameliorate complex, transnational, social problems. World citizens fulfill many functions in these organizations from financial support to volunteer service and social action and policy development.

One dramatic difference in today's global village is the capacity for simple, inexpensive, instant communication among concerned citizens. The opportunity for rapid information sharing, education, organization, mobilization, and participation in attempts to shape decisions affecting the world's citizens is available to people in the industrialized world through instant global communication—the Internet. In the last few years we have seen remarkable social action and civil disobedience responses at meetings of organizations such as the World Trade Organization, North American Free Trade Agreement, General Agreement on Trade in Services, and Multilateral Agreement on Investment. These large demonstrations have been marked by significant levels of information sharing, education, and sophisticated organization in preparation for the gatherings.

Rarely have we seen encounters with such diverse, interconnected constituencies—Third World, labour, environmentalists of many hues, concerned young people, farmers, indigenous peoples, religious organizations, and folks from different social strata. Despite the distinct lack of commonality of concerns or agreement as to means of protest, and wide variation in values, a common thread of concern has emerged in the protesters and demonstrators. It is opposition to the power of a very small group of non-elected or corporate officials to alter hard-won democratic rights, threaten social welfare programs, and attack domestic sovereignty. These citizen protests and challenges have become a strong voice of left-wing perspectives as traditional left-of-centre parties no longer occupy centre stage as challengers of the power elites.

People in Western democracies have taken for granted that they have the democratic right to influence basic social policy directions for their national, provincial, and local governments. This is now cast in doubt, as international negotiations and agreements seek to override national and local preference. For many, a move in the direction of world order would not be so threatening if the advantages of the First World were being sustained and distributed more equitably around the planet. Unfortunately, the evidence is quite the opposite. With globalization of world economy and trade, the disparities between the rich and poor of the world have widened, rather than receded (Klein, 2000).

Conclusion:
Citizen
participation
in the twenty-
first century

The opposition to such immense international forces of global economic and cultural homogenization has taken the form of significant grassroots demonstrations designed to challenge and disrupt planning meetings. Simultaneously one marvels at the apparent level of organization of large groups representing such diverse constituencies in the face of overwhelming economic, organizational, and oppositional odds, while despairing that this protest is the form of "participation" left to disenfranchised global citizens facing grave social problems and political choices. Klein (2000), in her international best-seller *No Logo*, describes grassroots social activism by citizens around the world against transnational corporations and the monopolies they hold that elected governments have been ignorant of or impotent against. While the demands of vocalizing and mobilizing around issues of personal choice are decidedly different from those made by citizens who become involved in local governance or volunteer activities, its purpose is not—to effect change at the most personal of levels—the clothes we wear, the gas we use, the food we eat.

> All around the world, parties and protests were held in financial districts, outside stock exchanges, superstores, banks and multinational headquarters...a collection of protectionists getting together out of necessity to fight everything and anything global. But as connections have formed across national lines, a different agenda has taken hold, one that embraces globalization but seeks to wrest it from the grasp of the multinationals. Ethical shareholder, culture jammers, street reclaimers, McUnion organizers, human rights hacktivists, school-logo fighters and Internet corporate watchdogs are at the early stages of demanding a citizen-centred alternative to the international rule of the brands. (Klein, 2000, pp. 444-446)

At the present time citizens trying to open the doors of elite decision making are expending an enormous amount of organizing and participatory energy.

Whence citizen participation in this era of globaliation? On one hand, we see that the means of sharing information, education, organization, and participation are present in ways never before imagined. On another, we see planetary inequality at unprecedented levels accompanying the relentless march of global capitalism. While we are at a point where the means and opportunities for global citizen participation have unbounded potential, the values and ideologies of those who dominate the world's resources represent only a fraction of the world's citizens.

Conclusion: Citizen Participation in the Twenty-First Century

The concluding comments of this chapter contained in both the first and second editions of *Canadian Social Policy* remain as relevant today as they were in 1978 and 1987: namely that the participation of citizens in the devel-

opment and implementation of social policy remains very much at the margin. To be sure, many middle- and upper-class citizens with the time and
freedom from financial worries do participate in the affairs of health and
social service agencies in the voluntary sector. And low-income citizens
demonstrate enormous commitment in participating in local agencies and
particularly those concerned with poverty. While the work of these agencies
is important to the health and well-being of communities, they represent the
most ordinary of the ordinary issues of social policy. Indeed, from our point
of view, the regrettable reality is that citizen participation in social policy is
most evident where it matters the least.

There are a few, but only a few, opportunities for citizens to participate in
the ordinary issues at municipal and provincial levels. In most provinces citizens can stand for election in school boards and some provinces have created
health boards composed of locally elected or appointed citizens to govern
health care on a regional basis. Yet, as noted earlier, only the well-educated,
well-spoken, and well off, are members of school and health boards. Policy
development and implementation in provincial ministries or departments
remains an exclusive responsibility of politicians and civil servants.

Again, from our point of view, a particularly distressing example of the
absence of citizen participation occurs in public sector human service organizations. The social work profession is committed to

> The values of acceptance, self determination and respect of individuality.
> Social workers are dedicated to the welfare and self realization of human
> beings, to the development and disciplined use of scientific knowledge
> regarding human and societal behaviours; to the development of resources
> to meet individual, group, national and international needs and aspira-
> tions and to the achievement of social justice for all. (Canadian Association
> of Social Workers, 1994)

We argue that this commitment is consistent with and supports the principle
of affected interests. No one is more deeply affected by the absence of social
justice and by inadequate resources than those in receipt of human services.
Hence, those served have a primary reason to be involved in the development and implementation of the policies that affect them. Yet few public sector organizations have seen fit to honour this principle and the social work
profession has only intermittently and occasionally advocated for the inclusion of those being served in the policy process.

Participation in the grand issues of social policy at the national level takes
the form of reacting to the announcement of policies already developed.
Organizations like the Canadian Council on Social Development, the National
Anti-Poverty Organization, and the National Council of Welfare have an excellent record of responding to policy decisions made by the federal government. But in recent years federal government ministries have shown little
interest in involving these and similar organizations in the initial stages of
policy development. However, as noted earlier, the reverse situation is true

with respect to the business community. Indeed, the Business Council on National Interests is not only a powerful lobby organization but its contacts and resources have enabled it to anticipate the agenda of the federal government and prepare draft legislation that suits its interests. A conspicuous example concerns the competition law.

Conclusion: citizen participation in the twenty-first century

> During the next three years the BCNI spent $1 million on the project, hired its own team of twenty-five lawyers headed by Toronto's Bill Rowley and by 1985 had produced a 236-page master plan which became Canada's new competition law. It was the only time in the history of capitalism that any country allowed anti-monopoly legislation to be written by the very people it was meant to police. (Newman, 1999, p. 156)

In a recent review of the experience of citizen and community participation in health care, White (2000) concludes that participation does not lead to community control, nor does it empower individuals. Nevertheless, she asserts that health care planners and administrators continue to be enthusiastic about citizen participation. Why support a phenomenon that clearly does not achieve its stated objectives? In explaining this apparent contradiction, White notes first that the favoured form of participation is to consult citizens about established plans and, second, that having done so, administrators and planners can then present their recommendations as having the support of the public. "Lay participation as it is preached and practiced is clearly about administrative and political efficiency not democracy, consumer empowerment or community control. It derives its value principally from its role as an administrative strategy" (White, 2000, p. 477). In our view, it would be preferable to dispense with participation than to use it in such a shallow fashion.

A hopeful example of citizen participation is occurring at the global scene where citizens have organized effective protests against the actions of multinational organizations and have forced these powerful organizations to pause in their headlong rush to establish corporations as the dominant ruling force in the world. Canada can lay claim to considerable contributions to these protests through the work of the Council of Canadians and of young activists like Naomi Klein. If multinational organizations can be throttled back through citizen action, it is theoretically possible that the same energy and commitment could be brought to bear on social policy matters that affect children and families in a most immediate fashion. Both Canada and the United Kingdom are desperately seeking ways to improve the delivery of health and social services. One path might be to finally implement the recommendations of numerous commissions of inquiry, such as the CELDIC Report (Commission on Emotional and Learning Disorders in Children, 1970) and New Directions for a Healthy British Columbia (British Columbia Ministry of Health and Ministry Responsible for Seniors, 1993) that services should be provided on a decentralized basis and governed by boards of elected citizens.

References

Anderson, M., Meaton, J., & Potter, C. (1994). Public participation, an approach using aerial photographs at Ashford, Kent. *Town Planning Review, 6*(1), 41-58.

Arai, S.M., & Pedlar, A.M. (1997). Building communities through leisure: Citizen participation in a healthy communities initiative. *Journal of Leisure Research, 29*(2), 167-182.

Banting, K. (1987). Visions of the welfare state. In S. Seward (Ed.), *The future of social welfare systems in Canada and the United Kingdom.* Halifax: Institute for Research on Public Policy.

Berry, J.M., Kent, E.P., & Thomson, K. (1993). *The rebirth of urban democracy.* Washington, DC: Brookings Institute.

Bregha, F.J. (1973). *Public participation in planning, policy and programme.* Toronto: Ministry of Culture and Recreation.

British Columbia Ministry of Health and Ministry Responsible for Seniors. (1993). *New directions for a healthy British Columbia.* Victoria: Author.

Brown, C. (1989). Citizens' rights. *New Statesman and Society,* (April), 28.

Brown, M.P. (1994). The work of city politics: Citizenship through employment in the local response to AIDS. *Environment and Planning, 26,* 873-894.

Brownlea, A. (1987). Participation: Myths, realities and prognosis. *Social Science and Medicine, 25*(6), 605-614.

Canadian Association of Social Workers. (1994). Code of ethics, reprinted in F. Turner & J. Turner (1995), *Canadian social welfare* (3rd ed.) Scarborough: Allyn & Bacon Canada.

Chrislip, D. (1995). Pulling together—creating a constituency for change. *National Civic Review,* (Winter), 21-29.

Church, J., & Barker, P. (1998). Regionalization of health services in Canada: A critical perspective. *International Journal of Health Services, 28*(3), 467-486.

Clarke, T. (1997). *Silent coup.* Toronto: Canadian Centre for Policy Alternatives and James Lorimer & Company.

Commission on Emotional and Learning Disorders in Children. (1970). *One million children.* Toronto: Leonard Cranford.

Crawshaw, R. (1994). Grass roots participation in health care reform. *Annals of Internal Medicine, 120*(8), 677-681.

Dahl, R.A. (1970). *After the revolution.* New Haven: Yale University Press.

Drover, G. (2000). Redefining social citizenship in a global era. *Canadian Social Work,* Special Issue, *2*(1), (Summer), 29-49.

Foley, P., & Martin, S. (2000). A new deal for the community? Public participation in regeneration and local service delivery. *Policy and Politics, 28*(4), 479-492.

Freedman, T.G. (1998). "Why don't they come to Pike street and ask us?": Black American women's health concerns. *Social Science and Medicine, 47*(7), 941-947.

Gorham, E. (1995). Social citizenship and its fetters. *Polity, 28*(1), 25-47.

Graham, J., Swift, K., & Delaney, R. (2000). *Canadian social policy.* Scarborough: Prentice Hall Allyn and Bacon Canada.

Henderson, L.J. (1990). Metropolitan governance: Citizen participation in the urban federation. *National Civic Review, 79*(2), 105-117.

Hemingway, J.L. (1999). Leisure, social capital and democratic citizenship. *Journal of Leisure Research, 31*(2), 150-165.

Hunt, S. (1990). Building alliances: Professional and political issues in community participation. Examples from a health and community development project. *Health Promotion International, 5*(3), 179-185.

Jewkes, R., & Murcott, A. (1998). Community representatives: Representing the community? *Social Science and Medicine, 46*(7), 843-858.

Jones, F. (2000). Community involvement: The influence of early experience. *Canadian Social Trends*, (Summer), 15-19.

Julian, D., Reischl, R., Carrick R., & Katrenich, C. (1997). Citizen participation—lessons from a local United Way planning process. *American Planners Association Journal, 63*(3), 345-355.

Kathlene, L., & Martin, J.A. (1991). Enhancing citizen participation: Panels designs, perspectives and policy formation. *Journal of Policy Analysis and Management, 10*(1), 46-63.

Kingwell, M. (2000). *The world we want: Virtue, vice and the good citizen.* Toronto: Viking.

Klein, N. (2000). *No logo—Taking aim at the brand bullies.* Toronto: Vintage Canada.

Lindblom, C. (1979). Still muddling, not yet through. *The Public Administration Review,* (November/December), 517-526.

Lomas, J., & Veenstra, G. (1995). If you build it, who will come? *Policy Options,* (November), 37-40.

Marshall, T.H. (1977). Class, *citizenship and social development.* Chicago: University of Chicago Press.

McLuhan, M. (1962). *The Gutenberg galaxy: The making of a typographic man.* Toronto: University of Toronto Press.

Merzel, C. (1991). Rethinking empowerment. *Health/PAC Bulletin,* (Winter), 5-6.

Midgley, J. (2000). Globalization, capitalism and social welfare: A social development perspective. *Canadian Social Work,* Special Issue, *2*(1) (Summer), 13-28.

Newman, P. (1999). *Titans: How the new Canadian establishment seized power.* Toronto: Penguin Books.

O'Neill, M. (1992). Community participation in Quebec's health system: A strategy to curtail community empowerment? *International Journal of Health Services, 22*(2), 287-301.

Pateman, C. (1970). *Participation and democratic theory.* Cambridge: Cambridge University Press.

Phillips, A. (1993). *Democracy and difference.* Cambridge: Polity Press.

Prior, D., Stewart, J., & Walsh, K. (1995). *Citizenship: Rights, community and participation.* London: Pitman.

Putnam, R. (2000). *Bowling alone, the collapse and revival of American community.* New York: Simon and Schuster.

Rappaport, J. (1985). The power of empowerment language. *Social Policy, 1,* 5-21.

Rice, J., & Prince, M. (2000). *Changing politics of Canadian social policy.* Toronto: University of Toronto Press

Richardson, R., & Waddington, C. (1996). Allocating resources: Community involvement is not easy. *International Journal of Health Planning and Management, 11,* 307-315.

Rittel, H., & Webber, M. (1973). Dilemmas in a general theory of planning. *Policy Science, 5,* 155-169.

Rosener, J. (1978). Matching method to purpose: The challenges of planning citizen-participation activities. In S. Langton (Ed.), *Citizen participation in America* (pp. 109-122). Lexington: D.C. Heath.

Scanlan, A., Zyzanski, S., Flocke, S., Stange, K., & Gravagubins, I. (1996). A comparison of U.S. and Canadian family physicians' attitudes toward their respective health care systems. *Medical Care, 34,* 837-844.

Schulz, A.J., Israel, B.A., Zimmerman, M.A., & Checkoway, B.N. (1995). Empowerment as a multi-level construct: Perceived control at the individual, organizational and community levels. *Health Education Research, 10*(3), 309-327.

Sen, R. (1994). Building community involvement in health care. *Social Policy,* (Spring), 32-43.

References

Shackleton, D. (1977). *Power town: Democracy discarded.* Toronto: McClelland and Stewart.

Smith, D. (1995). *First person plural, a community development approach to social change.* Montreal: Black Rose Books.

Smith, N., Baugh Littlejohns, L., & Thompson, D. (2001). Shaking out the cobwebs: Insights into community capacity and its relation to health outcomes. *Community Development Journal, 36* (1), 30-41.

Syme, G.J., & Nancarrow, B.E. (1992). Predicting public involvement in urban water management and planning. *Environment and Behavior, 24* (6), 738-758.

Tewdwrjones, M., & Thomas, H. (1998). Collaborative action in local plan-making. *Environment and Planning, 25,* 127-144.

Wandersman, A., Florin, P., Friedmann, R., & Meier, R. (1987). Who participates, who does not and why? An analysis of voluntary neighbourhood organizations in the United States and Israel. *Sociological Forum, 2,* 534-555.

Warren, R., & Weschler, L.F. (1975). The costs of citizenship. In R. Warren & L.F. Weschler (Eds.), *Governing urban space* (pp. 10-23). Newark: University of Delaware Press.

Wharf Higgins, J. (1992). The healthy communities movement in Canada. In B. Wharf (Ed.), *Communities and social policy in Canada* (pp. 151-189). Toronto: McClelland and Stewart.

Wharf Higgins, J. (1999). Citizenship and empowerment: A remedy for citizen participation in health reform. *Community Development Journal, 34* (4), 287-307.

Wharf Higgins, J., Vertinsky, P., Cutt, J., & Green, L.W. (1999b). Using social marketing as a strategic approach to understanding citizen participation in health reform. *Social Marketing Quarterly, 5* (2), 42-55.

White, D. (*2000*). Consumer and community participation: A reassessment of process, impact and value. In G. Albrecht, R. Fitzpatrick, & S.C. Scrimshaw (Eds.), *Handbook of social studies in health and medicine* (pp. 465-480). London: Sage.

Younis, T. (1995). The Allende community experiment in empowerment: Participation too far? *Local Government Studies, 21* (2), 263-279.

Additional Resources

Canadian Council on Social Development. On-line at <www.ccsd.ca>.

Canadian Policy Research Networks. On-line at <www.cprn.org>.

Harvey, J. (2001). *The role of sport and recreation policy in fostering citizenship: The Canadian experience.* Ottawa: Canadian Policy Research Networks.

Jenson, J., & Papillon, M. (2001). *The changing boundaries of citizenship. A review and research agenda.* Ottawa: Canadian Policy Research Networks. On-line at <www.cprn.org>.

Laker, A. (2000). *Beyond the boundaries of physical education: Educating young people for citizenship and social responsibility.* London: Routledge/Falmer.

Phillips, S., & Orsini, M. (2002). Mapping the links: Citizen involvement in policy processes. Canadian Policy Research Network Discussion Paper No. F21.

Valentine, F. (2001). *Enabling citizenship: Full inclusion of children with disabilities and their parents.* Canadian Policy Research Networks. Discussion Paper No. F13. On-line at <www.cprn.org>.

Evaluating Social Welfare Policies and Programs

17

Anne Westhues

S ocial policy is evaluated in an environment that is just as political as the one in which it is formulated. This means that evaluators have to be aware of the larger political context in which a study takes place, as well as the politics within the organizations delivering the programs intended to implement a policy. They must also be aware of how they believe knowledge is created and the implications of this perspective for their role as evaluators. The perspective taken will shape the evaluators' research design, sampling, the means they will use to collect data, the generalizability of the findings, and any responsibility they understand themselves to have beyond carrying out research and reporting the findings. In this chapter I will briefly review the larger political context of social policy evaluation, outline shifts in thinking over the past twenty-five years about the questions to be answered by evaluation, and describe the evolution of evaluation research functions since it has been recognized as an essential part of the policy-making process by the federal government in Canada in the 1970s, showing how this evolution has been influenced by both the political context and the debates about epistemology. I will close with a discussion of the impact that a shift to a more humanist approach to evaluation has had on the development of social policy.

The Larger Political Context

The 1960s and 1970s were a time of great hope among social workers in Canada, with the passage of many progressive pieces of social policy legislation, including the Canadian Bill of Rights, the Canada Assistance Plan, the Medical Care Act, the Canada/Quebec Pension Plan, and the addition of maternity benefits to the Unemployment Insurance Act (Guest, 1985). Consequently, expenditures for health and social services increased dramatically, from $2,257 million in 1960-1961 to $61,490 million in 1982 (Guest, 1985) continuing on to $154,836 million by 1997-1998 (Statistic Canada, 2001). Spending growth increased steadily over this period, with the largest increases in times of high unemployment. This growth slowed in the 1980s when a Conservative

The larger political context government under Brian Mulroney replaced the Liberals federally. A neo-conservative policy environment gave rise to international agreements like the Free Trade Agreement in 1989 and the North American Free Trade Agreement in 1993, and a commitment to reduced taxation, all of which created pressure to reduce spending for health, education, and social services as the federal government attempted to "harmonize" our social policy and taxation levels with the United States. Most provincial governments during the 1990s shared this philosophy.

The perception of high levels of government spending, a more conservative political environment, and substantial growth in the number of social scientists trained to do evaluation research all contributed to the conditions that gave rise to a concern with accountability that went beyond a narrow emphasis on financial management (Muller-Clemm & Barnes, 1997). While the profit sector has the bottom line of profit and loss to tell them how well they are doing with respect to business ventures, the non-profit sector has no comparable indicator to assess what is being achieved through social spending. The promise of a method that would allow the federal government to systematically measure the impact of social programs led them to commit to program and policy evaluation.

Evaluation of programs became routine, with the Treasury Board approving its first formal policy requiring deputy heads to evaluate all programs within their jurisdiction in 1977 (Muller-Clemm & Barnes, 1997). Programs were understood to be the mechanism by which policy was implemented, so program evaluation was seen as the way to evaluate policy as well. The Neilsen Task Force review of 989 federal programs in 1984 concluded that evaluations of these programs were inadequate, however, in part because they were often internal evaluations and therefore seen as self-serving. They were also criticized for failing to question a program's basic rationale, focusing instead on impact (outcomes) and delivery (process). A further criticism leveled at federal program evaluations was that they were not "objective" but "political" and therefore value-laden (Sutherland, cited in Muller-Clemm & Barnes, 1997).

These critiques led to a revised policy in 1991, reaffirming a commitment to program evaluation as a mechanism for improved cost-effectiveness, and for decision making with respect to program changes including whether a program should continue to operate (Senate of Canada, 1991). Notwithstanding a twenty-five-year experience with program and policy evaluation, and an apparent recommitment to an "objective" approach to evaluation by the federal government, evaluators continue to explore questions of methodology, epistemology, and the role of the evaluator (See *Canadian Journal of Program Evaluation, Evaluation Review* and *Evaluation and Program Planning*). Primary among these is the role of the evaluator.

Role of the Evaluator

In the early days of evaluation research, the role of the evaluator was defined as that of a detached, value-free researcher engaged in the primarily "rational" process of assessing whether a program was meeting its objectives or outcomes (Rossi & Freeman, 1982; Suchman, 1967; Weiss, 1972). Over time, researchers realized that they might discover that a program met its objectives, but not know why. They began to redefine their role to include interaction with those who had designed, delivered, and managed the programs being evaluated to learn about the program elements and why it was thought the program would deliver the expected results; that is, there was increased recognition of the theory of the program, as well as the political and ethical aspects of evaluation (Abma, 1997; House, 1980, 1993).

More recently, the roles of program consultant or program developer have been recognized by some evaluators as appropriate practice in some cases (Patton, 1997), with the evaluator internal to the organization rather than external (Love, 1983). This role requires the evaluator to be even less detached, entering into in-depth discussions with service providers and service users within their workplace after the evaluation is completed about what the results suggest should be changed based upon study findings. The politics of this relationship are clearly different and more complex than for the external evaluator.

The debate as to the appropriateness of the role of program developer within the context of evaluation research continues, as well as how much responsibility the evaluator carries for ensuring that the recommendations are implemented, and how neutral the researcher should be in presenting the results of a study with public policy implications (Roach & Youngman Berdahl, 1999). In addition to the discussion about internal versus external evaluators, terms like "critical evaluation" (Everitt, 1996; VanderPlaat, 1997) and "empowerment evaluation" (Worthington, 1999) have begun to appear in the literature. This debate can be understood as the manifestation of a fundamental discussion within the social sciences: whether the researcher should adopt a philosophy of science that is positivist, or one that Maguire (1987) describes as humanist. This debate raises a number of issues that recommend different practices to the evaluator, summarized as follows by Maguire:

- objectivity versus selectivity
- research distance versus closeness to subject
- generalizations or universality versus uniqueness
- quantitative versus qualitative
- social control versus local self-determination
- impartial advice versus solidarity and action

The positivist approach posits that there are observable social facts that the researcher must discover using research methods borrowed from the natural

sciences. The humanist perspective, a blend of what others have called naturalistic and transformational (Westhues, Cadell, Karabanow, Maxwell, &
Sanchez, 1999), argues that human reality is socially constructed. That is, it is
a consequence of the interplay between an individual's values and experience (Baum, 1987; Gergen, 1985). Hence it is critical to capture the experience or perception of participants in the study. In the case of evaluation, this
means those involved in providing a social program as service deliverers,
managers, and funders and those who receive services through the program.
The humanist perspective argues that meaningful insights cannot be gained
without close interpersonal interchange. In contrast, associated with the positivist belief in objectivity is the need to maintain distance from the people or
systems being studied.

The very purpose of research is conceptualized differently by the positivist and the humanist. For the positivist, generalization to a larger population is the intent of research, whereas for the humanist the purpose is to
understand the workings of a given group or program at a specific time in
history. Positivists and humanists also differ with respect to the type of data
that they collect. For the positivist, the more quantifiable the data, the better.
Humanists are likely to supplement quantitative data with qualitative data, or
use only qualitative data, which they believe provide insight and a depth of
understanding that just the quantitative data lack.

Positivist and humanist researchers also differ with respect to their definition of the political impact of research. For the positivists, the goal is to
develop understanding of human behaviour, which permits control of those
behaviours by the knowledge holders, in this case policy makers, program
developers, and managers. For the humanists, the goal is one of self-determination or empowerment. They feel that both the research process and its
outcomes should put increased power in the hands of those who are the focus
of the study. This understanding of the evaluation researcher's role is consistent with what Vaillancourt (1996) calls "new progressive social work."

Finally, positivists leave it to policy-makers and politicians to decide how
to use the results of the research findings—they see their job solely as providing the most objective and impartial assessment possible. By contrast,
humanist researchers recognize the policy implications of their work and
advocate for those changes.

Changes in evaluation practice over the past twenty-five years have moved
the field away from a more purely positivist orientation toward one that fits
with Maguire's conceptualization of humanist practice. This has occurred
through the addition of two research functions to the field of evaluation
research—needs assessment and evaluability assessment—as well as through
changes in practice in the traditional research functions of process and outcome evaluation. Developments in each of these functions are analyzed
below with respect to their contribution to the evolution of the field of evaluation research, and their support of this epistemological shift.

Evolution of Evaluation Research Practice

Outcome Evaluation

The primary focus of evaluation efforts in the early years of practice was on outcome evaluation. The questions answered by an outcome evaluation are: Is the program having the desired effect? At the desired level of cost? (Pancer & Westhues, 1989). The research techniques traditionally associated with this approach are experimental and quasi-experimental designs.

Reflecting the shift to a more humanist philosophy in evaluation, social workers have argued for the utility of the single case design in assessing outcomes (Bloom, Fischer, & Orme, 1999; Briar & Blythe, 1985; Jayaratne, 1978; Mutscheler, 1979; Thomas, 1978). The single case approach may use quantitative or qualitative data, but focuses upon the achievement of an individual participant's goals within the program. This shows increased concern with the unique rather than the universal or generalizable. It also shows a move toward greater subjectivity, as the assessment of whether the individual has achieved his or her goals is often a self-report measure like Hudson's self-esteem or peer relations indexes (Hudson, 1982).

Another way in which a move is seen toward the subjective is the use of client satisfaction surveys to assess the effects of participating in a social program (Atkisson & Zwick, 1982; Giordano, 1977; Nguyen, Atkisson, & Stegner, 1983). Again, the focus of these questionnaires is often upon people's experience within the program and their perception of its effects upon them. This is in contrast to a more behavioural approach, which might have the service deliverer or a trained observer assessing individual behaviours that have been defined as indicators of the program participant achieving his or her goals, perhaps increased self-esteem or improved peer relations. While it is now more common to collect client satisfaction data, questions are being posed about the extent to which it actually influences program design or delivery (Holosko, 1996)—an ethical challenge for evaluators.

Social impact assessments, though not yet widely used, are a means by which one can measure the effects of programs that are intended to have a community-wide impact, like a public education campaign with respect to family violence. These effects would be clearest in small or well-defined communities experiencing few other changes (Bowles, 1981; Finterbusch & Wolf 1977; Tester & Myles, 1981). Their design is participatory and action-oriented. The findings of the assessment are fed back to the community with the intention of helping it assess whether it is meeting its goals, such as a reduction in family violence.

To determine whether the program is achieving its effects at a desired level of cost, evaluators borrowed cost-benefit and cost-effectiveness analysis from economists. Both cost-benefit and cost-effectiveness analysis involve a calculation of the costs and the benefits of a program. In cost-benefit analysis, the benefits are assigned a monetary value so that a benefit-to-cost ratio can be calculated. If a program is found to have greater benefits than costs, or a greater benefit-to-cost ratio than a specified level, then it is concluded that it is meeting its objectives at an acceptable level of cost (Stokey & Zeckhauser, 1978; Yates, 1985).

A further refinement of the cost question is the development of cost-outcome analysis (McCready & Rahn, 1983, 1986). With this approach, costs are calculated for the program, a determination is made of what proportion of clients are successfully treated within the program, and then a cost-per-successful outcome figure is calculated. Thus, if a program is expensive for each person served, but has a high success rate, it would have a higher cost-outcome benefit than a program that was less expensive on a per capita basis but which also had a lower level of successful outcomes.

Evaluability Assessment / Program Logic Models

One of the difficulties that evaluators encountered from the beginning when undertaking outcome evaluations was that program and policy objectives were often implicit rather than explicit. Or they had in fact shifted from what was explicitly written when the program was first begun a number of years earlier. Or there were different understandings among service providers, managers, funders, and program participants as to program objectives. If evaluators selected objectives for the program, or if they took as objectives what was stated in the original program description, those choices could well be at variance with the current focus of program activities. As a consequence, the program would be evaluated against objectives that were no longer valid in the perception of service providers, service recipients, or perhaps funders. When this happened, or was perceived to happen, the research findings were not utilized (Patton, 1997). To address this problem of non-utilization, evaluators began to write about "pre-evaluation work" (Suchman, 1967), "developing a program model" (Weiss, 1972), evaluability assessment (Rutman, 1980; Wholey, Nay, Scanlon, & Schmidt, 1975;) or more recently program logic models (McLaughlin & Jordan, 1999; Montague, 2000; Petrosino, 2000; Rush & Ogborne, 1991; Wong-Rieger & David, no date).

Rutman, a Canadian who played a major role in developing these ideas, suggested that the purpose of the evaluability assessment is twofold: to determine whether an outcome evaluation is appropriate for the program at this time; and to ensure that the program managers and the evaluator have agreed upon realistic, measurable objectives, appropriate performance indicators, and intended uses of the information prior to the evaluation (Rutman, 1980). The evaluability assessment answers the questions: What are the components of the program? Are the intended effects (goals) and unintended effects of the program clearly specified? Can the program realistically achieve the specified goals or produce the anticipated effects? (Pancer & Westhues, 1989). The technique associated with this aspect of evaluability assessment is called a program logic model (Rush & Ogborne, 1991) and in addition to telling the evaluator whether it is reasonable to proceed with an outcome evaluation, it can also be used to help explicate the theory of the program (McLaughlin & Jordan, 1999) and to define outcome objectives for performance measurement (McEwan & Bigelow, 1997).

Evolution of evaluation research practice

A second aspect to the evaluability assessment is to complete what Rutman calls a purpose analysis. This addresses another difficulty that evaluators experienced—the reality that evaluation can be carried out for many reasons, including a desire to whitewash a poorly functioning program, or to torpedo a well-functioning one (Suchman, 1967). By purpose analysis Rutman means that the evaluator should attend to the political concerns pertaining to the evaluation, answering these questions: Why is this evaluation being proposed at this time? Who are the various stakeholders, or interest groups? Whose interests are primary, that is, which of the stakeholders is pushing for the evaluation right now—the managers, the consumers, or the funders, for instance? (Rutman, 1980).

It can be seen from the above description that the development of the research function called evaluability assessment rests upon an acceptance of humanist principles. It builds upon the assumption that program objectives are socially constructed, and hence can be identified only in discussion with program providers and perhaps program participants. The process of reaching agreement on the objectives of the program creates a trust and closeness in the working relationship between the evaluator and program staff that is unlikely to occur if the evaluator remains distant from them in an attempt to retain objectivity. The literature is full of articles outlining the tensions between practitioners and researchers, an indication of the pervasiveness of this problem (Carrilio, 1981; Casselman, 1971/72; Davies & Kelly, 1976; Fanshel, 1966; Gordon, 1984; Saleeby 1979; Stiffman, Feldman, Evans, & Orme, 1984). The use of an evaluability assessment also recognizes that when a program is delivered in a number of sites, the sites share common objectives, but they may have additional unique ones. This shift may be at variance with the funders' expectations if they are interested in "apolitical" assessments against predetermined outcomes, a reversion back to the thinking in the early days of program evaluation, which we see being articulated by neo-conservative governments today (Muller-Clemm & Barnes, 1997).

The intent of the staff consultation with respect to specification of objectives and input into the design of the research is to empower those involved in delivering the program by giving them the opportunity to have questions asked in the data collection that will be helpful to them in program development. Finally, it is argued that an evaluation that is based upon an evaluability assessment is more likely to be used by program managers and staff because they understand the research process and have had input into its design. This is congruent with the humanist position that a researcher has responsibility for ensuring that the results of his or her work are utilized.

Process Evaluation

Another issue that became evident for evaluation researchers was that the programs they were asked to assess were often "black boxes." That is, the actual service delivered was not clearly articulated, and there was little or no monitoring to ensure that it was implemented as it had been designed (Weiss, 1972). This meant that if the evaluator found that the program was meeting its objectives, it wasn't clear how to replicate that program in another setting. If the finding was that it was not meeting its objectives, it wasn't clear if this was a failure of theory, or a failure of implementation. The response to this realization was to invest in developing the aspect of evaluation research that is called process evaluation, or monitoring (Rossi & Freeman, 1982) or auditing (Posavac & Carey, 1997).

A process evaluation answers the primary question: Is the program operating as planned? More specifically, Is the *quantity* of service intended being delivered? and Is the *quality* of service intended being delivered? (Pancer & Westhues, 1989). Information systems, peer review ratings, and client satisfaction surveys are the research techniques most often utilized in process evaluation. To determine whether the quantity of service is sufficient, data would be gathered on how many clients are being served; whether they are the intended client group; and whether they are receiving the intended types of service (Caputo, 1986; Hanbery, Sorenson, & Kucic, 1981). All these questions are routinely answered with data from a well-constructed information system.

To answer the question of whether the intended quality of service is being provided is more complex. Data sources might include periodic case reviews like those that are now common with children in foster care (Backus, 1978; Chappell, 1975; Claburn & Magura, 1978); comparison to standards that have been set by the program funder or a professional body (Ontario, Minister of Community and Social Services, 1981); judicial reviews to determine the constitutionality of a policy or whether it has been implemented according to principles of due process and accepted administrative law (Howlett & Ramesh, 1995); or a quality-assurance approach that relies upon peer review to determine whether the appropriate service was provided (Frankel & Sinclair, 1982; Sinclair & Frankel, 1983). Observational techniques might also be used, as in an evaluation of a distress line where quality of service was assessed by means of pseudo-calls made to the distress line by an actress (Crocker, 1983). Observation through a one-way mirror might also be possible to assess the quality of counselling being offered. Client satisfaction surveys may also focus on process as well as outcomes (Williams et al., 2001). The health care and education "report cards" now being issued in many provinces are an example of a fairly comprehensive process evaluation that draws upon a mix of the approaches outlined above.

While process evaluation was recognized early as important to the understanding or interpretation of the results of an outcome evaluation (Suchman,

1967), the argument is now made that process evaluation is useful in and of itself when the purpose of the evaluation is formative (Posavac & Carey, 1997). This position reinforces the legitimacy of the evaluator's role as program developer. As such, it reflects a humanist perspective because it recognizes the uniqueness of each program, and its potential to unfold in a way that is unlike any other program. Process evaluation also emphasizes the importance of qualitative data such as client comments with respect to satisfaction with the program, as well as quantitative data such as how many clients are being served, and whether they are demographically the same as the intended group.

Evolution of evaluation research practice

Needs Assessment

The final evaluation research function that has evolved since the 1960s is needs assessment. Needs assessments were first developed to answer the question: Can we justify our claim that we require a service or a program in this community? (Pancer & Westhues, 1989). With community expectations that are often greater than our resources, it has become necessary to demonstrate more clearly that there is a need for a service, the magnitude of that need, and the nature of the need. As program developers became sensitive to the fact that the specific form of the program needed in one community might vary from that in another community because of resource availability, religious and ethnic culture of the community, or size of the community, for instance, it became clear that we needed to communicate with the community in some way to determine what they see as necessary (Batsche, Hernandez, & Montenegro, 1999; Weaver, 1999).

Milord (1976) and McKillip (1987) identify three approaches to assess community need: the social indicators approach, the survey approach, and the community impressions approach. The social indicators approach involves the use of statistics like age distribution within a geographic area to project the need for a service. You might be trying to assess the need for child care, for instance. Agreement would have to be reached on a reasonable standard of service provision, for instance, that group child care facilities be able to accommodate 25% of children between the ages of three and five. These standards, to be widely accepted, must be created in consultation with service providers and consumers of service. The number of children in this age group in your area, times the proportion specified in the standard, is then used to determine the number of daycare spots that should be available in that area.

Another social indicators approach that is commonly used is based upon the demand for service. Estimates of need are based upon the number of families that have requested child care but could not be accommodated and are therefore on a waiting list. The difficulty with this approach is that it may not provide a valid indicator of need. If resources are limited, people may fail to leave their names on a list anywhere, resulting in an underestimate of need. Conversely, they might have their names on every available waiting list, with the result that the need for service would be overestimated.

It is generally more expensive to use the second approach to needs assessment—the survey—than the social indicators approach. It is also often difficult to generate a random sample of potential users of service for the study. This approach has the advantage, however, of providing detailed information about people's need for service. It can tell you how many parents would use group child care, for instance; the ages of their children; what they would be willing to pay; and which hours of service are preferred. The answers to these questions would permit program development to proceed in a way that is based more upon the needs identified by potential users of the service than upon the best guesses of program planners.

The community impressions approach can provide similar information to the survey, but at a lower cost. Its primary drawback is that the opinions of those who come out to a community forum may be less representative of the broader community than are those who respond to a survey, especially if the response rate is high.

The development of the needs assessment research function is an important indicator of the shift toward a humanist philosophy of science within the program evaluation field. Where once the need for a new service was defined only by service delivery "experts," the people who are potential users of the service are now also seen as "expert" for this purpose. Further, all of the approaches outlined by Milord (1976) recognize that need is defined by the opinions and preferences of potential consumers of service, not by a standard created by a planner in isolation from consumers.

Needs assessments also recognize the uniqueness of each community, as they do not attempt to generalize their findings beyond the community where they are carried out. Needs assessments support local self-determination as well by permitting the opinions and preferences of community members to define which services should be provided. Finally, needs assessments are quintessentially action-oriented; their purpose is to provide data that will help decide whether a program is needed in a given community, and what form that program should take.

Effects of the Shift toward Humanism on Social Policy Development

I have argued that there has been a shift toward humanism in the philosophy of science guiding the practice of program evaluation over the past twenty years. This means that evaluators have added qualitative and participatory research approaches to their tool kit, and understand that they may become engaged in program development and advocacy activities that result from their evaluation studies. Needs assessment is now an integral part of evaluation research, sometimes at the program development stage and sometimes as a "zero-based approach" to determine whether a program is continuing to meet the needs of service users. Program logic models are commonly used, again, sometimes in the program development stage and sometimes as a means of helping service deliverers articulate the theory of the program they are offering, and reach agreement on what the program is intended to achieve. Multiperspectual research designs, including the client perspective, are common. Research processes that are shaped by service users are less common, but beginning to occur. And multimodal studies are understood to assess a program in ways that are useful not only to managers but also to service deliverers and to service users (Church, 1995).

Effects of the shift toward humanism on social policy development

The effect of this shift toward humanism has been fourfold on policy development. The greatest impact has been what might be called the democratization of the process. Where once policy development was the domain of politicians and a small number of bureaucrats, the input of the service provider and the consumer is now a greater consideration in the decision-making process. In Ontario, for instance, the Social Assistance Review Committee (Ontario, Ministry of Community and Social Services, 1988) held twenty-three public hearings in fourteen communities. They received more than 1,500 submissions and briefs, many from individual citizens. The input from this broad array of citizens shaped the recommendations of the Review Committee, and ultimately the policy that was passed by the Peterson government with regard to social assistance. At the federal level this same pattern appeared in the work of the Royal Commission on Aboriginal Peoples (1996). While some recently elected governments have shown less regard for the input of what they define as "interest groups," the tradition of consultation remains strong with others. The just-completed report of the Commission on the Future of Health Care (also known as the Romanow Report) (Romanow, 2002), headed by Roy Romanow and charged with identifying how to maintain a public, universal health care system, is an example of continued broadly based consultations as a precursor to policy change.

A second effect of the shift toward humanism has been to provide policy-makers with a perspective that was not heard, or was given much less credence in the policy-making process in earlier times. The subjective experience of the individual is captured through the use of qualitative data—the actual words used by people in written submissions or in presentations to the task force at community meetings. *Transitions* (Ontario, Ministry of Community and Social Services, 1988) captures this effectively in the sections titled "Voices," which appear throughout the report. Both the Royal Commission on Aboriginal Peoples (1996) and the Romanow Report (2002) used a similar approach, with powerful effect. The consequence of hearing these experiences as a policy maker is to give a sense of urgency to the policy-making process—to tear oneself away from the detachment traditionally associated with it. Policy makers are more likely to then become advocates for change.

A third effect of the shift toward humanism is to make clearer the link between policy and program, what some describe as "thinking globally, but acting locally" (Health and Welfare Canada, 1990). In recognizing the link between policy objectives and program objectives, it becomes possible to assess not only how well we are realizing policy objectives, but to identify the

In conclusion programs that are intended to realize them and the extent to which programs make differential contributions to the achievement of the objectives. This provides us with guidance as to which programs should be continued or expanded and which might reasonably be discontinued.

The final effect of the shift toward humanism is the provision of a framework that makes it possible to recognize the uniqueness of each program, and the uniqueness of each community's objectives within the context of that program, while still seeing that program as part of a larger policy direction. This permits a community to address its own particular needs with respect to its cultural or religious values or ethnic and racial makeup while still permitting the community to be connected with the broader policy initiatives of its province or country. Another way of saying this is that the humanist perspective allows us to meld the rational focus on common outcomes with the more subjective or political focus on the needs of a specific community.

In Conclusion

In spite of the progress made in developing a perspective that allows us to make multimodal, multiperspectual evaluations that provide a more comprehensive understanding of the effects of a given policy, challenges remain for the evaluator. Some are more technical/rational and others more political. None are easily addressed, but perhaps most challenging is the pressure currently exercised by politicians like Neilsen, who demand that evaluations be less "political" and more "objective" (Muller-Clemm & Barnes, 1997) at a time when we have come to a postmodern understanding that there is a plurality of opinions about what constitutes a good and just society (Abma, 1997).

We are now seeing governments emphasize performance measurement, outcomes, and results. Who defines which outcomes will be measured, and how? Who defines whether they are symptomatic of success or failure? Is placement in a job a success indicator even if the person is earning below the poverty line, for instance? Is a program successful if service users are satisfied with their experience, but show no change in "objective" measures like reading scores, parenting skills, or knowledge of community resources?

The evaluator is more likely to be able to ask these questions and utilize a humanist perspective to influence the design of evaluations at the agency or local level than at the provincial, federal, or international level. But given the essentially political nature of evaluation, there will always be some perspective missing or not given sufficient emphasis. Our job as social workers committed to furthering social justice is to bring a critical perspective to the design or reading of evaluation studies with a view to identifying these omissions and advocating for their inclusion in our judgments of which policies work.

References

Abma, T.A. (1997). Voices from the margins: Political and ethical dilemmas in evaluation. *Canadian Review of Social Policy, 39,* 41-53.

Atkisson, C.C., & Zwick, A. (1982). The client satisfaction questionnaire: Psychometric properties and correlations with service utilization and psychotherapy outcome. *Evaluation and Program Planning, 5*(3), 233-237.

Backus, T.K. (1978). Foster care review: An Ohio example. *Child Welfare, 57*(3),156-164.

Batsche, C., Hernandez, M., & Montenegro, M.C. (1999). Community needs assessment with Hispanic, Spanish-monolingual residents. *Evaluation and Program Planning, 22,* 13-20.

Baum, G. (1987). Humanist sociology: Scientific and critical. In K. Westhues (Ed.), *Basic principles for social science in our time* (pp. 77-91). Waterloo: University of St. Jerome's Press.

Bloom, M., Fischer, J., & Orme, J.G. (1999). *Evaluating practice: Guidelines for the accountable professional.* Englewood Cliffs, NJ: Prentice-Hall.

Bowles, R.T. (1981). *Social impact assessment in small communities.* Toronto: Buttersworth, 1981.

Briar, S., & Blythe, B.J. (1985). Agency support for evaluating the outcomes of social work services. *Administration in Social Work, 9*(2), 25-36.

Caputo, R.K. (1986). The role of information systems in evaluation research. *Administration in Social Work, 10*(1), 67-77.

Carrilio, T.E. (1981). The impact of research in a family service agency. *Social Casework, 62*(1), 87-94.

Casselman, B. (1971-72). On the practitioner's orientation to research. *Smith College Studies in Social Work, 42,* 211-233.

Chappell, B. (1975). Organizing periodic review in foster care: The South Carolina story. *Child Welfare, 54*(7), 477-486.

Church, K. (1995). *Forbidden narratives: critical autobiography as social science.* New York: Routledge.

Claburn, W.E., & Magura, S. (1978). Administrative case review for foster children. *Social Work Research and Abstracts, 14*(1), 34-40.

Crocker, P. (1983). *An evaluation of the quality of service at a volunteer-run telephone distress line.* Unpublished master's thesis. Wilfrid Laurier University, Waterloo, Ontario.

Davies, M., & Kelly, E. (1976). The social worker, the client and the social anthropologist. *British Journal of Social Work, 6*(2), 213-231.

Everitt, A. (1996). Developing critical evaluation. *Evaluation: International Journal of Theory, Research and Practice, 2*(2), 173-188.

Fanshel, D. (1966). Sources of strain in practice-oriented research. *Social Casework, 47*(3), 357-362.

Finterbusch, K., & Wolf, C.P. (Eds). (1977). *Methodology of social impact assessment.* Stroudsberg, PA: Dowden, Hutchison, and Ross.

Frankel, M., & Sinclair, C. (1982). Quality assurance: An approach to accountability in a mental health centre. *Professional Psychology, 13,* 79-84.

Gergen, K.J. (1985). The social constructionist movement in modern psychology. *American Psychologist, 40,* 266-275.

Giordano, P.C. (1977). The clients' perspective in agency evaluation. *Social Work, 22*(1), 34-39.

Gordon, J.E. (1984). Creating research-based practice principles: A model. *Social Work Research and Abstracts, 20*(1), 3-6.

Guest, D. (1985). *The emergence of social security in Canada.* Vancouver: University of British Columbia Press.

References Hanbery, G.W., Sorensen, U., & Kucic, A.R. (1981). Management information systems and human resource management. *Administration in Social Work, 5*(3-4), 27-41.

Health and Welfare Canada. (1990). *The report of the special advisor to the minister of National Health and Welfare on child sexual abuse in Canada: Reaching for solutions.* Ottawa: Author.

Holosko, M. (1996). Service user input: Fact or fiction? *Canadian Journal of Program Evaluation, 11*(2), 111-126.

House, E.R. (1980). *Evaluating with validity.* Beverly Hills: Sage.

House, E.R. (1993). *Professional evaluation, social impact and political consequences.* Newbury Park, CA: Sage.

Howlett, M., & Ramesh, M. (1995). *Studying public policy: Policy cycles and policy subsystems.* Don Mills: Oxford.

Hudson, W.W. (1982). The clinical measurement package: A field manual. Homewood, IL: Dorsey Press.

Jayaratne, S. (1978). Analytic procedures for single subjects designs. *Social Work Research and Abstracts, 14*(4), 30-40.

Love, A.J. (1983). *Developing effective internal evaluation.* San Francisco: Jossey Bass.

Maguire, P. (1987). *Doing participatory research: A feminist approach.* Amherst: The Centre for International Education, University of Massachusetts.

McCready, D.J., & Rahn, S.L. (1983). *The feasibility of cost-outcome analysis in Ontario social services: Six case studies.* Toronto: Ontario Economic Council.

McCready, D.J., & Rahn, S.L. (1986). Funding human services: Fixed utility versus fixed cost. *Administration in Social Work, 10*(4), 23-30.

McEwan, K.L., & Bigelow, D.A. (1997). Using a logic model to focus health services on population health goals. *Canadian Journal of Program Evaluation, 12*(1), 167-174.

McKillip, J. (1987). *Needs analysis: Tools for the human services and education.* Beverly Hills: Sage.

McLaughlin, J.A., & Jordan, G.B. (1999). Logic models: A tool for telling your program's performance story. *Evaluation and Program Planning, 22*, 65-72.

Milord, J.T. (1976). Human service needs assessment: Three non-epidemiological approaches. *Canadian Psychologist, 17*, 260-269.

Montague, S. (2000). Focusing on inputs, outputs, and outcomes: Are international approaches to performance management really so different? *Canadian Journal of Program Evaluation, 15*(1), 139-146.

Muller-Clemm, W.J., & Barnes, M.P. (1997). A historical perspective on federal program evaluation in Canada. *Canadian Journal of Program Evaluation, 12*, 47-70.

Mutscheler, E. (1979). Using single case evaluation procedures in a Family and Children's Services agency. *Journal of Social Service Research, 3*(1), 115-133.

Nguyen, T.D., Atkisson, C.C., & Stegner, B.L. (1983). Assessment of patient satisfaction: Development and refinement of a service satisfaction questionnaire. *Evaluation and Program Planning, 6*, 299-314.

Ontario Ministry of Community and Social Services. (1981). *Foster care: Proposed standards and guidelines for agencies placing children.* Toronto: Author.

Ontario Ministry of Community and Social Services. (1988). *Report of the Social Assistance Review Committee: Transitions.* Toronto: Author

Pancer M., & Westhues, A. (1989). A developmental stage approach to program planning and evaluation. *Evaluation Review, 13*(1), 56-77.

Patton, M.Q. (1997). *Utilization-focused evaluation: The new century text.* Thousand Oaks, CA: Sage.

Petrosino, A. (2000). Answering the why question in evaluation: The causal-model approach. *Canadian Journal of Program Evaluation, 15*(1), 1-24.

Posavac, E.J., & Carey, R.G. (1997). *Program evaluation: Methods and case studies.* Englewood Cliffs, NJ: Prentice-Hall.

Roach, R., & Youngman Berdahl, L. (1999). Lessons from the field: Surveying hard-to-reach populations. *Canadian Review of Social Policy, 43,* 101-110.

Romanow, R.J. (2002) Building on values: The future of health care in Canada— Final report. Ottawa: Minister of Supplies and Services.

Rossi, P.H., & Freeman, H.E. (1982). *Evaluation: A systematic approach.* (2nd ed.). Beverly Hills: Sage.

Royal Commission on Aboriginal Peoples. (1996). *Report.* Ottawa: Minister of Supplies and Services.

Rush, B., & Ogborne, A. (1991). Program logic models: Expanding their role and structure for program planning and evaluation. *Canadian Journal of Program Evaluation, 6*(2), 95-106.

Rutman, L. (1980). *Planning useful evaluations.* Beverly Hills: Sage.

Saleeby, D. (1979). The tension between research and practice: Assumptions of the experimental paradigm. *Clinical Social Work Journal, 7,* 267-284.

Senate of Canada. (1991). *Report of the Standing Senate Committee on National Finance: The program evaluation system in the Government of Canada.* Ottawa: Minister of Supplies and Services.

Sinclair, C., & Frankel, M. (1983). The effect of quality assurance activities on the quality of mental health services. *Journal of Quality Assurance, 8,* 7-15.

Statistics Canada. (2001). National economic and financial accounts. On-line at <www.statcan.ca/english/freepub/13-010-XIE/20022003/nef20022003.htm>.

Stiffman, A.R., Feldman, R.A., Evans, D.A., & Orme, J.G. (1984). Collaborative research for social agencies: Boon or bane? *Administration in Social Work, 8*(1), 45-57.

Stokey, E., & Zeckhauser, R. (1978). *A primer for policy analysis.* New York: W.W. Norton.

Suchman, E.A. (1967). *Evaluative research: Principles and practice in public service and social action programs.* New York: Russell Sage Foundation.

Tester, F.S., & Myles, W. (Eds.) (1981). *Social impact assessment: Theory, method and practice.* Calgary: Detselig.

Thomas, E.J. (1978). Research and service in single case experimentation: Conflicts and choices. *Social Work Research and Abstracts, 14*(4) 20-31.

Vaillancourt, Y. (1996). Remaking Canadian social policy: A Quebec view. In J. Pulkingham & G. Ternowetsky (Eds.), *Remaking Canadian social policy* (pp. 81-99). Halifax: Fernwood.

VanderPlaat, M. (1997). Emancipatory politics, critical evaluation and government policy. *Canadian Journal of Program Evaluation, 12*(2), 143-162.

Weaver, H.N. (1999). Assessing the needs of Native American communities: A Northeastern example. *Evaluation and Program Planning, 22,* 155-161.

Weiss, C.H. (1972). *Evaluation research: Methods of assessing program effectiveness.* Englewood Cliffs, NJ: Prentice Hall.

Westhues, A., Cadell, S., Karabanow, J., Maxwell, L., & Sanchez, M. (1999). The creation of knowledge: From paradigm to practice. *Canadian Social Work Review, 16*(2), 129-154.

Wholey, J.S., Nay, J.N., Scanlon, J.W., & Schmidt, R.E. (1975). Evaluation, when is it really needed? *Evaluation Magazine, 2,* 89-93.

Williams, A.M., Caron. M.V., McMillan, M., Litkowich, A., Rutter, N., Hartman, A., & Yardley, J. (2001). An evaluation of contracted palliative care home care services in Ontario, Canada. *Evaluation and Program Planning, 24,* 23-31.

Wong-Rieger, D., & David, L. (n.d.). *A hands-on guide to planning and evaluation.* Ottawa: National AIDS Clearinghouse.

References

References   Worthington, C. (1999). Empowerment evaluation: Understanding the theory behind the framework. *Canadian Journal of Program Evaluation, 14* (1), 1-28.

Yates, B.T. (1985). Cost-effectiveness analysis and cost-benefit analysis: An introduction. *Behaviour Assessment, 2* (3), 271-82.

Additional Resources

Knox, C. (1996). Political context and program evaluation: The inextricable link. *Canadian Journal of Program Evaluation, 11* (1), 1-20.

Light, R.J., & Smith, P.V. (1971). Accumulating evidence: Procedures for resolving contradictions among different research studies. *Harvard Education Review, 41,* 429-71.

Ristock, J.L., & Pennell, J. (1996). *Community research as empowerment.* Toronto: Oxford.

Tortu, S., Goldsamt, L.A., & Hamid, R. (2002). *A practical guide to research and service with hidden populations.* Toronto: Allyn & Bacon.

Tyson, K. (1995). *New foundations for scientific social and behavioral research: The heuristic paradigm.* Toronto: Allyn & Bacon.

Weiss, C. (1987). Where politics and evaluation research meet. In D.J. Palumbo (Ed.), *The politics of program evaluation* (pp. 100-145). Beverly Hills: Sage.

Westhues, K. (1987). Basic principles for social science in our time. Waterloo: University of St. Jerome's College Press.

Looking to the Future   Part IV

18

The Challenges Ahead

Anne Westhues

The overriding challenge now confronting people concerned with producing social policy that promotes a more just world is how to accomplish this at a time when Canadians have shifted from a dominant ideology that can be characterized as nationalist and reluctant collectivist (George & Wilding, 1985; Guest, 1997) to one best described as global and neo-liberal (McQuaig, 1998; Teeple, 1995). This means that the policy environment—whether local, national, or international—is now dominated by values that are less friendly to the promotion of equality in the distribution of goods, services, and rights than in the immediate post-World War II period. However reluctantly, most Canadians at that time acknowledged that an unfettered market system did not distribute sufficient income to the poorest Canadians to meet their basic needs for food, shelter, and clothing. There was a tolerance for—not an embrace of—the need for government to intervene to ensure that these basic needs were met. The previous chapters show us that the neo-liberal shift of the 1980s means that a majority of Canadians now believe that everybody—without regard to income level, gender, age, ability, or immigration status—will be better off if we compete in a world market, with a minimum of government regulation. If there is a role for government programs, it is to focus on helping people to be more employable, so they can compete for the opportunities in this new economy.

A majority does not mean that all Canadians share this neo-liberal perspective. It is a rare social worker who would adhere to such a belief system. So how do you position yourself to play a role in influencing policy in the context of this new reality? There are five defining questions that can help you decide on the way or ways you want to influence policy. The answers to these questions may change at different points in your life, so they should be revisited from time to time, perhaps when you change jobs, change province or country of residence, or when you achieve a developmental milestone like becoming a parent or reaching the age of thirty or fifty.

The first of these questions is: What is your vision of "the better world" that you are trying to create? Another way of saying this is: What is the theory or model that frames your thinking about the kinds of changes that need to be made? This should go beyond a broadly defined ideological perspective

like "social democratic" in order to give definition to the policy priorities that
you want put in place. Midgley (2000) argues that having such a framework
helps move you from a reactive to a proactive stance with regard to policy
development, thus counteracting the "Culture of Impotence"—the belief that
unfettered global capitalism is inevitable—which McQuaig (1998) says now
dominates Canadian thinking.

Midgley offers the social development perspective, supported by the
United Nations since the 1950s, as a useful framework. This perspective
understands social well-being to be inextricably linked with the health of the
economy, he explains, so requires the linking of economic and social planning. While this approach has been adopted in a number of developing
countries over the years, it stands in contrast to the "gift" or entitlement perspective that has dominated social policy thinking in most developed
countries. This is the idea, which Midgley attributes to Richard Titmuss, that
the way to achieve equity is to appropriate a share of the resources generated
by the economy and redistribute them to those in need. The difference
between these two approaches appears to be whether the policy developer
assumes that resources will be there for the taking, or understands the need
to plan to generate resources, which can then be reallocated.

A more recent framework that might be adopted, proposed by the World
Health Organization (WHO), is the social determinants of health framework
(Wilkinson & Marmot, 1998). Assuming a health promotion perspective, it is
grounded in the empirical evidence we have about the conditions that support good health. The broad goals to be addressed in this framework include
stress reduction; fostering a good start in the early years; reducing indicators
of social exclusion like homelessness and poverty; reducing stress in the workplace; job creation and support for people who are unemployed; promotion
of strong social support networks; reduction of alcohol, drug, and tobacco
use; provision of an adequate food supply; and promotion of transportation
alternatives to driving, such as walking, cycling, and public transport. This
vision had been implemented through the Healthy Communities initiative,
which now has projects in over 3,000 urban and rural communities worldwide (Directory of Pan American Healthy Cities Network, 2002). Conceived
in Canada in 1984, and adopted by the WHO in 1986, this approach emphasizes participatory planning practices in trying to realize the vision chosen
by each community.

The second question to ask is: At what level are you most comfortable
working—within your organization, community, provincially, nationally, or
internationally? Figure 1.1 shows that policy is made at a number of levels in
any country. This question is intended to help you think about which level or
levels you want to target. You may seek the opportunity to work at the United
Nations, or with an international NGO as described by Wichert in chapter 12.
Or you may decide, as advocated by Ife (2000), to work at the personal or local
level and attempt to influence policy at the agency/organizational, municipal, or community level, always cognizant of the global issues. Often, we

address policy issues on more than one level at a given time, the organiza- tional and the provincial or federal, for instance. The challenge that Ife identifies is being able to continue to combine a focus on the public, which is increasingly defined in global terms, with one on the personal/local or service delivery issues when the gap between the two worlds is so great.

Third, are you most comfortable promoting system transformation or system change (Friedmann, 1987)? System transformation assumes that you will work outside the policy-making or service delivery system through the mobilization of a political community. This community may be defined in relation to a specific social movement like the anti-globalization movement or through a political party as described by Wharf Higgins, Cossom, and Wharf in chapter 16, or through the activities of NGOs as described by Wichert in chapter 12. A systems change perspective, by contrast, means that you have chosen to work within a policy-making system, perhaps like the government policy analyst described by Kenny-Scherber in chapter 14. Friedmann (1987, p. 32) describes this stand as one in which "radical proposals become integrated with the structure of the guidance system of society." He notes that this process is riddled with conflict and compromise, and thus requires policy makers who have well-developed process and political skills. Some people will be most effective working only within the system, others only outside the system, and others will be successful influencing policy, at different times and on different issues, as both insiders and outsiders.

Fourth, following Kenny-Scherber's suggestion, ask yourself what issues energize you. That affront your sense of justice and mobilize you to action? These may be broadly defined as concerns about children, women, people who are seriously mentally ill, people who are homeless, or the promotion of human rights. They may be more specifically focused, with a concern about the injustice of the barrier to the right to marry for people who are gay or lesbian, the lack of accommodations in the workplace for people with physical disabilities, the high levels of poverty among Aboriginal children, or the inadequacy of home care services for the frail elderly.

Finally, ask yourself the question that Linda McQuaig posed to the audience during a keynote address at the annual conference of the Canadian Association of Schools of Social Work in June 2002. Are you comfortable being on the losing side of a policy debate? Because, in this environment, if you do not share the values associated with a neo-liberal perspective, the policy positions you support are unlikely to be acted on by the governments of the day. There may be occasional dramatic wins like the Council of Canadians' ability to stall the signing of the Multilateral Agreement on International Trade, which would have given private corporations the legal status of nation-states, and tools to enforce these newly acquired rights that would have compelled nation-states to safeguard corporate interests over those of their own citizens (Council of Canadians, 1999). Or the recent success in preventing the government of Ontario from selling Hydro One to private sector investors (Mackie, 2002). Much of the work to be done will be educational, however— planting the idea of what could be, but not seeing it germinate at this time.

Having said all of this, what are the priority issues that face us as Canadians living in a global context over the next ten years? The primary issue at the international level can be framed many ways, but I like the framing Senator Doug Roche chose in a speech to the Church Press Convention in May 2002. In the wake of the September 11, 2001, attack on the twin towers of the World Trade Center, he called for a resistance to the "culture of war" (*Getting the Word Out*, 2002). The culture of war calls for increased spending on guns, an incursion into long-accepted human rights, and the fostering of a belief that all people are either "friends" or "enemies." It promotes a world view supporting the belief that our friends are unconditionally right and that our enemies are unconditionally wrong.

Instead, he argues, we should participate in the UN Right to Peace initiative, which means educating people in all parts of the world to a set of values that rejects violence and fosters understanding of others. He reports that UNESCO is currently involved in hundreds of projects with this goal—some focused on human rights, some on gender, others on democratic participation, and still others on cross-cultural understanding. In keeping with Midgely's recommendation that we adopt a social development perspective, he might also have added that the most certain way to maintain peace in wartorn countries like Afghanistan or Iraq, or between Israelis and Palestinians, is to invest in economic development. This was Marshall's great inspiration after World War II, which led to the development of the Economic Recovery Program, better known as the Marshall Plan (For European recovery, 1997). This investment led to prosperity and peace in an area that might have erupted into yet another world war.

It is difficult to choose among many critical priorities at the national and provincial levels. The chapters that have been selected for this book reflect issues that I felt were of greatest significance at this time—the need to reduce child poverty, resolving long-standing issues between Aboriginal and non-Aboriginal peoples that are a consequence of colonialism; homelessness; the role we define for single mothers; workfare; heterosexism; how many immigrants should be admitted each year; what characteristics we should look for in immigrants; ensuring universal access to health care; providing care to people in their old age; and how best to support people with disabilities.

The debates will continue between provincial and federal governments about how much of the responsibility each has in these areas. As we have seen historically in areas like Mother's Allowances and medicare, a provincial government may decide that an issue is important enough that they go ahead and pass legislation to deal with it, even without federal funding. Quebec has done this most recently in passing the Act to Combat Poverty and Social Exclusion, legislation intended to reduce child poverty in Quebec to the lowest level among industrialized societies over the next decade (Séguin, 2002). We can hope that other provinces will follow, adding some of their own revenues to the federal spending on the Canada Child Tax Benefit.

Ford (1998) says that there are two broad themes that will influence operational or service delivery policy in the years ahead. The first of these is "contracting out" by which he means a reduction in government-provided services. Service provision is being shifted to community-based, not-for-profit agencies in some cases and to for-profit service providers in others. It remains to be seen if these service deliverers are actually more efficient—meaning they can provide quality service at lower cost—than the public sector. If they are able to, it may be because they pay lower salaries to service deliverers, and provide fewer benefits than the public sector. Stein (2001), in a recent book titled *The Cult of Efficiency*, argues that the dominant neo-liberal perspective has turned efficiency into a cult, with its pursuit in the delivery of services in the not-for-profit and public sectors divorced from a larger purpose—that is, pursuit of efficiency has become an end in itself.

The second theme identified by Ford (1998) is "new approaches to clients." By this is meant a greater shift in responsibility for provision of care and support from the public sector to families; an emphasis on community living and community care; increased emphasis on early intervention and prevention; and the provision of targeted rather than universal programs. None of these shifts occurs without consequences, of course. A shift in responsibility to the family for care of elderly parents or disabled children usually means increased demands on the time of female family members—wives, daughters, or daughters-in-law—who are increasingly also in the paid labour force. Community living or community care, unless well thought through, can leave an individual more isolated than if he or she were living in institutional care. While early intervention and prevention are laudable, programs have to be carefully evaluated to determine whether they make any difference for the children, families, or individuals they are directed toward. Finally, however appealing intuitively, there is no evidence that targeted programs are more cost-effective than universal programs. This research also must be undertaken.

Perhaps more than at any time in history, the social policy issues facing us are enormously complex. It is easy to feel that there is no way to make progress on them. But, as Linda McQuaig said in the address mentioned earlier, "It's always been hopeless." Advocates for social justice have always pressed for change against all odds of actually achieving what they called for. And look what we have achieved anyway—a society where much remains to be done, but much has been accomplished in regard to social justice.

References

Council of Canadians. (1999). Mᴀɪ Inquiry: Confronting globalization and reclaiming democracy. On-line (June 13, 2002) at <www.canadians.org>.

Directory of Pan American Health Cities Networks. On-line (June 13, 2002) at <www.healthycommunities.org>.

Ford, R. (1998). *Changing roles, changing systems. Recent trends in social services restructuring.* Calgary: Canada West Foundation.

For European recovery: The fiftieth anniversary of the Marshall Plan. (1997). On-line (June 13, 2002) at <www.lcweb.loc.gov>.

References   Friedmann, J. (1987). *Planning in the public domain: From knowledge to action.*
Princeton: Princeton University Press.

George, V., & Wilding, P. (1985). *Ideology and social welfare.* Boston: Routledge &
Kegan Paul.

Getting the word out in perilous times. (2002, June 16). *Catholic New Times,* 10-11.

Guest, D. (1997). *The emergence of social security in Canada.* (3rd ed.) Vancouver:
University of British Columbia Press.

Ife, J. (2000). Localized needs and globalized economy: Bridging the gap with social
work practice. In W. Rowe (Ed.) *Social work and globalization* (pp. 50-64).
Ottawa: Canadian Association of Social Workers.

Mackie, R. (2002, June 13). Stopping Hydro sale gratifying. *Globe and Mail,* A10.

McQuaig, L. (1998). *The cult of impotence: Selling the myth of powerlessness in the
global economy.* Toronto: Viking.

Midgley, J. (2000). Globalization, capitalism and social welfare: A social development perspective. In W. Rowe (Ed.), *Social work and globalization* (pp. 13-28).
Ottawa: Canadian Association of Social Workers.

Séguin, R. (2002, June 13). Quebec bills sets target to reduce poverty. *Globe and
Mail,* A12.

Stein, J.G. (2001). *The cult of efficiency.* Toronto: Anansi.

Teeple, G. (1995). *Globalization and the decline of social reform.* Toronto: Garamond
Press.

Wilkinson, R., & Marmot, M. (1998). *Social determinants of health: The solid facts.*
World Health Organization.

About the Contributors

Mike Burke is an associate professor in the Department of Politics and School of Public Administration at Ryerson University. He has published articles on community modes of health care delivery in Canada, the political attitudes of women physicians, the limitations of health promotion research, and the policy implications of the social-environmental paradigm in health. He co-edited a book with Colin Mooers and John Shields, entitled *Restructuring and Resistance: Canadian Public Policy in an Age of Global Capitalism* (2000), in which he examined recent transformations in Canadian health care policy and new trends in labour market inequality in Canada.

Lea Caragata is an associate professor in the Faculty of Social Work at Wilfrid Laurier University. She teaches social policy, planning, and community development, following extensive practice experience working with marginal communities, developing social housing, and developing and analyzing public policy. Current research includes work in the areas of the social construction of knowledge, civil society, and international social work practice.

John Cossom is professor emeritus, School of Social Work, University of Victoria. His practice was in child welfare, family services, and corrections. He also taught at Wilfrid Laurier University and the universities of Waterloo and Regina.

Peter A. Dunn is an associate professor at the Faculty of Social Work, Wilfrid Laurier University. His research interests include disability policies, poverty concerns, gender issues, and alternative interventions. He has been involved in disability research dealing with barrier-free housing, issues confronting seniors with disabilities, the development of government independent living policies, the impact of independent living and resource centres, and the empowerment of adults with developmental disabilities.

John English is a professor of history and political science at the University of Waterloo. He served as member of Parliament for Kitchener between 1993 and 1997. Between 1993 and 1995 he was parliamentary secretary to the minister for Intergovernmental Affairs and the president of the Privy

Council. He has written several books, including a two-volume biography of Lester Pearson. He is currently working on a history of Canada since 1967 and a biography of Pierre Trudeau. He was awarded the Order of Canada in 2002.

Usha George is an associate professor in the Faculty of Social Work at the University of Toronto. Her scholarship focuses on the development of culturally competent social work practice. Usha's research interests are in the areas of newcomer settlement and adaptation; organization and delivery of settlement services; and community work with marginalized communities. She has completed research projects on the settlement and adaptation issues of various immigrant communities in Ontario. She is currently involved in three studies: a national study of social work; developing culturally appropriate interventions in child maltreatment; and barriers that prevent immigrant women from accessing health care.

Garson Hunter is an assistant professor of social work at the University of Regina. He has taught courses in direct social work practice, social policy, research methods, and field education, and has published on welfare and child poverty. Currently he is researching with government social workers the impact of program cuts and policy changes on their work.

Carol Kenny-Scherber is a PHD student in the Faculty of Social Work at Wilfrid Laurier University. Carol has worked as a senior policy adviser within the Ontario government in five different ministries during the twenty-four years of her social work career. The focus of most of her work has been on education, training, and employment policy.

Iara Lessa is an assistant professor at Ryerson University School of Social Work. Her research interests are focused on bridging issues of subjectivity with social policy. In particular, Iara is interested in exploring the lives and situations of certain groups of subjects, such as immigrants and single mothers in contemporary Canadian policy environment.

Sheila Neysmith is a professor in the Faculty of Social Work, University of Toronto. Her research and writing has focused on social policy issues important to women as they age, in particular the effects of unpaid work and caring labour. She is co-editor of *Women's Caring: Feminist Perspectives on Social Welfare* (2nd ed.) (1998); editor of *Critical Issues for Future Social Work Practice with Aging Persons* (1999); and *Restructuring Caring Labour: Discourse, State Practice and Everyday Life* (2000).

Brian O'Neill obtained his MSW from Carleton University in 1971, and subsequently worked in child welfare management in Toronto until 1988. He received his PHD from Wilfrid Laurier University in 1994, after conducting a study of Canadian social work education from the standpoint of gay men. He is currently a faculty member at the University of British Columbia School of Social Work and Family Studies in Vancouver, where he teaches interprofessional practice in relation to HIV/AIDS, research design, and social service management. His current research focuses primarily on issues in social service policy and management for gay men and lesbians.

Malcolm A. Saulis was born on the Tobique Indian reserve. He is a Malicite Indian of the Negoot-gook tribe. He was educated at St. Thomas University in Fredericton, New Brunswick, where he received a BA Honours degree in psychology. He went on to get an MSW at Wilfrid Laurier University. He sought guidance from his elders to determine where he should put his efforts to better the reality of First Nations peoples, and was told to work in making communities better places to live. He subsequently dedicated his life to making the reality of First Nations better, primarily through community-based university educational processes. He has helped communities develop programs, services, and institutions in health, child welfare, restorative justice, education, and social policy. He has consulted with government departments on various social development areas. He is a trained Traditional Circle keeper, and works extensively in holistic healing processes.

Susan Silver is an associate professor in and director of the School of Social Work at Ryerson University. In addition to her interest in health policy, her current research projects include: a study examining structural job displacement and social exclusion in the new labour market; applying principles of participatory action research to the development of an evaluation framework for community-based models of family support; and the normative analysis of the shared values and frames of reference in relation to family well-being.

Linda Snyder is an assistant professor and member of the social work faculty at Renison College, University of Waterloo. Her research focuses on means of addressing poverty and her particular interests include women's employment initiatives and comparison of Canadian and Latin American endeavours. Prior to her doctoral studies, Linda held policy and program administration positions in Waterloo Region's Social Services Department.

Barbara Waterfall (White Buffalo Woman, Crane Clan) is of Anishnabe-Cree and Iroquoian lineages and descends from Great Lakes Métis peoples. She has eighteen years of experience working in the human services field. She became a faculty member in the Native Human Services program at Laurentian University in 1995 and recently accepted a faculty position in the Faculty of Social Work at Wilfrid Laurier University. Barbara has a BA degree from St. Thomas University, an MSW from Carleton University, and is a doctoral candidate in the Sociology and Equity Studies Department at the Ontario Institute for Studies in Education/UT. Her doctoral dissertation addresses the topic of "Decolonizing Native Social Work Education."

Anne Westhues is a professor in the Faculty of Social Work at Wilfrid Laurier University where she teaches research, social policy, and community practice. Her research interests include evaluation of policy and practice, social and strategic planning, and evidence-based practice. Her publications include articles on adoption (international adoption, disclosure, disruption, and reunions); family violence (elder abuse and prevention of wife assault); and planning (conceptualizations of social planning, human resources study of the profession of social work).

Brian Wharf is professor emeritus, University of Victoria. During his career at this university he was director, School of Social Work, dean, Faculty of Human and Social Development, professor in the graduate multi-disciplinary program focused on connecting policy and practice, and acting director of the School of Public Administration. He is the author/editor of numerous books and journals, including *Connecting Policy and Practice in the Human Services* (1998) with Brad McKenzie, and is past president of the Canadian Association of Schools of Social Work.

Joan Wharf Higgins is an associate professor in the School of Physical Education at the University of Victoria. She has degrees in Leisure Studies (BA), Adult Health and Fitness (MA), and Health Promotion (PHD). Joan's research and teaching interests include planning and evaluation, social-marketing, community and population health, and participatory action-research methodologies.

Tim Wichert, LLB, has spent ten years working with the Mennonite Central Committee in Nairobi, Geneva, New York, and Canada. Much of his work has focused on policies related to refugees. In Geneva he was seconded to the Quaker United Nations Office. Prior to MCC, he worked as a refugee lawyer in Toronto.

Bill Young received his PHD in history from the University of British Columbia. Since then he has taught at several universities (Simon Fraser, York, McGill), worked on the memoirs of the Rt. Hon. Paul Martin, and since 1987 has worked in the Parliamentary Research Branch. He is currently a senior analyst with general responsibilities in the area of social policy and has served as acting director of the Political and Social Affairs Division. He has provided research assistance to many committees of Parliament (currently the Standing Committee on Human Resources Development and its subcommittees on people with disabilities and children).

poverty
  absolute measure, 32
  feminist theory of poverty, 37
  human capital theory of poverty, 37
  Low Income Cut-Off, 30-31, 32, 34,
    110
  Market Basket Measure, 32
  relative measure, 30
  structural (capitalism, market
    system) theory of poverty, 38-40
  subculture of poverty theory, 36
privatization, 164
Progressive Conservative Party, 117

Reform Party, 243
refugee policy
  children and, 231
  definition of refugee, UN, 225
  Immigration and Refugee Board,
    Canada, 231-232
  internally displaced persons (IDP),
    236
  People Oriented Planning (POP),
    230
  women and, 229-231
relative measure of poverty, 30
residential schools, 55-57
residual programs, 164
Romanow Report, 169-170, 329
Royal Commission on Aboriginal
  Peoples, 62, 329

Safe Streets Act, Ontario (1999), 69
sexual orientation, 129-130
  Criminal Code and, 134
  identity and, 131
  Immigration Act and, 134
  knowledge about, 130-131
  psychiatric classification, 134-135
  theories of causation, 130
single motherhood
  changing meaning of, 91-95
  child care as an obstacle to
    employment, 98-101
  demographics, 102
  mothers as employees first, 101-104
  paying for mothers' caring work,
    95-98
  status/perception of women in,
    91-92
social assistance
  characteristics of recipients,
    109-110
  defined, 108
  "deserving" and "undeserving"
    poor, 109

"employable," defined, 109
  programs promoting independ-
    ence, mandatory, 114-117
  programs promoting independ-
    ence, voluntary, 113
Social Assistance Reform Act, Ontario
  (1997), 117
social change
  system change, 339
  system transformation, 339
social democratic perspective, 26,
  123-122
social determinants of health, 338
social development, 338
social exclusion, 84
social policy
  debate about meaning, 6
  definition, 8, 302
  evaluation of policy, programs,
    319-334
  democratization of evaluation
    practice, 329
  evaluability assessment, 324-325
  evolution of practice, 323-324
  giving voice to marginalized, 329
  link between policy and
    program, 329-330
  needs assessment, 327-328
  outcome evaluation, 323-324
  political context, 319-320
  process evaluation, 326-327
  role of evaluator, 321-322
  uniqueness of each program, 330
  levels, or dimensions, of policy, 7,
    303, 338-339
  participation (citizen), 273-274,
    303-304
  spending, 319
  values, 8, 301
social problems
  as social constructions, 68-69
social service delivery:
  and heterosexism, 137-139
Social Union Framework Agreement,
  Canada, (1999), 171, 255, 256, 257,
  259
social work education:
  and Native peoples, 50
social work profession in Canada:
  and active citizenship, 265-266,
    272-275
  as policy entrepreneurs, 275 –281
  Canadian Association of Social
    Workers (CASW) Code of Ethics,
    2, 7, 62, 112

Name and Institution Index